DANIEL WEBSTER

DANIEL WEBSTER

Irving H. Bartlett

W · W · NORTON & COMPANY · INC ·

New York

12709r

Copyright © 1978 by W. W. Norton & Company, Inc.
Published simultaneously in Canada by George J. McLeod Limited,
Toronto. Printed in the United States of America.

All Rights Reserved

First Edition

LIBRARY OF CONGRESS CATALOGING IN PUBLICATION DATA

Bartlett, Irving H.
  Daniel Webster.

  Includes bibliographical references and index.
  1. Webster, Daniel, 1782–1852. 2. Legislators
—United States—Biography. 3. United States—
Politics and government—1783–1865.
E340.W4B26 1978   973.5′092′4 [B] 77–27542
ISBN 0–393–07524–9

1 2 3 4 5 6 7 8 9 0

For Virginia,
who, as usual,
contributed far more
than she realizes

CONTENTS

LIST OF ILLUSTRATIONS

ACKNOWLEDGMENTS

The research for this book was begun in the fall of 1966 with the help of a grant from the Guggenheim Foundation and was later facilitated by a sabbatical leave from Carnegie-Mellon University. Over the years I have accumulated many debts to institutions and to individuals. A former student, Ruth Fleishman, assisted me with a summer of arduous research in antebellum newspapers. Erwin Steinberg and Ruth Corrigan arranged for the purchase of the microfilm edition of the Webster Papers by Carnegie-Mellon's Hunt Library. My debt to the entire staff of this library has grown steadily over the years and is especially great to Marilyn Albright, Dorothea Thompson, and Joan Tieman, who serve so assiduously and creatively in the Reference Department. I would also like to thank Edwin Latham and Kenneth Cramer for making my extended visit to the Archives of the Baker Library at Dartmouth College in the early stages of research both pleasant and productive.

My interest in Daniel Webster is part of a continuing fascination with the history of New England, which first became apparent a long time ago at Ohio Wesleyan University under the tutelage of Benjamin T. Spencer. My work as a teaching fellow under the direction of Edmund Morgan and Donald Fleming at Brown University led me eventually to a study of one of Webster's most eloquent critics, Wendell Phillips, and later to Webster himself. I began my research, trying to explain why so many of Webster's contemporaries, even those who hated him the most, thought he was so great. In writing the book, which attempts to answer this and the multitude of other ques-

xi

tions that arose along the way, I have been aided by numerous friends and colleagues. Repeated discussions over the years with Richard Schoenwald and William Stanton have always been supportive and of great help to me in the development of what I hope is a convincing psychological and historical perspective toward Webster. My friend and neighbor, Glenn Cambor, helped me at an early stage in research to understand some of the less obvious implications in Webster's brief *Autobiography*. Although his own work in preparing the microfilm edition of the Webster Papers was then incomplete, Charles Wiltse willingly shared his discoveries with me. Mary Gordon, Matthias Von Brauchitsch, David Humphrey, and Richard Schoenwald all helped overcome my reluctance to see that an earlier version of the manuscript needed substantial revision. Margaret Neff, Mary Zarroli, and Angela Napoleone have cheerfully and carefully handled the typing of the manuscript and have brought many errors to my attention that I would otherwise have overlooked.

Finally, I would like to thank Edmund S. Morgan not only for his encouragement and advice with this book, but for his continued support for more than twenty-five years—and for his superb example.

DANIEL WEBSTER

1

THE BLACK DAN–
GODLIKE MAN PARADOX

At his farm in Marshfield, Massachusetts, on the morning of October 23, 1852, Daniel Webster announced that he would die sometime that night. At 2:37 A.M. on October 24 he fulfilled the prophecy. He left instructions to be buried "without the least show or ostentation but in a manner respectful to my neighbors." They laid him out underneath a tree in front of the house in his blue coat with gold buttons and a white neck cloth to set off the most famous head in America. A special train with more than fifty cars came down from Boston, and the procession of mourners in wagons, carriages, on horseback, and on foot filled the narrow country lanes for miles around. As the solemn crowd filed silently past the open coffin they could hear the painful lowing of the cattle penned up in the barns. Meanwhile the eulogies began to pour out across the country. Webster's intellectual power had been unrivaled in the history of the world, according to the *New York Times*. But there were other ways to make that point. One of "the greatest intellects," a cooler judgment went, "God ever let the Devil buy."[1]

No American in the first half of the nineteenth century was more visible to the American people than Daniel Webster. For forty years, from 1812 to his death in 1852, he played a dominant national role as lawyer, orator, congressman, senator, secretary of state, leader of two major parties, and perennially unsuccessful presidential candidate. It was his remarkable versatility as well as the length of his political career that helped keep him before the public mind. In an age of great orators, few of Webster's contemporaries challenged his pre-eminence. He was compared to other distinguished ora-

3

tors as Michelangelo was to Raphael. Men marked the anniverary date of his speeches with a solemnity usually observed for the birthdays of great men, and later generations of American orators were brought up on Webster's speeches the way writers fed on Shakespeare. In 1900 a distinguished senator observed that whenever debate in Congress turned to large and weighty issues, Webster would be quoted "twenty times as often as any other public man in our history."[2]

Like other men Webster was capable of ordinary performance. Unlike ordinary men he was frequently called upon to serve the grand occasion, and the opportunities for great oratory offered by the centennial celebration at Plymouth, by the almost simultaneous deaths of Jefferson and John Adams, by the commencement and completion of the Bunker Hill Monument, and, above all, by the question of the durability of the Union have never been surpassed in American history. Although it would be dangerous to argue that Webster could regularly fascinate an audience more completely than other famous orators, it is clear that his eloquence had a unique staying power. Given the state of communications in the mid-nineteenth century, most Americans were introduced to Webster through reading his speeches. Webster's success as an orator depended only in part on his extraordinary presence and a voice which could carry to the far edges of a crowd of tens of thousands; it was dependent to a degree not generally understood on his ability as a writer. He was not one to rush into print with a major effort, and the published speech was usually a much revised edition of the spoken version. The famous Plymouth address was not published until a year after it was given, and the printed speech was longer than the original presentation. The peroration in the reply to Hayne, which thousands of schoolboys over several generations would commit to memory, was not a verbatim report of what Webster said in the Senate, but a consciously shaped literary effort which Webster revised afterward. The fact that Webster was read so much more widely than any other public man of his time, that he was looked upon as a literary giant as well as a great lawyer, orator, and statesman contributed heavily to his enormous visibility before the American public.[3]

We know today that visibility of celebrities is not necessarily a natural phenomenon. It can be bought, and today when educated people talk complacently about "the engineering of consent," it frequently is. In Webster's case the danger was not that he would be ignored, but that his image would be identified too closely with the rich industrialists and great cities of the northeastern states. At a time when Americans still clung tenaciously to the agrarian ideal, but poured their fortunes and their energies into building railroads and factories, such an image was a distinct liability for a politician with presidential aspirations. As a result Webster's supporters attempted to produce an image of "the great farmer." He was described in loving detail returning to his ancestral farm in New Hampshire or working in the fields of his estate at Marshfield. He liked to be interviewed while standing in a bed of onions or feeding his prized ram Goliath. It has been said that Americans distrust presidential candidates who are photographed fishing in their street clothes. Webster was painted in his hunting jacket, and his admirers saw to it that anecdotes about his skill with the rod and gun circulated in the press. However consciously it was shaped, the image of a rustic Webster was not completely false. No one can read his letters without realizing that as hard as he worked in Washington to serve the interests of factory owners, bankers, and merchants, his heart more often than not longed for the peaceful meadows and sweet breezes of Marshfield. The point is that a man so rich in other accomplishments, who could also be seen as a simple lover of the soil, was a man likely to stick in the American mind and imagination.[4]

Webster's remarkable visibility in a variety of roles does not explain why so many of his contemporaries seemed to think of him in superhuman terms. "Mr. Webster had a giant's brain and a giant's heart" one of them wrote, "and he wanted a giant's work." Visbility hardly explains this kind of language, or why he was likened to remarkably disparate figures like Charlemagne and Dante. And it certainly does not explain why the expression "Godlike" was regularly applied to Webster both before and after his death, an extravagrance of rhetoric equaled only by the religious imagery which attached itself to the assassinated Lincoln.[5]

Obviously Webster was richly endowed with that mysterious quality that we label charisma. Difficult to explain by its very nature, charisma is, among other things, a gift of presence closely related to the size, personal appearance, dramatic style, voice, and personality of the person perceived.

Much of Webster's charismatic appeal must have depended on his physical appearance. He was little more than average height, but he gave the impression of a giant. He had been rather fragile as a boy, but in his prime what people noticed most about him was his massive chest (the bellows for the famous Webster voice), leonine head, and the heavily browed black eyes so often compared to furnaces. The size of his head was considered to be highly significant. "His brow," it was said, "was to common brows, what the great dome of St. Peters is to the small cupolas at its side." In an age of phrenology, when mental strength was equated with the size of the brain, the Webster dome was the subject of a good deal of speculation. It was measured at 25 inches around as compared to 23 for Henry Clay and 23 for John Quincy Adams. After he died, Webster's brain was weighed and the phrenologists were delighted to discover that against an average weight of 50 ounces, the Webster brain weighed 63¾, close to the largest brain on record (Turgenev's at 65 ounces). Even today one can find in the Dartmouth Archives a picture of one of Webster's straw hats with a careful notation of its inside measurements.[6]

There are many people who possess charismatic qualities, but the politician becomes a charismatic leader of the first rank by finding a clearly defined role to play in a time of crisis. By ministering to a people in psychological or material distress, the charismatic leader is perceived as responding to a transcendent call, as possessing more-than-human power. The leader henceforth becomes a symbolic figure of heroic dimensions, capable of moving the people not only through practical accomplishment but through the projection of a public image. Symbolic leaders find their power in various roles, as revolutionaries, dictators, crusaders, martyrs, and spiritual leaders. The names of Lenin, Hitler, Saint Joan, and Gandhi come readily to mind. Since World War II, many charismatic leaders have risen to power in third-world nations where people struggle with profound identity problems as traditional societies are modernized and colonies move rapidly into nationhood.[7]

Daniel Webster became a symbolic leader by playing the role of the "guardian" or "defender."

> The guardians express the ideals of the community. In art drama, celestian choric groups of angels, spirits or gods are solemn, majestic and sublime. In community celebrations the guardians embody the dignity and honor of community ideals. . . . When community guardians address individuals struggling to make sense out of conflicting loyalties, they speak with deep conviction and power, because they speak as the conscience of the community.[8]

The need for "guardians" and "defenders" in antebellum America is suggested by a number of recent monographs which show how deeply ambivalent Americans were during the first half of the nineteenth century about the velocity of change in their society. On the one hand, they felt that their spectacular social and economic growth might be a sign that they were the chosen people. On the other, they feared they might be captured by materialism and cut off from the more heroic virtues of their past. The age of the "great triumvirate" of Webster, Calhoun, and Clay was, in other words, an age of anxiety, and in no part of the nation was the level of anxiety higher than in New England.[9]

During the second quarter of the nineteenth century Webster ministered to the distress of New Englanders and other Americans by convincing them that the great gift of their fathers and grandfathers, on which their own liberty and prosperity depended, was the Union under the Constitution. It was an unparalleled heritage and Webster called his countrymen to preserve and defend it. By 1830 his name had become symbolically attached to the concepts of Constitution, Union, and the stability and virtue of the age of Washington. In 1860 it was essentially Webster's vision of the Union which Lincoln articulated and the North responded to with massive enthusiasm. And after the war, when the principle of Union had been vindicated at terrible cost, the great speeches of Daniel Webster seemed even more prophetic than before, and the lesser New Englanders who played such an important role in writing the textbooks for American schools in the last half of the nineteenth century made sure that his memory would stay green. No matter how controversial Webster's political career had been, no matter how many frailties could be found in his private and public life, on the great subjects— Constitution, Union, the American Past—Daniel Webster's guardianship, like a great natural law, never wavered. "He was independent, self-poised, steadfast, immovable," wrote one eulogist, "you could calculate him like a planet."[10]

Although multitudes praised Webster, lavished him with attention, and probably read, wrote about, and listened to him more than any other leader of his time, the American people never came close to making him president. The political explanations for this phenomenon emphasizing the liabilities of his New England Federalist-Whig lineage in an increasingly democratic society, do not tell the whole story. A certain intimation of weakness, the perception of a marked streak of dependency within the magnificent carriage of the man, raised doubts even among his admirers. Those who hated him were more direct. As one congressman said on the floor of the House in 1846, Webster seemed to have two characters which he could play off against each other as he chose, "the God-like and the Hell-like—the Godlike and *Black Dan.*"[11]

Webster had been called Black Dan ever since he was a boy, but toward the end of his career, the nickname which had originally referred to his dark complexion was regularly applied to his character. It is commonly believed that the abolitionists fastened the Black Dan image in the American mind by their eloquently vituperative attacks on Webster after he supported the Fugitive Slave Law, but the fact is that Webster's character had been under attack for years before 1850.

To his enemies Black Dan was the real man. To his admirers it was a slanderous image, but even they sometimes caught glimpses of a darker side. Webster's ambition was a case in point. It seemed to clash with his Godlike image, and haters like John Quincy Adams confidently denounced his "rotten heart" and "ravenous ambition" while his admirers responded in a more subtle, interesting way. One of them remembered telling Webster in front of Henry Clay that he demeaned himself by trying to be president when by remaining the "great Senator" he could wield a much greater power over the people. When Webster persisted in his impossible quest, it suggested that he was "wanting in some of the small qualities that are necessary to true greatness."[12]

Even if he had been as selfless as a saint, Webster would have had trouble maintaining the exalted image he projected as a symbolic leader. It is a dangerous thing to be labeled Godlike in a democracy, especially for one who finds his calling in the rough and tumble of American politics. And a saint Webster certainly was not. Few American leaders have had a greater appetite

for the good things of life. Toward the end of his life the Webster belly had
become as much a national landmark as the great dome surmounting it.
Contemptuous of Spartan ways, the guardian bragged openly about his
knowledge of good food and drink. Eventually, people said he drank too
much, even in public—and they were sometimes right. They said he pursued women, a harder matter to judge, but there were thousands of intelligent Americans who never doubted it. Above all, Webster seemed to
give the lie to his superhuman reputation by his incredible improvidence
with money. Perhaps the highest paid lawyer in the country, Webster made
a fortune of his own as a relatively young man and took at least another fortune in gifts from his constituents. How much he made in other ways from
his career in public service was a matter of dark speculation for more than
twenty years. Despite these munificent sources of income he could never
pay his debts. At the crest of his career, Webster was put before the people as
the nation's greatest fiscal expert. When he died even his closest friends said
that to live off other people's money had become a governing principle in
his life.

It has been argued that a distinguishing characteristic of any charismatic
leader is the capacity to arouse hatred as well as devotion. The revolutionary
excites the passionate opposition of those at the head of the standing order;
the guardian inflames those who demand change. In Webster's case, however, the worshiper and the denigrator frequently combined in the same person. One antislavery writer called Webster, "a sensualist, a libertine and a
pauper supported by the contributions of his party," but only a few lines
earlier he had written, "I have no question that he is the ablest man in public
life on the stage at this time, and has been since the day of Fox and Pitt." The
radical Boston preacher, Theodore Parker, whose funeral sermon on Webster was intended as an antidote to the fulsome eulogies flooding the public
presses in 1852, asserted that no living man had done so much "to debauch
the conscience of the nation." But he also confessed that since Charlemagne
there had "not been such a grand figure in all Christendom."[13] Whittier's
famous poem "Ichabod," filled with echoes of Webster's former glory,
likened him to a fallen angel. The most famous and eloquent of all the
Webster watchers was Emerson. Upon reading Webster's reply to Hayne,
Emerson wrote, "The beauty and dignity of the spectacle he exhibits should
teach men the beauty and dignity of principles. This is one that is not blown
about by every wind of opinion, but has mind great enough to see the majesty of moral nature and to apply himself in all his length and breadth to it
and magnanimously trust thereto." Later Emerson wrote that Webster's
speeches represented "the utmost that the unpoetic West has accomplished
or can." These remarks were written before Emerson became sympathetic
to abolitionism. In 1850, when Webster supported the Fugitive Slave Law,
Emerson denounced him with exquisite vehemence. "The word *liberty* in

the mouth of Mr. Webster," he wrote in his journal, "sounds like the word *love* in the mouth of a courtezan." What appeared to be a final judgment was summed up with the words "The fame of Webster ends in this nasty law." Less than two years later, on an October Sunday in 1852, Emerson stood on the beach at Plymouth watching the spray blow off in the direction of Marshfield where Daniel Webster lay still warm in death.

The sea, the rocks, the woods, gave no sign that America and the world had lost the completest man. Nature had not in our days, or not since Napoleon, cut out such a masterpiece. He brought the strength of a savage into the height of culture. He was a man *in equilibrio;* a man within and without, the strong and perfect body of the first ages, with the civility and thought of the last. . . . And what he brought, he kept. Cities had not hurt him; he held undiminished the power and terror of his strength, the majesty of his demeanor.[14]

No one has done more to keep the transcendent image of Daniel Webster alive than Stephen Vincent Benét. In his famous story *The Devil and Daniel Webster* in which Webster convinces a jury handpicked by the Devil to free a condemned New Hampshire farmer, Benét depicts a man who when alive could bring the stars and stripes "right out in the sky," and from the grave threatens to make the ground shiver and trees shake if the Union is in danger. But even Benét seems to suggest that Webster had a darker side. When the Devil confronts him "with his eyes glowing like a fox's deep in the woods," Webster stares back and his eyes are "glowing too." We leave the story suspecting that all of Webster's power may not have come from above; that to beat the Devil at his own game, one has to have learned something about the Pit from the inside.[15]

Almost without exception Webster's biographers have concerned themselves with the outer man, the politician, statesman, orator, constitutional lawyer. Some of them actually despaired of getting beyond the outer man. "This colossal task of *Webster* weighs like a cloud upon my spirits," Gamaliel Bradford wrote early in this century. It was not just the "brooding presence of the man, that gigantic personality, so intense, so positive, so affirmative, so dwarfing and dwindling" his own that discouraged Bradford, but the massive "emptiness" of a correspondence which always seemed "limited to the basest practical detail . . . never by any chance giving a touch of vivid insight or an illuminating comment on the man himself." In the end Bradford decided that Webster did not have an inner life. Like other obsessive politicians, he was "so busy with the external gesture" that his soul ran to seed.

Claude Fuess, a much more comprehensive and sympathetic biographer than Bradford, confessed that despite the wealth of material available on Webster's life it was difficult "to uncover his essential personality." Nevertheless, Fuess believed that the Webster who appeared in detailed public display was the real man. He lacked the "weird phobias and morbidities" which commonly afflicted other great men because he was "elemental, not subtle, simple not complex." It was Webster's hugeness rather than his strangeness that set him apart from ordinary men.[16]

It is true that Webster rarely gave much of himself away. He never confided in a diary, and the overwhelming mass of his correspondence is concerned with the practical business of life—law, politics, financial transactions, farming, and housekeeping. The thrust of his thinking as revealed in his letters was usually outward. He was not introspective, rarely confessed to doubt on serious matters, and seldom let public controversy or criticism invade his private composure. From his middle years on, when he was constantly before the public eye, a large part of Webster's appeal lay in this ability to project an image of monumental serenity. "Fidgety men were quieted in his presence," James Parton recalled, "women were spellbound by it, and the busy, anxious public contemplated his majestic calm with a feeling of relief."[17]

Webster at his peak was a person of such overwhelming appearance and accomplishment that even intelligent, critical-minded observers have been encouraged to believe that what they saw was all there was. He liked to present himself as a man of simple pieties and profound convictions, and those who admired him perceived him that way. Bronson Alcott called him a cross between the Roman and the Indian, "solid, columnar, formidable," and Emerson recalled how a few simple words from Webster after the showy performance of a lesser orator was "like a cup of cold water to a man thirsting among hogsheads of lavender." But great men are rarely simple, great politicians never, and in Webster's case the outward simplicity frequently masked an inner complexity.

The mask is an essential part of theater, and almost everyone who knew Webster remarked on his dramatic talent. A lawyer who worked closely with him at the beginning of his career said that Webster was a born actor, and that touring the courts with him in New Hampshire was like being on a caravan. Everything Webster did in the Congress was dramatic. His customary dress, the black long-tailed coat with gold buttons, buff-colored vest, and blue pantaloons, was a dramatic reminder of the Revolution. He was a master of late entrances, and the mere sight of him approaching his seat in the Senate would command attention. When he got up to speak it was "not a mere act; it was a process," like an elephant's rising with an intellectual dimension to it. And one cannot escape the feeling that the frequent references to Webster's self-absorption, the likening of him to a slumbering giant or lion, unwilling to vent his fantastic power on trifling matters, was in part, at least, the product of a studied effort.[18] Like other great actors he insisted on top billing and once threatened to withdraw from the first Bunker Hill celebration unless a rival orator canceled a competing ceremony with Lafayette a few weeks earlier. Webster played the leading role throughout his adult life, carefully staged his own deathbed scene, and died on cue.

But acting is more than technique, and there is a depth to the really great performance that even the actor himself cannot fully explain. If Webster's monumental simplicity was part of a conscious effort to sustain his Godlike image, it was also, along with the darker side of his personality and reputation, rooted far more deeply than he, himself, could know. The effortless eloquence on behalf of the Constitution and Union along with his incessant panting for the impossible presidency, his willingness to accept tainted money, and his inability to pay his debts can all be traced back to the struggles he endured in boyhood and adolescence to claim his own autonomy without giving up the warmth and security of childhood—a struggle he continued throughout life.

What follows is an attempt to understand three Daniel Websters, the Godlike Daniel and Black Dan, along with the person in between—the man behind the image, who succeeded, failed, laughed, loved, and sometimes found himself ensnared in webs of his own making but beyond his understanding—even as his less celebrated countrymen.

2

SALISBURY, EXETER, AND HANOVER

Although he would become closely identified with the Boston aristocracy and was proud to trace his lineage back to the first generation of New England settlers on both sides of his family, there was nothing Brahmin about Daniel Webster's background. Except for Stephen Bachelder, the first settled clergyman in New Hampshire, from whom his father's mother had descended, he came from a long line of tough pioneer farmers who had battled bears, wolves, Indians, Frenchmen, and the granite-laden soil of New Hampshire for almost 150 years in order to survive.

Daniel was the product of four generations of New England Websters. His father, Ebenezer, had been born the son of a plain farmer family in Kingston, New Hampshire, in 1739. Without ever having gone to school, Ebenezer had been on his own since the age of fourteen, when he ran away from a hard master to work as a teamster in Portsmouth. While still a boy he signed up with Roger's Rangers and saw action in the French and Indian War under General Amherst in Canada. After the war he married a Kingston girl and in 1762, blazed a trail through the wilderness to claim two hundred acres of land in the rugged hill country west of the upper Merrimack River. The site of his log cabin in what would become Salisbury, New Hampshire, was on the extreme northern perimeter of the American frontier. Daniel was born January 18, 1782, in a four-room frame house near that cabin. Two years later his father moved the family to a much larger building three miles to the east in the more fertile Merrimack valley. It was here on Elms Farm that the boy passed the formative years of his childhood.

The experiences which shaped him in the beginning were pastoral. The smell of the barnyard, a great expanse of field and meadow stretching out from the house toward the broad glistening river, the rugged granite peaks of Kearsarge and Ascutney Mountains dominating the western sky. These were the boy's primary sensations, and with them came a sense of security. His earliest specific recollection was when the Merrimack rose so quickly that it swept away the great barn of a neighboring farmer. The water came to their very doorstep, but the Webster house and farm buildings stood fast.[1]

The boy could not have imagined any natural phenomenon powerful enough to dislodge his father. Ebenezer Webster, the towering figure in Daniel's childhood and the most dominant influence in his whole life was about fifty when Daniel first remembered him, "with a broad full chest, hair still of unchanged black, features rather large and prominent, a Roman nose, eyes of brilliant black."[2] A big man, six feet tall, the father seemed to dwarf the surrounding mountains. He carried himself like the old soldier that he was—like a man who was proud of what he had done in the world—and he had reason. He kept a mill up near his old cabin and sometimes took the boy there. There was plenty of time, when the mill was not working, to recall what life had been like in the wilderness, how he had been forced to walk many miles with a sack on his back to get his corn ground while his wife stayed behind to cope with Indians who had never visited a settler before except in search of scalps. He told his son what it had been like to battle the trees and the boulders, to survive the mountainous winter snows in isolation. He described the other children who had been born and died in the cabin, the time the sickness had been so bad that one child lay dying while he and his wife prayed over the coffin of another. These stories became a part of the boy's ancestral memory. It was almost as if he had been born in the cabin himself. Fact and legend faded into one another in old New Hampshire. There was a ruined Indian fort on his father's farm, and Daniel once talked to a neighbor who could remember hiding behind the chimney in her cabin while the Indians killed her mother. He heard about Peter Bowen, who had murdered two savages in secret and had then gone off to live with their tribe as an act of atonement. As a man, Webster never forgot the pioneer spirit which had touched him during his earliest years.[3]

The Webster household was a bustling place when Daniel was growing up. His father's first wife had died in 1774 leaving three surviving children. Ebenezer then married Abigail Eastman, a plain-faced, strong-bodied spinster of thirty-seven who gave him five more children. Daniel was the youngest son and the next to youngest of the eight Webster children. He remembered little about his mother and although she outlived his father by several years, he made almost no mention of her in his autobiography or in his letters. This may simply be a reflection of the dominant personality of Ebenezer, but it is also likely that Abigail Webster was so overwhelmed

Ebenezer Webster.

Abigail Webster.

with work, taking care of her husband's first family, raising one of her own, and helping out with the farm work and the tavern her husband operated out of the farmhouse, that she had little special attention to pay to Daniel or any other child. She was thirty-seven when she was married and forty-five when Daniel was born—all of which may help explain the visitor who remembered that she was "the worst housekeeper he ever saw."[4]

With plenty of older brothers and sisters in the family, Daniel did not want for instruction or companionship, no matter how busy his parents were. Quickly taking to the outdoor sports that were part of every New Hampshire country boy's upbringing, he learned to slide, fish, swim, and skate, and would play with such single-mindedness that he once froze his feet while sledding. His brothers also showed him what a farmer's work was like. He learned how to milk, to tend the horses in the barn and follow them in the field when the plowing and the raking needed to be done. But for all his love of the outdoors, he never took to farm work. Some basic skills, like mowing with a scythe, he never learned, and of all the Webster boys he contributed the least toward operating the farm. He was much more comfortable back at the tavern where he helped out by watering the horses of the teamsters and other travelers passing by on horseback.[5]

It is not surprising that Daniel's father should have found himself engaged in tavern keeping. That activity was closely regulated in New England in post-revolutionary days, and only respected leaders in the community, usually retired militia officers, were given the privilege. The big farmhouse where Ebenezer moved his family in 1784, was about fourteen miles north of the state capitol at Concord on one of the few substantial roads in New Hampshire—an ideal place to locate a tavern. Salisbury was still a small, scattered settlement of subsistence farmers isolated from the rest of New England. But in Salisbury, the Webster tavern was a link with the outside world. Post riders with newspapers, and travelers passing through from Concord and Boston encouraged the boy to think in terms of a larger world than that circumscribed by the Merrimack valley.[6]

The tavern in old New England was a place for the rest and refreshment of the traveler, but it also served as the political hub of the community and the landlord was usually at the center of the politicking that took place. The boy would sit in a dark corner watching his father huddled before the fire plotting with political cronies to keep their part of the state under the right kind of political control. There was one simple test of political loyalty in Ebenezer Webster's tavern. If a man was not willing to support George Washington, the Constitution, and the Federalist party, he had better look for hospitality somewhere else. In these discussions as elsewhere the boy always saw his father as the man at the center. He was not only the legendary pioneer who had fought in the Indian wars and had blazed a trail into the wilderness.

He was also Captain Webster, who had commanded a company at Bennington and White Plains and had personally guarded General Washington's tent
the night after Benedict Arnold's betrayal. He was also the town moderator,
selectman, town clerk, and state representative, and as an elector from New
Hampshire had helped make Washington president in 1789.[7]

The boy realized early that he was different from the other children in his
village. The first thing that set him off was his father, the most famous and
respected man in the community, as big a man as Salisbury could ever hope
to hold. He must also have sensed something different about his own appearance. Although slight for his age, he had an unusually large head topped
with jet black hair and huge black eyes. He would not remember where the
nickname started, but the teamsters putting up at the tavern had started to
call him "little Black Dan" even before he was ten years old. Most of the
boys in the village took to books grudgingly if at all and strained impatiently
for the day when they would be farmers themselves. Daniel cared nothing
for farm work, but seemed to have been born knowing how to read. And
whatever he read he learned. An illiterate British army veteran by the name
of Robert Wise lived on his father's place, and the boy read newspapers to the
old man in exchange for romantic tales about soldiering in Gibraltar and the
Moorish coast. He memorized Watts's Psalms and recited them to the teamsters as he took care of their horses. The teamsters were his first audience.

The local schools, which taught only reading and writing, were held in
different parts of the township at different times of the year. The first school
Daniel attended was held in a log cabin. There he found that he was at least
the equal of his first teachers and that most of his early education would have
to come from his own reading. Books were hard to come by in the village,
but he read everything he found, discovering Addison in a tiny circulating
library, committing Pope's *Essay on Man* to memory from a pamphlet edition brought home by his father, mastering a Latin grammar that fell into his
hands by chance. The one family chore that he tried to make his own was at
his father's saw mill up at Punch Brook. Once he set the saw and lifted up
the gate, he could read while the boards were being cut. The rest of the family made fun of his apparent lack of aptitude for work in the field. The boy
took the teasing well enough but would not be challenged when it came to
something he had gotten out of a book. He was closer to his brother Ezekiel
than to anyone else in the family. Two years older, a youthful giant matur-
ing physically much more rapidly than Daniel, Zeke seemed to be a replica
of Ebenezer, and everyone assumed that he would manage the farm and tavern after the father's death. Daniel admired his brother tremendously but insisted on his own pre-eminence when it came to matters of mental ability.
One night in bed he fell into an argument with Zeke over the exact wording
of a poem in a newly arrived almanac. Unwilling to let the matter rest, he

took a candle, went to another room and searched out the passage. Finding that he was wrong, he returned to bed without properly extinguishing the candle and almost burned the house down.[8]

A traveler pausing in Salisbury might have noticed something exotic about Ebenezer Webster's youngest son. Sharing his father's features, wearing the same homespun clothing that his brothers wore, showing the same simple manners of any other country boy, he still commanded special attention. His parents thought him sickly and his mother once took him all the way to Portsmouth on horseback, hoping the salt air would help him fill out. There was something about the boy's blazing black eyes, however, that seemed to belie his slight stature and playful, almost indolent personality. He kept a gamecock that could vanquish any rooster in the village, and when his bird was finally bested the boy walked twenty miles to bring home another champion.[9] Did a burning inner intensity explain his dusky pallor? Was there a connection between the fire in his eyes and the fire that was started after he lost the argument to his brother? No one could answer questions like that, and perhaps no one ever asked them. But any perceptive observer could recognize the power in the boy. Thomas Thompson certainly did. Thompson was a newcomer to the village. A Harvard graduate and lawyer, he hired the thirteen-year-old Daniel to sit in his office when he was away and act as a receptionist for prospective clients. Impressed by his intellectual curiosity and initiative, Thompson encouraged Ebenezer to think of sending his son away to school. None of the Webster children had ever been sent to an academy. Only two Salisbury residents had ever gone to college. Money was always scarce around the Webster household, and Ebenezer needed as much help from his sons as he could get. The father measured all these factors carefully and set against them the fact that Daniel seemed the brightest of all his sons and the one least equipped to run a farm. Finally, despite the solid accomplishments of his own life, Ebenezer had always felt the lack of formal education in himself. In July, 1795, while working in the fields with the boy, he revealed his decision. Webster recalled the moment in detail a half-century later.

Of a hot day in July, it must have been in one of the last years of Washington's administration, I was making hay with my father, just where I now see a remaining elm tree. About the middle of the afternoon, the Honorable Abiel Foster, M. C., who lived in Canterbury, six miles off, called at the house, and came into the field to see my father. He was a worthy man, college learned, and had been a minister, but was not a person of any considerable natural power. My father was his friend and supporter. He talked awhile in the field, and went on his way. When he was gone, my father called me to him, and we sat down beneath the elm, on a haycock. He said, "My son, that is a worthy man, he is a member of Congress, he goes to Philadelphia, and gets six dollars a day, while I toil here. It is because he had an education, which I never had. If I had had his early education, I should have been in Philadelphia in his

ningly, that I would venture; but I could never command sufficient resolu-
n the occasion was over I went home and wept bitter tears of mortification.

oy who had frequently recited before audiences in Salisbury, and
uld become famous for his declamations at Darmouth less than two
er, was totally paralyzed at Exeter. A simple case of stage fright in a
o had never left home before? Perhaps, but like any other pattern of
r, stage fright is not always simple. People experience stage fright
e they are afraid—afraid of failure, afraid of ridicule, afraid of
ing—or afraid of something else. The last possibility suggests that
right can have a hidden meaning. Why was Webster for the only time
life struck with an extreme case of stage fright at Exeter? The boy
that he had come to the academy to realize unfulfilled ambitions in his
. He was thus simultaneously confronted with challenging oppor-
es and with equally frightening possibilities. He worshiped his father
anted to please him, but was terrified at the thought of leaving him.
ake a formal declamation was to surpass his father in ability—to leave
ehind. Here was a problem Webster would struggle with one way or
er for the rest of his life. At Exeter he resolved the inner conflict by
ng silent. At Darmouth, he would declaim with eloquence, but it
d take years before he could work out the problem of separating from
ather in a way that allowed him to turn all his power out upon the
ld.

benezer's original plan had been to turn his youngest son into a teacher
in December, 1796, he called Daniel home from Exeter and put him to
rk teaching at a one-room school in Salisbury. Within a few weeks, how-
r, a minister in the neighboring community of Boscawen convinced
enezer that the boy was meant for better things than school teaching and
ered to prepare him for Dartmouth College. Ebenezer agreed and in Feb-
ary, 1797, packed the boy in a sleigh and started off with him for Bos-
wen.

It would be difficult to overemphasize the importance of this decision for
aniel Webster's future. Only about two of every thousand Americans
ent to college at this time, and they almost automatically became a part of
e elite group of merchants, landed gentry, and professionals that com-
osed the "upper class" and ruled American politics at the higher levels. To
e launched on such a course from a Salisbury tavern was enough to turn any
oy's head, and Daniel remembered how he felt when his father told him
why he was being sent to Boscawen for more schooling.

On the way to Mr. Woods', my father first intimated to me his intention of sending me to college. The very idea thrilled my whole frame. He said he then lived but
for his children, and if I would do all I could for myself, he would do what he could
for me. I remember that I was quite overcome, and my head grew dizzy. The thing

place. I came near it as it was. But I missed it
ther," said I, "you shall not work. Brother a
hands out, and you shall rest." And I rememb
recollection. "My child," said he, "it is of no
my children. I could not give your elder brothe
can do something for you. Exert yourself, impi
and when I am gone, you will not need to go thr
dergone, and which have made me an old man

On May 25, 1796, Daniel Webster rode
enroll in Phillips Exeter Academy. The scho
mous by Webster's standards, and presided o
the celebrated American schoolmasters of the
came from New Hampshire and some of them
Saltonstall, had eminent careers before them.
minimal entrance requirements, which involve
read from the Bible, he was unprepared for h
never been away from home," he later recall
powered me. I hardly remained master of my
boys who had seen so much more and appeared t
I did."[11] He envied the expensive clothes and
students along with their ability to do mathematic.
from the classics. Back home he had enjoyed be
Now he was the center of a different kind of attent.
crude homespun suit, his clumsy boots, and awk
apart from his fellows both in their eyes and his ow
ridicule in silence, worked as hard as he could, an
the warmth and security of his native village. Years
youngest son, Edward, to Exeter, Webster would re
his own first months there and carefully instruct his
stay at his brother's side until he was fully adjusted t
Even though he made good progress, we must co
Webster passed through the most traumatic experienc
most striking evidence can be found in his own word

I believe I made tolerable progress in most branches which
this school, but there was one thing I could not do. I could not
could not speak before the school. The kind and excellent Bu
tutors] sought especially, to persuade me to perform the exercis
other boys; but I could not do it. Many a piece did I commit to
and rehearse, in my own room, over and over again; yet when
the school collected to hear declamations, when my name was
eyes turned to my seat, I could not raise myself from it. Somet
frowned, sometimes they smiled. Mr. Buckminster always pre

appeared to be so high, and the expense and sacrifice it was to cost my father, so great, I could only press his hands and shed tears. Excellent, excellent parent! I cannot think of him, even now, without turning child again.[12]

Whenever he thought about his father he became a little boy again. Webster wrote this in 1829 when he was famous and near the height of his powers. Without knowing it, he was explaining why he had been unable to recite before his classmates at Exeter. He wanted to be a worthy son, and this meant making the most of opportunities in a world his father had never seen. At the same time he depended for his own strength upon his father and would do nothing that might threaten that childlike bond. As a village schoolteacher he might have remained under Ebenezer's protection indefinitely, but in deciding to send him to college, his father was telling him that he expected more than that. The implications of this decision were both exhilarating and bewildering. In the long run they would produce serious anxieties, but in the short run the boy was free to move well beyond the circumscribed life style of a respected New Hampshire farmer and local politician. Although he would continue to depend upon his father in ways that decisively shaped his own behavior, as he prepared for a role in the larger world, Webster would never again suffer the childish stage fright that had victimized him on that modest platform at Exeter.

Dr. Samuel Wood was one in a long line of older men who recognized the special talents of Daniel Webster and volunteered to push him forward. A Dartmouth graduate, himself, and one of the leading clergymen in the Merrimack valley, Wood prepared more than a hundred young men for college, many of them at his own expense. Under Wood's tutelage from February to August, 1797, Webster began to study Greek and to read the Latin classics. He also discovered the Boscawen Social Library with about two hundred volumes, including works by Milton, Pope, Thomson, and Cowper. It was here that he first encountered *Don Quixote,* a book which so fired his imagination that he devoured it in a single sitting. In August the boy returned to Salisbury, only three miles distant, and prepared for the more momentous journey to Dartmouth. He made the trip on horseback, his head crammed with new knowledge, and a feather bed tied to his saddle. He was fifteen years old.

With an enrollment of about one hundred forty students, Dartmouth was one of the new nation's largest colleges, but its campus, cut out of a pine forest, surrounded by the fir-clad New Hampshire mountains, and served by the village of Hanover, was not the kind of place to overawe someone from Salisbury. In fact some of Webster's classmates got so tired of picking dung off their shoes from the cows grazing on the college common that one night a group of them rebelled against these rural delights by chasing the cows across the Connecticut River into Vermont. Whether or not Daniel himself participated in this prank, we don't know. We do know that despite his youth (his classmates, on an average, were about four years older), his shaky hold on Latin and Greek, and his unsophisticated country ways, he soon made an impact on the college.

In later years few things irritated Webster more than the circulation of stories claiming that he had been a lazy, careless student at college. In a revealing outburst to a close friend he said, "I studied and read more than all the rest of my class, as if they had all been made into one man. And I was as much above them all then, as I am now!"[13] The testimony of Webster's classmates, almost all of it collected long after he had become famous, supports his own recollection. His style of work, not only then but throughout his life, was distinctive. Because he could focus all his intellectual energy on a single point, and because he possessed powers of almost total recall, he could begin an assignment at the last minute and still be ready. Where other students needed to fill their notebooks to be sure of a subject, Webster needed only to get the thing clearly in his mind the first time. A classmate later recalled that Daniel could read a twenty-page passage twice and repeat it almost verbatim and that whenever he spoke he seemed to have "an intuitive knowledge of whatever subject he was considering."[14]

Webster's ability to concentrate his intellectual energies into relatively short periods of time was helpful not only to himself but to his brother Zeke. Once Daniel grasped the full scope of the opportunities which college would open up to him he began to worry about his older brother who seemed to have nothing to look forward to but a farmer's life in Salisbury. In the spring of 1799 he convinced his father that Zeke also deserved a chance for college, and when Ebenezer agreed Daniel undertook to pay some of the expenses by working as an editor for a small local paper in Hanover and during the winter of his senior year by teaching school in Salisbury.

Aaron Loveland, who was Webster's roommate, remembered that when Ebenezer, who was known to be "in embarrassed circumstances" economically, visited Daniel, "He said that if he had received an education in youth, he could have done anything he chose." The son still had some of the rough awkwardness of his father, but now he was also beginning to show the father's drive and self-confidence. Loveland recalled that he was "very ambitious in college from the first, and took every opportunity to make himself conspicuous. He had unbounded self-confidence, seemed to feel that a good deal belonged to him, and evidently intended to be a great man in public life."[15]

The best evidence of Webster's leadership in the college can be found in the records of the United Fraternity, one of the two leading literary societies on the campus. Freshman Webster was admitted to the fraternity almost immediately, and within two weeks the brothers were meeting in his room. He was the only freshman and later the only sophomore to be elected to office. By his junior year he was recognized as the outstanding orator in the fraternity and was made president during his senior year.[16]

Webster was a good but not outstanding student (one of twelve juniors elected to Phi Beta Kappa out of a class of thirty). He never fully overcame his limitations in Greek and mathematics, was never the top scholar in his class, and tended to find more intellectual stimulation outside than inside the classroom. As George Ticknor, who was a year or two behind Webster later recalled, the teaching at Darmouth then was "exceedingly meagre" and the texts were "miserable." Neither President Wheelock, the hook-nosed, stiff-necked head of the college, nor any of his three senior professors commanded special respect from the students, and without their leadership, the curriculum featuring classical languages, mathematics, and such texts as Paley's *Political Philosophy,* Locke's *Essay on Human Understanding,* Jonathan Edwards's essay on free will, and Burlamqui's *Principles of Natural Law* was hardly designed to spark the imagination of talented students. In later life Webster admitted that some of his classmates, outshining him in the classroom, had been more favored by "the authority," while he had concentrated more on "general reading" and attainments that counted for less "in the recitation room."[17]

The accomplishments to which Webster referred were in literature and oratory, and the approval he sought outside the recitation room was the esteem of his peers. Soon after he came to Darmouth Webster developed a reputation as a poet. He was known for his ability to write long gossipy letters in verse, some of which appeared in the local literary paper. The first of these to have been preserved was written to his classmate George Herbert on December 20, 1798, and is as graceless as most poetry written by the ordinary untalented sophomore. Webster had a way of reading, however, that made bad poetry sound good, and one of his classmates remembered many years later that he had once hypnotized an entire class with a long narrative poem dramatizing the encounter between a British and French frigate. Naturally, being Ebenezer's son, he dispatched the French ship into the depths with all guns blazing. Another poem addressed to Herbert in February, 1799, shows Webster's growing ability to handle more serious matters in verse form. The final lines end on a deistic note which would have grated harshly on pious ears in Salisbury.

> When thus, dear George, you see with wondering eye
> Systems on systems roll along the sky
> Then, friend, consider that there is a God
> Who rules this vast machine, and governs with a nod.[18]

The four lines which Webster wrote about God ruling over a machinelike universe tell almost everything there is to know about his religious development at college. Back in Salisbury he had been taught to read his Bible, say his prayers, and go to church with his father. Ebenezer was a practical-minded, hymn-loving Presbyterian with the most booming voice in the township and a decided dislike for theological controversy and religious prudishness.[19] He brought Daniel up in the "nurture and admonition of the Lord" without ever expecting him to suffer through the intense spiritual crisis that was a part of growing up in so many New England Calvinist families at this time. Thus the revival which swept through Salisbury when he was ten years old left Daniel untouched.[20] He grew up accepting religion as a natural part of life, taking Scripture, prayer, and sermons as part of the good things in life, like food and drink. He had no difficulty reconciling this simple faith with the Enlightenment writers that he read in college, and it served him well for the rest of his life. On the other hand, because he was never shaken to the foundations by religious experience himself, he would never be able to understand those who were.

Although he would have denied any interest in pursuing politics while he was at Darmouth, Webster's career there foreshadowed his later political life. He was using language to gain favor and advancement from his peers. In this sense the Fourth of July oration which he gave in Hanover in his junior year should be considered his first significant political triumph. This speech, his first published oration, despite its undergraduate overtones is remarkable for a boy of his age and anticipates his mature work in both tone and substance.

Beginning with a traditional recital of the heroic events leading up to the revolution and creation of a new nation, Webster called the infant Constitution "undoubtedly the greatest approximation toward human perfection the political world ever yet experienced . . . which, perhaps, will forever stand in the history of mankind, without a parallel." In good Federalist fashion, he lamented the passing of Washington "the man, who never felt a wound, but when it pierced his country, who never groaned, but when fair freedom bled," praised Adams, and warned against the dangers of encroachment by France. "Neither a supercilious, fire-headed Directory, nor the gasconading pilgrim of Egypt will ever dictate terms to sovereign America."[21]

That Webster should have been invited to deliver the Fourth of July oration while still a student shows that he had come a long way since his tongue-tied days at Exeter. The man who would become known as America's pre-eminent orator was beginning to show as a college student the qualities that would later make him famous. Indeed, the more closely we look at Webster during this period the more we begin to see that the strengths and weaknesses of the man were already apparent in the boy. His personal style was beginning to change. By the time he was a junior Webster had thrown away his homespun and had earned a reputation for being somewhat of a dandy. The account books of Richard Lang's general store in Hanover document his purchases of cotton stockings, silk gloves, and velvet trousers. By the summer of 1801, he had run up one of the highest accounts of any student, and storekeeper Lang had advanced him money in addition. Half of all his purchases were for gin, brandy, port, lemons, and sugar. Being in debt was nothing new. His father was always in debt, and everyone respected him.[22]

From his college days on, Webster was always idolized by a close circle of admirers. His center of power at Dartmouth was within the United Fraternity, where one of his friends recalled that he "received almost unbounded flattery. They thought he was great." Among his fraternity brothers Webster's word was law.

Such was his standing among them that no enterprise would be undertaken until Webster's advice was obtained. A number of students were one day playing ball on the common, when a man came up to a student near me, and stated that he wished to open a dancing school if he could have the patronage of students. The student did not express any opinion, but said, "I will consult Webster."[23]

George Ticknor remembered how when Webster visited the campus a few months after his graduation, "the young men seemed rejoiced to have him with them, and treated him very caressingly and affectionately." In some ways he was like most students. He knew what horseplay was and once knocked down a door to get at a friend who splashed water on him. The handful of letters which we have from his own hand during this period show that he maintained an affectionate, confiding relationship with close friends. He had at least one soulmate, Jeremy Bingham, whom he described as "the friend of my heart, the partner of my joys, griefs and affections," and in his letters to Bingham and other friends he seems to have been as willing to gossip about the Hanover girls and poke fun at the "longtitude" of President Wheelock's nose as any other student. At the same time it is clear that this was no ordinary college boy. Although he was really younger than most of his fellows, and still physically immature, there was a weightiness about Webster, a gravity of manner that made him seem older and inspired deference. It is hard to read his own letters or the recollections of his classmates without suspecting that he deliberately played on these qualities in order to set himself off from the others. He was always conscious of his dignity, rebuking one friend for having said something which "argues a suspicion of my sincerity," counseling another about his courtship ("If you are seriously and honorably inclined I can tell you enough to give you perfect confidence of success; if you only wish to amuse yourself and sport with the girl, I beg you not to make me your instrument."), and like some aging Federalist senator predicting that Jefferson's administration would ruin the country.

I already see in my imagination the time when the banner of civil war shall be unfurled; when Discords' hydra form shall set up her hideous yell, and from her hundred mouths shall howl destruction through our empire; and when American blood shall be made to flow in rivers by American swords![24]

His roommate Loveland, who had occasion to observe Webster closely at Darmouth, noticed "something rather amusing and pompous in his bearing as well as his style, He was, and felt himself to be a kind of oracle." While some students actually thought Webster was an oracle others thought he was overly ambitious and pretentious. Loveland recalled that students outside Webster's fraternity thought he was overestimated, and disliked his Olympian ways.

He was not very popular with the class, owing to his being so independent and assuming. On one occasion, when some matter was discussed before the class, the side which he advocated received but few votes: whereupon he got up and left the room. He would appear rather stuffy if things did not go to suit him, though he took no special pains at electioneering.

And yet Loveland's final judgment was that despite unpopularity in some quarters Webster was "generally regarded as our ablest man," and usually selected for important student assignments which he performed well.[25]

The silk gloves and velvet trousers were outward manifestations of important inward changes taking place in Webster at Dartmouth. The inhibitions which had troubled him at Exeter were momentarily overcome, and the young man was beginning to show the kind of aggressive concern for public advancement and acclaim that would later become so closely associated with his name. At the same time he seems to have been aware of what was happening to himself and anxious about the possible implications. Here, for example, is what he wrote in a manuscript on ambition three months after his Fourth of July oration.

Ambition is what? The grand nerve of human exertion; the producer of everything excellent in virtue and . . . in vice. . . . Whoever would irradicate [sic] it from his breast must tear it from the inmost fibres of his soul. . . . To talk of this subject more coherently ambition is an inflection of the will, by which men are inclined to seek for eminence in some direction or other. Ambition in Caesar and in Washington is radically the same; in each it is the wish of excelling. But there is an essential difference in its direction. Caesar's ambition was not subordinate to his virtue. . . . In Washington ambition was a secondary principle. It was subservient to his integrity "and rose and fell by virtue's nicest rule. . . ." He united glory with the good of his country, and every stroke of his arm that added a laurel to his brow, erected a new pillar in the temple of freedom.

Thus various are the effects of ambition. It can enslave a nation, or it can burst the manacles of despotism, and make the oppressed rejoice. . . .[26]

Webster had a good chance to test his philosophy of ambition at the end of his senior year. Ordinarily the Dartmouth students elected their own valedictorian for commencement. During his junior year, however, the students had been unable to agree and the faculty made the choice. This procedure was followed for Webster's graduating class and Thomas Merrill and Caleb Tenney, both ranked above Webster in the class, were asked to give the Latin oration and valedictory address. Webster was offered the opportunity to give an oration on English literature or some similar subject, but since this would have placed him in a lesser position on the program, he refused. Several of his friends who were to have appeared on the program also refused to participate, and Daniel stood in the ranks with them to receive his diploma without special recognition. In later years a story was circulated saying that he was so enraged by what had happened that he tore up his diploma. The story is without foundation, but there is no doubt that he was disappointed. He tried to make light of the matter shortly afterward in a letter to his friend Jeremy Bingham. "You will see the propriety of apologizing as much as possible for the sterility of our Commencement," Daniel wrote. "Tell people it is because they discouraged genius."[27]

Daniel Webster was denied the opportunity to deliver the valedictory address at commencement, but that did not keep him from saying a few final words to those friends who wanted to hear him. At about the same time as the commencement he gave an oration before the United Fraternity on the subject of "Opinion." His purpose in the oration was to warn his friends against "the blind obsequiousness to received opinion" whether this came from prescription or the "new-fangled rights of man," and remind them that the great man was he who, like Washington, could stand erect "amidst the conflict of the winds and waters of party and opinion. . . . For his greatness was altogether internal; it consisted in a regular and compacted system of passions and powers arranged in a manner that gave him at once energy and moderation; and the brilliant achievements were only the outward expressions of what existed in his mind."[28]

Washington had become great not just because his principles were great, but because he believed in himself and knew what he wanted. During the years just ahead Webster would struggle to attain the inner strength necessary to sustain his own long career in public life.

3

RITES OF PASSAGE
To Be an Eagle or a Sparrow?

Daniel Webster was nineteen when he returned to Salisbury as a college graduate. He had already learned far more from books than his father would ever know, but he was still a boy in many ways. His father at nineteen had been on his own for five years—had been a teamster and a runaway apprentice and had fought as an equal with hard-bitten veterans in Rogers Rangers. Like most poor boys on the frontier, Ebenezer was plunged immediately into the resonsibilities of independent adulthood and never had time to worry about what he would do with his life. The case with Daniel was quite different. At nineteen he was still dependent on his parents. Pale, thin, and frequently sick, his physical development had not kept pace with the improvement of his mind, and on at least one occasion he was dismissed by girls his own age as "awkward and rather verdant." Despite his educational triumphs he was not prepared to make the fundamental commitments to career and family that commonly mark the beginning of adult life.

Some young people graduate from college in an exultant mood; they cannot wait to conquer the world. When Webster came home to Salisbury in the fall of 1801 he wrote to his friend Bingham that he was "sunken in indifference and apathy." Hanover had been a hard place to leave. There he had encountered new books and ideas and surrounded himself with sympathetic friends and admirers. Hanover had meant adventure. Salisbury promised a return to the dull routine of provincial life. To be sure, he would continue his education by reading law in Thomas Thompson's office, but he knew that his professional preparation would not provide him with the satisfac-

The "awkward and rather verdant" Daniel Webster by
an unknown artist.

tions he had enjoyed in college. In fact he can hardly be said to have chosen law as a career at this time. The only other practical alternatives were medicine or theology, neither of which interested him, and so, as he admitted himself, he "fell into a law office, pretty much by casualty." Whatever attention he gave to his law books that fall was desultory at best. Shakespeare appealed to him more than Blackstone, and his chores for Thompson, such as bringing charges against the surly Puritan farmer who smashed a fiddler's violin at a husking dance, were hardly challenging. Yet, in late October when it appeared that his father's financial distress might force him to give up his study and return to school teaching, Daniel's heart sank and he wrote Bingham that he "never was half so much dispirited—as now." Ebenezer's money troubles were temporarily patched up with the help of a few hundred pounds from Governor Gilman, and Webster limped through the fall and early winter in a state of generalized dissatisfaction.[1]

By the turn of the year the family was strapped again, and it was clear that Daniel would have to go to work if Zeke were to finish college. Accepting his fate with good grace, and perhaps secretly relieved at being able to leave his law books behind him for a while, he left Salisbury in early January, 1802, to become master of the academy at Fryeburg, Maine.

Fryeburg was a prosperous farming and lumbering center in the Saco valley. An attractive, elm-shaded village with stately homes marked off by white picket fences, it was a more sophisticated community than Salisbury and enjoyed what Webster described as "a pretty little society." He and a Dartmouth friend, James McGaw, lived and boarded with the local register of deeds and had access to the library of Judah Dana, a Fryeburg attorney. In some ways Webster's life at Fryeburg was an extension of his Hanover experience. When he was not teaching or copying deeds to help pay his board, or fishing in the Saco, he was reading history and literature and stretching his mind in extended dialogues with McGaw. "Nothing here is unpleasant," he wrote to Bingham, "the people treat me with kindness and I have the fortune to find myself in a very good family. I see little female company, but that is an item with which I can conveniently enough dispense."[2]

Brave words but false. In fact Webster was drifting. His life at Fryeburg may have been pleasant enough on the outside, but his inner life was in turmoil. There were two big problems to resolve before finding the course that would ultimately take him to greatness, and despite his cavalier remarks about how easy it was to dispense with "female company," one of them involved women.

At Dartmouth there had been a lively social life between the students and the Hanover girls. Webster was drawn into the local society during his last two years at college, and his letters show that he alternated in characteristic adolescent fashion from romantic moods of erotic playfulness to moments of near despair as he became more deeply involved.

The playfulness can be seen in this excerpt from an early letter to his classmate Thomas Merrill.

I could do no less than to say yes to an invitation to go in to a Miss whom I last night attended home from a visit or dance & warm myself by the fire as the night was chilly. As I was leaning carelessly over her shoulder a fragrance accosted my olfactories, such as before I had never known. Delightful [   ] creature thought I—thou art sweeter than the spicy gales of "Araby the blest." Nature has chosen to make thee all up of incensed essences—In truth I thought her altogether the *sweetest* girl I had ever seen. The very next Eve I took tea in a polite family, & when the cake was handed around I instantly recognized the same luxury of sweet smell that had regaled my nerves the Eve before—Mercy! Thought I—you have certainly here a piece of the cheek, or neck, or bosom of that angelic creature!! . . . No such thing in nature! The woman who made the cake was very harmless. Unravelled the whole affair is thus— the nymph who so much charmed me had taken the liberty to burden herself with *rose-water*, which happened also to be an ingredient in the cake.[3]

Webster would not marry until 1808, seven years after he graduated from college, when he was more than twenty-six years old. His bachelorhood was prolonged about two years beyond that of the average American male of his generation, and it is natural to wonder if he limited himself during this period to sniffing rose water. Probably not. The evidence in his letters strongly suggests that during the nine years between his junior year at Dartmouth and his marriage, he attempted to marry at least once, became anxiously involved with several other young women, and openly envied those friends who preceded him into marriage.

During the winter of his junior year at college, Webster wrote to Bingham that he had heard from another classmate twitting him about a possible engagement or marriage. "What does he hint at here?" Webster asked. "How should he know that I was just about to (try to) be married? My amour, you very well know, had not commenced the last time I wrote to him." Bingham presumably knew who the girl was, but Webster did not mention her by name. Ten months later, again writing to Bingham, he expounded on the necessity of controlling desire. "I am fully persuaded that our happiness is much at our regulation, and that the 'Know thyself' of the Greek philosopher meant no more than rightly to attune and soften our appetites and passions till they should harmonize like the harp of David." Then Webster went on to say that he expected Bingham was already "surfeited with Hanover reports, and it will not gratify you to learn that your friend is implicated in them." The reports involved Webster's relationship with a girl he identified as "S." He did not specify the nature of the relationship but was obviously worried about it. "Perhaps I have been imprudent," he told Bingham, "but nobody shall be unhappy for my imprudence, but myself; for the fulfillment of this promise I pledge my honor. If I ought to I will.

Nobody knows whether I wish to." Was "S" the girl Webster had sought to marry, or was she another friend? What was the imprudence which elicited his pledge of honor? The letter yields more questions than answers, but the tone of it, and the serious note on which Webster closed, reminding Bingham that the real purpose of life was to assure oneself an easy resting place in the "narrow house" of the grave, suggest that he had overcommitted himself with a girl and was seriously concerned about the outcome of the affair. If we assume that "S" was "Sally" we discover in another letter to Bingham written in Salisbury a few weeks later why Webster was not called upon to fulfill his pledge.

I have next to tell you that I am in no inconsiderable consternation. About ten minutes ago friend Gilbert and I were taking a walk a few rods down street, when we perceived a chaise, containing a gentleman and lady, the latter of whom we concluded looked very well, while at a distance; judge my surprise, when I saw, as the carriage passed me, that its fair inhabitant was no other than SALLY! The chaise drove so fast I only had time to bow and blush, and receive a smile and a look as the carriage passed on.

I hoped she would stop at the tavern, but no. On inquiring of my father, I found the gentleman to be a young major, by the name of Hale.

So Sally you see is gone; yes, gone! gone![4]

Piecing together the evidence we can be sure that Webster lost his heart on more than one occasion at Dartmouth without finding a bride. In January of his senior year he wrote enthusiastically about the charms of "an arch coquette" from Salem, and later in the same month, after a visit to Boscawen, he confided to his classmate Fuller about his feelings toward a critically ill friend, identified only as "Miss O." "There can be no danger in avowing a passion after its object has ceased to exist. If ever I had a wish; but what am I saying? . . . Pardon me for the ideas I have suggested."[5]

When he went to Fryeburg, Webster was actively trying to disengage himself from still another entanglement. He wrote some sentimental verse representing himself as a disappointed lover turned away from "those fragrant lawns of Love," but a letter which he received from Hanover at about the same time tells a different story. "My Dear Friend," it began. "Suffer me once more to ask you if you have entirely forgotten one whose anxiety to hear from you makes her completely unhappy. Not one syllable have I heard from you since your letter of Nov. 20th accepting [sic] by accident that you was at Fryeburg. Had an earthquake shook the house to its foundations am confident I should have had more command of my feelings than I had when in a large circle of company was asked if I knew that you had taken the Academy at Fr . . . g." Then after a brief diversion, the writer reported that she had spoken to a mutual acquaintance who "makes the same warm professions as usual," and told him "he must never think of me but as a friend."

And then pointedly, "I feel myself perfectly free as if I had never seen him." The following paragraph closed the letter.

> Do not forget one who thinks of you with the same tender friendship, a friendship which causes her to go so far from you with the greatest reluctance but in so doing follows your better judgment.
>
> Yours with the truest affection
CD[6]

Webster's reply to the disappointed "CD," if he did reply, has not been found. Content to let her find happiness without him, he managed to steer clear of other entangling alliances during the six months residence at Frye-burg, but the problem of women and what to do about them remained very much on his mind.

Along with women Webster worried about his vocation. The Fryeburg students liked him and performed so well at the academy exhibitions that the trustees voted him a special gratuity. His high standing in the community was confirmed when he was asked to give the Fourth of July oration, and the trustees promised him a raise in salary plus a house and a patch of land to cultivate if he would stay on at the school. He was not tempted. It was one thing to be approved, but something else to contemplate a prolonged future as a teacher. He put his feelings on the subject into verse.

> *Tied to my school, like cuckold to his wife*
> *Whom God knows he'd be rid of, runs my life*
> *Six hours to yonder little dome a day*
> *The rest to books, to friendship and my tea*

Webster obviously did not feel called to be a schoolmaster. Where, therefore, should he turn? Once more he opened his heart to Bingham. Whatever his talents might be, he felt responsible to put them to good use. Despite his hesitancy at making a living out of the dishonesty or misfortune of others he would go back to Salisbury and have one more try at the law. He would do this to please his father, not because he expected to achieve eminence as a lawyer. In what he said about his father Webster was obviously sincere, but his eschewing ambition is more difficult to interpret. In later life this would become a pose which everyone could see through, but he was not posing now. Still young and unsure of himself in many ways, he was unwilling to give himself up to expectations that might prove false, yet afraid that he might be getting off to an unfortunate start. As he wrote to his friend Fuller, "The world is nothing but a *contra-dance,* and everyone *volens, nolens,* has a part in it. Some are sinking, others rising, others balancing, some gradually ascending towards the top, others flamingly leading down." Webster was afraid that he might have slipped a foot and was "fairly on the knee" at Freyburg. [7]

Back in Salisbury in the fall of 1802 he sometimes felt that he was down on both knees. At Fryeburg he had been forced to sell his horse and his watch to raise cash, but he had at least been able to pay his way and contribute something to the cost of Zeke's education. At home he was dependent on his father, who had left the tavern for a comfortable farmhouse nearby and now relied on his three-hundred-dollar salary as judge of the Court of Common Pleas to support a household in which penury had become a way of life. "We are all here just in the old way," Daniel wrote to Zeke in early November, "always behind and lacking; boys digging potatoes with frozen fingers, and girls washing without wood." [8]

Webster would have tolerated his penniless state more easily if he had been less ambivalent about his apprenticeship in Thomas Thompson's law office. In those days a young man prepared for the law by attaching himself to an attorney and performing various clerical duties in exchange for the privilege of reading his books and studying his notes. That Thompson was willing to let Webster read in his office without charge was itself a considerable boon. Thompson was an alumnus of Harvard where he had served as a tutor. After studying with Theophilus Parsons, one of the most learned lawyers in the country, he had moved to New Hampshire and become a leading citizen in Salisbury. He would soon become a congressman and a trustee of Dartmouth. Against the advantages of beginning his professional study with a solid man like Thompson, Webster weighed the negative attributes of law as a profession. Growing up in the New England countryside at the end of the eighteenth century, he knew the low opinion most Americans had of lawyers. Before the Revolution many leading lawyers had been royalist, identified with the prerogatives of the crown. After the Revolution the business of the law fell into the hands of men with inferior training who were able to turn the economic chaos of the period to their own advantage by enforcing contracts, collecting debts, and sending thousands of hapless debtors to jail. By seeming to thrive on the misfortunes of honest patriots the provincial American lawyer lost the professional standing he enjoyed in England. As young John Quincy Adams said, just a few years before Webster began his own studies, "the mere title of a lawyer is sufficient to deprive a man of the public confidence." Daniel had grown up in the New Hampshire back country, where honest men like his father were constantly in debt. He had spent much of his boyhood in a tavern and he knew what his neighbors thought about the "bandits," "vampires," and "windbags" who plied their trade in local courts. [9]

It is hardly too much to say that Webster fought the law as much as he studied it during his two-year stay in Salisbury. He worried about his character, noting that a lawyer with an unspotted reputation deserved a place in the calendar of saints. He fretted over his health, which he suspected was being undermined by his incarceration in a musty office. A bout with the measles seemed to confirm this suspicion.

Pills and pukes and vivisections & blisterings and all the apparatus for patching up nature's works are what my soul loathes, tho sometimes I can but approve them. These factitious substitutes are poor, very poor exchanges for the high vigor which those enjoy who can labor upon the earth—upon the business which God originally set us about. "No learned finger ever need explore their vigorous pulse." Nature that made their system, keeps it in repair. . . . When man seeks to avert the curse of living by the sweat of his brow, when he drives himself into offices, close rooms and airless closets, headaches & heartaches & consumptions are his just punishment. These reasons . . . sometimes in a fit of the rheumatism quite persuade me to relinquish every kind of literary pursuit & have no more to do with the sedentary life. Yet health returns, a ray of hope shoots thru my bosom & pride & vanity & the fame's curse erase every vestige of reason & moderation.[10]

A large measure of Webster's discomfort at this time can be explained as sheer intellectual frustration. At Dartmouth he had earned a reputation for his ability to master books at a single reading, but now he found that repeated attempts to penetrate the thicket of archaic technicalities in *Coke on Littleton* left him baffled. It was little wonder. There was no "teaching" of the law in those days. The student was given the hardest books first and forced to make his way alone. Joseph Story, soon to be Webster's confidant and the leading legal scholar in the country, was reduced to tears by Coke, and even the tenacious John Quincy Adams floundered in the "incoherent mass" of learning piled up in the book. Eventually Webster put Coke aside and concentrated on more intelligible texts like Blackstone's *Commentaries,* Espinasse's *NIUS PRIUS,* and *Saunders' Reports,* but he continued to complain about a literature that was "dry, hard and stubborn as an old maid," and reluctantly concluded that to be a good lawyer one first had to consent to be "a great drudge."[11]

As Webster himself confessed, what kept him going despite poverty, measles, headaches, and Lord Coke was "the fame's curse." The inability to sound the depths of his own ambition and to know exactly where it might lead him was still every much on his mind. He repeatedly insisted in letters to friends that he sought no more out of life than what would be due any other simple country lawyer, but his near obsession with the subject spoke more eloquently than his professed modesty. Dramatizing the plight of the young man clutched by the temptation of "Madame Fame's" caresses, he wrote

If he take her to his bosom, she has no flesh and blood to warm it; if he search her pocket, he finds nothing but poverty; if he taste of her lip, there is no more nectar in it than there are sunbeams in a cucumber; every rascal who has been bold and fearless enough, Nimrod, Catiline, Cromwell, and Tom Paine, all those have had a smack at her before him; they have all, "more or less," become famous, and will be remembered much longer than better men.[12]

Although he tried to pass it off to his friend as a matter of morals, Webster's problem in coming to terms with ambition involved more than that. Put quite simply, he was terrified by the half-conscious knowledge that the torrent raging within himself might be the kind of force that had driven a Caesar and a Washington—that was even then propelling Napoleon, like a canon shot, across the face of Europe. Should he acknowledge the force and ride out his destiny toward an unknown glory or disaster, or should he settle for a safer but more ordinary life? One would hardly expect him to put the dilemma this explicitly, but he came surprisingly close in a poem which apparently was written at Fryeburg.

> Bursting thunder racked the sky
> Lightning dazzled every eye
> Winds in conflict roared aloud
> And floods dropped from the frosting cloud
>
> The daring eagle then with manly strength
> Long bent his wing in air, at length
> Tossed by the storm in mizzy whirlwinds round
> Feeble and cold he fell to ground
>
> Safe on her poplar limb the sparrow sat
> And all this scene surveyed
> A sigh escaped her for the eagle's fate
> And thus the moralizing songstress said
>
> Thus greatness dies, in the wild world's alarm
> While meek humility endures no harm!
> The storm that hurls yon bird of might along
> Rolls oer my poplar nor disturbs my song [13]

How to aim higher than the sparrow while avoiding the eagle's crashing fall—that was the problem. Webster thought he saw a way out when he told Bingham that they should pursue an ambition "consistent with the duties and the honest pleasures of life . . . enabling us to treat our friends as they deserve and to live free from embarrassment." Such a degree of ambition, Webster said, was "rational and necessary." [14]

But was it rational to think that the intelligent and diligent young American in 1804 could satisfy his reasonable ambitions by practicing law? After a good deal of wrestling with the subject, making due allowances for the present low estate and corruptive tendencies of the profession, Webster decided it was. When Bingham wrote desparingly that poor young men like themselves could not aspire to eminence in law or any other profession because their concern for money-making would keep them from serious study of the subject, he disagreed. America might not produce great scholars like a Locke or Newton, but "Mansfields and Kenyons" (famous eighteenth-century English jurists) were within reach, the reason being that in America "eminence will be sought with more ardor in the lucrative professions than in the abstract sciences and the fine arts." A rational and almost prophetic analysis in view of the importance which historians would later place on the creative role of the law in nineteenth-century America.[15]

Webster was attempting to rationalize and control his ambition and his sexuality at the same time. In a manuscript essay he depicted the ideal maiden as one who was chaste, retiring, sensitive, born with "a capacity to return affection, not to originate it," knowing insinctively that "fruit" that falls without shaking is too ripe." Although this is about as close as he ever came to making a direct statement about sex, we have to assume that he knew what it meant to be tempted by overripe fruit. The letter he received from "C.D." in Fryeburg does not sound as if it came from the hand of a blushing virgin. Webster had been born and brought up on a farm. Sex was hardly a mystery to him, and living at a time when about every third bride in New England went to the altar pregnant, he knew how easy it was for a young man to be tripped up by his desires. Writing for the Boston *Monthly Anthology* three years after his Fryeburg experience, he praised an American book of satirical verse for its moral tone—the fact that its wit was not "corrupted with the sensuality of Moore." In a footnote he wrote "the author who cannot please without endangering the morals of his readers, had better study ethics than write poetry. On the restraints which youth, with infinite pains, imposes on its passions, Mr. M. breathes the effusions of licentious ingenuity, and they dissolve like scorched wax."[16]

Upon first returning to Salisbury, Webster tried to continue the fiction he had begun at Fryeburg about not being interested in women. "To tell you the truth," he wrote to Fuller after a visit to Hanover in December, 1802, "I am hungry twice where I am lovesick once." But his friends knew better, and chided him for trying to hid his interest in Professor Woodward's daughter, Mary, who attracted him with her beauty and her position in Hanover society. In a letter to Merrill in August, 1803, Webster finally confessed that he was drawn to Mary but did not know how she felt about him. Whatever happened, he was not about to lose his head.

In this little Mary matter I feel *serious* (don't laugh) but moderate. The object I think worth an effort, but then I have no intention of dying in event of failure. I am not yet quite deep enough in the [   ] to resolve either to succeed or else in despair to depart in hemp or hurling stream. Hanging or drowning has still more terrors to me than a *refusal*.

Apparently Mary Woodward was never given the opportunity to refuse. Webster vacillated over the matter until November, when Merrill, now tutoring at Dartmouth, told him she had promised herself someone else. Pledging his friend to secrecy, the bashful lover in Salisbury retired from a contest he had never fully entered with mixed feelings of disappointment and relief. A few weeks later one of the local Salisbury belles cut her foot on the afternoon preceding a dance causing him to write the following lines.

> Rust seize the axe, the hoe, or spade,
> Which in your foot this gash has made!
> Which cut thro' kid and silk and skin,
> To spill the blood that was within:
> By which you're forced to creep and crawl,
> Nor frisk and frolic at the ball!
>
> But Clara, Clara! were thy heart
> As tender as thy pedal part;
> From thy sweet lips did love but flow,
> Swift as blood gushes from thy toe,
> So many beaus would not complain
> That all their bows and vows are vain! [17]

As an old man Webster would be accused of having mistresses. As a young man he appears to have been better at writing poetry than making love.

By the spring of 1804 Webster began to feel that he had gone as far as he could with his legal studies in Salisbury. He grumbled about the "small society" of the village, called it a "vale of tears," and complained bitterly at the absence of real friends like Bingham. He still anticipated setting up as a country lawyer but felt he needed some experience in a larger town first. When Zeke, who had taken a school in Boston, offered to pay his room and board in exchange for tutorial duties in Greek and Latin, he jumped at the opportunity, arriving at his brother's doorstep in Boston on July 17. [18]

Except for what he had learned during a brief visit a few months earlier, Webster knew nothing about Boston. His only friend there, besides Zeke, was Cyrus Perkins, a former Dartmouth classmate now practicing medicine. His anonymity along with the fact that he had neglected to bring letters of introduction with him complicated the problem of finding a good place to read. He had approached several lawyers without success when he arrived unannounced at Christopher Gore's Tremont Street office on July 20. Gore was just returning to his practice after serving eight years in London as commissioner under the Jay Treaty. One of the leading New England Federalists ever since Washington named him the first United States district attorney for Massachusetts in 1789, Gore was wealthy, aristocratic, and owned one of the best law libraries in Boston. That Webster could suddenly impose himself on a man of such great reputation and in the matter of a fifteen-minute interview get himself accepted as a clerk in his office says a good deal about the young man's developing poise and confidence. No doubt Webster's ability to rattle off the names of prominent New Hampshire Federalists helped his case, but it was a giant step forward to move from Thomas Thompson's simple Salisbury office to the handsomely outfitted quarters of Christopher Gore, and he knew that he was fortunate to have negotiated it. As it was it took more than a week before the famous lawyer and statesman could remember the name of the pale young man with the conspicuous black hair and huge eyes who had so suddenly taken up residence in his office.[19]

Webster made the most of his opportunity and methodically went through Gore's library, reading Vattel, Bacon, Pufendorf, and Viner and abstracting from Latin and Norman French into English the folio edition of *Saunders' Reports*. He concentrated on the common law and regularly attended sessions of the Massachusetts Supreme Court and the United States Circuit Court, reporting all of their decisions.

He learned even more from the lawyers of Boston than he did from books. In New Hampshire his appetite for study had been cooled by the fact that unlearned judges openly ridiculed the great classical texts from the bench. In Boston he came into close contact with a man like Gore who was both an eminent lawyer and "a deep and varied scholar," and in the Boston courts he had an opportunity to watch some of the best legal minds and practitioners in the country. One of these was Samuel Dexter who had served in the House of Representatives, the Senate, and President Adams's cabinet before returning to the law two years earlier. A big man with what Webster described as a "strong, generalizing and capacious mind," Dexter was not a great student but was immensely powerful in the application of great principles. Deliberate and unostentatious he was said to make five thousand dollars a year from his practice and had once earned the royal sum of fourteen hundred dollars for arguing a single case. The leader of the Boston Bar was Theophilus Parsons, with a long career of public service dating back to the Massachusetts constitutional convention, a remarkable general knowledge of such disparate subjects as Greek, astronomy, and carpentry, and the best law library in the United States. Parsons had a great following among young lawyers and a reputation among Jeffersonian Republicans for being "as cunning as Lucifer and about half as good." After studying Parsons in court, Webster described him in his notebook:

Theophilus Parsons, Esq. is now fifty-five years old; of rather large stature and inclining a little to corpulency. His hair is brown and his complexion not light. His face is not marked by any striking feature, if we except his eyes. His forehead is low and his eyebrows prominent. He wears a blue coat and breeches; worsted hose, a brown wig, with a cocked hat. He has a penetrating eye of an indescribable Color. When couched under a jutting eyebrow, it directs its beam into the inmost recesses of his soul. When Parsons intends to make a learned observation, his eyebrow sinks; when a smart one, for he is, and wishes to be thought, a wit, it rises. The characteristic endowments of his mind are strength and shrewdness. Strength, which enables him to support his cause; shrewdness, by which he is always ready to report the sallies of his adversary. His manner is steady, forcible, and perfectly perspicuous. He does not address the jury as a mechanical body to be put in motion by mechanical means. He appeals to them as men, and as having minds capable of receiving the ideas in his own. Of course, he never harangues. He is never stinted to say just so much on a point, and no more. He knows by the juror's countenance, when he is convinced; and therefore never disgusts him by arguing that of which he is already sensible and which he knows it impossible more fully to impress. A mind thus strong, direct, prompt, and vigorous is cultivated by habits of the most intense application. A great scholar in every thing, in his profession he is peculiarly great. He is not content with shining on occasions; he will shine everywhere. As no cause is too great, none is too small for him. He knows the great benefit of understanding small circumstances. 'Tis not enough for him that he has learned the leading points in a cause; he will know every thing. His argument is, therefore, always consistent with itself; and its course so luminous that you are ready to wonder why any one should hesitate to follow him.[20]

The description of Parsons is notable for many reasons, in addition to its value as a vivid piece of expository prose. It shows how intense Webster had become in his application to the law in Boston. He literally absorbed Parsons, and it is striking that some years later when Webster himself was becoming a familiar figure in Boston courtrooms, Emerson would describe him with words very similar to those he employed in getting the measure of Parsons.[21] It is no accident that Webster's complaints about his chosen profession came to an end after his Boston experience. In men like Gore, Dexter, and Perkins he had found the professional models that he needed.

Boston was crowded with young men from the New England hinterland like himself, and most of the outlanders fell in with each other, but Webster made a point of searching out "the aboriginal Bostonians." He was apprehensive of mixing in this kind of society, noting that a man "with a fortune to spend is not a fit companion for one who has a fortune to make," but he managed to borrow enough to get by and spent liberally on repertory tickets and accessories to his wardrobe (thread gloves and a seven-dollar hat) in a manner befitting the clerk of Christopher Gore, who traveled in a liveried coach and six.[22]

At the Boston boarding house where he stayed Webster met a wealthy eccentric named Taylor Baldwin who invited him to be his companion on a trip to Albany and back. The two men traveled in style "in a hackney coach, with a pair of nimble trotters, a smart coachman before, and a footman on horseback behind." In Albany Webster met Abraham Van Vechten and Stephen Van Rensselaer both leading Federalists in upstate New York. Upon their return, Baldwin paid him one hundred twenty-five dollars for his company. Already there was something about Webster that seemed to attract gifts from friends and associates.[23]

By the end of December, Webster had begun to grow impatient about setting up in practice and discovered that it would be to his advantage in gaining early admission to the bar if he could show that he had been studying law while at Fryeburg. To accomplish this purpose he dispatched the following letter to Judah Dana, a Fryeburg attorney.

Circumstances exist which render it desirable to me to be able to show that during the eight months in which I instructed in the Fryeburg Academy I considered myself destined for the profession of the law, and had myself to the library of a practitioner. If you can, salvo honore [to safeguard honor], say this of me, it would gratify me that you should.

A "student at law" I certainly was not unless "Alan Ramsay's Poems" and "Female Quixotism" will pass for law books. Besides, I should not expect a man of your habit to certify me to have been a student at anything during the time I loitered away in your country. Persuing rather my male and female friends than any books.

To be serious, however, you would really oblige me by writing me a line and stating in it, if you can, that while I was within the academy six hours in the day, you understood me to have made choice of the law as a profession and that I had access to your library—I will immediately excuse you, if there is anything in this request incompatible with propriety—otherwise I will entreat your attention to it as soon as may be, as I should be glad of an answer in three weeks. You will, if you please, reveal this to no one.

Dana promptly replied with the words that Daniel needed, "On your arrival you informed me that as you had commenced, you intended to pursue the study of the law; and asked for the use of my library during said term and you had access to the same—and I expect that you devoted the principal part of your leisure hours while you were at Fryeburg in the study of the law. If a certificate of the above statements will be of any benefit to you, I can truly and cheerfully make it."

When Webster's letter first came to light it was published under the heading "Tricky Daniel Webster."[24] The caption is unfair. Webster was candid enough in explaining what he wanted and what the problems might be in granting his request. The important thing, however, is that he managed to get more than he asked for. He asked only for a statement that he had indicated his commitment to law and had permission to use a library. He received, and presumably used, a statement implying that he had been seriously studying law during this period, which by his own admission was not true. Surely there is no great sin revealed here, and even if there is something about the tone of the whole affair—the concern for secrecy and the willingness to tolerate a certain looseness with the truth in matters of his own convenience—that anticipates the less attractive aspects of Webster's later career, the more important point to note is that his ambition was finally taking hold. The inwardness of his post-college years was giving way to an aggressive outward thrust aimed at protecting his own self interest.

This new-found assurance was put to the test in January, 1803. Largely through the influence of his father, Webster was appointed clerk for the Court of Common Pleas in Hillsborough, New Hampshire. As he recalled in his autobiography, the appointment which carried an income of fifteen hundred dollars a year and promised a competency for the whole family "was equal to a Presidential election." When he rushed in to Christopher Gore with the good news, he was immediately told to decline the offer. At first this seemed like chilling advice, but a little reflection about his dislike for clerical duties and the fact that the clerkship would keep him from building his own practice convinced him that Gore was right. Finding a place in a country sleigh, he went back to Salisbury, his heart as frigid as the landscape at the prospect of confronting his father on the issue. He found the old man sitting before the fire, filled with satisfaction at having done so well by his youngest son. Daniel had rehearsed his speech and spoke it through in a kind of trance. "I felt as if I could die, or fly," he remembered later, "I could hardly breathe." However this near-paralysis did not keep him from saying that although he was honored by the clerkship opportunity, he thought he could do better for himself as "an actor, not a register of other men's actions." At first incredulous, Ebenezer soon relented and contented himself with reminding Daniel of his mother's prediction that he would "come to something or nothing, she was not sure which." From now on that would be up to Daniel himself.[25]

He had begun to take charge of his own life. Internalizing his father's unrealized ambitions, Daniel had mixed them with his own to outreach the father's vision. The roots of that ambition, more powerful than he could ever admit, would eventually support one of the great driving personal energies in nineteenth-century America. Yet at the same time he was asserting his strength and independence, he was reinforcing a feeling of obligation and dependence toward his father. Long after Ebenezer's death, as he strove to prove that he had come to something after all, he would continue to rely for support on others who seemed to stand in his father's place but had little to give except money.

After being admitted to the bar in March, 1805, Webster began to practice law in Boscawen, New Hampshire, the village near Salisbury where he had gone to be tutored by Dr. Wood about ten years earlier. That this would be a temporary situation, not to be extended beyond his father's death, was clear in his mind from the beginning. A year or two earlier he had been assuring friends that he aspired to nothing higher than an honest competence as a village lawyer. Now he emphasized his intention to remain mobile. "The disagreeable incumbrances of houses, lands and property need not delay me a moment," he wrote to Bingham, "Nor shall I be hindered by love, nor fastened to Boscawen by the power of beauty." With Zeke just beginning to study law himself, and his father increasingly feeble and anxious about money, Daniel was willing to launch his career within the shadow of the family farm, but his intention was to move to the metropolitan port town of Portsmouth as soon as he could.[26]

If we are to believe local tradition, Webster made a sensation in the courts in Hillsborough and neighboring counties almost from the day he began to practice. His own memory was a little different. Eight months after he opened his office he described his life as one of "writs and summonses." He applied himself to routine business with great diligence, and his sister Sally, up from Salisbury for a visit, reported to Zeke that Daniel was busy trying to make the most of small beginnings by scratching out writs for a dollar apiece. He did occasionally appear before a jury, the first time when Ebenezer himself was on the bench, a source of great satisfaction to both father and son. Another time he was narrowly bested in a trial with Jeremiah Mason, a luminary of the New Hampshire Bar who would soon become a close friend. For the most part, he tried to collect old debts and by his own admission sometimes raised a commotion by sending worthy neighbors to jail.[27]

Ebenezer Webster died in April, 1806. Visiting Elms Farm forty years later, Senator Webster remembered the day. "I neither left him nor forsook him. My opening an office at Boscawen was that I might be near him. I closed his eyes in this very house. He died at sixty-seven years of age, after a life of exertion, toil and exposure; a private soldier, an officer, a legislator, a judge, everything that a man could be, to whom learning never had disclosed her 'ample page.' "[28]

His father's death removed one of the main reasons for staying in Boscawen. Missing the excitement of Boston, Webster's appetite for a more stimulating environment was whetted by letters from Zeke and from the editors of the *Monthly Anthology,* a leading literary journal published in Boston, which had published a review of his in the spring of 1805. During the year following Ebenezer's death he and Zeke reached an agreement which made it possible for him to move. His brother would take over his office in Boscawen and would also oversee the family farm in Salisbury, while he would try to improve his own fortune at Portsmouth.[29]

The Webster who moved to Portsmouth in September, 1807, was an incomparably more confident young man than the boy who had graduated from college six years earlier except in one respect—he remained without a wife and worried about it. By this time almost all of his friends had long married, and he could no longer claim that bachelorhood was a financial necessity. What was wrong? He had confessed his own perplexities about the matter to Bingham in January, 1806. "The example of my friends sometimes excites me," he wrote, "and certain narratives I hear of you, induce me to inquire why the deuce female flesh and blood was not made for me as well as others; but reasons, good or bad, suppress hope and stifle incipient resolution." More than a year later he was still sounding a negative note. "I rejoice that you have so comfortable a cage," he wrote to his friend Merrill, "A bird you cannot but find easily. Your friend Webster has neither cage nor bird. However he lives in hopes."[30]

One of the reasons Webster may have tried to keep his hopes up about finding a wife is the fact that while he was at Boscawen he had a chance to see at firsthand the trouble into which a young bachelor might fall. Samuel Fessenden, who had been one of Webster's students at Fryeburg, was teaching school in Boscawen at the same time Daniel started his law practice. The two must have become close friends because one wintry day in 1806, Daniel drove "20 miles in a snow storm to stand godfather" at the christening of Fessenden's bastard son. Fessenden took the baby back to his family in Fryeburg while Daniel is supposed to have raised some money to settle on the unwed mother.[31]

Just before leaving for Portsmouth Webster wrote to Thomas Worcester, minister of the Congregational Church in Salisbury, enclosing "a few propositions in the shape of articles, intending to exhibit a very short summary of the doctrines of the Christian religion as they impress my mind." The list of Christian doctrines which he sent to Rev. Worcester is essentially a summary of the orthodox faith most New Englanders subscribed to, emphasizing the providence of God, the divinity of Christ, and the authority of Scripture. If there is anything at all distinctive about Webster's statement it is the calm and rational language in which it is presented. Nothing is said about natural depravity, damnation, conversion, or the exclusiveness of any form of church polity. Shortly thereafter, at the age of twenty-five, Daniel Webster formally united with the church in which he had been baptized.[32]

Webster joined the church on August 8, 1807. Less than a month later, on September 4, he wrote the first letter of which we have any record to his future bride, Grace Fletcher, an intelligent and deeply religious minister's daughter living with a married sister in Salisbury. We know almost nothing about the courtship except that it had been going on at least since 1805 and that Grace's cousin once described her suitor by saying "Father and Uncle Chamberlain think him a man of great promise, but we girls think him awkward and rather verdant."[33]

Verdant or not, this time Daniel persisted. In his letter to Grace, he described a *"solitary* ride" home after visiting her. This was a condition he was determined to remove. One day in the late spring of 1808, without sharing his mission with anyone, he left his bachelor's apartment in Portsmouth and rode off to Salisbury where he was married to Grace Fletcher by Thomas Worcester.[34]

Despite the paucity of information about Webster's courtship and about his wife before their marriage, it is easy to see why he decided on a woman like Grace Fletcher. Coming from the same kind of village background that he did, she had grown up in a minister's house where books and ideas were considered important, had attended an academy herself and had taught school. Webster's unsatisfactory experiences with the Hanover girls had tended to involve him with aggressive or inaccessible women (C.D. and Mary Woodward). Grace was an attractive, gentle woman without being a great beauty, and as an unmarried woman of twenty-seven in danger of being considered a spinster. Physically and emotionally delicate, and without personal ambition of her own, she was the kind of woman content to stay in a husband's shadow. At the same time she had other qualities that he needed. His decision to take up formal church membership was probably triggered by his courtship, because Grace would not have been likely to accept an unaffiliated suitor. Much more religiously intense than Webster, she retained the Puritan's tendency to look inward and constantly measure her own performance against the stern moral requirements of Calvinism. Seven years before her marriage, when she was twenty years old and a recent graduate of Atkinson Academy, Grace wrote to a former school friend. The letter is a plea for the importance of humility and resignation in a life which must constantly confront the pain of separation from the death of loved ones. She closed by writing, "But such is our stupidity that we neglect the all important realities of eternity for the trifling follies of this vain, delusive world, and scarce a thought aspires to heaven. Let us rouse from our stupor, and oh! may we be prepared for the momentous period which surely awaits us." A solid rock to hold on to for a young man who had worked so hard to come to terms with passion and ambition.[35]

Webster had finally taken the last step to prepare himself for the challenges and responsibilities he would encounter in later life. He had committed himself to a profession, made his peace with his family and with God, and taken the kind of wife he needed. The doubting and inward looking were behind him forever.

4

LAW AND POLITICS IN
NEW HAMPSHIRE

Portsmouth was a good place for the young couple to make their start. A proud, thriving seaport with a population of about five thousand, it claimed some of the best ships and sailors in the world and exuded an exotic atmosphere unknown to sleepy inland villages like Salisbury and Boscawen. Bustling wharves, dwarfed by the soaring spars of ships from Liverpool, Canton, and Jamaica, the cries of stevedores and seamen, a breeze heavy with the scent of brine, molasses, rum, and spices, dockside taverns crowded with pigtailed sailors—all this was heady stuff for country folks. Still the town was not really large enough to be intimidating, and Grace had the security of knowing that her husband, with an assist no doubt from Christopher Gore, had already ingratiated himself in some of the best Portsmouth drawing rooms.

After temporarily renting quarters, Webster purchased a house not far from his office near Market Square. Two stories high with a gambrel roof, diamond-glass windows and probably four rooms to a floor, the house was an eminently respectable residence for a fledgling lawyer and a good measure of his ambition. He paid six thousands dollars for it, about three times his annual income. Within the neighborhood, however, the Webster place was modest enough. Not far down the street was the Governor Langdon House, a handsome, three-storied, elegantly paneled mansion which had offered hospitality to a host of famous visitors including George Washington. Webster would not entertain presidents in Portsmouth, but he was on the way.

Playing hostess to presidents was the last thing on Grace Fletcher Web-

46

ster's mind. A slender, sweet-faced, gentle woman with natural social charm, she made a good companion for her husband at formal gatherings in the neighboring mansions, but she was happier in her own parlor in the company of close friends like the Jeremiah Masons and Eliza Buckminster, a literary-minded spinster whose brother had tutored Webster at Exeter. Here she was content to sit quietly by her husband's side as he talked law and politics and sometimes entertained friends with readings from Shakespeare. Here, after April 29, 1810, she proudly showed off their first child, a black-haired, sparkling-cheeked little girl whom Daniel insisted on naming Grace after her mother.[1]

It was at Portsmouth that Webster's physical appearance began to change. His pallid complexion started to take on the swarthy hue of his father, while his figure expanded into a more fitting support for the remarkable Webster head and voice. He began to project the kind of elemental vitality that encouraged friends to compare him to a lion and would later compel Emerson to observe at Bunker Hill that as a magnificent personal spectacle, Webster almost overshadowed the monument. Recognizing years later that his "remarkably good" health dated from his Portsmouth years, Webster was inclined to give the credit to God, but any impartial observer would have to say that God's instrument in the work was Grace Fletcher.[2]

Most of Webster's time at Portsmouth was taken up following the sessions of the Superior Court through the counties of New Hampshire. He was quickly thrown into close contact with the leading attorneys of the state, not only in the competition of the courtroom, but in the rough fellowship of inns and taverns where lawyers clustered as they made their way around the state. The unfavorable image of the lawyer, carried over from the eighteenth century, was changing and the courtroom, like the pulpit, was beginning to hold the same attraction for rural New Englanders then that the stage and screen would hold for later generations. Each important trial, as Claude Fuess wrote, "was a tournament in which champions were matched against each other, and farmers drove in from all the surrounding country to hear a case argued by two famous advocates." Competition was keen and the quality of the antagonists was high, as Webster discovered when he found himself matching wits with the likes of older men like William Plumer, Jeremiah Smith, and Jeremiah Mason.[3]

Plumer was an experienced politician who had already served both in the state legislature and as United States senator. A shrewd, self-contained, and self-taught lawyer, he had no flair for rhetoric or theatrics, but knew how to handle himself in a fight. Smith, a former congressman and United States district attorney, held a Doctor of Laws degree from Harvard, and was one of the best conversationalists Webster ever met. A judge during one of Webster's first court appearances, Smith was profoundly impressed by what he heard and became quite close with the younger man.

Jeremiah Mason was the most important influence on Webster during these years. Easily one of the most impressive physical specimens New England had produced, Mason towered six feet seven inches, and his intelligence was as impressive as his bulk. A master of detail in every case he undertook, Mason was fourteen years older than Webster and renowned for the number of cases he had won. "He had a habit," Webster recalled later, "of standing quite near to the jury, so near that he might have laid his finger on the foreman's nose; and then he talked to them in a plain conversational way, in short sentences, and using no word that was not level to the comprehension of the least educated man on the panel." Webster soon decided to pattern his own style after Mason's, to simplify his language and concentrate on the power of fact and logic rather than on literary allusions. The lucidity of many of his famous arguments later on can be explained in part by Mason's example. For nine years he and Mason competed against each other in the New Hampshire courts, and the competition, rather than creating tensions which pushed them apart, forged the bonds of a lifelong friendship. After he left Portsmouth, Webster frequently called on Mason for advice in political and legal matters, and he took pains to make the debt he felt to his older colleague a matter of record long before Mason died.

He has been of infinite advantage to me, not only by his unvarying friendship, but by the many good lessons he has taught, and the example he set me in the commencement of my career. If there be in the country a stronger intellect, if there be a mind of more native resources, if there be a vision that sees quicker or sees deeper into whatever is intricate, or whatsoever is profound, I must confess I have not known it.[4]

Nine years competing against and associating with men like Mason and Jeremiah Smith turned Webster into a tough-minded, self-confident professional, able to hold his own in any court in the land. He sometimes shared cases with his brother Zeke at this time, and one sharp-eyed New Hampshire reporter later recalled how the two young Websters came sweeping into Grafton, New Hampshire, the day court was being held.

I can see them now, driving into that little village in their billows-top chaise—top thrown back—driving like Jehu, the chaise bending under them like a close-top in a high wind. . . . I could have told either of them thirty miles among a thousand men.

Once he had made his dramatic entrance Webster had the kind of magnetic personal attraction that commanded attention even when he did nothing.

He was a black raven-haired fellow, with an eye as black as death, and as heavy as a lion's—and no lion in Africa ever had a voice like him; and his look was like a lion's—that same heavy look, not sleepy, but as if he didn't care about anything else. He didn't look as if he was thinking about anything; but as if he would think like a hurricane if he once got waked up to it.[5]

Sometimes Daniel would undertake to argue a case just before it was coming to trial. Ignoring the law books he would pace about restlessly, throw his hands through his hair and suddenly stop a colleague to ask where certain authorities could be found. When the case came up for trial he would stand up "and pour out the law and cite his authorities, as if he had spent months in poring upon it." Every point of law he learned became a part of him forever. His memory was prodigious and his ability to recall the intricate detail of a case years afterward never ceased to amaze other lawyers.

But it was not just intellectual power that made Webster such a tough adversary in the New Hampshire courts. He learned how to flatter vain witnesses and browbeat the weak ones. He intimidated one hapless perjuror to such an extent that the latter not only admitted giving coached testimony but fished a piece of paper out of his pocket to prove it. He learned how to charm a country jury. A witness for the other side testified that he had heard a certain statement about "a hundred times." The testimony reminded Webster of a hunter of low credibility who once told of seeing one hundred black snakes each twenty feet long lined up in a row. His friends refused to believe his story, prompting the hunter to reduce the number of snakes. Finally getting down to two snakes, he took his stand, saying "I won't give up another snake; I'll give up the story first."[6]

It was Webster's virtuosity as much as anything that impressed those who saw him outside the courtroom. Mason once said that the stage lost a great actor when he took up the law, and those privileged to hear Webster read the great speeches of Hamlet, Othello, and Macbeth in the privacy of his own parlor agreed. He was also developing a reputation as a writer in the prestigious Boston *Monthly Anthology*. The *Anthology* featured work by some of the leading intellectuals in New England, but if Webster was flattered to appear in their company he did not show it. When asked to comment on a volume of political philosophy by an English radical he scornfully disposed of the book by saying he had "never made a worst bargain with an honest man" than when he paid a dollar for a book so hastily thrown together. "But perhaps it is well," he went on, that the rash Englishman had written so hastily, "for if he had taken longer time, there is reason to fear that instead of writing better, he would have written more." He knew almost nothing about modern European languages, but this did not stop him from reviewing a book on French, and from saying

If I might have my choice, I would make love in Italian; converse with wits and connoisseurs in French; say my prayers in Spanish; and talk to my dog in some of the dialects of the Baltic; but my funeral eulogy should be written in English by Doctor Johnson.[7]

The *Anthology* was established in 1803, the year before Webster went to Boston. It was modeled after the famous English *Gentleman's Magazine,* and its founders represented the intellectual elite of Boston, including men like Ralph Waldo Emerson's father, William, John Kirkland, president of Harvard, and the scholarly young George Ticknor. Liberal in theology and conservative in politics, the *Anthology* was the ornament of the Federalist mind in New England, and according to Henry Adams it "far surpassed any literary standards then existing in the United States and was not much inferior to any in England." The men behind the *Anthology* were alarmed at the decline of Federalist power. They tended to associate democracy with barbarism and were among the first American intellectuals to seriously grapple with the problem of finding a place for humanistic culture in the new Republic. It is no wonder that they welcomed a young man like Webster to their ranks. A Federalist by inheritance, temperament, and conviction, he had personally experienced the kinds of anxieties repeatedly expressed in the pages of the *Anthology* about the national obsession with money-getting and the neglect of letters and public virtue. To the editors of the *Anthology* Webster represented a level of sophisticated literacy that was hard to reconcile with life in the hinterland, and they were reclutant to see him leave Boston. "Do not let the cares of the world and the deceitfulness of riches choke the growth of literature in your mind," one of them wrote to Webster after he had settled in Boscawen. "New Hampshire has yet to produce its portion of eminent men."[8]

Perhaps he remembered these words as he rode up through the hills with Grace and the Jeremiah Masons during the summer of 1809 to give the Phi Beta Kappa address at Dartmouth. At any rate he chose to speak on "The State of Our Literature," and what he said could have been taken out of the pages of the *Anthology*

An inordinate ambition to accumulate wealth forms a prominent feature in the character of this country. The love of gold is the ruling passion, and of all passions this is the most hostile to literary improvement. There is a liberal pursuit of wealth which well consists with the interests of science, which while it accumulates princely private fortunes, endows colleges . . . and there is a mean, monkish, idolatrous devotion to it, which when once enthroned in the heart, banishes thence every generous sentiment. Where this grovelling, dust-loving propensity predominates, literature can make little progress.

A second obstacle to the advancement of literature was "the pursuit of politics." By this Webster meant not the pursuit of political science, but

. . . The mad strife of temporary parties, the rancor of conflicting interests and jarring opinions. These are vials of wrath the contents of which scorch and consume all that is desirable and lovely in society. The strife of politics never made a great or good man. Its unvarying tendency is to belittle greatness, and corrupt goodness. It contracts the mind, and hardens the heart.[9]

George Ticknor, the brilliant young scholar in the audience, and soon to become one of Webster's most fervent admirers, reported that although the speech was not much, the mere presence of Webster and Mason in Hanover caused a flurry of excitement. Webster admitted, himself, that he had not had time to prepare for the occasion. Nevertheless, it must have given him satisfaction to return to his alma mater in the role of pundit after his rather petulant exit nine years before. Of course, the irony of the performance would have escaped him. No amount of preaching against money-making would ever keep him from scrambling for dollars, and even as he bemoaned the enticements which beguiled the young into the "contentious paths" of party politics, he found himself being drawn into the leadership of the Federalist party in New Hampshire.

Although Webster had been much more concerned with his own personal development than with politics during the time between his graduation from college and his residence at Portsmouth, there was no question about where his political loyalties lay. Political identity was not one of his problems. He had been brought up to revere George Washington and to assume that the Federalists were Washington's legitimate political heirs. These were the men who had governed New Hampshire when he was a boy. They opposed social conflict and partisan spirit and believed in strong government by the elite with the people's consent. Far from believing in democracy, they sought to hold on to "a *speaking* aristocracy *in the face of a silent* democracy."[10]

The "speaking aristocrats" in New Hampshire were local leaders like Ebenezer Webster, with his long tenure as town moderator, and John Gilman, the perennial Federalist Governor. Their leadership during Daniel's boyhood seemed as certain as the stars. Then came the trauma of 1800 when a new Republican party, led by Jefferson, came into power. In New Hampshire it was not so much Jefferson's election, but the fact that Gilman was seriously challenged for the first time that shocked people. The Federalist response, led by Congregational clerics who identified Republicans with the fanaticism of the French Revolution, can only be described as hysterical. A minister in Concord warned that a Federalist defeat could mean "our towns and villages laid waste and plundered by French soldiers; and your *mothers,* your *wives.* . . . ravished before your eyes." A Federalist paper put the matter even more bluntly.

Jog round the country, then ye disorganizers—publish your electioneering pieces—hold your private meetings—foment malicious falsehoods—exert every nerve—make use of every species of intrigue—but before any person you propose is chosen Governor, you ALL will be suspended by a single rope.[11]

Webster was eighteen and still at Dartmouth when Jefferson was elected. The year before he had helped organize a Federal Club in Hanover. Like other members of the club, he found Jefferson's victory hard to take, but unlike the older Federalists he was able to shrug it off by reminding Bingham that "what cannot be cured must be endured."[12]

During the acrimonious years between 1800 and 1805, when the Federalists finally lost the governorship for the first time, Webster was less interested in politics than he was in trying to come to terms with his own future. Although politics was not his major concern, he did not try to hide his anger over what was happening from his friends. Privately he called the Republicans in Salisbury "a pack of Jackasses," and assured Bingham that "the path to despotism leads through the dirt and mire of uncontrolled democracy." In public, as at the Fourth of July celebration in Fryeburg in 1802, he took more philosophic ground, warning his audience after the manner of a Yankee Edmund Burke that

> The politician that undertakes to improve a Constitution with as little thought as a farmer sets about mending his plow, is no master of his trade. . . . our government is good because it is practical. It is not the sick offspring of closest philosophy. It did not rise vaporous and evanescent from the brains of Rousseau and Godwin, like a mist from the ocean. It is the production of men of business, of experience, and of wisdom. It is suited to what man is and what it is in the power of good laws to make him.

When it became clear in 1804 that Jefferson's popularity was more than a passing delusion, Webster grew impatient with the futile croaking of some of his friends. He saw that the ability to adjust to changing party leadership not only indicated the basic strength of the system, but required vigorous countermeasures on the part of the opposition. "Sighs and tears and broken hearts" were "not worth a biscuit"; they could not "get a vote."[13]

During a visit to Salisbury in February, 1805, Webster wrote his first political pamphlet in a last-ditch attempt to save the governorship for his father's friend and creditor, John Gilman. Employing standard Federalist rhetoric, he likened Gilman to the saintly Washington and warned that the opposition candidate, John Langdon might bring the guillotine to New Hampshire. It was just as well that he published the pamphlet anonymously, but as he told Bingham, he did get the pleasure of seeing it "kicked about under many tables." That was the only satisfaction he received from it, because Langdon, for all his alleged Jacobinism, became the new governor.

Webster obviously did not believe his own rhetoric, because he lived amicably with a family of Republicans during his residence in Boscawen and kept his politics pretty much to himself. At the same time his old mentor, Thomas Thompson, was a Federalist congressman in Washington, and he was able to experience vicariously through Thompson's letters some of the excitement of a political career at the national level.[14]

After he moved to Portsmouth Webster became more actively involved with politics. The city was strongly Jeffersonian at the time, but as William Plumer, Jr., later recalled, "Webster was indefatigable in bringing it over to his way of thinking." His timing was good, because the overriding issue of the day, which involved American policy toward the warring nations of England and France, was one in which the people of Portsmouth had a compelling interest. Each of these powers was trying to prevent the other from enjoying the advantages of American trade with the result that American shipping was constantly harassed. Since England had the more powerful navy, English interference became the more serious problem, and Jefferson tried unsuccessfully to contain it by applying economic sanctions aimed at preventing the importation of English goods. In December, 1807, the Congress, acting on his recommendation, went far beyond this by passing an Embargo Act which prohibited practically all seaborne commerce between the United States and foreign nations. The Embargo Act promised to have a devastating effect on New England seaports, and Webster was quick to see that the marriage of Federalist principles to sea-coast interests might be strong enough to break the hold of the Jeffersonians in New Hampshire and Washington. He campaigned actively for the Federalist cause in the fall of 1808 and wrote a pamphlet attacking Jefferson's embargo as an unconstitutional step which would destroy American commerce and "surrender" American liberty and independence "to the protection of Bonaparte." Whatever influence this may have had, the results were mixed. Although the embargo was repealed and New Hampshire voted for the Federalist presidential candidate Pinckney, the strong Republican tide elsewhere in the country carried Jefferson's protégé James Madison into the White House. Meanwhile the Republican John Langdon remained governor of New Hampshire.[15]

During the next four years Webster remained moderately involved in New Hampshire politics. He helped put his friend Jeremiah Smith into the governor's chair in 1809, only to see John Langdon take it back again the following year. In March of 1810 he wrote Zeke exhorting him to help keep Boscawen and Salisbury in the Federalist camp, and a few months later he himself was named head of a committee to do the same for Portsmouth.[16]

In Washington President Madison, inheriting Jefferson's problems with England and France, had been turning American trade on and off in a vain effort to make the seas safe for American shipping. When Napoleon pretended to allow trade with America, Madison imposed an embargo on England alone. This action, odious in New England, was applauded by westerners who wanted war with England in order to acquire new territory in Canada and Florida and remove the border menace of Indians whom they suspected of being supported by the British. In July of 1811 William Henry Harrison and one thousand troops threw back an Indian attack at the famous battle of Tippecanoe which further increased anti-British sentiment. The nation drifted steadily away from peace, and in June of 1812 Congress declared war on Great Britain. The vote in the Senate was 19 to 13 in favor of war. New Hampshire and all the other New England states except Vermont voted for peace.

In March of 1812 Webster was chosen town moderator of Portsmouth by the narrow margin of twelve votes. He was the first Federalist to hold the post in thirteen years, and in a natural position to reap political advantage from the unpopularity of the war. On July 4 he addressed the members of the Washington Benevolent Society, and contrasting Washington's wise policy of neutrality with Madison's rashness, warned his audience that while Federalists intended to obey the law they had no intention of being drafted as allies of France. "French brotherhood is an idea big with horror and abomination," he said. "There is no common character, nor can there be a common interest, between the Protestants, the Dissenters, the Puritans of New England, and the Papists, the Infidels, the Atheists of France."[17]

In August Webster prepared a memorial endorsed by local Federalists which emphasized that although the war was allegedly being fought in the interests of American commerce, New Hampshire merchants did not support it. The document warned that the specter of disunion might already be on the horizon, and that if it ever did occur it would be because "one portion of the country undertakes to contrive, to regulate, and to sacrifice the interest of another."[18]

Daniel Webster was only thirty-one years old, but he had already become the voice of the New Hampshire Federalists. It was natural that they should want him to be their candidate for Congress. When Jeremiah Smith first mentioned the possibility, he refused, saying that he could not spare the time away from his practice. The next day he changed his mind: "As to he law," he said "I must attend to that too—but honor after all is worth more than money." He was nominated and easily elected.[19]

When Webster set off for Washington the first time, life must have seemed sweet to him. He was healthy, young, and handsome, with a talented and affectionate wife who had already borne him one child and was about to give him another. He had attained professional and political recognition far beyond what his father had sought for him. And he had not yet even begun to make the most of the power that lay within him.

The image of Webster which predominates during this period is the image of the young lawyer and politician with almost limitless powers. The testimony of older observers like Jeremiah Mason and Jeremiah Smith, two of the most intelligent men in New England, that they had never seen such a young man before, must be taken at face value. Add to this the extraordinary effect which he seemed to have whenever he addressed an audience, and his apparently effortless ability to lavish charm upon friends in small social situations, and we begin to get a sense of the princely qualities the young Webster seemed to embody. George Ticknor Curtis, Webster's close friend and authorized biographer, after collecting as much personal testimony as he could find from friends who had known him in Portsmouth wrote:

> . . . I can scarcely open one of the numerous communications that are before me from those who knew him as a young man, that does not speak with peculiar zeal of his general powers. It seems as if they felt that the world had set its seal upon all that was great in his genius and majestic in his deportment and character or imposing in his intellectual achievements and public service, yet that there was a charm, a grace, a perfume in his social existence which they fear the world has not known, and of which they bear their testimony more fondly than of all things else that cluster about his name.[20]

The other image of Webster at this time is more cloudy. Everyone, even his political opponents, remarked on his ability, but some observers who fell outside the spell of his charm noticed that he did not try to please everybody. William Plumer, Jr., remembered him at this time as being "haughty, cold, and overbearing," and recalled how the young lawyer had once disposed of New Hampshire Common Pleas judges. "They are too contemptible to be noticed," he quoted Webster as saying, "ignorant, indolent, vain. I trust them as they deserve, that is, as if they had no authority, and deserved no respect." Webster's father had been one of those judges.

Dr. Goddard, a leading New Hampshire Republican, thought that Webster's professed aversion for factional politics was hardly borne out by his political behavior, which included joining other Federalist lawyers in a successful attempt to have a prominent local Republican politician jailed for debt. "Webster has talent for any office," Goddard said, "but he is as malignant as Robespierre, and not less tyrannical." Finally there was the fact that Webster was known to be careless in matters involving money. Friends and opponents alike knew that he was quick to borrow and slow to repay. Jeremiah Smith was willing to pass this off with a smile. "The imprudent dog that he is," Smith said, "he does not know the value of money, and never will. No matter, he was born for something better than hoarding money-bags."[21]

5

IN CONGRESS ON THE
WRONG SIDE OF THE WAR

Like most other visitors making their first trip to Washington in the early nineteenth century, Webster was disappointed. "It is not the wealth nor the People which I expected," he wrote to a college friend. "From Baltimore to this place, the whole distance, almost, you travel thru woods & on a worse road than you ever saw. There are two or three plantations looking tolerably well—all the rest is desert."[1]

There was abundant reason for Webster to have been put off by his first impressions of the new capital. Accustomed to tidy New England villages and the Georgian elegance of Portsmouth and Boston, he was appalled by the emptiness and unfinished quality of Washington. Five miles of scattered shacks and houses interspersed with woods and gravel pits, it looked "more like Hampstead Heath than a city." The main government buildings, in various stages of incompletion were separated from each other in a manner consistent with the principle of the separation of powers, and the distances between them were so great that on at least one occasion a party of congressmen lost its way within a mile of the Capitol and spent the night floundering in the gullies, thickets, and swamps that composed so much of the local terrain.

Then there were the people. New Hampshire had abolished slavery when Webster was one year old. The 24,000 people in the District of Columbia in 1812 included more than 5,500 slaves and 2,500 free blacks, and the slave market had become one of the liveliest forms of commerce in the city. Most of the other business in Washington was almost as unsavory, since it involved trying to tap the federal treasury, an activity which attracted paupers, petitioners, petty confidence men, and pamphleteers as well as wealthy speculators and lawyers. For all its august pretensions there was a carnivallike atmosphere about the capital city. The Indian delegations decked out in paint and feathers, and turbanned envoys from countries like Tunisia contributed to this effect, along with the grizzly bears penned up in front of the president's mansion.

Then there was the weather. Webster arrived at the end of May. As the summer heat settled over Washington, and the steam rose from the privies behind the houses lining the way from the Capitol to the president's house, the city began to smell more like a zoo than of magnolias, and the local papers pointedly urged the citizenry to perform a public service by patronizing the newly opened public baths.[2]

Determined to hold on to his New England moorings amid so much strangeness, Webster immediately took up lodgings with his old mentor, Christopher Gore, now Senator Gore, in a Georgetown boarding house. Senator Rufus King, from New York, was also in the house, and both Gore and King had brought with them a liveried coach and four, thus managing to impart an aristocratic tone even to boarding-house living. Once Jeremiah Mason joined the group as a newly elected senator from New Hampshire, Webster felt secure. His domicile, at least, would be an island of congeniality and sound New England principle.

As a boy Daniel often heard his father say that if he had been given the opportunity for an education he would have risen higher in life, including, perhaps a place in the Congress. Now the son was realizing the father's ambition, and he was prepared to execute it in the father's spirit. Ebenezer was dead, but Federalists of the old school, like Massachusetts congressman Timothy Pickering, who sought to organize a northern Federalist confederacy to oppose Jefferson's policies, were still alive. Before leaving Portsmouth, Webster wrote to congratulate Pickering as one of "the Masters of the Washington School of Politics" and to say that he would "imbibe the spirit of the first administration" by following his example. As an earnest of this partisan commitment, he was prepared to bring suit against a "dirty little paper" in New Hampshire for libeling Pickering. Few freshman congressmen have been afflicted with more self-confidence. Scornfully observing that some of his colleagues (almost all of them men of greater political experience), were too limited to make anything but routine motions, he described one of them "as insipid an animal as one would wish to see," and passed off his formal visit to President Madison by simply saying, "I did not like his looks any more than I like his Administration."[3]

It did not take Webster long to discover that although party leadership was almost nonexistent in the Congress there were men of great individual talent in the House. Most congressmen lived in boarding houses grouped according to political and regional interest, and most significant legislation was plotted off the floor of the two houses by boarding house coalitions. During Jefferson's administration the president had been able to dominate Congress, but with the embargo policy and the coming of the war the balance had begun to shift to the House of Representatives, where the rank and file were beginning to fall with increasing regularity under the spell of the militant War Hawks like Henry Clay and John C. Calhoun.[4]

Henry Clay was Speaker of the House. Five years older than Webster, Clay came from a poor- to middling-class Virginia family. He had lost his father at an early age and enjoyed only a smattering of formal education. As a boy of fifteen, however, he had been lucky enough to attract the attention of George Wythe, a signer of the Declaration of Independence and one of Virginia's leading lawyers, who took him on as secretary. This was all the start Clay needed. Once admitted to the bar, he moved to Lexington, Kentucky, where he immediately prospered as a lawyer and plunged into politics. He was first sent to the United States Senate in 1806 at the age of twenty-nine. Thereafter he served as speaker of the Kentucky legislature, filled another unexpired term in the Senate, and was chosen a congressman and Speaker of the House of Representatives in 1811. Clay was only thirty-six when Webster first met him, but already an old hand at politics. He was lanky and fair-skinned with a long, narrow face set off by a wide, gay mouth that could be shaped to laugh, curse, weep, and cheer within the limits of a single breath. Whatever his mood, Clay was the kind of man who always generated excitement. By nature a social creature, his vices (drinking, gambling, smoking, swearing) were the vices of a boisterous frontier democracy, and made him seem more human. Clay was a natural orator who tended to pour out words in fiery profusion until he hypnotized or overwhelmed his audience. He had none of Webster's deliberate manner before a crowd, and his effect was more likely to be electric and immediate rather than intellectual and lasting. Above all he commanded personal loyalty and love among his followers. As Speaker he had begun to bring party discipline to bear in the House, and as a leader of the War Hawks he was committed to an American military victory over England.

John C. Calhoun was Clay's chief lieutenant. Calhoun had been born on the South Carolina frontier the same year as Webster and under the same simple conditions. His father, a zealous, tough-minded Scotch-Irishman from Donegal, had earned a reputation for fighting Indians, aristocrats, lawyers, and the Constitution of the United States. Although John grew up to be an aristocratic lawyer and, during the early phase of his career, a supporter of strong national government, he inherited from his father a fierce confidence in the power of his own mind and an unwillingness to accept anything as truth that he could not confirm by his own reasoning. Calhoun had graduated from Yale, practiced law, and served a term in the South Carolina legislature before he came to the Congress in 1811. Even at this stage he was a walking paradox. His mind was cold, analytical, brilliant, and once he made it up on any subject he would no more think of changing it than he would of trading on the honor of his wife. But his spirit was hot. The gleam in his eye and the set of his jaw might have belonged to any frontier revivalist. Although he knew how to be hospitable and charming, Calhoun had little patience with the kind of conviviality to which Clay was addicted. Like Clay he was a man of great ambition, but there was another fire burning within him which would burn hotter with the years and ultimately consume him—a burning desire to make society conform to the image of social justice painstakingly and logically worked out in his own mind. Calhoun was that strange combination of qualities, a life-long politician born to be a martyr.

Webster was hardly settled at Washington before he got a letter from Zeke reminding him that he had been sent to Congress "at a time when men who love their country and have talents to promote her best interests, would like to be there. It is a time for men to act in." No doubt. The problem was to plot some initial form of action that would not only be good for the country but would also tell leaders like Clay and Calhoun that Daniel Webster had arrived.[5]

Five days after Zeke's letter, Webster took his first significant action in Congress. Many Federalists believed that Madison had learned of Napoleon's intention to revoke French sanctions against American trade as early as 1811 and had kept the information secret for fear that England might also revoke her sanctions, thus removing the pretext for war the next year. Webster introduced resolutions, which he had worked up with Pickering, demanding a full investigation into the matter. It would have been hard for a freshman congressman to have done anything more audacious. He chose to introduce himself to his colleagues by directly impeaching the integrity of the president. And yet so clearly and impressively did he make his argument that the members of the House listened to him in fascinated silence. Clay had assigned Webster to Calhoun's Committee on Foreign Relations and we can only conjecture about Calhoun's thoughts as the black-browed newcomer from New Hampshire spoke. Calhoun was quick to see that the administration could only lose by debating the issue, and he quickly passed the word to let the resolutions pass. This action surprised and disappointed Webster who had relished the possibility of extended debate with administration leaders. However, he was appointed to carry a copy of the resolutions to the president, then seriously ill, a mission he performed with relish.

Eventually Madison proved that the French information had not been received until after war was declared, but politically and personally Webster had made a good beginning. However flimsy and politically contrived his charges against the administration, they created excitement and brought attention to the man who introduced them. The *New York Evening Post* wrote that Madison's illness was really caused by an overdose of medicine from New Hampshire.[6]

Early in July, 1813, while the debates over his resolutions were still being reported in the press, Webster took leave of the House and returned home to attend the birth of his first son and accept the plaudits of his constituents for having belled the Republican cat. Meanwhile the blundering war went on. American troops made an ill-coordinated campaign against Montreal, which culminated with the burning of Buffalo by the British. At the same time, Madison's embargo of the New England coastline aroused the fury of people in Portsmouth, thus encouraging their respresentative to step up his attacks on the administration after he returned to Washington at the end of December.

No sooner had Webster returned to his seat in Congress when he learned that a fire in Portsmouth had destroyed his house, leaving his family safe but homeless. He considered giving up his office and going home. "This life tho great, does not much move me," he wrote to a friend, "when I reflect on the dangers my family were in." Assured that Grace and the children would be comfortable with friends until they could find a new house, he decided to stay in Washington, showing by the decision how strong his commitment to political life had become.[7]

It was January, 1814. Madison's government was reeling and Webster wanted to be in on the kill. Ridiculing the abortive invasion of Canada which had resulted in the invader becoming the invaded, he reminded the House that this was "not that entertainment to which we were invited . . . not that harvest of greatness and glory, the seeds of which were supposed to be sown, with the declaration of war." Now the government sought a bounty to encourage enlistments—to put muscle and bone behind an effort which the people would not support out of enthusiasm alone. Webster opposed the bounty and accused the administration of trying to muzzle the opposition with charges of disloyalty. His opposition was constitutional and conscientious, "as undoubted as the right of breathing the air or walking on the earth. Belonging to private life as a privilege" and "to public life as a duty." The Federalist press chortled at finding a young man of their own capable of matching the arrogance and eloquence of Clay and Calhoun. They put Webster in the front rank of parliamentary speakers on either side of the Atlantic, and even the pro-administration *National Intelligencer* commented favorably on the "elaborate and ingenious" oratory and the level of debate which it elicited. Following up this triumph with a sarcastic speech which helped sink the embargo, Webster went home for the spring recess.[8]

Back in Portsmouth, Webster moved his family into a rented house and tried to dig himself out of debt. The six-thousand-dollar house which had gone up in smoke had not been insured, and he was forced to borrow heavily to set up housekeeping a second time. When he was not working up cases or following the courts, he was at home enjoying what had become the too infrequent company of his wife, their black-eyed little girl and Daniel Fletcher, their new baby son. Visitors who called made it clear that Portsmouth Federalists were proud of their congressman. He was unanimously endorsed for a second term and re-elected by a handy margin in the August elections.

While New Hampshire voted for the Federalist "Peace Ticket," the war moved closer to New Hampshire. Having obtained a foothold on the coast of Maine, the British were in a position to threaten the entire New England seaboard. The man whose father had once been charged with the responsibility of guarding General Washington's tent was now made chairman for the local committee for defense, and on September 10 a handbill appeared over his name summoning all able-bodied men to assemble with whatever arms they owned on the Portsmouth parade ground. This was Webster's only venture into military life, and we can only guess how he would have fared in battle since the crisis passed without an attack.[9]

If he had remained in Washington, Webster would have had a better chance of confronting the enemy directly. While he was ordering out the militia at home, the British fleet in Chesapeake Bay, a threatening presence for months, launched a raid on the capital city which left most of the government buildings in ruins. Called back for an emergency session of Congress in October, 1814, Webster joined his colleagues in the makeshift quarters of the Patent Office, one of the few official buildings still standing. He was appalled by the ease with which the British had been able to sack the city and at the dismal prospect which they left behind. Even with a good government Washington would be a "hideous place," he wrote. "At present it is abominable." The executive mansion lay in ruins, and Madison had taken refuge in a private residence known as the Octagon House, but Webster had no sympathy for him. When the British came, the president and his family had fled along with everyone else. Instead of providing for the defense of the city, he had "acted the part of a faint-hearted, lily-livered runaway," and Webster wanted as little to do with him as possible.[10]

One might have thought that the calamitous course of events would have had the effect of bringing him, at least temporarily, to rally support for the beleagured administration, but this was not the way Webster saw his duty. His constituents believed that "Mr. Madison's war" was being waged to make Mr. Madison's party rich and powerful, and they were dead set against any measures that might help him win it. Letters from home, especially from Zeke, who now sat in the New Hampshire legislature, urged Webster not to relent. "For what purpose should you put men or money in their hands?" his brother demanded. "With all the men & money asked for, how have they defended the capitol? I am confident that the people would support almost any attack that should be made on the administration, especially any which should expose their imbecility and their incompetency to fill their offices."[11]

Zeke, sitting in New Hampshire, made his brother's duty look deceptively simple, but Daniel, sitting in Washington, knew that he was involved in something more than a simple moral exercise. In the first place, despite the obvious short-term advantages to be gained by flogging a government which had blundered into a war it did not know how to win, he did not want to build his career on a reputation for having sabotaged the national defense. In the second place, he had to work with Federalists outside New Hampshire who opposed Madison and feared New England in about equal measure. Given this situation he sought a strategy of responsible partisanship in which all Federalists could agree. He made the matter quite explicit in a letter to an unnamed Massachusetts correspondent even before Washington was raided.

> . . . the Southern Federalists, you know, are themselves alarmed at everything which looks like dissolution. The severance of the Union would give them over to be buffetted. Their will is that N. England would be moderate & reserve itself to act hereafter. If the war lasts, they are confident of being able to oust Democracy out of the Genl Government.
>
> My own opinion is that you ought, in N-E. to go no further than the People drive you. Take care to carry your elections by strong Majorities; keep alive the public attention; convert the honest; silence the brawlers; let the War of the Embargo drive away from Democracy all men of any honor, principle or property & in the end, if the Government will not relieve you from the evils of its oppression, act as the case shall require. In the mean time, forbear talking *big*—hold a cool but a determined & fixed resolution. They speak a good deal here of the scolding, blustering spirit of Massachusetts.[12]

When it came time during the special session to take up the administration's tax bill, Webster showed what this kind of advice could lead to in practice. The bill proposed to double the direct taxes on land so as to provide revenue for the war effort. Webster voted against it but claimed that since it would pass anyway he could not be accused of withholding the means of defense. At the same time he recognized that other Federalists might "choose to vote for revenue, without making themselves in any degree responsible for its probable misapplication." Such tortured reasoning would hardly satisfy the enthusiasts back home, and Webster lamely confessed to his brother that although he would have preferred "a fuller tone of opposition" he did not want to break with Federalists from other states who relied on the federal government to protect them.[13]

The hotbed of Federalist radicalism was in Massachusetts, and Webster, who was already thinking of moving to that state, and had a direct line into the party councils there through Christopher Gore, knew that temporizing in Washington would not win friends in Boston. Some of the radicals were openly ready to encourage New England to go it alone even if that meant disunion; others were anxious to hold a New England convention to discuss how best to protect New England interests. Without saying anything about disunion Webster was quick to support the idea of a convention. "You perceive now that there is no peace," he wrote to William Sullivan in Boston on October 17, 1814, "I am perfectly confident you will see in three months that the Govt could not if it would, protect N. England. Indeed its inability to do so is already sufficiently manifest. Why then not prepare to defend yourself next campaign?[14]

The Federalist convention which Webster endorsed in advance began to hold secret sessions in Hartford on December 15. Would the delegates support open defiance of the law? Would they advocate secession? Webster did not know, but he was prepared to act a part in Washington that was consistent with the spirit of rebellion in New England. The administration, frustrated by the refusal of some New England governors to free detachments of state militia for service in the national army, wanted Congress to pass a draft law. Webster condemned the proposed legislation as unjust and unconstitutional. It was unjust to force young men to shed blood for a cause they did not support, and unconstitutional to conscript an army for purposes of conquest. Furthermore the law could not be enforced. Claiming the same rights for the people of New Hampshire and Massachusetts that Jefferson and Madison had claimed for Virginia and Kentucky during Adams's administration, Webster would advise his constituents to resist this law.

It will be the solemn duty of the State Governments to protect their own authority over their own militia, and to interpose between their citizens and arbitrary power. These are among the objects for which the State Governments exist; and their highest obligations bind them to the preservation of their own rights and the liberties of their people. I express these sentiments here, sir, because I shall express them to my constituents. . . . With the same earnestness with which I now exhort you to forbear from these measures, I shall exhort them to exercise their unquestionable right of providing for the security of their own liberties.

New England had no intention, Webster insisted, of dissolving the Union, having "too strong a recollection of the blessings which the Union is capable of producing under a just administration of government." It was the party in power that threatened the Union by proposing measures which would destroy "every principle, every interest, every sentiment and every feeling which have hitherto contributed to uphold it."[15]

In denouncing conscription Webster invoked the right of nullification that Calhoun would later hold so dear. It was to be his last speech against the war. He delivered it on December 9, 1814, wrote it out carefully afterward, and then decided against printing it because he thought it would not live up to the expectations of his friends. That was the excuse he gave, but there may have been a darker wisdom involved. Although he continued to sound supremely confident in letters ("The Govt. cannot execute a Conscription Law if it should try. It cannot enlist soldiers—it cannot borrow money—what can it do?" he wrote on December 22), he was Calvinist enough to know the hazards of trying to predict the future. He could not be sure of what the Federalists would do in Hartford, any more than he could know the outcome of peace negotiations then being conducted in Europe or the result when General Jackson's untrained troops would meet British regulars in the coming battle at New Orleans. Confronted by these uncertainties Webster's decision not to publish the speech made excellent sense.[16]

The Hartford Convention issued a report in early January supporting the principle of states' rights and calling for constitutional amendments curtailing federal power to lay embargoes, conscript troops, declare war, and admit new states. These and other recommendations amounted to little more than a resanctification of Federalist orthodoxy, and Webster was quick to commend them. On January 11, 1815, he wrote to a correspondent identified only as "Reverend Sir":

We rec'd yesterday the proceedings of the Hartford Convention. They are esteemed moderate, temperate and judicious.

The Federalists who belong in the middle & southern states are very highly gratified. . . .

If New England *reforms her morals* & maintains her religious, literary & social institutions, she will have the best securities for her prosperity, which the case admits. These constitute her real strength. With these, if she should be compelled *to take care of herself*, she will have nothing to fear. She is sufficiently powerful to resist all encroachments on her civil liberties; she is so situated as to command more or less commerce & she has the means of subsistence. All the reflecting men in the Nation know how important New England is to the Union & all the reflecting men in New England feel that the Union also is important to her. I am sure—at least I have a high degree of confidence—that she will never dissolve it. But I do not conceal my apprehension, that if the war lasts, & our affairs be as much mismanaged as they have been—this Government will almost cease to exist—& dwindle to nothing—as to the protection & defense which it will be able to yield.[17]

Three days before Webster wrote these words Andrew Jackson's riflemen, behind a barricade of cotton bales on the edge of a swamp outside New Orleans, destroyed a carefully trained British army of five thousand men. With a loss of only sixty-three Americans, Jackson killed almost two thousand redcoats. More importantly, he and his woodsman soldiers vindicated the American character, and by the time the news reached Washington during the first week in February, American cities only recently threatened by the British torch were glowing in the light of victory parades. The country was still vibrating to the news of the Battle of New Orleans when word came that a treaty of peace had been signed at Ghent. No matter if it had been negotiated before that battle and did not really resolve the issues over which the war had been fought—Jackson made it possible for Americans to believe that they had won the war.

Webster left no record of how he received the news of Jackson's victory, and he was back in Portsmouth when Madison celebrated the treaty by hosting a glorious candlelight reception in the Octagon House in Washington. "Mr. Madison's war" had ended with rapturous victory, and Webster would have plenty of time to calculate the cost of having been on the wrong side.

In later years Webster's political opponents would tirelessly contrast his early sectionalism with the nationalism that had become his trademark. This was easy enough to do with respect to the war but more questionable when applied to the positions he took on the tariff and the bank. His earliest statement on the tariff was made in 1814 in connection with the repeal of the embargo. A question came up over the advisability of protecting American manufactures which had sprung up during the war in response to the shortage of British goods. Webster had never thought much about the subject. He told friends he was undecided but leaned toward the principle of protection. Yet when the time came for him to speak he opposed tariffs because "Habits favorable to good moral and free Governments" were "not usually most successfully cultivated in populous manufacturing cities." At this point, as he conjured up a picture of sturdy American yeomen deteriorating under the assault of "dust, and smoke, and steam, to the perpetual whirl of spools and spindles, and the grating of rasps and saws," Webster's federalism seemed to merge into the agrarian philosophy of Jefferson. He was also speaking for his constituents who were farmers, merchants, and sea captains, but not manufacturers. Webster would not be converted to the tariff until many years later, and even then, although he would be accused of being the paid representative of New England factory owners, he would never forget his own rural background and his affection for the land and those who worked it, sensitive "to the bleatings of their own flocks, upon their own hills, and to the lark that cheers them at the plough."[18]

When it came to federal finance policy, Webster wavered. His natural tendency was to follow Hamilton and support a strong national bank that would pay in "hard money" and "command the solid wealth of the country." At the same time he was reluctant to support any scheme that would shore up the shaky financial structure of Madison's government. When the administration, at its most desperate, proposed a bank backed by paper money which gave special borrowing privileges to the government, Webster helped to defeat it. He later teamed with Calhoun to support a bank bill which Madison vetoed. The president finally got the bank that he wanted

despite Webster's opposition. The latter was instrumental, however, in getting a currency act passed, requiring that all revenues due the government be
paid in coin or notes redeemable in specie. His position on banking in these
early years was generally consistent with the position he took later on and
expressed the fiscal conservatism of the first-generation Federalists. He was
reported in one of his speeches on the subject as saying that "though young,
he found that he possessed antiquated notions; and that, to be useful, he
ought to have been with generations that had gone by."[19]

Webster spent most of 1815 in Portsmouth, returning to Washington in
January, 1816. Although he had two more years to serve in Congress, he
was discouraged by declining Federalist prospects and by his own financial
needs, and began to look forward to quitting his seat. He supported a move
to raise the compensation of congressmen to $1,500 a year plus mileage and
was bitterly surprised at the outcry that went up even among Federalists.
"No respect for talents, services, character of feelings" restrained them, he
complained, "from joining with the lowest democracy in its loudest cry."[20]

By the spring of 1816 Webster had decided to leave Portsmouth for either
Boston or New York. He wanted to find a more lucrative law practice and
be closer to the center of national power. "Our New England prosperity and
importance are passing away," he wrote Zeke. "If any great scenes are to be
acted in this country within the next twenty years, New York is the place in
which those scenes are to be viewed." In April his mother died, thus sever-
ing his last parental tie with New Hampshire. That August, having been
convinced by friends, apparently, that the capital of New England was still a
place of some importance, Webster moved his family to Boston.[21]

Although now a resident of Massachusetts and thus ineligible for renomi-
nation as a New Hampshire congressman, Webster was still obligated to attend the final session of his term. He did not look forward to going through
the motions as a lame duck, and despite the expense determined to turn the
occasion into a celebration by taking Grace with him. They arrived in Washington with the Masons at the end of October, 1816, taking up quarters in a
boarding house almost directly opposite the ruins of the Capitol. Webster
had previously complained about the "unrelieved masculinity" of Washington social life and it pleased him to be able to escort his wife to the diplomatic dinners, receptions, and balls which had seemed so boring without
her. He even broke a long-standing rule and accepted the president's invitation to dine. Although these diversions helped him endure the bickering of a
Congress bogged down with the problems of trying to provide indemnities
for citizens who had lost property during the war, they were cut short when
he and his wife were called back to Boston by the illness of their daughter,
who died in late January, 1817. Leaving his grieving wife in the care of
friends in Boston, Webster returned once more to the capital where he tried
to relieve his own sorrow by attending to the routine business of the House

and absorbing himself in work before the Supreme Court. He remained there until March when he observed the inauguration of James Monroe, who had overwhelmingly defeated the Federalist presidential candidate, Rufus King.

New Hampshire Federalists, of course, were sorry to see Webster go. The *Portsmouth Oracle* had proclaimed him "second to none in the House" before he was fairly settled in his seat, and after his speech on the bank had rhapsodically quoted a passage from the *New York Evening Post* praising Webster for "more sound sense, more practical knowledge of the subject, in a style plain and unadorned, yet precise and chaste, than we have seen from any other man. Hamilton himself were he living, might be willing to acknowledge it as his own."[22]

The Republican-controlled *New Hampshire Patriot* drew quite a different picture of Webster. The *Patriot* was edited by Isaac Hill, a hard-hitting journalist and tough-minded political organizer who was to become one of Webster's most tireless and vehement critics. Before Webster went to Congress the *Patriot* was content simply to suggest that Webster, like other Federalists, was suspected of being "under *British* influence." As his public reputation became greater the paper began to lampoon him for an alleged aristocratic style. On May 17, 1814, for example, the *Patriot* reported

The Portsmouth Oracle of May 7th informs the good people of New Hampshire that Mr. Stockton [probably Richard Stockton, the federalist representative from New Jersey] and Mr. Webster took dinner on their way home from Washington, and that after dinner, "Mr. Stockton and Mr. Webster *bowed*—and went out." *That's a nice boy!*

A little later when Webster was drawn into a local election dispute and asked by the New Hampshire legislature to aid in the investigation, the *Patriot* said his "imperative and haughty manner" was enough to disgust the Federalists themselves. Two weeks later the *Patriot* was referring to "Mr. *Daniel Webster* and his high toned Jackals in Portsmouth." As the end of Webster's first term approached the *Patriot* was accusing the Federalists of talking as if all the "talent and respectability in the world . . . this whole monstrous weight" lay in Daniel Webster's head, a man who had been flattered so much that he was actually beginning to believe in his own divinity. One writer for the *Patriot* who identified himself as "A Farmer" reported that on some of the pages of Webster's speeches the particles *"I my* and *me* are as thick as the bristles on a hog's back."[23]

An objective observer would have to say that Webster's entrance on the national political scene had been impressive. He upheld his party's cause with intelligence and style during the war years, and showed from the start that as a thinker, speaker, and law maker he could hold his own with Clay,

Calhoun, or any other American politician. Despite the *Patriot*'s jibes about his lofty, aristocratic manner, Webster did lend dignity to the Congress. The best example of this is his conduct when John Randolph challenged him to a duel. Randolph, the shrill-voiced, neurotic, and imperious representative from Virginia, who liked to bring his hunting dogs onto the floor of the House with him, had a fantastic sensitivity to what he fancied were matters of honor and was always challenging someone to a duel. In the spring of 1816, Randolph took offense at the way Webster objected to a proposed tax on sugar and promptly sent his challenge to decide the matter on the "field of honor." Webster was opposed to dueling in principle, especially when the issue involved "words of a general nature used in debate." The letter of refusal which he had delivered to Randolph was cool, confident, and precise.

> It is enough that I do not feel myself bound, at all times and under any circumstances, to accept from any man who shall chose to risk his own life, an invitation of this sort; although I shall always be prepared to repel in a suitable manner the aggression of any man who may presume upon such a refusal.[24]

Webster handled Randolph's challenge in a way any conservative could admire. He preserved his honor without risking his life. This is appropriate to note because conservatism was the most dominant theme in his thinking and speeches during these four years. When he wanted to cite authority he usually found it in the past, in the wisdom of Washington. When he opposed conscription, banks, and tariffs he did so by calling them unconstitutional or dangerous innovations. He would never depart from the basic conservatism expressed during his first years in Congress.

Unfortunately Webster's conservatism did not extend to all matters of personal life. In politics he preached conservatism and warned against unnecessary risks. As a man who had yet to establish his own economic security, he spent freely, sought shortcuts to fortune, and eventually accepted the bounty of others. Although this pattern of behavior would not emerge fully until later, some of the seeds of future difficulty were already being planted. Apparently even before he got to Washington Webster entered into some kind of agreement to act as a legislative agent for Charles March, a New York merchant whose parents lived in New Hampshire. Beginning the day after his arrival, Webster wrote regular letters to March reporting on all legislative matters relating to commerce. On May 31, 1813, he included in one of his reports a request that March pay $150 on a bill he owed in Portsmouth, and on June 14 he wrote *"You must contrive some way for me to get rich, as soon as there is a peace."*[25]

No one could ever keep Webster rich, and there is no reason to believe that March or anyone else was giving him regular financial support at this time. In view of the later purses that his friends made up for him, however, it is interesting to notice Webster's reaction when he heard a rumor in January, 1814), that a movement was afoot in Portsmouth to raise money for him. "I have no knowledge that any such thing is contemplated," he wrote to a friend, "and if it were, should act as I think every other man would in like circumstances. I mention this to the end, that if any such report is prevalent among you, you may stifle it." The language is ambiguous enough to suggest that Webster may not have wanted to say no, but felt appearances demanded it. On the other hand, it is only fair to recall that this letter was written shortly after the Websters lost their home through fire.[26]

The ironic thing about Webster's first years in Washington is that the man who became not only famous but venerated by whole generations of Americans as a spokesman for American nationalism began his career by opposing the war which more than any other single event in the first quarter of the nineteenth century made national sentiment possible. His opponents accused him of having plotted sedition with other Federalist leaders at the Hartford convention. He tried to defend himself from these charges for the rest of his life, pointing out that he had advised Governor Gilman of New Hampshire against sending delegates to the convention, which may have been true, and that he was in Congress when the convention met, which was certainly true. When the charges persisted he denied that he had ever approved of or concurred in "the objects or the results of that convention," which was false. Webster had encouraged Federalists to hold the convention and he had applauded the results. Not only that. He had given a speech on the floor of Congress which embraced most of the sentiments held by the Federalists at Hartford. That speech would not be printed in his lifetime, but his opponents knew where Webster had stood during the war and they would not let American voters forget it. Without mentioning his name, the *Patriot* predicted what this might mean for his political future.

Some twenty years hence, when the glory achieved by our gallant naval and military heroes shall shine like a star of the most resplendent lustre . . . when we shall have seen that foreign nations will dare no longer trample on our rights, because we have had the courage to resist them . . . what will then be thought of the party which belittled and decried our resources, which exulted in the prospect of a depreciation in the national credit, which exulted in the successes of the enemy and in our own reverses . . .? They will find that the longer the lapse of time after any great epoch in which was preeminently involved the destinies of a country, the greater and more pointed will be the detestation of those who have acted the disgraceful part. . . .[27]

The editorial was entitled "The Fall of Federalism."

6

THE GODLIKE MAN
ARRIVES IN MASSACHUSETTS

One morning, soon after Webster had quit Washington for the comfort of his Beacon Hill home in Boston and the security of his own law office, he was visited by a group of men who sought his services in a highly publicized criminal action about to be tried in nearby Essex County. The case involved a Major Goodridge of Maine who claimed to have been assaulted, robbed, and shot on the highway between Exeter, New Hampshire, and Newburyport, Massachusetts. The accused were a pair of brothers named Kenniston, toll-keepers on the Exeter-Merrimack Bridge. There were no witnesses to the robbery, but the major exhibited a gunshot wound in his hand and some pieces of marked gold presumably found in the Kenniston's cellar as evidence of their guilt. Although the evidence was convincing enough on the surface, some of the people in Essex County had begun to ask questions. Goodridge seemed like an eccentric stranger; why had he marked his own money before coming into their law-abiding neighborhood? What motive would inoffensive citizens like the Kennistons have for committing such a crime? When these doubts began to appear in public, Goodridge responded by discovering alleged accomplices to the Kennistons. Invariably in searching a suspect's house the major would poke into an obscure hiding place and come up with one of his marked gold pieces or a paper wrapper in which he said he had kept his money. By the time of the trial many people had begun to suspect that the Kennistons were innocent and that Goodridge, for reasons of his own, was no more than a mischief maker.

Webster had heard about the case even before he reached Boston, but he knew nothing of the details. Pleading ignorance and the need to rest after his trip from Washington, he tried to decline. When his visitors persisted and told him that William Prescott, one of Boston's top lawyers, would represent Goodridge he began to show interest. He took the case and arrived in Ipswich the night before the trial to defend the Kennistons.

It was Webster's first appearance before an Essex County court, but his reputation had preceded him and the courtroom was packed. He had been unable to study the testimony or examine witnesses in advance, but he listened carefully, locking every word of Goodridge's direct testimony into his memory, and decided to stake everything on cross examination. Webster's scowl, black enough to remind the urbane Harrison Gray Otis of the terrors of the Holy Inquisition, was too much for the distracted witness. Webster growled, and as the befuddled major began to contradict himself his credibility crumbled. Webster stopped growling and turned benevolently to remind the jurors of the high reputation their community had enjoyed before Goodridge appeared. Perhaps the plaintiff, for reasons of his own—to avoid paying debts or merely to attract publicity—had pretended to be robbed and had even shot himself in the hand to make it look plausible. Stranger things had happened. They were hard put, those Essex County jurors, to tell where the logic stopped and the magic began, but they believed what they heard and promptly acquitted Webster's clients.[1]

The Kennistons furnished Webster with a spectacular vehicle for entering the Boston scene. His legendary unmasking of Major Goodridge made him an instant celebrity whom every well-informed Bostonian would want to see in action. Over the next two years, as he continued to perform in what was perceived as disinterested service to the community, Webster would grow enormously in public stature. He would become a myth before he was forty.

Naturally the Websters entered Boston society at the top. Indeed, Harrison Gray Otis, perhaps the single most influential man in the city, confessed that he had "decided" Webster to come to Boston—another way of saying that he had helped to subsidize him. Exactly how much money the local elite furnished to set Webster up in their city is unknown, but it was apparently several thousand dollars although not enough to cover all of his Portsmouth debts. Since Otis and his friends would raise purses for Webster several times over the next thirty years, it is important to understand why they would do so in the beginning.[2]

In the first place Webster fit into the Boston mold. The city leaders were so overwhelmingly Federalist that a Jeffersonian had about as much chance as a cow of seeing the inside of a Beacon Hill drawing room. Webster was a young Federalist of national reputation and they were anxious to claim him as one of their own. He promised to fit socially as well as politically. When the talented young George Bancroft came back to Boston after years of sub-

An unfinished portrait by Gilbert Stuart during
Webster's early days in Boston.

sidized study in Europe and began to parade around the city in velvet trousers and greet people in an affected European manner by kissing them on both cheeks, he was quickly disowned by his former benefactors in the establishment. Boston abhorred anything "outre or bizarre" which might keep a man from "respectable and useful" service to the community. Not the velvet-trousers type, Webster had the kind of home-bred stability and elegance that Bostonians cherished.[3]

His combined reputation as a man of letters and practical affairs enhanced his promise. Harvard was about to be transformed from a provincial college for the training of ministers, merchants, and lawyers to a place of genuine intellectual excitement. The transformation would be led by two young professors, Edward Everett and George Ticknor, who were returning to Cambridge fresh with the most recent learning of the greatest European scholars, and would soon launch a new generation of American scholars, including Emerson, with their lectures on classical and romance language and literature. Webster had taught the precocious Everett some years before at his brother's school in Boston, and he knew Ticknor as a Dartmouth alumnus and through his association with the Boston *Anthology*. He could count on them to be among his warmest admirers. Along with other leaders of the Boston-Cambridge establishment they would seek his advice on the government of Harvard as naturally as others sought his opinion on law and politics.

When Van Wyck Brooks said that Unitarian minister William Ellery Channing spoke for the inner life of Boston while Webster spoke for its outer life, "it's property sense and a kind of patriotism that largely represented its mundane pride," he did not give Webster enough credit. Bostonians welcomed him because they knew he could speak for all of their elite. His own cool and rational approach to religion made him perfectly at home with Unitarianism. His professional experience established his position with men of affairs, and his reputation as an orator and man of letters assured his standing in the scholarly community. Membership in the Massachusetts Historical Society, the Atheneum Library, and the celebrated Saturday Club came almost as a matter of course.[4]

Finally, there was the superb timing. Boston leaders and Webster needed each other in ways that were deeper than either understood. Under siege for almost two decades, they had been losing power in national councils ever since Adams's administration. Their ill-timed participation in the Hartford convention had been more than a protest against unpopular war policies. It was also a reaction to the steady democratization of political and economic power under Republican rule. Still believing in statesmanship as a high calling, but increasingly shut out of that calling at the highest levels, they needed new leaders who could be true to the spirit of the old Federal tradition in a way that would be acceptable to a new generation of Americans. It was because Webster promised to fill this role so magnificently that the wealthy Federalists of Boston subsidized him in the beginning.[5]

To understand the full extent of what Boston would mean to Webster we must go back to that frozen day in the winter of January, 1803, when he refused the law clerkship which his father had worked so hard to secure for him. In spurning that position with all its short-run advantages Daniel had irrevocably committed himself to "come to something" on his own. He was committed to achieving the wealth and fame denied his father—without surrendering the father's cherished political principles. He had tried to do this in New Hampshire, but his native state offered no more than modest financial rewards and was becoming politically wayward. Boston still stood where Ebenezer had stood, foursquare in the old Federalist tradition, and offered fortune too. Boston would depend on Webster to succeed just as Ebenezer had, and Webster would continue to be nurtured by Boston and the wealthy men who ran the town much as he had depended on his father. He would serve them well for more than thirty years, but he would never get out of their debt.

There could be no question about the fact that he needed money. His uninsured Portsmouth house had been lost in fire, and his new four-story residence on fashionable Mount Vernon Street, was far more handsome and expensive than any place he had yet lived. The obligations which he left behind him were so substantial that soon after he came to Boston in August, 1816, Webster sent a copy of his receipt book to a Portsmouth creditor to assure him that his law business was flourishing and would eventually allow him to pay his debts. According to this record his income for the first month in fees and retainers was almost two thousand dollars—the equivalent of a full year's work in Portsmouth.[6]

The tendency had been developed in New Hampshire, but in moving to Boston he embarked on a life style more elegant than anything he had known before. As a newcomer to Boston society he aspired to a way of life like that of his neighbor Harrison Gray Otis. The Otis mansion at 45 Beacon Street was considered by many to be the most gracious house in Boston. It contained eleven bedrooms, was served by as many servants, and was presided over by Otis himself, whom John Quincy Adams called the perfect host and who was said to buy as much from his provisioner as any large hotel keeper. Webster learned how to live well and expensively by watching Otis, who would start out the day with a tureen of *pâté de fois gras,* do his own marketing in the morning accompanied by a servant, and set a ten-gallon bowl of punch for thirsty visitors outside his drawing-room door in the early afternoon. This was the kind of life that Webster took to naturally. Whether it was a grand cotillion with three hundred guests or a small bachelor supper over Madeira and oysters he was a congenial guest and would soon become a famous host. Although he and his family began on a more modest scale than that attained by Otis and other wealthy Bostonians, theirs was the style on which Webster would always insist even if it kept him poor.[7]

Although Webster would not actually represent Boston in Congress until 1822, he continued to make his presence felt there through his appearances before the Supreme Court. The Court was held in a dingy basement auditorium in the Capitol, an unpromising but intimate setting which Webster came to love. He loved the Court because it was the one place in Washington where Federalism still dominated. In theory the Republicans were supposed to have a majority on the bench, but the experience of sitting next to Chief Justice John Marshall had a way of converting Republicans into Federalists. Webster had come to know Marshall when they were both boarding at the same house with Christopher Gore, and he respected him more than any man in Washington. Although Marshall was seventeen years his senior, lanky in build, shambling in deportment, and slovenly in dress, the two men had much in common. Marshall had been born in a frontier log cabin, was self-taught as a boy on books like Pope's *Essay on Man,* and had soldiered at Valley Forge before carving out a career for himself in law and politics to rise to the head of the Federalist establishment in Virginia. Like Webster, he was an earthy man who liked good food, good drink, and the pleasures of the field. Like Webster his success as a lawyer rested less on a scholarly mastery of the law than on his ability to learn quickly from the work of others and reduce technical details to easily understood basic principles. His power of leadership was so great that he almost always took the rest of the judges with him. Webster said that he had never met a man whose mind he respected more.

Webster also loved the Court because it gave him an opportunity to compete against the best lawyers in the country and encouraged elaborate arguments and long orations. During routine sessions, the chamber might be nearly empty, but it would be jammed with spectators, including a multitude of fashionably dressed ladies if a renowned performer like Wirt, Pinckney, or Webster were about to make a major speech. The attorney general, William Wirt, a Virginian of grace and literary accomplishment as well as a fine lawyer, was a favorite of Webster's. William Pinckney was more of a problem. An experienced diplomat who had served the nation with distinction in a number of important assignments abroad, Pinckney was considered the top lawyer in Washington when Webster went there. He was a big man of incredible vanity, and people laughed at his corsets and cosmetics and the way he would arrive at the Capitol on horseback, dismount, strip off his overalls, pull on a fresh pair of gloves, and stride into court like a Versailles courtier. But for all his foppish ways Pinckney was a hard man to argue down. He loved to chew up young lawyers, and was surprised to discover how tough his new young rival from New Hampshire was. Webster was later quoted as saying that he once coaxed a public apology from Pinckney by locking him in a room and threatening him with a beating. The story is probably apocryphal, but there is no reason to doubt that he demanded respect and got it from Pinckney and everyone else.[8]

Although Webster's reputation as a great constitutional lawyer is based on a career which numbered over a hundred fifty cases before the Supreme Court over a period of thirty-eight years, the foundation for this career was laid during his first years in Boston, when he was out of formal politics, and really starts with the famous Dartmouth College case. During Webster's student days Dartmouth had operated under the authority of a royal charter granted by the colonial governor of New Hampshire to Eleazar Wheelock in 1769. The charter put the power of administration in the hands of Wheelock and a self-perpetuating board of trustees. In 1779 Eleazar's son, John Wheelock, succeeded to the presidency of the college. Almost everyone who had studied the history of Darmouth agrees that the younger Wheelock was an autocratic administrator who was able to run the college pretty much according to his own whim until about 1793. From that point on the trustees began to play an increasingly important role, and by 1809 a majority of the board opposed Wheelock's policies. The issue of how the college should be governed became complicated by an additional quarrel that Wheelock got into with the Hanover church, a majority of whose members organized as Congregationalists while Wheelock and his supporters remained Presbyterian. By 1815 the dispute which had been bubbling below the surface for several years finally burst into public view. Wheelock published a pamphlet attacking the trustees, and they retaliated by dismissing him and appointing Francis Brown as the new president. At this point, since the board of trustees was largely Federalist, Wheelock looked to the Republicans for help. A Republican governor, John Plumer, succeeded in getting the legislature to revise the college charter, changing the name to Dartmouth University and creating a new board of overseers with powers over the trustees. When the overseers made Wheelock president of the university, there were two institutions of higher education contesting for the right to occupy the same campus, and the struggle was transferred to the courts.

In a dispute of this kind it was natural that both sides might want Webster's support since he was both a distinguished alumnus and a celebrated lawyer. Wheelock talked to Webster about the matter in the winter and spring of 1815 and felt that he had received some kind of a commitment from him. On August 15 he sent Webster a twenty-dollar retainer and asked him to attend a legislative committee meeting in Hanover saying, "I have made dependence on you as counsel, agreeably to our conversation at Concord." A few weeks earlier, however, Webster had assured his old friend Thomas Thompson, one of the college trustees, that he would represent their case.

When Wheelock's friends accused Webster of double dealing, he replied that he did not consider the request to appear before a legislative committee a professional matter and that he had severe doubts as to the justice of Wheelock's case. There were, of course, many reasons for Webster to have sided with the trustees. The Federalists were on this side, including close friends like Thompson, Mason, and Jeremiah Smith. There is also the fact that he disliked Wheelock and held him responsible for the inferior place he was awarded at commencement. It is easy to see why Webster should not have wanted to go into the battle on Wheelock's side. It is not quite so easy to see why he should have held on to Wheelock's twenty-dollar retainer fee, but if he did return it we have no record of the fact, although the *New Hampshire Patriot* made the matter public in October, 1815.[9]

To the people of New Hampshire who watched the whole thing develop, the contest between Dartmouth College and Dartmouth University must have seemed more like a political brawl than a confrontation over weighty constitutional issues. Isaac Hill made the cause of the university the cause of democracy and filled the columns of the *Patriot* with angry columns designed to prove that the trustees of the college were out to take over both the educational and religious system of the state in order to maintain an aristocratic society. The *Portsmouth Oracle,* on the other hand, took the more lofty and legalistic position that property rights invested in the trustees by charter could not be destroyed by legislative action. That was the high ground. The low ground they left to the "malicious reptile," Hill, who "probably never saw the inside of a college."[10]

When the case was called before the Superior Court of New Hampshire on September 19, 1817, Webster joined Jeremiah Smith and Jeremiah Mason as counsel for the college. Mason and Smith opened by arguing that the legislature had exceeded its authority and violated both the state and federal Constitution by altering the college charter. Webster closed for the plaintiffs in a two-hour speech which was not preserved, but which left some of his audience in the New Hampshire court almost as affected as his later speech did the justices and spectators of the Supreme Court. A correspondent for the *Patriot* who claimed to have been sitting almost in front of him claimed that at the end of his remarks Webster

> . . . like a profligate heir, who at the funeral of his wealthy ancestor *endeavors* to weep, began to snuffle and sob and make wry faces, and ever and anon speak a word about a certain person at Rome, but he would not name him, as how he drew a "red dagger" against his friend, another man who also lived at Rome. . . . And looking around . . . I discovered a platoon or two of orthodox Dons, and here and there a corporals guard of their poor, distressed devotees, all gaping with apparent wonder, and motionless from amazement—their necks stretched forward, and, in a few instances I believe, drops of water furrowing their way down faces which would not have been injured by a basin full. About this time some person behind me observing

to another—"I guess he's being pathetic, aint he?" I instantly said to myself, "right fellow"—you have seen asses shed tears before today.[11]

Webster had no illusions about the effectiveness of his eloquence before the New Hampshire judges. It was a Republican court appointed by a Republican governor and he correctly predicted a decision favorable to the university. This decision, given on November 6, was based on the assumption that the college trustees formed a public corporation subject to modification by the legislature.

The case now moved to the Supreme Court of the United States. Webster agreed to serve as chief counsel for a fee of one thousand dollars and selected Joseph Hopkinson of Philadelphia as his associate. The university, which had been ably represented by Ichabod Bartlett and George Sullivan before the New Hampshire Court, was represented by John Holmes, a mediocre lawyer from Maine, and William Wirt.[12]

On the morning of March 10, 1818, Webster rose before John Marshall's Court and made history in a speech which has been variously estimated as lasting from three to five hours. He spoke from notes carefully prepared from the briefs which Mason and Smith had written. He based his argument on the assumption that the original charter was a contract which established "a private eleemosynary corporation"; the Court could not allow it to be revoked without threatening the existence of all similar institutions and the sanctity of contracts themselves.

There is no verbatim report of what Webster said before the Court. The printed report, which he prepared himself, runs to less than forty pages and is obviously a carefully revised summary of his argument. The famous peroration which presumably reduced the justices to tears does not appear in the formal record at all. It relies for its authenticity on the recollection of a spectator in the courtroom which was not made public until after Webster's death thirty-five years later. According to this account Webster concluded his argument as follows:

This, sir, is my case. It is the case, not merely of that humble institution, it is the case of every college in our land. It is more. It is the case of every eleemosynary institution throughout our country, of all those great charities founded by the piety of our ancestors to alleviate human misery, and scatter blessings along the pathway of human life. It is more. It is, in some sense, the case of every man who has property of which he may be stripped,—for the question is simply this: Shall our state legislature be allowed to take that which is not their own, to turn it from its original use, and apply it to such ends or purposes as they, in their discretion, shall see fit? Sir, you may destroy this little institution; it is weak, it is in your hands! You may put it out; but if you do, you must carry on your work! You must extinguish, one after another, all those great lights of science, which, for more than a century, have thrown their radiance over the land! It is, sir, as I have said, a small college,—and yet there are those who love it. . . .

Sir, I know not how others may feel, but, for myself, when I see my alma mater surrounded, like Caesar in the senate house, by those who are reiterating stab upon stab, I would not, for this right hand, have her turn to me and say,—*et tu quoque, mi fili!*,—*"and thou too, my son!*[13]

It is highly unlikely that Webster said these actual words, but the forcible and dramatic impact which he made on the Court is a matter of record. Moreover the *Patriot*'s satirical account of Webster's peroration before the New Hampshire court is close enough to the last paragraph of the Supreme Court peroration to suggest that Webster probably gave the same kind of effective closing in both places. When he finally prepared his speech for the printer Webster wrote Mason "All the nonsense is left out," little knowing that some day that nonsense or some apocryphal likeness of it would become even more famous than his legal arguments.

Webster was not impressed by the quality of the arguments made by opposing counsel and looked forward to a favorable decision. When the Court adjourned on March 14 without a decision, he did what he could during the summer and autumn recess to strengthen the college's position even further. He carefully revised his own argument, had it privately printed, and sent five copies of it to his friend on the Court, Justice Joseph Story, for distribution among "such of the judges as you feel proper." A copy was also sent to Chancellor Kent, the redoubtable legal authority in New York, who was known to exert an influence on some of the judges. On February 2, 1819, the Supreme Court reconvened and John Marshall read his famous decision upholding the cause of the college on the basis of the fact that the Dartmouth charter was a contract creating a "private eleemosynary institution," the obligation of which could not "be impaired without violating the Constitution of the United States."[14]

By establishing the protection of the contract clause not only for educational, but for all kinds of corporations at a time of great economic expansion, the *Dartmouth College* case became a landmark in American constitutional history. It also established Webster's position as one of the leading constitutional lawyers in the country. Although he admitted that the original arguments used in the case had been developed by Mason and Smith and that his role had been mostly one of exposition, Webster did not underestimate the effect that the case would have on his own career. *"You must therefore write out your argument,"* he wrote to his associate Hopkinson when they were preparing the case for the press, "This is a work which you must do for *reputation*. Our college cause will be known to our children's children."[15]

Webster agreed with Marshall on the great constitutional question of the day and favored a loose interpretation of the Constitution and the expansion of the powers of the federal government. Two of the more than twenty cases which he argued before the Supreme Court between 1819 and 1824 became almost as famous as the *Dartmouth College* case. In the first, *McCulloch v. Mayland,* Webster argued for the constitutionality of the Bank of the United States and against the right of an individual state to tax it. Marshall's opinion upheld his argument and expounded the famous Hamiltonian principle that the federal government was "limited in its powers" but "supreme within its sphere of action." In the second, *Gibbons* v. *Ogden* (1824), Marshall followed Webster's reasoning very closely in affirming the pre-eminence of federal over state powers in the regulation of interstate commerce. In view of the enormous amount of federal legislation which would later be justified under the commerce clause, it would be hard to overestimate the importance of this decision, and Webster correctly felt that his role in it represented one of his most important legal contributions. In all three cases he used his influence to protect ancient principles. In the first case he was guarding private property rights secured by contract; in the second and third cases he was guarding the work of the founding father by protecting constitutionally derived federal powers against state encroachment.[16]

Webster had quit his seat in Congress under the clear apprehension that the results of the war and new economic developments in the country would force changes in party organization. Although he professed little interest in resuming an active political career, he continued to spend a good deal of time in the company of politicians, especially when he was in Washington. The partisanship of the war years seemed to be giving way to a consensual politics during Monroe's administration, and Webster expressed the new sprit of "good feeling" when he advised his New Hampshire friends to keep the Federalist press "from triumphing too much" over the college decision. In the same spirit, he encouraged the president to make a good-will tour of New England, and himself played host to Secretary of War John C. Calhoun when the latter visited Boston in the summer of 1820.[17]

Nobody knew better than Webster that these ceremonial gestures of political good will reflected the weakness of Federalism more than a Republican change of heart. When the Fifteenth Congress had adjourned in March of 1819, the question of admitting Missouri to the Union as a slave or free state had been left unresolved. At the end of August an anti-Missouri protest meeting was held in Burlington, New Jersey. Although Webster had nothing to do with the meeting, Joseph Hopkinson, his legal associate in the *Dartmouth College* case, helped to plan it. Given this information the *New York National Advocate* announced that Daniel Webster was behind the whole thing, plotting "for the *erection of a northern party, the triumph of federalism,* or the *separation of the Union.*" Webster made only one public statement opposing the admission of Missouri (at a Faneuil Hall meeting in December, 1819), but from August, 1819, until March, 1820, when the famous compromise was reached pairing the admission of Missouri with Maine, he was regularly accused of masterminding *"a Second Hartford Convention business."* The moral was clear. Webster's enemies would seize every opportunity to touch up the partisan colors he had worn in the House during the bitter war years. He would not be allowed to forget his political past.[18]

Although the Missouri debates did not improve Webster's image in the South, they did help to keep his name before the public. Meanwhile, his reputation as the leading statesman in New England was enhanced by his performance as a delegate to the Massachusetts Constitutional Convention which opened in November, 1820. This was the kind of public assembly in which Webster felt comfortable. The venerable John Adams presided as honorary chairman and the other delegates included the best in Massachusetts brains and property regardless of party, although Massachusetts being what she was, the Federalists dominated. Besides Adams, the two closest students of government among the delegates were Webster and Joseph Story, whom Webster had come to know through his work before the Supreme Court. Easily one of the most interesting men whom Webster had met in Massachusetts, Story had graduated from Harvard as an enthusiastic Jeffersonian, and had returned to Federalist Essex County where on at least two occasions he was forced to defend his political principles with his fists while beginning a stormy career in law and politics. As he grew older Story managed to tame his prejudices, and he had served as congressman and Speaker of the Massachusetts House of Representatives before Madison appointed him to the Supreme Court in 1811. Once established beside Marshall, Story's latent conservatism began to flower, and after about 1813 he and Webster became close personal friends and intellectual soul mates. Eventually they developed a kind of professional partnership in which Story agreed to advise Webster on points of law while Webster looked out for the interests of the judiciary in the Congress.[19]

Story and Webster played the part of friendly rivals in assuming the leadership role of the Massachusetts convention. There was a good deal of technical debate at the outset about rules and procedures in the course of which Webster carried several points. He later boasted that this early attention to detail proved helpful in keeping the radicals in check. The most important issue before the convention involved the establishment of districts for representatives and senators. According to the constitution of 1780 representatives to the lower house were divided into districts by population while senators were divided into districts by the amount of taxable property. The move to amend the constitution so that all legislators would be chosen in proportion to population was consistent with the spirit of the time and the practice in other states, but Massachusetts Federalists opposed it, and Story spoke for many of them when he warned that such a change would give too much power to poor people and threaten the protection of property. "Poverty leads to temptation," intoned the judge, "and temptation leads to vice, and vice to military despotism." Sound Federalist doctrine, but dull in Story's interminable presentation. When Webster began to say the same thing, the delegates picked up their ears. Some of them remembered years later how he quoted Harrington to show that political power without economic power invited anarchy and despotism, and argued that forty years of prosperity and stable government in Massachusetts had been built on respect to that basic principle. Webster was bucking the popular tide; state after state was moving toward a greater reliance on popular suffrage and away from property restrictions in general. But in Massachusetts he seemed to speak with the same authority that John Adams had exercised forty years before, and the convention voted to keep the basis of representation in the Senate as it was.[20]

After the convention adjourned Webster wrote to Mason that although "there was a good deal of inflammable matter, and some radicalism in it," the voice of reason had prevailed and "some of our friends have increased their reputation a good deal." Webster was talking about friends like Joseph Story but thinking about himself. No one had played a more active role and his influence had been felt on a host of important issues. The patriarchal Adams, too full of age and experience to be easily impressed by anyone was quoted as saying Webster was "head and shoulders above them all." And Story himself thought his friend's appearance before the constitutional convention had been dazzling.

> It was a glorious field for him, and he has had an ample harvest. The whole force of his great mind was brought out. . . . He always led the van and was most skilful and instantaneous in attack and retreat. . . . On the whole I never was more proud of any display than his in my life.[21]

It was Webster's virtuosity that drew people toward him as much as anything else in these early Boston years. He seemed to be as much at home before the Supreme Court as before a local jury, as effortless on the floor of the legislative chamber as in the parlor of a Beacon Street mansion, as fluent with his pen as with his tongue. When New England's self-esteem was rudely jolted by the publication of a book attacking General Putnam, the hero of Bunker Hill, it was gratifying to find Webster offering his services for the defense. He wrote a long article for the *North American Review,* carefully disposed of the testimony designed to discredit Putnam's role in the famous battle, and reminded his readers that they had an interest in preserving the reputations of their national heroes.

The public . . . has an interest in the reputation of its distinguished men, which, when it ceases to preserve or protect, it will cease to deserve distinguished services from any of its citizens. The characters of its great men are the real treasurers of the country. They are the regalia of the Republic. What has it but these for its glory? What but these for the themes of its poets and orators? What but these for the examples of its emulous youth?

The defense of Putnam appealed to Webster's conservative instincts. The general reminded him of his own father, uneducated, trained in "the militia and in the school of Indian and colonial warfare, of integrity above suspicion, and of courage not to be doubted, much esteemed by the people . . . and a warm friend of the Revolution." Anything that reminded Webster of Ebenezer and the strength, patriotism, and integrity which he represented was to be protected. He treasured few things more than the "pair of silver *sleeve buttons*" made from material his father had picked up on the battlefield at Bennington.[22]

To a man with Webster's strong ancestral sense, it must have come as a special honor to be invited to give the oration at the bicentennial celebration of the landing of the Pilgrims at Plymouth on December 22, 1820. The ceremony was held at the First Church and Plymouth was overflowing with visitors for the occasion. Some twelve hundred of them crowded together to hear a two-hour oration. The performance made such an impact on some members of the audience that they could only recall it with wonder decades later. Webster's friend, George Ticknor, as scholarly and sophisticated a young man as the nation could provide, and one who had visited most of the great romantic figures in Europe in a spirit of cool detachment, described his response in a letter written that evening.

I was never so excited by public speaking before in my life. Three or four times I thought my temples would burst with the gush of blood; for, after all, you must know that I am aware that it is no connected and compacted whole, but a collection of wonderful fragments of burning eloquence, to which his whole manner gave tenfold force. When I came out, I was almost afraid to come near him. It seemed to me as if he was like the mount that might not be touched and that burned with fire. I was beside myself, and am so still.[23]

It is easier to report the rapture of people like Ticknor to Webster's speech than to explain it. There was first of all the emotion-laden spirit of the occasion. Ticknor said that on the afternoon before the address he stood on Plymouth Rock and then walked up the hill to where the Pilgrims suffered through their first winter. He stopped at the unmarked burying ground and at the mound where the survivors had conferred with Massasoit the following spring. He had seen the best that Europe could offer, but he felt now as an American, and especially as a New Englander, that he stood on ground as classical as that occupied by the Colosseum, the Alps, or Westminster Abbey. Webster spoke directly to this feeling when he announced

We have come to this Rock, to record here our homage for our Pilgrim Fathers; our sympathy in their sufferings; our gratitude for their labors; our admiration of their virtues; our veneration for their piety; and our attachment to those principles of civil and religious liberty, which they encountered the dangers of the ocean, the storms of heaven, the violence of savages, disease, exile, and famine, to enjoy and to establish . . .[24]

Even granting Webster's ability to exploit the symbolism of his setting and the drama of the occasion, it is still difficult to read the speech today, with its lengthy historical passages comparing the colonization of New England with other colonization movements going back to the Greek and Roman Empires, and grasp the dynamic force which connected the orator to his audience. To do that it is necessary to enter the mind of that audience. The men and women who sat before him that day were well educated and comfortable with classical allusions. They also knew that he was not just talking to them about the past but about their own place in history. The two hundred years since the settlement of Plymouth weighed less heavily in their minds than the half century since the Revolution. They knew what extraordinary things had transpired since that time. They knew how prosperous they were compared to the early Puritans, how preoccupied with getting and spending. And what they could say about themselves they could say about the nation—how what had once been a simple and virtuous republic presided over by heroic leaders like Washington and John Adams had become a vast, complex nation, materially prosperous but ideologically discordant. It was a proud story but worrisome. Was history pushing them too rapidly toward an unknown and possibly disastrous future? Were they in danger of being cut off from their glorious beginning? What Webster did at Plymouth—transcendently for some, like Ticknor, who actually heard him, and powerfully for thousands of others who only read the speech—was to recreate a vital connection with the best in their past. He not only made his audience feel this connection, but he reassured them by explaining why the American experiment had prospered. Here Webster simply rephrased the same arguments he was making at the constitutional convention, which was still in session. The genius of American politics was that it based political power on a wide distribution of property thus making it to the interest of almost every citizen to support the system. Despite the problems and tensions caused by economic and territorial growth and political controversy, America more than any other country had built-in guarantees of stability for the future—if only present and future generations of Americans would preserve and cherish the ideals and institutions of their virtuous fathers.

Toward the end of the address Webster spoke harshly about the continuation of the slave trade.

If there be, within the extent of our knowledge or influence, any participation in this traffic, let us pledge ourselves here, upon the rock of Plymouth, to extirpate and destroy it. It is not fit that the land of the Pilgrims should bear the shame longer. I hear the sound of the hammer, I see the smoke of the furnaces where manacles and fetters are still forged for human limbs. I see the visages of those who by stealth and at midnight labor in this work of hell, foul and dark, as may become the artificers of such instruments of misery and torture. Let that spot be purified, or let it cease to be of New England. Let it be purified, or let it be set aside from the Christian world; let it be put out of the circle of human sympathies and human regards, and let civilized man henceforth have no communion with it.

I would invoke those who fill seats of justice, and all who minister at her altar, that they execute the wholesome and necessary severity of the law. I invoke the ministers of our religion, that they proclaim its denunciation of these crimes, and add its solemn sanctions to the authority of human laws. If the pulpit be silent whenever or wherever there may be a sinner bloody with this guilt within the hearing of its voice, the pulpit is false to its trust.[25]

Ticknor said that Webster gave this passage "with a power of indignation" that he had never witnessed on any other occasion. It was the strongest anti-slavery statement he would ever make in public and spoke directly to the deeply felt but still inarticulate anxieties of thousands of Americans who feared that the true destiny of the nation would never be realized while slavery endured.

The Plymouth oration was Webster's first permanent contribution to American literature. It helped take American oratory out of the political forum and establish it as a literary form in its own right. Generations of American schoolboys would memorize it along with other orations which he would give over the next decade. The man who had burst on the Boston scene to defend the Kennistons was emerging as a Homeric figure who, more than any other leader of this generation, could create a heroic past for his countrymen. In combining this with his activities in law and public life, Webster was taking on a symbolic role as guardian for thousands of people in New England. He would continue to play this role for the rest of his life, and in his finest moments, he would appear to many Americans, in New England and beyond, as he appeared to Ticknor at Plymouth—an inspired leader with almost Godlike gifts.

Meanwhile what of the immediate future? A man with his gifts, reputation, and ambition could not be expected to stay out of politics indefinitely. Harrison Gray Otis, who had watched Webster with detached admiration during these years mused over the possibilities for his future.

Webster is a man whose talents are of a very high order beyond all doubt. He has also the good fortune which attends newcomers to Boston of being surrounded by Puffers who do him full justice. If he does not get spoiled by praise and inflated by vanity (of which those who know him best say there is some danger), he will make a great figure in the world.[26]

7

ONE PRICE FOR FAME
Grace Fletcher Webster

Triumph piled on triumph for Webster in the 1820s. He was elected to the House of Representatives in 1822 and moved up to the Senate in 1827. During the same period he made a fortune arguing maritime claims cases in Washington, appeared in almost fifty cases before the Supreme Court, and found time to draft, deliver, and revise several of his most celebrated orations. What made Webster's performance all the more remarkable was the seemingly effortless way in which he accomplished it. But this was a false perception. Fame and success always exact their price, and if the great man does not pay it himself, someone close to him usually does. In Webster's case the price was paid by his first wife. The more than seventy letters which Grace Webster wrote during the middle of the 1820s reveal the recurrent and at times the desperate depression of a young wife and mother trying to keep her family together without losing contact with a husband who belonged as much to the world as to his own family.

Coming from a simple New Hampshire village like Webster, Grace rejoiced in his success and grew along with him. In 1824 she moved her growing family into a mansion on Summer Street. One of the handsomest residential avenues in Boston, Summer Street would later be described as "a winding river of elm and horsechestnut trees and sunshine, bordered with beautiful houses, lawns and gardens—the homes of merchant princes and of Daniel Webster." Their new three-story brick house, flanked by deep gardens and set off from the street by a heavy ornamental railing, gave Webster the solid residential base he had always wanted. The Webster house shared a common wall with the city's richest merchant, Captain Israel Thorndike, who obligingly cut a passage so that his neighbors could use both houses for entertaining. If Grace sometimes felt uncomfortable as hostess in such munificent surroundings she did not show it. Naturally shy and introspective, she behaved with an unobtrusive dignity and poise which blended nicely into her husband's more magisterial presence. Fully equal to the grand occasion, like the great candlelight reception given in the combined Webster-Thorndike establishment for Lafayette, Grace was at her best in smaller, informal dinner parties. When the aristocratic and somewhat disdainful British visitor Mrs. Basil Hall attended one of these affairs she noted that the Webster "dinner arrangements" were the most impressive she had seen in America.[1]

Daniel Webster was a man born to be at the center of things, and he loved being there, even at home. Even in repose he seemed to dominate the household. After an exhausting day in court he would throw himself on a couch to rest while his children clambered over him as if they were playing on a mountain. Fiercely awake every morning at dawn, he would summon the rest of the family with a lusty rendering of his favorite hymns before setting off on his morning ride "dressed in a frock coat, with tight pantaloons, a pair of blucher boots, reaching to the knee and adorned with a tassel, a bell-crowned beaver hat set a little on one side of his head, and a riding whip in his hand. . . ."[2]

Although Webster could do the work of two or three men at once, he could not be in Boston and Washington at the same time. Most of his work as a congressman and a constitutional lawyer was in the latter city, and by 1823 his family had grown too large to consider moving it to Washington with him. His oldest son, Daniel Fletcher, a serious-minded boy who would increasingly feel the pressure of trying to live up to his father's name, was ten years old and in school in Boston; Julia, a sensitive five year old who took after her her mother, was about to enter school. Three-year-old Neddy, the most high-spirited of all the Webster children, was at an age when he needed constant watching, and the baby Charley, a great favorite, was still in the cradle. Since Grace was understandably reluctant to leave her children in Boston, Webster was confronted with the possibility of returning to Washington as a bachelor. He had tried this before back in 1813 and had complained bitterly about the "unvarying masculinity" of his company. In 1816 he had brought Grace to Washington with him, but they had just started to enjoy life together with the Jeremiah Masons when Grace was called home by the fatal illness of their youngest daughter. It was with great apprehension, therefore, that she agreed to accompany her husband to Washington again in the fall of 1823. This time she took the two middle children, Julia and Edward, with her, while Fletcher and Charley stayed with friends in Boston.

Grace Fletcher Webster.

While still en route to Washington on November 12, Grace wrote to Fletcher urging him "to enjoy all your sports and little pleasures as if your mother were near. It was inexpressibly painful to leave you and dear little Charley." A month later she found herself trying through correspondence to get Fletcher to stop "a certain manner of speaking which I very much disapprove as by it you do yourself great injustice. Anyone not acquainted with you would think . . . that you were a very silly boy." The usual tone of her letters, however, was not of admonition but one of guilt and yearning. "You must write and tell me all about yourself and Charles and how much he has learned to talk and if he looks just as he did when Mama left him. I wish you and he were here . . . and then I should be very happy—but now I do want to see you too much. You must not let Charles forget 'Mama, Mama.' . . . Papa is engaged in writing as usual."[3]

During the relatively brief time that they spent together in Washington, Grace was a good companion for Daniel. She was attractive without being beautiful, poised without being artificial, and had a good supply of the common sense which Daniel liked to attribute to New England. She took their four-year-old Edward to hear John Randolph speak in Congress, but when Randolph failed to show up and the long-winded McDuffie took over the floor, agreed with her fidgety son that it was "a pretty dull way of passing a forenoon." Webster circulated freely at the top level of Washington society and Grace soon grew accustomed to dining with famous political leaders like Calhoun and Adams, but she showed an independent spirit by developing a very un-New England attraction for Andrew Jackson. "It is astonishing how intercourse liberalizes the feelings," she wrote to her brother. "I have always felt that he was a perfect savage—but he is very far from it in his appearance; his manners are very mild and gentlemanly. I begin to think it is only for him to be seen to make him the most favorite candidate."[4]

That Grace Webster's outspoken approval of Jackson was a function of the general's personal appeal and not an endorsement of what would eventually become known as "Jacksonian democracy" is made clear by another letter which she wrote to her brother in February, 1924, describing a patriotic ball which she and Daniel attended with their friends from Boston, the Blakes. They were invited to the ball with the understanding that it would be a full-dress affair

and to our amazement found a large hall crowded with "tag rag & scanderbag" [sic]. There was not a person we had ever seen before or ever hope to again. There were three or four gentlemen belonging to our class, and as to the rest anyone was there who could by hook or by crook, raise a dollar. We took a turn round the room and saw such dancing . . . as does not often meet the eye. As to Mrs. Blake and Mr. Webster, they were so much diverted at all they saw I was glad to come off lest they should offend the company by their laughter.[5]

This anecdote tells us a good deal about Webster and his wife. Although they both descended from humble beginnings in rural New Hampshire, they had spent their married life together as members of the elite in Portsmouth and Boston, and despite the many misfortunes of the Federalists as a political party, they still clung fast to the old Federalist sense of class in an increasingly democratic age.

When Webster returned to Washington in the autumn of 1824, his wife remained in Boston. "I feel now as if I could never again be spared from home," she wrote, "and since it seems to be so ordered that you must be away we must be separated, I hope it will be for our mutual good." For his part, Daniel was pleased to learn how many people in Washington missed Grace and wrote proudly that she had become known as "a favorite of the whole city." Once again he resigned himself to a bachelor's winter, a prospect that always made him irritable, depressed, and prone to colds and occasional curt notes to his wife. "I hoped I should have another letter today," Grace wrote to him on December 11, "written in better spirits than your last which was when you had just arrived and things did not go right and you had a headache—and you did not like my letter and I know not how many other things were wrong." In the same letter Grace reported the serious illness of their three-year-old son Charley, writing pointedly, "I cannot be sufficiently grateful that I am at home with him—am able to bestow so much care upon him."[6]

Eight days later Charley died. Daniel was visiting Jefferson at Monticello at the time and did not get the mournful news until he returned to Washington. Outwardly he showed little emotion. "I know that my presence at home could not have altered the course of things in respect to our little boy," he wrote to Everett, "the loss I feel heavily, but I hope not to be too much depressed by it." Inwardly he grieved over the mysterious Providence that sent the son to an earlier grave than the father. His thoughts took the form of a poem which he sent to Grace with a copy to their close friends the Ticknors, with the precautionary note that it was intended for the eyes of "*no other human beings.*" The poem included the following stanzas

> On earth my lot was soonest cast
> Thy generation after mine
> Thou has thy predecessor past;
> Earlier eternity is thine.
>
> My father! I beheld thee born,
> And led thy tottering steps with care;
> Before me risen to Heaven's bright morn,
> My son! My Father! guide me there.[7]

At the time of his son's death Webster was at the center of the intense politicking in Washington that ultimately put John Quincy Adams in the presidency. The pressure of this activity undoubtedly helped to ease his own grief. His wife was not so fortunate. She yearned both for her lost son and for her absent husband. "In my sleep last night you were with us," she wrote on January 7, 1825, "but I awoke and the delightful vision fled! And long must it be ere I can hope to see you save in the visions of sleep or fancy." Having lost two children already, she worried about the three remaining living among the temptations and frivolities of Boston society. "There is the greatest folly at this day—children are *anticipating* all the *pleasures* and *amusements of Gentlemen & Ladies,*" she complained to her husband. "Boys even have supper parties and in some instances have drunk so much they could hardly be got home."[8]

Although she shared her husband's political and social values, unlike him Grace Webster was a true daughter of the Puritans, born with an uneasy conscience which no amount of worldly success could satisfy. Now, tormented by the memory of her dead son and the separation from her husband, she brooded over her own limitations and the disadvantages of being the wife of a famous man. "I have no letter from you today," she wrote to her husband on New Year's Day, 1925. "I fear you have grown weary with writing. Daniel [Fletcher] has several times begun to write you but has not accomplished a letter. He seems to recollect with some degree of pain that you did not write him a single line during your long absence over last year. I fear he has a little of the mother in him." Looking ahead, she doubted if she would ever go to Washington again. The prospect of continued separation depressed her, but the lonely nursery where "the busy feet, the sentimental prattle of our darling little boy is heard no more," reminded her of her obligations at home.[9]

Despite her social position Grace apparently saw few friends in Boston, and her confidante, Eliza Buckminster, accused her of contributing to her own loneliness. "You must permit me to say my dear friend," she wrote, "that when your husband and children are with you and you are more than happy in their society you do not quite do enough yourself to keep up the friendships that would be grateful to you in his absence. You find few like me who will not suffer themselves to be forgotten, but still cling . . . to the place where they have found warmth & comfort."[10]

For all her apparent poise and ability Grace feared she would never be the kind of wife her husband deserved. Once when Daniel reprimanded her for trying to make light of some matter which displeased him, she wrote back, "It is my prayer that I may never again offend either in word deed or thought." She was afraid on the one hand, of talking of things "too high" for her, and on the other, of writing dull letters. Even when Daniel did not write regularly, she could follow his activities through the press and learn that he was often wining and dining with the most fashionable and cleverest people in Washington. She was curious to learn more about one of the ladies living in Webster's boarding house because, as she wrote, "I have heard much of Mrs. Wool's uncommon conversation—extraordinary informa- tion, etc etc." Unwilling to write to any man except her brother and her husband ("my liege and lord"), she knew that Daniel regularly corre- sponded with other women, and was afraid of being overlooked. "I have not written you for several days," she wrote on one occasion, "but among your *numerous* correspondents I can hardly flatter myself that my poor epistles will be missed." By February 21, 1825, almost two months to the day after Charley's death, Grace revealed the depth of her depression in a long letter to her husband.

> I have not written for several days for I fear if I write oftener my letters will be en- tirely without value. I who never stir from my own fireside but to enter a church, can have nothing to communicate but the health or sickness of my family as it please Providence—the shining of the glorious sun, or the howling of the storm. My life is monotonous indeed, and somewhat dull—but it is doubtless best for me; it gives me time for reflections which the frequent intercourse with the world is too apt to banish . . . and I have many, very many painfully mortifying reflections. It is morti- fying to reflect how much I am behind you in everything. I know no one respects, but rather despises those they consider very much their inferiors. You will perhaps say I am unusually humble, but these are not the feelings of an *hour* or a *day*—they are *habitual*.

In the last paragraph of her letter Grace spelled out the kind of woman she felt Daniel should have married.

> I would not forget that Mrs. Ticknor desired me to mention her particularly to you. When you compare her letters with mine, my dear Husband, I am well aware that the difference in length would be the most trifling. You must have the mortifica- tion to reflect that Mrs. T. is the daughter of a man of *millions*, and has enjoyed since her infancy, every advantage which wealth can bestow, while your wife as the daughter of a poor country clergyman—all the early part of her life passed in obs- curity, toiling with hands not *"fair"* for subsistence. These are humiliating truths, which I regret more on your account than on any other.[11]

There is no record of Webster's reply to this letter from his wife. He al- most certainly would have tried to comfort and reassure her, and would probably have interpreted her outburst as the temporary derangement of a bereaved mother. And he would have been wrong. Depression does not necessarily put a person out of touch with reality. Grace was a realistic, in- telligent woman. She knew that in fact her husband had gone beyond her in many ways, how often, both in her company and without, he enjoyed the companionship of women more elegant, educated, and sophisticated than herself. Anna Ticknor was one of those women. Highly educated, beautiful, and independently wealthy, she could travel with her husband and discuss politics, literature, and art with the best minds in America and Europe. Webster had been dazzled by her company when he visited Monticello with the Ticknors. After the trip was over and the Ticknors had started back north, he playfully complained that Anna had spoiled him for returning to work. "She had no right, I shall say, to be so agreeable as to draw my attention from the weighty affairs of state while she was here, and to create depression, or a kind of I-am-not-quite-ready-to-go-to-work feeling by her departure." A little later he wrote Ticknor again, after dining with Calhoun, and said, "He talked to me among other things about your good fortune in picking up a *companion* on the road to life." The underlining was hardly accidental. Ticknor was married to a companion, and Webster was beginning to realize, if only dimly and half consciously, that for all her splendid qualities as a wife and mother Grace was still in many ways a simple village girl from New Hampshire.[12]

After Daniel came home that spring, Grace's spirits revived, and she joined her husband, the Storys, and Eliza Buckminster on a trip to Niagara Falls. The expedition was an arduous one, but Daniel seemed to welcome the opportunity of matching his own power against that of the falls. Marching up and down the walls of the falls with a vigor that discouraged his companions, he descended to the base, drew a line of the falls in the dirt with his six-foot walking stick, made his own calculation about their height, carefully studied the currents, and then ascended to his hotel room overlooking the spectacle to write a meticulously detailed 3,500-word letter to Mrs. George Blake describing what he had seen. "Mr. Webster has a giant's constitution and can bear every sort of fatigue," Story wrote afterward, "but I was a good deal overcome and returned in very indifferent health."[13]

After a vacation on Cape Cod, where Daniel refreshed himself fishing the trout streams and tramping the fields in search of pheasant and quail, the entire Webster family returned to Washington for the winter sessions of 1825–1826. Surrounded by her family, Grace found she could enjoy the capital more. This time she did get to hear Randolph speak. After going to an auction where he outbid her for a piece of fine linen, and then following him to the Senate where he poured his brilliant invective on Webster and the Adams administration, she decided that Randolph was "a deranged man" who needed to be horsewhipped. There were also formal dinners at the White House which the Websters went to more out of a sense of obligation than anything else. "I think they are hardly better for having ladies," Daniel wrote to Ticknor. "It is a solemn time when we are at a dinner table where numbers prevent us from being social, and politeness forbids us to be noisy." Webster liked to enjoy social life on his own terms—in small intimate gatherings centered about himself; and Grace wrote to her brother that he entertained "more company ten times than all the rest of the Gentlemen in the house." Those invited to one of the Webster dinners counted themselves favored indeed. Before hostile groups Webster would "shut himself up like an oyster. . . . 'We cannot safely play the fool,' " he would say, " 'with fools.' " But among friends he could relax, enjoy his wife, gossip charmingly with the ladies, and tell stories about himself, about the fact that the real tragedy during the Portsmouth fire had been the loss of his first pipe of wine—about the teamster who had reluctantly carried him from Baltimore to Washington because, as he confessed after their safe arrival, he was sure anyone so fierce and ugly looking had to be a bandit. Above all, those who visited Webster at this time were struck by the tenderness and affection which he showed his wife. Josiah Quincy claimed that those who never saw him with his first wife never knew the man "in his perfect symmetry."[14]

Too often the symmetry was missing. By January, 1827, Grace Webster was again left with her children in Boston while her husband made history in Washington. She celebrated Daniel's forty-fifth birthday by reading one of his speeches. "May heaven add blessings," she wrote him, "to a life so valued and so valuable." Under the strain of their separation, many of her old anxieties returned. She began to dwell more on religion and worried about her husband's leanings toward Unitarianism. "I cannot but fear that we are wrong to appear to be of that sect," she wrote Daniel. "I am anxious that our children should be taught the right way if it be possible to determine what that is. I fear my dear husband that you have not sufficiently considered the subject and I have been myself too easy." Webster was always in the news and always writing to friends in Boston, and whenever she was forced to get word about him through others rather than from his own hand she grew depressed. His letters seemed "like Angels visits, short and far between." "My husband is the center and height of my ambition," she wrote on January 29. "I fear you think it would be better if I were more so for myself. No one could more ardently wish to be all woman ought to be than I do, but I have not the courage to pursue a course that would make me what I would be." Two weeks later she wrote, "Amidst your cares, your business and your pleasures, my dear Husband, I sometimes feel that if I did not obtrude myself upon you I should be a thing quite forgotten."[15]

When Webster returned to Boston in the spring of 1827, Grace was in poor health but recovered enough to spend the summer vacationing with him and their children on Nantucket and Cape Cod. As the winter session of Congress approached, she decided after much agonizing to leave her children in Boston and go to Washington with her husband, who was about to make his maiden appearance in the Senate. En route that December she became seriously ill while visiting friends in New York. The difficulty, diagnosed as an inoperable tumor, was probably a tubercular lesion. She was too sick to be moved, and Daniel was torn between remaining with her or joining his colleagues in the Senate where he was badly needed. He finally left for Washington, heartsick and wracked with the rheutmatism that tended to afflict him in moments of disaster. Grace's last two letters to her husband, written from her New York sickbed were characteristically self-deprecating and concerned with his comfort and welfare. "I beg you will not be too anxious about me," she wrote, "nor too much enhance the value of this poor life by your love for me." After two gloomy weeks in Washington, Webster returned to his wife in New York, hoping to "be able to meet the greatest of all earthly afflictions with firmness." Grace lingered for a fortnight after his return, maintaining her melancholy serenity to the end. One of the last letters she received was from Eliza Buckminster, relating how handsomely Fletcher had comported himself at a New Year's dance. Toward the end, when she was asked what kind of clergyman should be brought in to pray for her, she said she would have to consult her husband.[16]

Grace died January 21, 1828. Webster had her body brought to Boston for burial, and on the morning of the funeral, bareheaded and bowed, his daughter in one hand and his eldest son in the other, followed the hearse on foot through puddled streets to St. Paul's Church, where Grace was laid to rest beside her son. When Ticknor went to call on him at Summer Street, Webster broke down completely. Ticknor never forgot how he alternated between moments of composure as he attended to details of the funeral and moments of collapse. "When exertion was no longer required he sunk down again in his chair & appeared almost to shrink in size under the pressure of deep affection."[17]

In the weeks and months that followed his wife's death, Webster sought to solace himself by returning to Washington and plunging into professional and public work, but found this to be a cure that did not readily take. "I am growing indolent," he wrote to his sister-in-law. "I do nothing in Congress, but what is clearly necessary." He confessed to Eliza Buckminster that he was growing more depressed. "I feel a vacuum, an indifference, a want of motive which I cannot well describe." He tried to take increased interest in his children's welfare, but they had been divided up among friends and relatives in Boston, and his only contact with them was through letters. His oldest son, Fletcher, was eighteen now, and a no more than indifferent student at the Boston Latin school. "I have nothing more at heart," the father wrote, "than your success and welfare, and the cultivation of your virtues. You will be in the common cause of things, coming into active life, when, if I live so long, I shall be already an old man, and shall have little left in life but my children, and their hopes and happiness." But Fletcher seemed to suffer from the same feelings of inadequacy that had troubled his mother. He had little of his father's ambition or capacity and eventually admitted that he lacked perseverance, "a fault of which I am as well aware as yourself."[18]

Throughout these trying times Daniel maintained his usual close relationship with his brother Ezekiel, whose first wife had died several years earlier and who was now happily remarried. The two commiserated with each other not only over Grace's death but over the disastrous political trends as well. They hoped to win a small victory for virtue by getting Ezekiel elected to the Congress during the spring elections in 1829. But Zeke had remained more dogmatically rooted in his Federalism than Daniel and was beaten decisively. A few weeks later, on April 10, 1829, he dropped dead while addressing a jury in the Court House in Concord, New Hampshire.

In some ways Daniel had been more dependent on his brother than he had been on Grace. Like their father, Ezekiel had sacrificed himself to send Daniel to school. Daniel had repaid that debt, but his older brother remained a father figure to him, always ready to give him money or encouragement and to admonish him to greater achievement. "He has been my reliance through life," Webster wrote to one friend. And to another, "His death was like tearing away one half of all that remained of myself."[19]

Shortly after Ezekiel Webster's death, Daniel received a letter from a woman correspondent who identified herself only as "Your Sympathizing Friend—W." The professed purpose of the letter was to offer condolences, but the real purpose was to remind Daniel that they had once been close and that she was still available. The record does not tell us how Webster parried this approach from an old sweetheart, but there is plenty of evidence to show that "W" was not the only person interested in learning about his plans for the future. Grace Fletcher was hardly cold in the grave before Edward Everett's wife decided they should name their new baby Grace Webster Everett. "There sh'd [sic] be something or somebody to revive occasionally in his mind the recollection of his poor wife—for the world has already begun to talk. . . . It is very cruel I think for people to talk so soon, for Mr. W. has really seemed much afflicted & has behaved throughout with great propriety."[20]

Eliza Buckminster, who had recently become Eliza Buckminster Lee, and was thus out of the running herself, urged Daniel to write her regularly, and Mrs. Langdon Elwyn, a wealthy Philadelphia socialite with a marriagable daughter, wrote that she was unhappy at receiving secondhand accounts of how Webster was adjusting to his bachelorhood. In January, 1829, not quite a year after Grace Webster's death, William Sullivan wrote that he had read in the press that Daniel was "accompanied" by a lady in Washington. "I pray to be allowed the honor of presenting my homage," Sullivan wrote, adding pointedly, "though I have never had the pleasure of seeing the fortunate lady to whom it is tendered."[21]

Despite the curiosity and speculation of friends, Webster kept his own counsel. Stephen Van Rensselaer, an old political acquaintance and head of one of the wealthiest families in New York State was one of the first to learn of his intentions. On May 15, 1829, Webster wrote a "Private & Confidential" letter to Van Rensselaer in Albany, asking "whether there be any objection to my visiting your house, & cherishing an acquaintance in your family." The person he wanted to cherish was Van Rensselaer's young daughter, Catherine, a renowed belle in Washington society. Webster had apparently approached the Van Rensselaers earlier with his interest in their daughter and had been told that she was not interested, for he now wrote, "Not unconscious that difficulties may appear to lie between me & my object, I hope, still, that I may be pardoned, if my feelings prompt me not to withdraw my attention from that object, until it should be intimated, from the proper sources, that those difficulties, or some of them, are deemed insurmountable." This was a labored and legalistic way of saying that when Daniel Webster asked for a lady's hand, he expected to hear from the lady herself. The documentation of the abortive courtship ends at this point, but the story that was passed down through successive generations of the Van Rensselaer family tells of Webster "going to Albany and calling on Mrs. Nat Thayer's mother—the 'Patroon's' wife—and asking one of her daughters in marriage whom he had never seen. The mother took the offer upstairs and brought it down again: Webster finally would only take 'no' from the young woman in person. His idea was that it would give him a powerful position in New York state."[22]

Failing in his object with the Van Rensselaers, Webster turned his attentions on Caroline LeRoy, daughter of a wealthy New York businessman who was one of his clients. The wedding took place on December 12, 1829, in the parlor of the Eastern Hotel in New York City. Only Julia Webster and the bride's immediate family were present. Along with his daughter, Herman LeRoy gave Webster a dowry of twenty-five thousand dollars.

There is not a great deal to be learned about Caroline LeRoy before her marriage. At thirty-one she was seventeen years younger than Webster, who described her as "amiable, discreet, prudent, with enough personal comeliness to satisfy me and of the most excellent character and principles." Edward Everett, who met the new Mrs. Webster in Washington before she came to Boston, told his wife that she was "a lady who owes much to full dress. In plain dress she is plain." Although Everett was mystified at Webster's being "smitten so deeply and so suddenly," there was obviously more calculation than romance in the courtship leading up to his second marriage. He had every reason to believe that he had made a substantial match. In a different way Grace Fletcher had been substantial—bred from pure New England stock, full of the virtues of a strong, rural Protestant, New Hampshire background. She had been a natural bride for the youthful Daniel Webster, and Caroline was a natural bride for the mature Webster. Coming from a prominent, sophisticated family (her father had been the Dutch consul in

New York) of wealth, in the most important political state in the country outside New England, she had many of the qualities that Grace Fletcher had wanted in order to be a more complete wife to her husband.[23]

Like most of their colleagues connected with the Congress, Daniel and Caroline were forced to find a boarding house. They soon found themselves comfortably settled in a doctor's residence, and complete with their own maid, footman, and carriage, began living in what Washington considered grand style. Everyone important in Washington, including all the foreign ministers, came to call, and Caroline worried about pronouncing the foreign names, and finding time to repay all the invitations that she had accepted at other houses. The Websters attended one of the president's small dinner parties and she reported in dazzling detail to her sister how Jackson escorted her to the table and helped her choose the wines. The social whirl seemed to suit them both.

A few months after their marriage Caroline went to New York to visit friends, while her husband remained with his work in Washington. It was their first separation, and when he wrote that he was getting along reasonably well alone, Caroline responded with words that she might have learned from Grace Webster. "I feel you are so happy without me," she wrote, "you will *feel disinclined* to *return to me.* Though surrounded by all my friends who are kindness & affection to me—still a blank exists within—I can't be supplied until you are with me."[24]

Other biographers have claimed that Webster's second marriage represented a fatal break with his humble New England antecedents, that Caroline LeRoy lacked the will and character to restrain him from the extravagant and self-indulgent life style which marred his latter years. This emphasis (New England chauvinism at its worst) is misplaced. What his second marriage does show is the strength of Webster's ambition. The double loss of wife and brother might have thrown a less determined man off his course. Webster could have retired from politics, married a woman like Grace, and settled in Boston to concentrate on his family. Instead he chose a woman who added wealth, family, and political connections to his own base of power. The world would never quite be the same, now that Grace Fletcher and Zeke had gone, but the great prizes were still there—and as Caroline LeRoy was already discovering, her new husband belonged very much to the world.

8

FEDERALISM AND THE
POLITICS OF FRUSTRATION

Death had become something to be reckoned with. Webster had lost a beloved son, wife, and brother within a four-and-a-half-year span, but throughout this staggering personal loss the thrust of his career remained upward. The sixty thousand dollars which he realized by representing eastern merchants before the Spanish Claims Commission made him a relatively wealthy man.[1] His fame as a lawyer, orator, and politician grew. At the same time the political party which he represented was dying.

Webster could resign himself to the reality of physical death because he had no power to prevent it. Political death was another matter. The Federalist party might die, but Webster would try to keep Federalism alive in principle by showing that the country could be governed without strong parties if talented leaders from different backgrounds would cooperate for the common good. In trying to accomplish this goal, so closely bound up with his own personal ambitions, he found himself forced to operate on two separate and sometimes conflicting levels. On the level of public address he emphasized lofty national themes, while on a practical level he often found himself supporting factional interests for his own immediate good. In the end the new politics never materialized, and Webster found that he could not transcend the burdens of his own partisan past. Meanwhile Andrew Jackson emerged to dominate the American scene and build an entirely new framework for American politics.

His experience in Boston helped to shape the position Webster took in national politics. Boston elections had traditionally been held at town meetings, where Federalists believed "the most respectable persons" could best exert their influence. As the town grew, people began to demand elections through separate ward polling places. Once this was accomplished over Federalist objections, the opposition to the local ruling elite began to work more effectively. In the spring of 1822 this opposition, which called itself "the middling interest," had taken on a decidedly anti-aristocratic tone. The chief issue involved the construction of homes in Boston. Most of the leading Federalists owned substantial brick homes and approved of state laws which kept down fire hazards and insurance premiums by prohibiting the construction of additional wooden buildings. Artisans and mechanics who could not afford to build with brick but wanted to construct their own homes felt discriminated against, and the middling interest capitalized on their resentment by defeating half the Federalist candidates in the May elections.

Throughout this controversy Webster sided with the Otis Federalists, but said or did nothing to publicly link himself with what the middling interest described as "proud and haughty aristocrats" who tried to rule Boston "by the influence of family connections." Thus it was almost inevitable, once the middling politicians decided to run their own candidate for Congress, that the Federalists would draft Webster for the race. He was represented as an experienced, disinterested statesman with an "unspotted reputation," the one man who would be sure to bring Boston's true influence to bear in national councils. In carrying the election that fall by a decisive margin he seemed to show that a leader whose appeal went beyond party could win.[2]

Upon taking his seat in Congress in the fall of 1823 Webster appeared nonchalant about returning to active political life. Referring to his election as "a case of *over persuasion,*" he told a friend that he did not expect to serve more than one term and thought that his most substantial achievement might be to help pass a law to provide for the actual payment of the Spanish claims. This was mere posture. William Plumer, a New Hampshire congressman and an old acquaintance of Webster, remembered strolling with the latter outside the Capitol when he suddenly began to talk of his desire to make a permanent place in history. "I have done absolutely nothing. At thirty Alexander had conquered the world, and I am forty," Webster complained, "but I have sometimes such glorious dreams!" For the next thirty years he would be almost constantly in public office trying to turn those dreams into "glorious realities." No American of his generation would live a more intense political life. It is important, therefore, to look beneath his superficial reactions and understand how Webster perceived the drift of American politics in the 1820s and what he really hoped to accomplish by returning to Washington as a congressman from Massachusetts.[3]

Webster contrasted the old politics of the war years with the coming politics of the twenties. The old politics had emphasized "the assiduity and impudence of office-seekers, the licentiousness of the Press, the abuse and perversion of the right of suffrage, and above all that violence of party spirit" which had dominated the years before and after 1815. The new politics would be one in which voters would abjure factional considerations for common interests and support men of talent and responsibility regardless of party labels. This simplistic analysis was consistent with old-fashioned Federalist theory and seemed to make sense in terms of Webster's own experience. The one party politics he had observed in Washington under Monroe and the circumstances of his own election in Boston suggested that the course of American politics was shifting in the right direction.[4]

Once settled in Washington, however, Webster discovered it was not easy to practice politics without party considerations. He could profess an interest in joining hands with Republican leaders for the common good, but they had the power and would do what suited their own self-interest. Henry Clay was a case in point. Webster expected Clay to be Speaker of the House again, and although he thought him "in many respects a liberal and honorable man," he doubted that Clay would pass out important assignments to Federalists. Party discipline had always been stronger among the Republicans than with the Federalists and Webster found it particularly irksome now. "It is time to put an end to *Caucuses,*" he wrote, "they make great men little & little men great. *The true source of power is the People*. The Democrats are . . . real aristocrats. Their leaders wish to govern by a combination among themselves, & they think they have a fee simple in the peoples' suffrages." We should not be deceived by what seems to be a strong Jacksonian flavor in these remarks. Webster's real concern was not so much to institute direct democracy as to get away from party rule and restore the old role of the elite by exploiting the popular prejudice against caucuses.[5]

In the same letter in which he attacked the caucus, Webster speculated about the wisdom of "doing or *saying* something about the *Greeks.*" He was referring to the Greek war for independence from Turkey which he had already decided upon as a vehicle to announce his return to national politics. As a fledgling congressman from New Hampshire he had made a splash by directly attacking the president, but such tactics were no longer appropriate. Now he needed a nonpartisan cause, and he believed he could find it by turning the Greek revolution to his own advantage. He knew the Greek struggle had become a popular cause with many Americans, who saw an analogy in it to their own struggles against England, and he knew that Monroe had expressed sympathy for the Greeks in his last message to Congress. What if he were to lay the whole issue before the Congress by proposing a resolution calling for tangible Greek support—to be followed later with a major speech? Here was an issue bigger than party which could command the ear of the administration and the public.

As Webster began to prepare a resolution calling on the president to send a commission to Greece (tantamount to recognizing Greek independence), he realized he knew a lot more about the politics of talking about Greece than he did about the Greeks themselves. Fortunately, his friend Everett had also been elected to Congress, and was even then writing an article for the *North American Review* on the Greek question. Confessing that his "real difficulty" was ignorance, Webster prevailed upon Everett, whom he implied might well become the first American ambassador to Greece, to join him as a silent collaborator.[6]

Although he introduced his resolution on December 8, Webster waited five weeks before speaking to defend it. The publicity which flurried up during the interval pleased him, and he boasted to Everett, "We shall have the nation, and if Mr. Monroe does not do speedily as much as I have suggested, he will soon be obliged to do more." On January 19 he addressed the House at length and argued that Americans, as custodians of liberty for the world, had an obligation to publicize their moral support for the cause of Greek independence.

What do *we* not owe to the cause of civil and religious liberty? to the principle of lawful resistance? to the principle that society has a right to partake in its own government? As the leading republic of the world, living and breathing in these principles, and advanced, by their operation with unequalled rapidity in our career, shall we give *our* consent to bring them into disrepute and disgrace? It is neither ostentation nor boasting to say, that there lies before this country, in immediate prospect, a great extent and height of power. We are borne towards this, without effort, and not always even with a full knowledge of the rapidity of our own motion. . . . Does it not become us, then, is it not a duty imposed on us, to give our weight to the side of liberty and justice, to let mankind know that we are not tired of our own institutions, and to protest against the asserted power of altering at pleasure the law of the civilized world?[7]

In the ensuing debates Webster was supported by Henry Clay. Republican congressmen found two big objections to Webster's proposal. The first, argued by his old Salisbury neighbor, Ichabod Bartlett, was that Americans had no more business interfering in the internal affairs of Turkey than Haitians would have trying to support a slave insurrection in the southern states. This was too much for Clay, who had hoped he would never hear the word slavery mentioned in the House again. He silenced Bartlett with a blast so brutal and withering that it almost provoked a duel. The second objection came from Republicans who objected to the quixoticism of an anti-war Federalist suddenly exposing such aggressive diplomacy. But Clay refused to play that game. Liberal sentiments were liberal sentiments no matter who proposed them, and Clay would not oppose a man just because he "happens to belong to a different party."[8]

Despite this kind of gratifying support Webster's motion eventually failed. When it came to a vote, the administration decided that to send a commissioner to Greece would mean an unnecessary involvement in European affairs. Webster was hardly a loser for that. He had improved his own reputation by identifying himself with the spirit of national pride and self-affirmation which had come after 1815. He had been on the wrong side then, but the Greeks were pushing him back into the mainstream of American public opinion.

Popularity is a highly unstable element for a politician. Webster's friend Joseph Hopkinson reminded him of this when he wrote on February 1, 1824, urging him to take pains in preparing the Greek speech for the press. "It is in one respect, a misfortune for a man to obtain a high eminence of character," Hopkinson wrote, "he is always required to maintain it, and this calls for constant vigilance and effort which are not always convenient." It was one thing to build up political credit by riding the wave of national pride rolling across the country, and something else to negotiate the treacherous shoals beneath the surface of Clay's ambitious "American System," which called for internal improvements and a protective tariff. Webster had no scruples about the constitutionality of internal improvements, but along with almost every other Massachusetts representative he was still afraid of a tariff that might hurt Massachusetts shipping interests. He knew he couldn't please everyone on this issue, complained that it was "a tedious, disagreeable subject," made a speech in early April that Clay thought argued both sides and ended up being more "New England" than "American," and finally voted against the tariff.[9]

The other issue in which Webster found himself forced to weigh factional considerations was the presidential election of 1824. Webster had originally been for Calhoun, but Calhoun had withdrawn, leaving the field to four other Republicans, Secretary of the Treasury William Crawford, Henry Clay. Andrew Jackson, and Secretary of State John Quincy Adams. As early as February of 1824 Webster predicted that the multiplicity of candidates would split the vote and throw the election into the House of Representatives. In this situation he believed Federalists would do well to sit back and hold their power until it was called upon to help tip the balance. During the interval, at least, they could expect to be treated civilly by Republicans. He felt that Jackson and Adams were the most promising contenders. The Websters had visited with Jackson on more than one occasion and were surprised and impressed by his "presidential" manners. Webster also sensed that Jackson had a powerful base of support as "the peoples' candidate in a great part of the southern and western country." He was ambivalent about Adams. On the one hand, Adams was a Massachusetts man and the son of one of the greatest Federalists. On the other hand he had early deserted to the Republicans, and Webster suspected that as Monroe's secretary of state he had been responsible for blocking Webster's Greek resolution. Webster disliked and distrusted Adams, a feeling which Adams reciprocated with vehemence.[10]

During the spring and summer of 1824 Webster kept Adams guessing as to whom he would support. Adams thought he knew what Webster wanted—a guarantee to take Federalists into the government—and for himself, the ministry to England. In November Jackson received 99 electoral votes to 84 for Adams, 41 for Crawford; and 37 for Clay. The choice then fell to the House, as Webster had predicted, and although the people of Massachusetts had clearly demonstrated their support for Adams, Webster pointedly refrained from indicating how he would use his personal influence to help decide the contest.[11]

In December, with the presidency still undecided, Webster spent two weeks traveling with Mr. and Mrs. George Ticknor on a visit to Jefferson at Monticello. The party passed five days with Jefferson and Webster took notes on the conversation that took place. There was little talk about current political matters, but Webster did note Jefferson's feeling about Jackson— that the general was much too violent and headstrong a man for the presidency. Mostly the talk turned to the Revolution, France as Jefferson had known it, and the University of Virginia. The former president was more than eighty, but he still had a lot to say on these subjects and he said it all well.

Jefferson was the most famous living American at this time, and it was natural that Webster should have wanted to meet him. The visit also fit nicely with the new nonpartisan role which he was seeking to create for himself. Before he left he wrote the following note marked *"Private"* to Gales and Seaton, editors of the *National Intelligencer:*

These are times when the most common & natural occurrences are often *conjectured* to be connected with some unavowed object. If any *wise acre* should intimate that my absence is connected with anything political, I will thank you to say—that you understand—(& so the truth is)—that I am merely gone with some private friends from Boston on a visit to Mr. [Thomas] Jefferson.

Of course, it was an election year, and Daniel Webster, the leading New England Federalist, was making a pilgrimage to the father of the Republican party. One didn't have to be a "wise acre" to know what that meant.[12]

Back in Washington in January, 1925, Webster continued to ponder his role in the House election which would decide the presidency. He wrote that "Mr. Adams might be chosen if he or his friends would act somewhat differently. But if he has good counsellors, I know not who they are." Webster would not commit himself to Adams until he had solid reason to believe that Adams would let Federalists into his administration. He secured the guarantee he wanted in an interview with Adams on February 3, six days before the balloting. At this time he showed Adams a letter from Henry

Warfield, a Federalist congressman from Maryland, asking Webster to reassure him of Adams's attitude toward Federalists. Webster had come prepared with a draft reply to this letter saying that he expected Adams "by some one clear and distinct case" to accept Federalists into the government. When Adams said he agreed to the spirit of Webster's reply, Webster wrote in a footnote to Warfield that Adams had read and approved the letter.

The Webster-Warfield correspondence, which later became known as the "Webster pledge," was contrived to force Adams's hand. Once he had the assurance he wanted, Webster went to work on key Federalist votes in the Maryland and New York delegations, and this influence, added to the Clay supporters who went over to Adams en masse, was almost enough to assure Adams's victory.[13]

It is important at this point to try and understand the difference between what happened in the election of 1824 and what Webster believed, or at least wanted others to believe, had happened. Two months after Adams was chosen by the House, Webster told a Faneuil Hall audience that the election showed that old parties and old political prejudices were no longer viable, and that his own accomplishments in Congress were "owing wholly to the liberal manner in which his efforts there had been received." The truth is that it had taken a lot of old-fashioned political dealing to make Adams a minority president, and Webster and Clay had been at the center of it. Clay had thrown his support to Adams only after reaching some kind of "understanding" with him. The famous "Webster pledge" was carried out in the same style—a classic use of political muscle. Webster admitted as much when he told Jeremiah Mason, "I took care to state my own views and feelings to Mr. Adams before the election in such a manner as will enable me to satisfy my friends . . . that I did my duty. I was very distinct, and as distinctly answered; and have the means of showing *precisely* what was said. My own hopes, at present, are strong that Mr. Adams will pursue an honorable, liberal magnanimous policy. If he does not, I shall be disappointed as well as others, *and he will be ruined.*"[14]

And if that were not enough, on the very morning of the day the House was to choose the president, Webster joined with Clay to extort the last vote necessary to elect Adams on the first ballot. Thirteen states were needed to elect; Adams was sure of twelve and the New York State delegation was deadlocked. Just before the balloting, the venerable New York Federalist, Stephen Van Rensselaer, was intercepted and taken to confront Webster and Clay in the Speaker's room. The old man had assured his friends at breakfast that he would vote for Crawford, but his resolution melted under the double magnetism of Clay and Webster, and he left the room shaken and confused. Perhaps they were right. Perhaps the country would fall into bloody anarchy if Adams were not elected on the first ballot. What would happen to wealthy old patroon families like the Van Rensselaers in such an event? The line between fact and folklore begins to cloud at this point. Did he vote for Adams out of fear or conviction or because after praying for guidance at his seat he providentially found an Adams ballot lying at his feet? The fact is Webster and Clay made Van Rensselaer their instrument to make Adams president.[15]

The maneuvering which took Adams to the White House guaranteed that Webster would be one of the leaders in the new administration. Clay became secretary of state and Webster became Adam's chief lieutenant in the House, where he supported the new president's program of internal improvements and as chairman of the Judiciary Committee was instrumental in establishing a new criminal code. Unfortunately, however, Adams's administration was doomed from the start. Jackson supporters claimed that the president had stolen the election from their hero by making a "corrupt bargain" with Clay and that he was repudiating traditional Republican principles by linking up with Federalists like Webster. The force of this criticism together with the president's unwillingness to use patronage to build a base of his own kept Webster and other administration supporters on the defensive most of the time.[16]

By the spring of 1827, Webster decided that his career could expand more successfuly in the Senate than in the House. The Massachusetts legislature was unable to agree on the choice of senator, and although Adams and many of Webster's Boston friends thought he would be more useful in the House, and although his young friend and political protégé Edward Everett was seeking the post for himself, Webster saw to it that his own name was presented, and the legislature promptly elected him. "I was forced into it very much against my inclination," Webster wrote in a private note to the editors of the *Intelligencer,* "but it could not be helped without trouble and perhaps disaffection." Although this was consistent with the disinterested-public-servant image Webster sought, those closer to the matter knew better. Edward Everett's letters show clearly that Webster wanted the Senate seat for himself and that many of his political friends in Washington and Boston acceded to his wishes against their own better judgment. Everett, who had had his own agents at work in the Massachusetts legislature in case Webster should change his mind and who had earlier admitted that there was a "universal" opinion in Washington that Webster "ought not to leave the House," explained why he was willing to accept the ultimate choice.

1.   A man like Mr. W. ought to be gratified by his political friends in anything he asks. His principles forbid his asking anything unreasonable, his talents and services ought to prevent his being refused.
2.   I consider Mr. W. a competent judge of this place where he can best serve his friends & his own interest is so completely identified with theirs, that whatever is best for him is best for them.

In the mind of Everett and a good many other people, what was good for Daniel Webster was good for Massachusetts.[17]

Becoming a senator and a widower at about the same time seems to have given Webster a new sense of urgency about the future. He was only forty-six, but he wanted to see Europe in the vigor of his maturity and not in his old age. He persuaded Clay to visit Adams and urge his (Webster's) appointment as minister to England. The president had to admit that Webster was the most able man for the office but still felt "the political considerations at the present moment are unfavorable to his appointment." Shortly after Clay left, Adams received a Massachusetts friend of Webster's who entreated the president to find five thousand dollars to help the political cause of Adams and Clay in the coming Kentucky elections. Later, Adams mused darkly over the coincidence of the two visits. Perhaps Clay's proposal that Webster be sent to England and Webster's proposal that the president "sport" five thousand dollars on the elections in Clay's home state was "all accidental," but Adams suspected the worst.[18]

Despite his inability to get the appointment he wanted, Webster supported Adams in the election of 1828. He expected New England to stand fast for the administration and hoped that enough Federalists would be able to cooperate with Adams Republicans in other key states to re-elect the president. The results of the election showed the bankruptcy of this strategy. Outside New England, Jackson's victory was almost complete, and one of the most telling arguments of the Jacksonians was their claim that Adams had sold out to the Federalists. In New England and elsewhere, influential Federalists themselves deserted Adams in substantial numbers so that they might share the spoils of victory.

Webster's dream of a new party based on national interests and willing to be led by men of vision and talent no matter what their political history seemed only a dream after all. The new party that was emerging would be even more alien than the Jeffersonians had seemed twenty-eight years earlier. Despite a continued succession of personal triumphs and and his own surging popularity at home, Webster was still without a national base on which to operate. "We are beaten . . . by private disagreements & individual partialities," he wrote, "it is eno' to disgust one with all public employment."[19]

9

A GREAT SPEECH
AT THE RIGHT TIME

Whatever Webster did, he did with style, and however trivial the event, there was usually someone to record it. "Webster was tremendously sick off Pt. Judith in our steamboat passage," Emerson wrote to his brother June 24, 1827. "He spouted like a whale and roared like a leviathan, yea outroared the steam engine and vomited as he wd. address the House." Despite his political disappointments, Webster's public reputation soared ever higher during the 1820s. This was partly because he cared very much about matters of reputation and consciously tried to shape his image when he could. It was also the product of historical circumstance. If we can understand how he stage-managed the first Bunker Hill celebration in 1825, why he sued his Boston Bramhin friend Theodore Lyman in 1828, and what the courtly South Carolinian, Robert Hayne did to enhance his national reputation in 1830, we can begin to understand why Daniel Webster emerged as one of the most celebrated Americans of his time and why perceptive observers like Emerson had an almost irresistible urge to portray him as a majestic figure no matter what he did.[1]

Webster was probably never happier or more successful than when he spoke at Bunker Hill in 1825. He was a trustee of the Bunker Hill Association, and when it was decided that the cornerstone of the monument should be laid on the fiftieth anniversary of the battle, his fellow trustees unanimously asked him to give the oration. Lafayette had agreed to be present for what promised to be one of the most impressive ceremonies in the history of the young Republic, and Webster had begun to think about his important

May assignment as far ahead as February, when he received the disturbing news that Edward Everett was planning to make a major address at Concord, with Lafayette in attendance, some two months before the Bunker Hill celebration was scheduled. Although younger than Webster and definitely in his shadow politically, Everett was a master orator in his own right and had recently made a spectacular impression with a speech before the Phi Beta Kappa Society in Cambridge. Webster had no intention of allowing a political protégé to stage a competing ceremony in the vicinity of Boston which might dull the luster of his own performance with Lafayette at Bunker Hill. His letter to Everett on the subject is a good example of the way in which he could combine directness with disingenuousness when a matter of personal vanity was involved.

I am sorry you have a speech to make at Concord. It would do better if you were not so well known all over the Country, as well as at home. If I were you *I would not do it.* Tell the good people, that you have, within a few months, made two Orations (both very good ones) & that you think it inexpedient to make another one so soon. This will satisfy all the reasonable. The truth is, the world will say, that in N. England we make too much of a good thing. I speak freely on this subject, because I am sure you will suppose I regard nothing but your permanent reputation. I would have you come out *next* in ~~my~~ your place in H.R.—To prove to you that I think of your case as my own, I will observe that I have not made a Speech this session, although I have on hand pretty full preparation for *two* interesting subjects; & the sole reason is that I may make an Address next June at B.H. . . .

Everett, no doubt, found it difficult to understand how he could be hurt by being "so well known all over the Country." Sophisticated enough to know that his own reputation was not really what was at stake, he was also smart enough to get the thrust of Webster's advice. When Webster wrote the word "your" over "my" in his letter, he was simply underlining the fact that Everett owed his place in the House to him. With the managers of the Bunker Hill ceremony he was not quite so subtle. If they let Lafayette go to Concord beforehand, Webster would not participate.[2]

When the great day finally arrived, it found the orator equal to his assignment. Demosthenes had prepared for his great triumphs by learning to speak with pebbles in his mouth. Webster rehearsed for Bunker Hill while standing knee deep in a Cape Cod trout stream, one hand grasped firmly to a fishing pole, the other extended in salutation to the imaginary throng. The real audience on June 17 was estimated in the tens of thousands, and the parade preceding the speech was so long that the first marcher had already reached Charlestown Bridge before the rear left Boston Common. Webster was to speak from a platform erected at the foot of Bunker Hill. Seating had been constructed in a semicircle extending part way up the hill for about a thousand ladies plus the Bunker Hill veterans and those who had marched in the procession. There were thousands of spectators jammed together near the top of the hill beyond the seats. After Lafayette had taken his place with the Bunker Hill veterans and the Reverend Joseph Thaxter, who had served as chaplain at this very spot fifty years before, had raised his ancient voice in prayer, Daniel Webster strode forward and began to speak. At this moment the crowd in the distance began to push forward in an attempt to get more clearly within hearing distance. Under this pressure some of the improvised seating began to collapse and the great ceremony seemed on the verge of degenerating into hysteria and confusion as constables and guards struggled to keep order. Then came one of those legendary moments in Webster's long career. When a member of the committee said it would be impossible to restore order, Webster retorted thunderously, "Nothing is impossible sir! Let it be done." Advancing to the front of the platform with a voice that seemed to come from Jehovah, he directed the marshals: "Be silent yourself and the people will obey!" Instantly the tumult subsided, and the orator continued with his address.[3]

The Plymouth Oration had been an attempt to evoke the spirit of peace consecrated by the Pilgrims and to reavow the high moral principles for which they sacrificed themselves. At Bunker Hill, Webster undertook to do much the same thing—to make his audience feel the sacredness of place and to call them back in time, before the living relics of a more glorious day, to the great principles of the Revolution. Reminding his audience that the number of states had doubled since 1775, that the American population had increased many times, that American prosperity was the envy of the world, Webster spoke for the need of a great symbol to remind Americans, through all progress and disaster yet to come, of their indebtedness to a virtuous past.

> . . . our object is, by this edifice, to show our own deep sense of the value and importance of the achievements of our ancestors; and by presenting this work of gratitude to the eye, to keep alive similar sentiments, and to foster a constant regard for the principles of the revolution.[4]

Webster's First Bunker Hill Address is considered one of his finest. It was printed and reprinted many times, and entire generations of American schoolboys were soon reciting it in classrooms across the country. As we return to it today, it is almost impossible to recapture the impact it had on the original audience. We must remember how charged the occasion was with pride and sentiment. The orator and his audience stood on hallowed ground. The survivors of those who had fought and bled to hold the ground a half-century earlier and who listened with tear-drenched faces as Webster recreated the battle before them, along with Washington's great lieutenant, Lafayette, provided a sounding board for Webster's rhetoric that few orators in our history have ever been able to command. A reporter to the *National*

Intelligencer, looking back from the perspective of five years, described the drama of the occasion.

The oration at Bunker Hill was literally delivered to the world. In the open air, exposed to sun and winds, stood an orator ripe with the thoughts of manhood, before all the impressions and glow of early days had gone; myriads of listeners were around him, among them the representatives of other hemispheres: holy men who were just entering eternity . . . the bones of friends & enemies were shaking in their graves beneath the feet of new & old generations, and passing time was announcing that half a century had elapsed since the roar of battle had broke over the sacred ground; the corner stone of a time-defying monument was then resting at his feet, and a hundred thousand bosoms in his sight were swelling and heaving with patriotism and republican pride; how sublime the scene! what a moment for "thoughts that breathe, and words that burn"; and is it not enough to say that all were satisfied.[5]

Little more than a year after the Bunker Hill celebration, John Adams and Thomas Jefferson died on the same day, July 4, 1826. On August 2, upon the request of the municipal authorities in Boston, Daniel Webster delivered a memorial address on Adams and Jefferson in Faneuil Hall. Once again the occasion was freighted with drama and symbolism. Once again Webster played the guardian's role, reconstructing this time not the Puritan past nor the revolution, but the climactic moment in the American experience when the Declaration of Independence was signed. Webster spoke for two and one half hours to what John Quincy Adams said was the largest crowd he ever saw in Boston, and "held the whole assembly mute." So successful was Webster in re-creating the debates over the Declaration that the speech which he imagined Adams as giving, beginning with the much-quoted lines "Sink or swim, live or die, survive or perish, I give my hand and my heart to this vote. It is true indeed that in the beginning we aimed not at independence. But there's a divinity which shapes our ends," was taken as Adams's actual words and not as Webster's dramatic reconstruction of the event.[6]

The trouble with these oratorical triumphs, as Webster knew, was that they did not build substantial political muscle for him outside the Northeast. After putting Adams in the White House and spending four years trying to steer legislation through the House for the Adams Republicans, he was still unable to get the appointment he wanted because the president could not risk trying to send a former Federalist of his reputation to England.

Webster no longer believed in party labels and was frustrated to find that he could not shed his own. At the same time he was disgusted with the spectacle of those once proud to call themselves Federalists scrambling to find a place on the Jackson bandwagon. It was little consolation to hear his Boston journalist friend, Theodore Lyman, explain the phenomenon as a response of human nature. "Pompey or Caesar said more worship the rising sun," he wrote to Webster in April, 1824, "the increase of democratic talent, respectability and wealth in Boston the last two years, entirely owing to gradual secessions, is very great . . . what can we do, therefore, having lost our own fortress, but take the enemy's?"

By 1828 Lyman had taken his own advice and was publishing a Jackson newspaper bent on destroying the Adams administration. On October 29 he wrote an article for this paper in which he charged Adams with having told Jefferson twenty years before that he was aware of a plot on the part of New England Federalists to destroy the Union. Although Adams had not named names, Lyman asserted that he was obviously referring to men like Harrison Gray Otis and Webster, who were now his own political associates. "We here beg leave to ask," Lyman wrote, "why for three years he has held to his bosom as a political counsellor, Daniel Webster, a man whom he called in his midnight denunciation a traitor in 1808?" Lyman and Webster had been Federalists together. They had belonged to the same eating club in Boston and had hunted and fished together on Cape Cod. There is no reason to believe that Lyman's admiration for Webster was in any way altered when he broke with Adams and took up the Jacksonian cause. Certainly the direct target in his article was not Webster but Adams. Therefore, when Webster responded to this piece of rather standard political journalism by bringing criminal charges against him, Lyman was amazed. "I have lived on friendly and occasionally intimate terms with Mr. Webster," he complained to a friend. "This extraordinary step he thought proper to take without making the least application, either in his own person or by means of a friend to me for an explanation. I need not say that his name was introduced as that of a conspicuous Federalist and to show what a rascal Adams must be to call his own friends traitors."

Although Webster said little about the libel suit in his correspondence, it is obvious from the way the action was drawn up that he was trying to do more than simply punish a political opponent for excessive language. By bringing a charge of criminal libel rather than a civil action, Webster prevented Lyman from testifying, and by filing the suit in the Supreme Court of Massachusetts, he assured that it would attract maximum public attention. The indictment itself was unusual, perhaps "unprecedented" according to one authority, since it was "framed upon a precedent under the law of *scandalum magnatum,* or slander of great men."

When the case came to court, Webster's attorneys had no difficulty in showing that their client had been living in New Hampshire in 1808 and had no intimate connection at all with the prominent Federalists named in the article. On the other hand it was admitted that he had opposed the embargo, and his early pamphlet on that subject was read into the record, Lyman's counsel simply argued that no intent to libel Webster was intended, and that the object of the journalistic attack was not Webster, but Adams. As it turned out, the law of *scandalum magnatum* was not invoked because the jurors failed to agree, and the case was dismissed.[7]

This was Webster's most desperate attempt to create a new public image. As the most eloquent spokesman for American nationalism, he could no longer tolerate being tarred with the charge of disloyalty for political opinions argued a generation earlier. He was compelled to fight back, not only for the sake of his own reputation, but for the memory of his father's as well. Yet, even if he had won his case in court, he could not have won it in the American mind in 1828. It was still not possible to reconstruct a positive image of the Federalists that a majority of Americans would accept.

After John Quincy Adams's defeat and while the libel suit was still in court, Webster received a consoling letter from Clay. "You have all my wishes for success in the prosecution against Lyman," he wrote. "In the midst of all the heat of former times I believed you as I have since found you, faithful to the Union, to the Constitution and to liberty under every vicissitude, believe me." This was doubtless a sincere statement on Clay's part, but it must have rankled Webster that it had to be said at all. He and Clay had pulled hard on a losing oar together in a vain attempt to keep Adams afloat. Each was now free to pull for himself, but Webster must have known that Clay, who had championed the right side back in 1812 was clearly in a more favorable position. He could hardly have expected events during the first year of Jackson's administration to move so quickly and positively in his own favor.[8]

Webster never really understood Jackson. He thought Jackson was weak and indecisive and would probably be led by others. He could not believe that the massive display of public affection for the president-elect was genuine. Washington was full of "speculation and speculators," he wrote on February 19, 1829, "too many to be fed without a miracle are already in the city, hungry for office." The inauguration spectacle itself was incredible. "A monstrous crowd of people is in the city," Webster wrote to his sister-in-law. "I never saw anything like it before. Persons have come five hundred miles to see General Jackson, and they really seem to think that the country is rescued from some dreadful danger." As the spring wore on Webster mused over "the infatuation of the times and the extravagance of personal devotion," and seriously considered leaving public life.[9]

Had Webster been able to gauge the reasons for Jackson's support more accurately, he would not have been so discouraged. For an important part of what was being expressed was not personal idolatry, but national pride. The people identified with Jackson because they saw in him what they wanted to believe about themselves. As an uneducated frontier boy he had fought and bled in the Revolution. As a self-trained soldier he had engineered the miraculous victory in the Battle of New Orleans. And as a self-made farmer, lawyer, and politician, he had overcome all obstacles to become the first "common man" to sit in the White House. A living link between the present and the past, Andrew Jackson was the reassuring symbol the American people needed—a custodian of traditional values prepared to guide them in the exciting but perilous task of building a powerful new nation out of the untested stuff of democracy.[10]

Webster, who consciously tried to identify himself with the Constitution and the founding fathers and whose oratorical success so largely depended on his ability to manipulate national symbols, was slow to see that under some circumstances Jackson's base of popular support might be turned to his own advantage. Even as he bemoaned the Jackson phenomenon, events were taking place in South Carolina and Washington that would soon thrust him on a pinnacle almost as lofty as that occupied by the new president.

By the middle of the 1820s, John C. Calhoun had given up the nationalism of his earlier years to lead a group of ardent states' rightists. The real cause behind the shift in political thinking was slavery, but the South Carolinians tended to argue their case over the tariff, which allegedly increased the price of manufactured goods while decreasing the price of agricultural exports like cotton sold on the open market. In South Carolina, the high duty tariff of 1828 almost instantly became a symbol for northern oppression. Plantation profits were down, fields were abandoned, and the state was losing population. Above all, the people of South Carolina, with the greatest slave density in the Union and a history of insurrection panics touched off by the Denmark Vesey Conspiracy in 1822, had already begun to feel that they could not trust their destiny to federal legislators who came from states where most people opposed slavery.

The situation in South Carolina put John C. Calhoun, vice-president under Adams, vice-president elect under Jackson, and a strong presidential contender in his own right, in a serious dilemma. He had to find a way to satisfy the separatists in his own state without sacrificing his own national position. He worked out a theoretical solution in the summer of 1828 when he wrote *The South Carolina Exposition and Protest,* which argued that the states had originally ratified the Constitution through state conventions. They had not abandoned their sovereignty by accepting the Constitution, and retained the right, acting again through state conventions, to refuse obedience to national acts they judged unconstitutional. It was this doctrine that Webster sought to refute in his famous debate with Robert Hayne.[11]

Although Webster would emerge from this debate with enormously enhanced prestige as the "Defender of the Constitution," the issue which started it all had nothing to do with the Constitution. In late December, 1829, Senator Foote of Connecticut introduced a resolution to consider limiting the sale of public lands. Thomas Hart Benton came roaring onto the floor to denounce the proposal as sectional legislation which would

Chester Harding's portrait of Webster the year before
the Hayne debate.

strengthen the settled, commercial, and industrial Northeast and hurt the unsettled, agrarian West. Benton was followed by Robert Hayne, senator from South Carolina and a leading Calhounite who saw the public-lands question as an opportunity to build a political alliance between westerners and southerners which might help Calhoun's presidential prospects. It was during Hayne's first speech, January 14, 1829, that Webster, who had been waiting to try a case in the Supreme Court on the floor below strolled into the Senate. He was just in time to hear Hayne charge that representatives from the manufacturing states wanted to sell western lands slowly at high prices in order to bring about "the consolidation of this government" and "create a manufactory of paupers." By this he meant that high revenues from land sales would increase federal power at the expense of state power while factory workers, unable to go West, would be forced to stay in their places and keep eastern capitalists rich.

Webster replied to Hayne the next day in a relatively short speech in which he defended a land policy which would dispose of public lands at prices high enough and in quantities small enough to encourage settlement and discourage large-scale speculation while at the same time providing some return to the states which had ceded the lands to the federal government. He defended New England's support of the tariff of 1828 because with southern support of earlier legislation a protective policy had become settled part of government policy and had thus encouraged New England money to flow into manufacturing. He ended his speech by flinging the challenge back at Hayne, drawing attention to two points over which South Carolinians were most sensitive. The first had to do with slavery. Webster argued that New Englanders had always pursued a pro-western policy and cited as evidence the fact that a New Englander, Nathan Dane, had authored the Ordinance of 1787, which kept slavery out of the Northwest Territory. The identification of anti-slavery with pro-western policy struck right at the heart of the South-West coalition that Calhoun sought. The second point was aimed at the specter of consolidation, "that perpetual cry both of terror and delusion," which Hayne had raised. Webster said that while he wanted no new powers for the federal government, he rejoiced in the "true, constitutional consolidation" which Washington had supported "in whatever tends to strengthen the bond that unites us and encourages the hope that our Union may be perpetual." Webster branded Hayne as a politician anxious to bring the whole value of the Union into question "as a mere question of present and temporary expediency; nothing more than a mere matter of profit and loss. The Union is to be preserved, while it suits local and temporary purposes to preserve it; and to be sundered whenever it shall be found to thwart such purposes." The "Carolina doctrine," in other words, didn't sound very American to Daniel Webster.[12]

A florid, intense, and proud man by nature, Hayne made it clear the next day as he stood up to reply, that Webster's parting shots had hit their mark. He launched into a sarcastic, detailed examination of Webster's Federalist record in the Congress, made a passionate defense of slavery, and with the help of encouraging notes passed down from the desk of Calhoun, who was presiding, finished with a ringing reaffirmation of the South Carolina theory of nullification.

Hayne's speech took parts of two days. Webster sat through the entire punishing performance and took careful notes, happy in the knowledge that he had succeeded in shifting the focus of the debate from tariff and land policy to the nature of the federal Union. Meanwhile, the Senate had become the center of attention in Washington. "Everyone is thronging to the capitol to hear Webster's reply," wrote Mrs. Harrison Smith. "A debate on political principle would have no such attraction. But personalities are irresistible. It is a kind of moral gladiatorship . . . the Senate Chamber is the present arena and never were the amphitheatres of Rome more crowded by the highest ranks of both sexes. . . . Every seat, every inch of ground, even the steps were compactly filled . . . the Senators were obliged to relinquish their chairs of State to the fair auditors who literally sat in the Senate." It was the kind of setting made to order for Webster. On the evening of the second day his friends found him calm and confidently predicting that he would "grind" Hayne "as fine as a pinch of snuff."[13]

Webster's Second Reply to Hayne was one of the two most important speeches he ever made in the Senate and must still be ranked as one of the greatest addresses ever made before a house of Congress. The speech was given from twelve pages of notes. It took several hours spread over two days to deliver and, after extensive revision, was printed in a form that takes up seventy-five pages in the national edition of Webster's *Works*. The speech has been remembered mostly for the eloquent "liberty and union forever" peroration, which every northern schoolboy would soon commit to memory, and for Webster's argument for constitutional nationalism. It was also notably successful as a political effort. Simply by commending the anti-slavery provisions of the Ordinance of 1789, he had pushed Hayne into accusing the nonslaveholding states of harboring plots to destroy the South. Webster was able to reply quite correctly that he had not uttered "a single word which any ingenuity could torture into an attack on the slavery of the South." Hayne's sensitivity on the subject was typical of the reaction of some southern politicians who sought "to unite the whole South against Northern men or Northern measures" on the basis of a feeling "at too intense a heat to admit discrimination or reflection." At the same time, while admitting that the federal government had no power to interfere with slavery in the states, Webster refused to agree with Hayne that the morality of the institution was a matter of political abstraction which statesmen could safely ignore. "I regard domestic slavery as one of the greatest evils, both moral and political," he said. "But whether it be a malady, and whether it be curable, and if so by what means—I leave it to those whose right and duty it is to inquire and decide."

During his assault on the American system, Hayne had implied that the people of South Carolina had no legitimate interest in canals or roads in other states. Webster skillfully picked this point up and turned it around so as to appeal to the self-interest of the patriotic sentiment of people in all the states.

"What interests," asks he, "has South Carolina in a canal in Ohio?" Sir this very question is full of significance. It develops the gentleman's whole political system; and its answer expounds mine. . . . On his system, it is true, she has no interest. One that system, Ohio and Carolina are different governments and different countries. . . . On that system, Carolina has no more interest in a canal in Ohio than in Mexico. . . .

Sir, we narrow minded people of New England do not reason thus. . . . In our contemplation, Carolina and Ohio are parts of the same country; states united under the same general government, having interests, common, associated, intermingled. . . . We do not impose geographical limits to our patriotic feeling or regard. We do not follow rivers and mountains, and lines of latitude, to find boundaries, beyond which public improvements do not benefit us. . . . Sir if a railroad or canal beginning in South Carolina and ending in South Carolina appeared to me to be of national importance and national magnitude . . . if I were to stand up here and ask, What interest has Massachusetts in a railroad in South Carolina? I should not be willing to face my constituents.

The last point carried special weight because Hayne and most other senators knew that only a few days earlier Webster had presented a petition from the South Carolina Canal and Railroad Company, asking the federal government to subscribe to its capital stock on the grounds that its projected railroad would aid the national welfare.[14]

The least effective part of Webster's speech was devoted to the defense of New England during the bitterly partisan years of the embargo and War of 1812. This was tiresome ground, and Webster, who had been over it countless times before, did the best he could with a bad case. He argued that the New England states had been sorely injured by government policy in those years, that they had exercised their right to protest, and that no matter how wrong-headed or potentially dangerous some Federalists had been in the Hartford convention, New England had in the end acquiesced to government policy.

Webster was most effective when he talked about constitutional power and appealed to national pride and sentiment. He began his refutation of Hayne's constitutional position by distinguishing it from the right of revolution, which, he said, every American would admit. After Hayne had interrupted to give his consent to this interpretation, Webster went on to show

how it was wrong in principle and bound to be disastrous in practice because the federal government was not the limited creation of sovereign states but a popular government with powers derived directly from the people and spelled out by the Constitution.

I hold it to be a popular government, erected by the people; those who administer it, responsible to the people; and itself capable of being amended and modified, just as the people may choose it should be. It is as popular, just as truly emanating from the people, as the State governments. It is created for one purpose; the State governments for another. It has its own powers, they have theirs. There is no more authority with them to avert the operation of a law of Congress, than with Congress to arrest the operation of their laws. We are here to administer a Constitution emanating immediately from the people, and trusted by them to our administration.

Who was to decide the constitutionality of state or federal? The answer, Webster said, was clearly given in the Constitution itself in the two clauses which made the Constitution "the supreme law of the land" and extended the judicial power "to all cases arising under the Constitution and laws of the United States."

These two provisions cover the whole ground. They are, in truth, the keystone of the arch! With these it is a government; without them it is a confederation. In pursuance of these clear and express provisions, Congress established, at its very first session, in the judicial act, a mode for carrying them into full effect, and for bringing all questions of constitutional power to the final decision of the Supreme Court. It then, Sir, became a government. It then had the means of self-protection; and but for this, it would, in all probability, have been now among things which are past.

To proceed on the opposite assumption—that the states were sovereign and could decide to obey or disobey federal laws at their pleasure, was to take a giant step toward civil war. Webster contrasted this bloody prospect with the harmony of the early Republic when Massachusetts and South Carolina had united to throw off British tyranny. "Would to God that harmony might again return! Shoulder to shoulder they went through the Revolution, hand in hand they stood round the administration of Washington, and felt his own great arm lean on them for support."

. . . When my eyes shall be turned to behold for the last time the sun in heaven, may I not see him shining on the broken and dishonored fragments of a once glorious Union; on States dissevered, discordant, belligerent; on a land rent with civil feuds, or drenched, it may be, in fraternal blood! Let their last feeble and lingering glance rather behold the gorgeous ensign of the republic, now known and honored throughout the earth, still full high advanced, its arms and trophies streaming in their original lustre, not a stripe erased or polluted, nor a single star obscured, bearing for its motto, no such miserable interrogatory as "What is all this worth?" nor those other words of delusion and folly, "Liberty first and Union afterwards"; but everywhere, spread all over in characters of living light, blazing on all its ample folds, as they float over the sea and over the land, and in every wind under the whole heavens, that other sentiment, dear to every true American heart,—Liberty and Union, now and for ever, one and inseparable![15]

Webster's Second Reply to Hayne did not reach the American public in written form until February 23, 25, and 27, when it appeared in three installments in the *National Intelligencer*. Soon it was being sold everywhere and in greater demand than any congressional speech in American history. A correspondent from Jackson's home state wrote that Webster was known "in every log house" in western Tennessee as "the champion of the Union."[16]

The Hayne debate not only nationalized Webster's reputation; it gave him a base of popular support from which he might reasonably seek the presidency, and also forged the final link in the magnetic chain which bound him to his worshipping followers in New England. The speech which was powerful enough to draw plaudits from an old adversary like Madison and from competitors like Clay, inspired reverence and awe among more intimate friends. Amos Lawrence wrote, "I thank you as a citizen of Massachusetts, of New England, of the United States, not only for myself but for my children." George Ticknor, who reviewed the first volume of Webster's speeches a year later, felt he could now explain Webster's power.

We feel as if the sources of his strength, and the mystery by which it controls us, were, in a considerable degree, interpreted. We feel that like the fabulous giant of antiquity, he gathers it from the very earth that produced him, and our sympathy and interest, therefore, are excited not less by the principle on which his power so much depends, than by the subjects and occasions on which it is so strikingly put forth. We understand better than we did before not only why we have been drawn to him, but why the attraction that carried us along, was at once so cogent and so natural.[17]

What Ticknor seems to have responded to was the fact that Webster had made possible a new perception of America, rooted in constitutional order and liberty, the present and future continuous with the wisdom and virtue of the past. Webster's friend, William Sullivan, wrote from Boston that the most valuable thing about Webster's replies to Hayne was "that they teach the citizens in general what their relation to the Federal government is," and Webster's oldest son, Fletcher, wrote to his father, "I never knew what the constitution really was, till your last short speech. I thought it was a compact between the states."[18]

What did it mean to be an American in 1830? Many of Webster's countrymen were troubled and confused by a question so fraught with implications for their own identity. Webster answered the question by demonstrating that to be an American meant to believe in the supremacy of the

Constitution and the Union. A stupendous accomplishment made possible partly by his masterful talents as a communicator and partly because the depth of his convictions seemed equal to the grandeur of the subject. He could no more doubt the wisdom of the Constitution and the blessings of Union than he could doubt the wisdom and integrity of his father. In his own mind paternal loyalty had fused with national loyalty, and he articulated it with an unshakable, awesome eloquence. Whatever calamities might befall him on other matters, on this great theme Webster's followers would always find him "independent, self-poised, steadfast." They would be able "to calculate him like a planet."

The image of Danield Webster, which had been an emerging phenomenon in the 1820s, became fixed in the minds of many Americans after 1830. Webster's name became symbolically attached to the concepts of Constitution, Union, and the wisdom and virtue of the age of Washington. He became guardian for the nation, defender of the constitution, preserver of the Union. By believing in him, thousands of Americans inside New England and out could continue to believe in their own future and the future of their country.

W. Lloyd Warner has said that symbolic heroes "release and free us, yet bind and control us, for they take us out of ourselves and permit us to identify with the ideals of our culture. The sacred ideals of godhead are never more than one step beyond: sometimes they are immediate and present, for in human history heroes often become gods."

It was Daniel Webster's destiny to become "godlike" while he lived, but in the end this was probably a dubious blessing, for as Warner has also said, "a champion in America . . . must be forever on his guard to be more the common man than champion, lest his followers look for new Davids to slay him."[19]

10

PRESIDENTIAL POLITICS
The Godlike Image Begins to Tarnish

The two years from 1830 to 1832 launched by his second marriage and the great Senate debate marked one of the most expansive periods in Webster's life. He began to live opulently, maintaining expensive establishments in Washington and Boston while supporting the family farm in New Hampshire and building up a great estate in Marshfield, Massachusetts. At the same time he showed the first overt signs of succumbing to what Van Buren would later call "an object which no man in the country ever pursued with more eagerness or with less prospect of success"—the quest for the presidency of the United States.

As a young lawyer and fledgling politician, Webster had envied the wealth of a man like Christopher Gore, who had been able to maintain a town house in Boston, a grand country estate in Watertown, and still take a staff of servants and a coach and four with him when he went to Washington. Sparked by his new marriage (and the dowry which came with it) he now embarked on a lavish life style of his own. After his brother died, Daniel purchased the Elms farm in New Hampshire and began to expand its holdings and operate it with a tenant farmer. At the same time, he invested almost forty-five thousand dollars for choice land in Boston next to his Summer Street mansion and rented an expensive three-floor apartment in Washington staffed by two servants plus a coachman and a two-horse coach.

Webster's acquisition of his Marshfield property during this period is particularly significant. He and Grace first saw the Thomas farm while driving back to Boston from a Cape Cod vacation in September, 1824. Webster was attracted to the spot for many reasons. In the first place, Marshfield was historic ground, settled and cultivated by the Pilgrims more than two hundred years earlier. In the second place, the 160 acres of meadows, fields, and woodlands were within sight of the sea less than a mile away. Finally, there was Captain John Thomas, himself, a sturdy veteran of the Revolution and a yeoman New England farmer of the old school like his own father. Once acquainted with the captain, the Websters made it a point to stop at his place whenever they went to the cape. In the spring of 1832 Webster bought the Thomas farm for $3,650. This modest sum was simply the first installment in a life-long investment intended to create something that would eventually put people in mind of Mount Vernon and Monticello. Every president except the Adamses had owned great country estates, and now Danield Webster had Marshfield.[1]

When Jackson was inaugurated, the matter of succession to the presidency could hardly have dominated Webster's thinking. He assumed that Calhoun and Van Buren would compete for the Democratic nomination if Jackson did not run again, and that the National Republicans would naturally call on Clay. Webster presumably would support Clay, just as he and Clay had supported Adams. Clay had run a strong race for the presidency eight years before, had served as secretary of state under Adams and would be supported by Adams in 1832. Moreover, Clay was the man most clearly identified with the "American system," the combination of protective tariffs and internal improvements which supplied the opposition party with its program. Webster would be called upon to be a chief lieutenant in Clay's campaign, but he would be a lieutenant and not the chief candidate.

By early January, 1830, Webster was watching the strange events taking place in Jackson's official family with amused detachment. The cabinet had fallen into complete disarray over the social acceptability of Peggy Eaton, the tavern keeper's daughter who had married Jackson's old friend and secretary of war Major Eaton. It was said that Vice-President Calhoun's wife had snubbed Mrs. Eaton, that other cabinet wives would do the same thing and that Martin Van Buren, the dapper little secretary of state from New York was turning the whole messy business to his own advantage. Webster could see at once that Van Buren was the man to watch. "He controls all the pages on the back stairs," he wrote to a friend, "and flatters what seems to be at present the Aaron's serpent among the President's desires, a settled purpose of making out the lady of whom so much has been said, a person of reputation." Unlike other leaders in Washington society the Websters did not pass judgment on Peggy Eaton. On January 4, 1830, they went to dinner at the president's along with Mrs. Eaton and about twenty-five others. Jackson was at his most gracious. He escorted Caroline to the table, put her on his right, advised her about the multitude of dishes, and asked her opinion of the wines. Daniel must have been pleased to see so much attention paid to his bride, but this did not prevent him from musing over the political implications of the Peggy Eaton affair for the future. "It is odd enough," he wrote a few days later, "but too evident to be doubted, that the consequence of this dispute in the social and fashionable world, is producing great political effects, and may very probably determine who shall be successor to the present chief magistrate."[2]

If the Jacksonians ended up fighting each other over Peggy Eaton, and if they alienated the public by making bad appointments and refusing to authorize a program of internal improvements, the National Republicans would have an easy time of it in 1832. Perhaps they would turn to Webster instead of Clay. This thought seems to have entered Webster's head sometime in the spring of 1830. It was prompted to a considerable extent by the public reception of his speeches against Hayne. Ever since the Federalists had fallen apart, he had been thinking of a new party based on great national principles. Loyalty to the Union and the Constitution were principles which men of every section could support—principles comprehensive enough to assimilate Clay's American system into a truly national party.

Webster's behavior between 1830 and 1832 was shaped by his desire to probe the sources of his own strength without openly challenging Clay. In March of 1830, he wrote to a Virginia correspondent that Clay would naturally be the National Republican candidate in 1832, but at about the same time he told Mason that the political future had never been so uncertain. The anti-Masonry movement, which had sprung up in western New York State after the mysterious disappearance of a man named William Morgan, who had threatened to publicize the secrets of the Masonic Order, was spreading "like an Irish rebellion," Webster said, and was bound to influence politics. Anti-Masonry was a spontaneous, democratic political movement nourished on the popular fear of a privileged, "aristocratic" secret society. The movement promised to steal votes from both the Jacksonians and the National Republicans, and Webster knew that Clay, a Mason himself, could hardly appeal to this faction, which might tip the balance in the key states of New York and Pennsylvania.[3]

On April 18, Webster wrote to Clay expressing his confidence that either Van Buren or Calhoun could be defeated in the next election. He said nothing about Clay's candidacy, and reserved judgment as to what the best course would be for the National Republicans if Jackson decided to run again. A letter from Story the previous day suggests that he was counseling his friends in Massachusetts to let other states take the lead in nominating Clay.

I have talked a little with the saints about a certain thing—they are satisfied with my views, to wait events, & agree that it is not well to say a word until a movement shall be made elsewhere—N. England never seemed less inclined to quarrel with her own than now. . . .[4]

By the end of May, prospects for a National Republican victory in 1832 seemed rather promising. The Peggy Eaton affair raged on and threatened to force Jackson to call for a new cabinet. The president had begun to suspect that Calhoun, the vice-president, was plotting against him, and had made it clear at the Jefferson Day Dinner on April 13 that he disapproved of Calhoun's nullification ideas. Looking straight at Calhoun, Jackson had toasted "Our Union; it must be preserved." Calhoun had cooly replied "The Union, next to our liberty most dear. May we always remember that it can only be preserved by distributing equally the benefits and burdens of the Union." The dinner had been planned to help unify the party, but it had the effect of driving the Calhoun and Jackson supporters further apart. Webster reported gleefully that when the Pennsylvania delegates found out in advance what the toasts were going to be they deliberately stayed away. He felt that the schismatic tendencies of the Democrats, together with Jackson's stubborn wrong-headedness in vetoing a bill for a federal road in Kentucky, provided the opposition with rare opportunities. "The present prospect is cheering," he wrote to Clay on May 29. "I think you cannot be kept back from the contest. The people will bring you out." But at the same time he confessed that he was against having the Massachusetts legislature nominate Clay just then "on the grounds that everybody knows we are safe and strong in Massachusetts, and a nomination there would only raise the cry of coalition revived. It has seemed to me the proper scene for the first formal action is Maryland." The impatient Clay swallowed his disappointment and agreed to postpone what would be "highly gratifying" to him personally to "what is most expedient."[5]

Meanwhile, Webster continued to do what he could to keep his own views on Union and the Constitution before the public. His friends gave him divided counsel. Some urged him to speak again while the Hayne debate was still ringing in the public memory. Others claimed he would be unlikely to approach the level of his earlier effort and should keep quiet. With Abbot Lawrence's help he had thousands of copies of the speech printed and distributed around the country. He also took pains to send a copy of the speech to James Madison and was delighted when Madison congratulated him for its "overwhelming effect on the nullifying doctrine of S. Carolina." Madison's letter was the next best thing to a blessing from Jefferson himself, and helped to demolish the argument of southerners like Hayne that nullification and secession were no more than the logical development of principles laid down in the Virginia and Kentucky resolutions. In his letter to Madison, Webster wrote that he had delayed sending the former president a copy of his speech because of Madison's role in the Virginia and Kentucky resolutions. He did not want Madison to feel pressed to take a further position now. Labored courtesy at best. As soon as Webster received the former president's answer, he wrote gloatingly to Mason, "Some time ago you expressed a wish that Mr. Madison might come out agst. this nullifying doctrine. *That object is secured.* In due time the public will have the benefit of his opinions in the most gratifying manner." Whether he knew it or not, Madison, who, as the beleaguered war leader, had been an object of amused contempt to Congressman Webster was now being enlisted in the campaign to make Senator Webster president.[6]

During the summer and early fall of 1830, Webster's law practice continued to be very heavy, and in the summer he added to his fame by participating in the celebrated Knapp murder case. On April 7, 1830, Captain Joseph White, a wealthy Salem merchant, was found murdered in his bed. For a long time the crime completely baffled the police and frightened the well-to-do community in Salem and Boston. "I never knew such a universal panic," Judge Story wrote to Webster, "It is not confined to Salem or Boston, but seems to pervade the whole community. We are all astounded and looking to know from what corner the next blow will come—there is a universal dred & sense of insecurity, as if we lived in the midst of a Bandetti." Finally, the police arrested a local criminal, Richard Crownshield, along with two brothers, Joseph and Frank Knapp. Joseph, who was married to the daughter of Captain White's niece, admitted that he had burned the captain's will and together with his brother had hired Crownshield to murder him in the hope of inheriting the White fortune through his wife. When Joseph Knapp confessed, Crownshield committed suicide in prison. Joseph thereupon retracted his confession. When it became necessary to try the Knapp brothers for a murder they had originally planned but not committed, the attorney general and the solicitor general of Massachusetts took the unusual step of inviting Daniel Webster to aid them in the prosecution. Webster agreed and performed before crowded courtrooms during three separate trials in the summer and fall. Every move he made was reported to the press in great detail, and the *Boston Transcript* devoted its entire first issue to his five-and-a-half-hour address to the jury. The Knapp brothers were convicted and their public execution served to enhance the special prosecutor's image as a guardian of the community. Whereever the threat appeared— from reckless insurrectionaries in South Carolina or from vicious murderers at home—Daniel Webster could be counted on to defend the interests of loyal, law-abiding citizens.[7]

During the winter of 1830 and the spring and summer of 1831, Webster continued to appear publicly committed to Clay while privately playing a delaying game to favor his own chances. On December 28, 1830, he wrote to a friend complaining about the "hollowness in Mr. Clay's support." The same day, Edward Everett confessed that Webster was using his influence to prevent a Clay nomination in Massachusetts. There were reports of Boston "mechanics and working men" getting up a public subscription to get Chester Harding to paint a full-length portrait of Webster, and early in 1831 Webster's collected speeches were published and favorably reviewed by

Ticknor. Somewhat later, Samuel Knapp published a laudatory biography. Both Ticknor and Knapp emphasized Webster's obscure origins and his identification with great national issues transcending ordinary party considerations. Although his undeclared candidacy was getting difficult to conceal, Webster assured Clay on March 4 that he agreed with him on the major issues of the day. He then went on to discuss possible problems involved in his own plans for a western trip. Friends advised him that he could not go to Kentucky at this time "without exposing *myself* & what is of more consequence, my *friends* to insidious and odious remarks, which might have a bad effect on the public mind. I am quite unwilling to give up the jaunt, not knowing at what other period I may hope to be beyond the mountains. Nevertheless, if there be well founded doubts about the prudence of such a thing, it ought to be omitted. My purpose was to go to Ohio, Kentucky & Michigan—but not down the river."[8]

Clay must have found Webster's delicacy about the western trip grimly amusing, in view of the fact that he was engaged in an open courtship with National Republican leaders in New York at the same time. The testimonial dinner held for Webster in New York City on March 10 was ostensibly to honor him for his service in defending the Constitution. It was really designed, as Everett confided to his wife, as a "feeler of the public pulse" regarding the possibility of Webster's candidacy. Everett thought the whole thing was unfortunate, because Webster could not possibly "succeed in opposition to Mr. Clay" but could alienate Clay supporters within the party. Joseph Gales, editor of the *National Intelligencer,* told Webster quite bluntly that Clay was the decided choice of the majority of the National Republicans and that he, Webster, should not be seduced away from his duty by the anti-Masons. Webster was in correspondence with leading anti-Masonic leaders at the time, and they were urging him to support their own presidential candidate, William Wirt. Although he would later go to extreme lengths to attract anti-Masonic support, he was able to see at this point that he could hardly build a new party on broad national principles by carrying a banner for those who felt that the greatest dangers America faced came from the Masons. Webster rejected the blandishments of the anti-Masons. He did not finally fall into line behind Clay, however, until shortly before the National Republicans held their national convention in Baltimore in December, 1831. In August, Stephen White, one of Webster's most intimate supporters in Massachusetts was asked point blank by another National Republican leader in the state where Webster stood with respect to Clay. White reminded his questioner that Webster also had a national following and that he was looked upon as a natural leader by those who sought to create a *"constitutional party."* White went on to say that Clay would be supported "until his defeat, if it should unhappily take place, should lead our friends to adopt some other more popular candidate rather than make a shipwreck of our hopes by an obstinate support of men instead of principles." The message could hardly have been clearer; Daniel Webster's days as a subordinate to Clay were numbered.[9]

Having reluctantly put on the party harness, Webster was content to let Clay dictate the strategy for the campaign. The original plan had called for the National Republicans to follow a moderate course, letting the Jacksonians make their own mistakes, and then to capitalize on the resulting dissatisfaction among the people. Such a strategy was based on the mistaken notion that Jackson's administration of the spoils system and his reluctance to support internal improvements would cause widespread discontent. But it at least had the virtue of counseling against a direct assault at that point where the opposition was strongest—at the president himself. Now Clay thought otherwise. He argued that new appointments of the president should be challenged and defeated in Congress in order to show that Jackson was not infallible. "The character of an eminent public man resembles a fortification," Clay said. "If every attack is repelled, if no breach on any point can be made, he becomes impregnable. But if you once make a breach, no matter how small, the work may be carried." When Jackson's secretary of state and chief advisor, Van Buren, resigned and was appointed minister to England, Clay advised voting against his confirmation. No one argued that Van Buren was not an able man and had not been a competent secretary of state. The pretext for opposing his nomination was that he had slandered the previous administration by informing England that American policy on West Indian trade under Adams had been a mistake. The real reason, as Clay confided in a letter to Everett, was to make Van Buren "powerless" as a future presidential candidate. Webster, although aware of the possible hazards of his action, went along with Clay and voted against Van Buren in January, 1832. Refusing to admit that he was influenced by partisan motives, he called his vote "the most unpleasant duty" of his public life. In retrospect, it must have seemed even more unpleasant. Recalled from London, Van Buren smiled all the way back on the boat. Most Americans thought he had been victimized by cheap political maneuvering, and his stock as heir apparent to Jackson rose higher than ever.[10]

The rejection of Van Buren also helped to insure the defeat of the National Republicans in their chief campaign issue—the attempt to recharter the Bank of the United States. Under the management of the brilliant Philadelphia financier, Nicholas Biddle, the Bank, which had played a significant and successful role in American economic life ever since 1823, operated on the basis of a congressional charter that was due to expire in 1836. The Bank was controversial. Its earlier mismanagement had helped to bring on a panic in 1819. Some state banks resented the fact that all government deposits went into the Bank of the United States. Debtor groups complained that the Bank restricted credit. Southern states' rights groups believed it was an unconstitutional use of federal power. On the other hand, the supporters of the Bank argued that it had provided a stable currency, allowed for the orderly expansion of bank credit, facilitated business transactions on a national basis, and carried out many operations for the United States Treasury free of charge. Jackson, who associated banks, speculators, paper money, and dishonest debts with financial disaster of his own many years earlier, was a declared enemy of the Bank. Webster and Clay supported the Bank and were close friends of Biddle. Yet it did not seem at the outset that the Bank would necessarily be a party issue. There was strong support in both houses of Congress for the Bank by men of all parties and some of Jackson's close advisors favored it. At first Clay and Webster advised Biddle to delay applying for a new charter until after the election. Sometime in the fall of 1831 they changed their minds, apparently thinking that if they stirred up Jackson's wrath over the matter they would have a good issue for the election. A bill for recharter was reported in the Senate in March 1832, and Webster spoke in support of it at the end of May.[11]

It was natural enough for Webster to be the bank's advocate in the Senate. He was personally close to Biddle, who was a man of wealth, family, and literary accomplishment—the kind of man Webster liked to see take an active role in public affairs. He had long represented the Bank in court and had been successful in getting favorable decisions, the famous *McCulloch* v. *Maryland* case being only one of many. Webster had been a director of the Bank himself and saw to it that the directors of the Boston branch were appointed from his friends. Along with many other members of Congress he was a borrower of the Bank, but his real problems in that connection had not yet developed. In addition, he acted as a kind of informal legislative agent for Biddle. On April 19, 1831, for example, Webster wrote to Biddle explaining why he was charging a substantial fee for a case in which little was done in court.

The case vs. Martin, the Alabama case, is one in which little was said in court. It was quite clear both to Mr. Sergeant and myself, that we could do nothing with it. Owing to a defect in the statute, the Alabama Court had no jurisdiction. I therefore went to work, in another quarter, to remedy the law & was successful. The amending law passed, without its being suspected anywhere that it was especially useful to the Bank. It opens the Courts of the U.S. to the Bks in 4 states, where there are or are to be offices—viz; Missouri, Louisiana, Alabama, Miss: this is of great importance in any event; and of very great, if the Charter is not to be renewed.

I bestowed good attention on this measure; which makes me willing to charge a *fee* in the cause itself.

Indeed I had half a mind to write 1000 instead of 500—but am well satisfied as it is.[12]

From our perspective, Webster's candor in this letter seems astounding. He was explaining why he expected a specific fee for getting a specific law passed. To be sure, congressional ethics in the 1830s were not what they are today; it was customary for members of Congress who were lawyers to appear on behalf of clients before the Supreme and lesser courts, and Webster apparently felt no sense of impropriety in what he was doing. Presumably, his interest, the Bank's interest, and the national interest all amounted to the same thing. From another point of view, he was placing himself in a highly vulnerable position.

Webster's speech for rechartering the Bank was argued ably enough on the grounds of its settled constitutionality and its usefulness in promoting commerce and supporting a stable currency. He maintained toward the end that his motives "were not drawn from any local considerations," because Massachusetts, unlike many other states, had strong banks of her own and could get along without the United States Bank. This was true, but could hardly disguise his political motives. The recharter bill passed both houses of Congress handily and was sent to Jackson early in July. Webster expected a veto but was not prepared for the message which Jackson sent along with it. Webster had argued for the Bank on rational grounds. His speech was directed at other senators and assumed some knowledge of public policy and finance. Jackson knew little about banking theory. He sent his message to Congress, but it was written for the people, who were told that the Bank's stock was falling into foreign hands and that the request for recharter was intended to perpetuate monopolistic privileges, "to grant titles, gratuities and exclusive privileges, to make the rich richer and the potent more powerful." Jackson intended to protect "the humble members of society, the farmers, mechanics, laborers, who have neither the time nor the means of securing like favors for themselves." Besides, the Bank was unconstitutional, no matter what the Supreme Court said. The President could decide that matter as well as the Court.[13]

The message had been drafted by Amos Kendall, the renegade Dartmouth graduate who looked like Ichabod Crane and wrote like Tom Paine. Kendall advised Jackson and had an uncanny way of translating his convictions into a pungent prose that the Old Hero would never have been able to manage himself. After the veto, the Jackson press claimed that their hero had written a new Declaration of Independence. But all Biddle could see in the White House was Robespierre lusting for anarchy. Webster was more restrained, but he must have realized that he was getting into more than he had bargained for. The *Washington Globe* had already begun to run articles about the fees he was collecting from the Bank. The venerable John Marshall had thought that Webster's argument in favor of rechartering the Bank was "unanswerable," but Jackson and his friends had apparently not even bothered to read it, let alone answer it. What irritated Webster the most was the casual way with which Jackson disposed of the constitutional issue. The authority of the Supreme Court did not control Congress or the president, Jackson had said, but had "only such influence as the force of their reasoning may deserve."[14]

Webster replied to the veto message on July 11, the day after it was issued. His speech, carefully revised for publication, emphasized the earlier arguments he had made for rechartering the Bank, and then concentrated on what he referred to in a note to Story as Jackson's "*trash* on the constitutional question." By seeking to put his own interpretation of the Constitution on the same level as that of the Supreme Court, Jackson was trying to convert "constitutional limitations of power into mere matters of opinion." He was seeking to replace a government of laws with a government of men. But this was not all—the veto was an invitation to class conflict and disunity.

It sows . . . the seeds of jealousy and ill-will against that government of which its author is the offiial head. It raises a cry, that liberty is in danger, at the very moment when it puts forth claims to powers heretofore unknown and unheard of. . . . It manifestly seeks to influence the poor against the rich; it wantonly attacks whole classes of people, for the purpose of turning against them the prejudices and the resentment of other classes.[15]

The vote to override the veto failed and the issue was taken to the voters. What had once been a legitimate and important question of public policy had now become hopelessly embroiled in political haranguing. It was not possible to be for Jackson and the Bank at the same time. The voters could figure that out even if they didn't know much about the intricacies of finance.

By the end of August it was obvious that the president would be a big winner. Much to Clay's embarrassment Jackson was even strong in Kentucky. Webster tried to pretend that the administration was still in trouble, but he knew better. When his speech against the veto came out in pamphlet form, he found it "too *forensic*" and legalistic to compete with Jackson's message for the public mind. Resolved to try and meet Jackson on his own ground and to help make sure that Massachusetts would not follow Kentucky into the enemy camp, Webster made a final slashing attack on Jackson at the National Republican convention in Worcester on October 12. The president was not only anti-Bank and anti-tariff, but a spoilsman who would turn a battle-scarred Bunker Hill veteran away from the White House door in order to reward one of his own illiterate henchmen. He was a tyrant willing to put himself above the law, and he held the nullifiers within the bosom of his own party. Webster painted the picture Massachusetts would confront if the president were re-elected.

Nullification will proceed, or will be put down by a power as unconstitutional as itself. The revenues will be managed by a treasury bank. The use of the veto will be

The so-called "Black Dan" portrait by Francis Alexander in 1835.

considered as sanctioned by the public voice. The Senate, if not "cut down," will be bound down, and, the President commanding the army and the navy, and holding all places of trust to be party property, what will then be left, Sir, for constitutional reliance?[16]

The more vigorously Webster attacked Jackson, the more bitterly was he attacked by the Democrats in return. Jackson editors liked to play rough, and they were given marvelous opportunities to exercise their ingenuity for sarcasm and invective when they discovered that some of Webster's enthusiastic admirers actually used the word "god-like" to describe him. When they had heard about the public subscription for a Webster portrait in Boston, they said that "the worshippers of the *God-like man*" would "extend devotion to his *images,* as well as himself" but would "give the *shadow* to the working men" and keep "the *substance*" for the Boston aristocracy. Now they jumped on him for defending the Bank as zealously as he had defended the Union, a cause which Jackson also took to heart.

Hear Him! Hear Him!, the God-like Daniel, Gen. Jackson has vetoed the mammouth Bank, and *therefore* the Constitution is in danger. True, he has declared *the Union must be preserved,* but what is the Union to me when the Bank is gone? Will the Union pay counsel fees? No, fellow citizens, I tell you that the Bank charter is the charter of your liberties.

Here was a theme that would never grow old for the writers of the *Washington Globe.* When they thought of Webster, they were reminded of the time Demosthenes refused to speak against Hepalius because he had a sore throat. "Some that were nearby said it was no common hoarseness he had got in the night; it was a hoarseness occasioned by swallowing gold and silver. . . ."[17]

When it was all over, Jackson had won sixteen of the twenty-four states and had piled up 219 electoral votes to Clay's 49. The victory was in large measure a tribute to the overwhelming popularity of the Hero, or to the "infatuation of the times," as Webster would have said. But there was more to it than that. Jackson was not only popular; he was also organized. He had won in 1828 not just because he was popular, but because he presided over a disciplined party organization which extended into every state and nearly every county in the country. By striking directly at Jackson in refusing to assent to Van Buren's nomination, Webster and Clay had forced a Jacksonian party threatened with disruption to close ranks. Men who believed in the Bank voted against it out of loyalty to Jackson and the party.[18]

Webster did not draw the correct conclusions from the election of 1832. He continued to think that a leader who stood above party and identified himself with the principles of Union and constitutionality could be made president, and failed to realize how much his own reputation was being chipped away in the Bank war which was just starting. For him it was enough to know that Clay had had his chance and exposed the "hollowness" of his support, while Massachusetts, as predicted, remained loyal to the National Republicans to the end. Webster spent most of the fall before the election in Marshfield planting trees, adding stock to his farm, and sailing his elegant new yacht *Calypso*. Marshfield, he thought, would make an ideal summer White House four years hence.

11

THE POLITICS OF
UNIONISM—A LOSING GAME

In a futile last-ditch attempt to help Clay, the National Republicans had flooded Maine with copies of Webster's speeches. There was so much papered Webster rhetoric in the state, chortled the *Washington Globe* on November 14, 1832, that people were wrapping seeds and lighting their pipes with it. Six months later the *Globe* was reserving its ridicule for opposition leaders like Clay and Calhoun and complimenting Webster for his "manly views" in defense of Jackson. When Webster visited Cincinnati in the summer of 1833 the *Globe* pointedly observed that "several distinguished friends of the Administration" were on hand to toast him as "the profound expounder of the Constitution, and the eloquent supporter of the *Federal Union,* and the uniform friend and advocate of the Western country." But by March of 1834, the editors of the *Globe* had dismissed Webster from his lofty perch and were scornfully describing him as a disappointed politician out "to establish the power of a moneyed aristocracy"—one of "the *natural enemies* of the rights of suffrage."[1]

His changing image in the columns of the country's leading Democratic paper is a good measure of Webster's fluctuating success in trying to make himself a strong presidential contender for 1836. His initial advantages were three. First, Clay had developed a reputation as a loser. Second, the opposition in 1836, whether Van Buren or some other Democrat, was bound to be less formidable than Jackson. Third, Webster could identify with an enormously powerful president in putting down nullification, the most serious threat to Union the United States had ever faced. But these advantages were not enough. After closing ranks with Jackson over nullification, Webster fell out again with the president over the Bank. Finding that he could not ride the politics of unionism into the White House, he was forced to play the old-fashioned sectional and factional politics with the Whigs—a losing game in every way.

The nullification crisis, which Webster had been warning about ever since the Hayne debate, actually came on more quickly than he expected. After a new tariff was passed with southern support in July of 1832, he believed the immediate threat was over, a miscalculation that did not take into account the intransigence of South Carolina and the ambition of John Calhoun. Late in August, John Calhoun wrote a public letter to Governor Hamilton defending nullification as a legitimate means of self-defense by the state. The governor, thereupon, called a state convention which met in Columbia on November 24 and adopted an ordinance nullifying the Tariff of 1828 and prohibiting the collection of tariff duties within the state beginning February 1, 1833. The legislature immediately passed laws to enforce the ordinance. Jackson responded by alerting army forces in South Carolina and by issuing a proclamation condemning nullification and asserting the supremacy of the federal government.

Now that the battle between the state and the federal government was finally joined, Webster's natural impulse was to support the president. But how? He had intended to write a formal reply to Calhoun's defense of nullification, but Jackson seemed to have made that step unnecessary. The president's proclamation was based on the same constitutional arguments Webster had made against Hayne, and Webster got some satisfaction in making this point a main theme in his remarks at a December 17 meeting in Faneuil Hall. In private he was willing to take all the credit for the government's position. "It is sometimes said," Webster wrote to a friend, "that in a changing world, if people but stand still, others, sooner or later, will come to them. Were you not struck with this truth in seeing the proclamation?" Daniel Webster might not be occupying the White House, but for the moment at least, his principles were. To add to this promising beginning, Webster began to appear more and more as a guest at presidential dinners and receptions. "I dined at the Palace . . . a few days since and found Mr. W. there in all his glory," wrote John Tyler on January 22. Tyler was a Calhoun man and predicted that Webster would lead the drive to perform Jackson's will in the Senate.[2]

Tyler did not appreciate the delicacy of Webster's position. For Jackson the supremacy of the federal government meant everything, the tariff very little. Webster was willing to give the president power to enforce federal law, but he could not, in loyalty to his constituents, agree to substantial tariff concessions. Thus he found himself supporting the so-called Force bill, which was designed to give the president a wide range of administrative legal and military authority to deal with nullification, and opposing the administration's Verplanck bill, which proposed to cut tariff duties in half.

Correctly judging that Jackson put a higher priority on the Force bill than on tariff legislation, Webster carefully watched its progress in the Senate. When southern Democrats tried to stymie the act, Webster rose to remind them that it was "the President's own measure." For his part, Webster said, he felt the president had no choice. "I give a hearty support to the Administration in all measures which I deem to be fair, just and necessary. And in supporting these measures, I mean to take my fair share of responsibility, to support them fairly and frankly, without reflections on the past, and without mixing other topics in their discussion." This display could not have done much to endear the harried southerners to their Massachusetts colleague. A few months earlier, he had been accusing them of supporting Jackson's executive usurpation in the Bank veto. Now he was flicking the Hero's whip over their backs.[3]

The heart of the debate over the Force bill took place about a week later in mid-February in a classic confrontation between Webster and Calhoun. The formal subject matter consisted of Calhoun's resolutions, which stated that the United States existed by virtue of a constitutional "compact" through which each state retained its sovereignty and could judge for itself whether or not the laws of the United States should apply in its case. The resolutions included a specific denial that the people of the United States were now or had ever been "one nation."

Calhoun spoke first. He was quiet, tense, logical, and determined. He concentrated mostly on the Force bill as an example of legislation in violation of the compact, an act of war really, against the sovereign state of South Carolina. He said nothing new; the arguments on which he based his case were the arguments he had already published—the arguments Hayne had used three years before.

Webster rose to reply on February 16. His speech was essentially a replay of his part in the Hayne debate. He disagreed with Calhoun over what had happened in 1787. He refused to consider what an ideal Constitution might be, but insisted on treating the United States under the Constitution for what it had become—one patriotic community bound together and secured in its liberty by a fundamental law which none could disobey. Where Calhoun was logical, Webster was pragmatic. How, he asked, could one state be allowed to secede without allowing two, three, or a dozen to secede? What would happen to the army in this case—to the navy, to private debts, treaties? The peroration at the end of the Hayne speech had been an appeal for unity, a mixture of hope and desperation. Now Webster was more confident.

Be assured, sir, be assured, that among the political sentiments of this people, the love of the union is still uppermost. They will stand fast by the Constitution and by those who defend it. I rely on no temporary expedients, on no political combination; but I rely on the true American feeling, the genuine patriotism of the people, and the imperative decision of the public vote.

When he finished, the crowded gallery broke into wild applause and had to be cleared before the Senate could be adjourned. Calhoun, who, as a young man had been so quick to serve the tide of patriotic feeling which had washed over the country back in 1812, had isolated himself. History was now on Webster's side. The Force bill passed 32 to 1. Calhoun and his supporters did not remain for the vote, and Clay was not recorded.[4]

Word spread rapidly among Webster's and Jackson's friends about the triumph. The president wrote to a friend that Calhoun was "in a state of dementation—his speech was a perfect failure; and Mr. Webster handled him like a child." Jackson had reason to be pleased. He had used Webster's rhetoric to get his way with the Senate; now he could relax while Webster, Clay, and Calhoun fought over a tariff bill which did not particularly concern him one way or the other.[5]

In what should have been a moment of triumph, Webster found himself frustrated. He had supplied the arguments, but Jackson would get most of the credit for routing the nullifiers. At the same time he faced defeat on the tariff. Although the Verplanck bill had failed, Clay had replaced it with a bill of his own, designed to lower all duties gradually until they reached a level of 20 percent or less by 1842. Although Webster had learned about Clay's general plan back in December, he was stunned by the bill itself for two reasons. First, it gave up the "protective principle" (larger duties on some commodities than others) so dear to the heart of New England. Second, it was apparent that the bill would become law. Webster poured his influence and rhetoric into a vain attempt to stop the Clay-Calhoun compromise. He accused Clay of selling out the interests of Massachusetts and filed away a copy of the original bill in Clay's handwriting for possible future use. To make matters worse, his friends in Massachusetts were not keen about battling Clay over the matter. Harrison Gray Otis thought that Clay's bill was probably the best that could be expected under the circumstances. Powerful businessmen like Abbot Lawrence praised Clay for his wisdom, and even Edward Everett was careful to advise his journalist brother to support Webster but still remain "tender to Mr. Clay."[6]

When it was all over and the senators had talked themselves out at the beginning of March, the Force bill passed together with Clay's tariff, and the president approved them both. South Carolina tried to save face by declaring the Force Act void, and the issue was closed with both sides claiming victory. The real winner was Jackson, with a powerful assist from Webster. But Clay had turned the crisis to his advantage and bolstered his sagging political stock by negotiating a genuine compromise on the tariff—with the help of the arch-nullifier himself. What, if anything, did this portend for the future?

The great advantage which Webster reaped from the nullification crisis was the possibility of gaining leverage with the administration. Jackson made it clear that he appreciated Webster's support. After the Calhoun debate, the president personally complimented him and subsequently a Democratic senator offered to consult with him about government appointments in the Eastern states. Although he declined this offer, Webster charted a course over the rest of 1833 designed to maintain his personal alliance with the president and disassociate himself from existing parties in the hope that a new party would emerge and make him its standard-bearer. The principles of the party would be adherence to the Constitution and Union, a tariff which recognized the "protective principle," and a sound currency and banking system. On the first principle, which he shared with Jackson, Webster would not budge. For the rest he was prepared to be flexible.[7]

Consistent with his goal, Webster stopped agitating the Bank issue, refused to identify himself with the Clay-Calhoun coalition, and continued to maintain a close relationship with key members of Jackson's cabinet. In April, Clay complained to Biddle that Webster had been trying to build a new party ever since their disagreement over the tariff. Biddle was less worried about the possibility of a new party than about his friend's reticence to use contacts within the administration to help the Bank, but Webster had no intention of stirring up Jackson's wrath on this point. The leader of the new party he had in mind could hardly afford to be known as a lackey to Nicholas Biddle.[8]

To help solidify his relationship with the administration, Webster arranged to have the president officially invited to Boston in late spring. At the same time he set out on an extended western tour of his own. Visiting Buffalo, Columbus, Cincinnati, and Pittsburgh, Webster took every occasion to praise the president for supporting the Union. The *Globe* repaid the compliment by noting that at his various stops Webster was honored by friends of the administration and pointed out that at Cincinnati there were no toasts to Webster *and* Clay because this would have been "an insult to Mr. Webster." Under the circumstances, it was probably just as well that Webster did not continue down the river to Kentucky. A local cholera epidemic provided an excuse for not going, but there were other reasons of which both men were aware.[9]

Webster did not get back to Boston in time to welcome Jackson on June 21, but his friends were conspicuous in extending their hospitality to the president. Shortly after Jackson left New England, Webster went to New York for a confidential political conference with Secretary of State Edward

Livingstone, who was anxious to get his continued support for the administration. We do not know what exactly transpired at that meeting except that the conversation must have touched upon possible courses of action regarding the mutual interests of Webster and Jackson.[10]

Webster's closest political supporters had already forgotten the hard words they had used on Jackson in early political battles. Now they supported the publication of a new Washington paper called the *Examiner,* which was intended to push Webster's presidential possibilities by exploiting his agreement with Jackson on the subjects of Union and nullification. Like such other explicitly pro-Webster papers as the Philadelphia *National Gazette* and *Boston Courier,* the *Examiner* attempted to show that distinctions formerly made between Federalists and Democrats no longer obtained. The important thing now was to get "Unionists" together in the same party to defeat the nullifiers. Even so, the Webster press remained tender on the subject of Webster's Federalist antecedents, and repeatedly denied his association with the Hartford convention. Documentary evidence was secured to show that he had been active in preparing Portsmouth to fend off an expected British attack in 1814.[11]

By the end of the summer, the romance between Webster and Jackson was well advanced and seemed to promise a permanent relationship. Webster was acting as if Henry Clay no longer existed, and he expected his friends in Massachusetts to fall in line. Rufus Choate, for example, felt obliged to send Webster a letter of explanation over a speech he had made at a political dinner on the Fourth of July. The thrust of his remarks had been to emphasize the importance of keeping Van Buren out of the White House in 1836, and, in the course of the speech, Choate had reminded his audience not to forget "our old tried trusting *absent friends,*" meaning Clay and Webster. There was some anxiety that the use of the plural may have offended Webster, so Choate sought to reassure him by explaining that he had treated Clay as "a retired statesman."[12]

The insurmountable obstacle in Webster's path was his inability to understand Andrew Jackson. When Jackson was first elected, Webster had called him weak-willed and predicted that he would be a figurehead for others. When Jackson vetoed the Bank bill, Webster called him a tyrant. During the campaign of 1832, Webster repeatedly said Jackson was too frail to survive a second term. After nullification, Webster embraced him as a vigorous, fearless leader concerned above all with maintaining the Constitution and the Union. In each instance he was wrong. The intuitive genius, the shrewd, complex, ruthless party leader, the president with a near-fanatical belief in himself as the people's instrument—the essential Andrew Jackson eluded Webster at every point. Jackson welcomed Webster's support at a time when it was particularly useful. The president's stand against the nullifiers had split his own party, and Webster had been the strongest man in Congress and the best-known political leader in the country to back him. But there is no reason to believe that he ever entertained the possibility of helping Webster develop a new party out of that controversy. He did have other goals, however, and the most important, now that he had slain the nullification monster, was to kill the Bank.[13]

Webster was unable to hide his differences with Jackson over the Bank, but he tried to minimize them and hoped that his accessibility to both Biddle and the president would allow him to mediate the issue in a way that would satisfy all parties. But the Bank war was not to be disposed of so easily. Biddle had begun to call in loans and tighten credit, ostensibly in preparation for shutting down the Bank when the charter expired in 1836, but really to create enough economic distress to put pressure on the administration. There were rumors that Jackson would retaliate by withdrawing government deposits from the Bank, but Webster chose not to believe them. Wrong again. The president had to flush out two successive secretaries of the treasury before he could get his way, but on September 25 the administration announced that it would henceforth deposit all federal funds in selected state banks rather than in the Bank of the United States.

The aggressive nature and questionable legality of the president's action immediately united the opposition, who argued that the issue was not just the continued existence of the Bank but executive usurpation of congressional power. "King Andrew" had gone too far and the congressmen and senators who looked to the Clay-Calhoun coalition for leadership began to liken themselves to the Whigs, who had fought the abuse of royal power a century earlier.

Webster returned to Washington in early December and continued to maintain his independent posture. Refusing to denounce the president, he urged Biddle to follow a prudent course in the hope of salvaging a reasonable compromise. Inevitably, the chasm between Webster and the Whigs widened. There was talk that the southern nullifiers might support Clay's candidacy in 1836 and that unionists in the South favored Webster. On December 10, Edward Everett wrote to his brother that it was being said "with great confidence and I believe with truth, that Genl. J. has said that he would not interfere between W & Van Buren." Two days later in the Senate, Webster supported a successful administration move to postpone the selection of committees. Clay had been counting on a coalition of National Republicans and Calhounites to appoint committees loaded in favor of the opposition. Webster and the other New England senators who followed him had enough votes to give control of the committees to the Democrats.[14]

Webster could go no further. He was willing to throw the balance of power in the Senate to Jackson—power the president could use in many ways, including his attack on the Bank. The overture to Jackson was also a thrust at Clay. On December 13, while waiting presumably to learn how the president would respond to this offer, Webster asked Everett to drop by "accidentally" and pass on to Nathaniel Silsbee (the other Massachusetts senator) the rumors about Clay and "chief of the nullifiers" Calhoun. He also suggested that Everett tell Clay that if Webster were to remain in the Senate, he would need a conspicuous appointment for himself—chairmanship of the Committee on Finance, for example. Thus Webster created a crisis which left him with three courses of action.

(1)   the development of a formal working relationship which would give him a permanent role in the leadership of the administration and might lead to the creation of a new party;

(2)   the displacement of Clay as leader of the opposition;

(3)   a "reconciliation" with Clay to be secured by putting himself at the head of the most powerful Senate committee.

As it turned out, it was the third alternative that he was forced to choose. Two days after Webster sent Everett on his "accidental" visits, Van Buren turned up at the White House for a meeting with the president and Felix Grundy, the senator from Tennessee who had cooperated with Webster in blocking the committee appointments. Grundy explained that "an arrangement could be made with Mr. Webster and his friends" to get "favorably constituted" committees in the Senate. Jackson asked for Van Buren's opinion and he immediately took issue with the proposal on the grounds that it would blur party lines and compromise the struggle with the Bank. The people could carry Jackson through—he didn't need Daniel Webster. Jackson listened a moment and then told Grundy to drop the matter. That was as close as Webster ever came to being elected president.[15]

Webster returned to the ranks of the opposition, but not until Clay had paid the required price by naming him head of the Finance Committee. If he had not been able to cement an alliance with an overwhelmingly popular president, he had at least established the fact that he would no longer linger in Clay's shadow.

Biddle was frantic and found Webster's actions incomprehensible. On December 15, he wrote to Webster imploring him to cooperate with Clay and Calhoun. "It is in your power to save us from the misrule of these people," Biddle said, "but you can only do it while you are united." Biddle seemed to have forgotten that Webster owed most of his national reputation to his success as Calhoun's adversary, but Webster ignored this in his reply, which played down the importance of the "little difficulties" over the committees and assured Biddle that he intended "to keep extremely cool" in the days ahead, although he feared "the temperature of others will rise higher and higher." Two days later, Webster sent Biddle the following note:

Since I have arrived here, I have had an application to be concerned, professionally against the Bank, which I have declined, of course, although I believe my retainer has not been renewed or *refreshed* as usual. If it be wished that my relation to the Bank should be continued, it may be well to send me the usual retainers.[16]

These two sentences have been repeatedly quoted to show that Webster expected to be paid for his political loyalty to the Bank. The allegation is not true. It was common practice at this time for members of Congress to supplement their income by representing clients before the Supreme Court. As a lawyer, Webster expected to be paid for the legal services he gave the Bank. As a senator he took up the cause of the Bank as a matter of personal conviction and political expediency. Although he and Biddle were close friends and shared the same general set of political beliefs, they frequently disagreed with each other. Webster's political behavior immediately prior to this letter is a case in point. Understandably a matter of immense importance to Biddle, the Bank meant much less to Webster, and he was perfectly willing to ignore it for a while in order to patch up his differences with Jackson. When this strategy failed, he returned to the Bank which he considered a viable political issue and an important part of the larger struggle to maintain the Constitution and the Union.

Webster accompanied his request for a retainer with the following explanation:

I thought it proper to write the enclosed letter, which, however, you need give no attention if you think it more *prudent* to wait a while. I shall not undertake professionally agt. the Bank whether you answer this or not. If such things have to go before the *Board,* I should prefer the subject should be *postponed*—Will you tell me whether you apprehend any changes from my writing to you, on account of infidelity in the P. Office—& tell me also if you are careful to burn *all* letters.

It is the second part of Webster's letter that reveals how vulnerable he really was because of his close ties to the Bank. He knew that to continue to accept a retainer from Biddle was political dynamite for the opposition, but rather than extricate himself from the situation he tried to hush it up. Biddle understood the problem and temporarily withheld Webster's fee out of fear that the *Globe* would immediately get word of it and use it to the Democrats' advantage. He urged Webster to join with Clay and reject Jackson's nominations for directors of the Bank, whom he suspected of being potential spies. When these men were voted down by the Senate, Biddle sent the retainer.[17]

As long as he remained in Jackson's favor, the Democrats overlooked

Webster's personal and professional relationship with the Bank, but once he reverted to the opposition, they resumed their old attacks with a vengeance. "The country demands a full account of Mr. Webster's FEES and LOANS, that the people may judge of his *disinterestedness* and *patriotism,*" wrote the *Globe.* "Let our *great statesman* stand out in the light of day *just as he is,* in all his relations with the institution he so zealously sustains [so] there can be no mistake about MOTIVES." There is no evidence that Webster's fees were excessive or that he profitted illegally from the Bank. In April, 1834, he told Everett that he "never had any particular or unusual accommodation from the bank to the amount of a single dollar." When he made that statement the Bank held four Webster notes totaling ten thousand dollars. Finding that he could not redeem the notes that July, Webster wrote to Biddle's assistant, Samuel Jaudon, saying "It is of great importance to get these matters out of the Bk. of U.S. I feel very anxious in this matter." A week later the notes were picked up by one of Webster's friends, and he prepared to make a public denial that he was in debt to the Bank. "In these times of the prevalence of slander and falsehood," he wrote to Jaudon, "it seems important to be able to make this declaration on some fit occasion in my place." Strictly speaking, Webster was telling the truth about himself and the Bank, but he was obviously unwilling to "stand out in the light of *day just as he is,*" and the Democrats would make the most of it. The Bank's practice of lending money to members of Congress had been common knowledge for years, but Daniel Webster was no ordinary congressman. His own constituents might overlook his chronic dependency on powerful creditors like the Bank because they were convinced he represented their principles and interest. What about the People? The Democrats would remind them that the great Whig guardian was acting very much like any other politician with something to hide.[18]

While intimacy with the Bank was tarnishing his public image, Clay and Calhoun were putting an end to Webster's career as a political independent. Although on record as strongly opposed to the removal of the deposits, Webster tried during the first three months of 1834 to remain independent of Clay and conciliatory to the administration. He took careful notice of reports from Stephen White that he had the support of many Jacksonian leaders in Massachusetts and he apparently hoped, with White, that the Clay-Calhoun love affair would eventually force more northerners from all parties to rally to his banner. He resisted making an open break with Jackson as long as he could, and on March 18 introduced a bill intended to compromise the Bank issue by providing for return of the public deposits to the Bank and a short extension of the charter. Although there was some support for this in administration ranks, Clay and Calhoun would have none of it. They wanted victory or all-out war, and insisted on terms for a new charter that

Jackson would never accept. Webster's bill was tabled on March 25 and three days later he was forced to state a position on the resolution censuring the president for removing the deposits. He voted for the resolution reluctantly, knowing that it marked the end of his hopes to make common cause with the most popular political leader in America since Washington.[19]

Webster had wanted to lead a new party based on the importance of preserving the Union and Constitution. What he got in the spring of 1834 was a position of partial leadership in the emerging Whig coalition. The American Whigs represented what was left of the National Republican party, former Jacksonites alienated by the administration's position on nullification and the bank, southern planters, northern merchants and manufacturers. The Whigs also hoped to absorb the anti-Masons. With such a mix the party was too disparate to unite on much more than the importance of getting Jackson and his crowd out of the White House. Thus, Webster, who for years had been warning about the danger of parties that attempted to turn opposition into a principle, found himself trying to lead just such a party. As early as February, 1834, he put Everett and Caleb Cushing to work on the matter of getting a nomination out of the Whigs in the Massachusetts legislature. Meanwhile, he conferred with important political leaders in New York City and made impressive public appearances in Philadelphia and Baltimore.[20]

In public meetings, Webster still put himself forward primarily as the great defender of Union and the Constitution, but many of his closest supporters found other reasons for wanting to make him president. Edward Everett spelled these reasons out in a candid letter to Thomas Ward, perhaps the single most powerful businessman in the country. "The present political contest," Everett said, was "nothing less than a war of *numbers* against *property* . . . carried on in the proscriptive and remorseless spirit of the French Revolution." American merchants and industrialists were now at the mercy of the government. Clay and Calhoun, "prompted by personal griefs and ambitious views," could not be counted on. "The power and weight of the warfare are in Mr. W's arm and there alone, and the party in power would put its foot tomorrow on the neck of the intelligence and property of the country but not for him." Everett went on to point out that Webster was not personally wealthy, and that he remained in the Senate at considerable financial sacrifice. If gentlemen wanted him to remain active in political life, they would have to help. One hundred men, each contributing $1,000, would make it posible to release Webster from the courts for full-time public service and would sustain a press to support his ideas. Implicit throughout the letter was the dreadful possibility of a man like Webster someday being forced to take the other side.

There is one consideration which I will suggest to you as a thoughtful observer of the state and tendency of things. What would have been the condition of public affairs in New England—in the Union at large—had Mr. W. taken the side of the Levellers, instead the side of security for property and government by law? He is the son of a poor father, brought up in poverty, has had to work hard and has the popular talent to have "wielded the fierce democracy" of the country with irresistible power. Instead of doing so, and turning his position and talents to selfish account, he has all his life long fought the battles of property, order and law.

Everett assured Ward that he was making his request on his own initiative, but it obviously had Webster's blessing because a few months later he wrote to Everett emphasizing "the *absolute necessity* of a fund for public purposes."[21]

We do not know exactly how much money Everett was able to raise for Webster in 1834, but we do know that this was only the first of several such funds collected during Webster's lifetime. Unlike his relationship with the Bank, Webster showed no signs of worrying about the effect these subsidies might have on his reputation. This is not quite as astounding as it seems when we realize that conflict of interest for public officials as we understand it today was an unknown concept in the 1830s. To congressmen who thought nothing of drafting laws and appropriating funds for the redress of claims and then interpreting those laws in the federal courts and representing clients in claims against the government, it seemed natural enough that a member might take advantage of the desire of constituents to help him maintain a proper standard of living. Representatives and senators have always had difficulty living on their salaries alone, and only a few years ago Webster was cited on the floor of the Senate to justify the acceptance of substantial gifts by senators.

Why Webster always needed money is a question which will be addressed in a later chapter. It is enough to point out at this time that whether he knew it or not, his willingness to accept subsidies, like his willingness to accept favors from the Bank, was bound to clash with his image as a disinterested public servant. And perhaps even more important, it suggests how naïve he was in thinking that he could build a party of his own on lofty political principles. The Everett letter, after all, was more than an appeal for funds; it was an appeal to class interest and a confession that the gut issue in American politics was no longer nullification but economic advantage. Webster would continue to stand on the surer ground of Union and Constitution but more and more over the years, he would find his special constituency in the kind of people to whom Everett was appealing—the men willing to pay the bills necessary to keep the great Webster frigate afloat.[22]

With able men like Cushing, Everett, and young Robert Winthrop working for him back home in Massachusetts, the campaign to get Webster before the people as a formal candidate for the presidency picked up momen-

tum in the spring and summer of 1834. The *Boston Atlas* was acquired as a
Webster paper, and the state elections that year put Massachusetts squarely in
the Whig camp. On December 17, the *Atlas* urged the state to endorse its favorite son and on January 21, 1835, the Whig members of the legislature
unanimously nominated Webster for president.

The Whig strategy, designed to achieve victory in 1836, was completely
inconsistent with Webster's basic convictions. He had sought to lead a party
which would appeal to the people's patriotic attachment to the Union and
respect for the Constitution. But the Whig coalition, representing strong
sectional interests, could not unite behind such a program, and the Whig
strategy, which Webster helped to plan and implement, was to exploit the
deep ideological and sectional differences in the country by supporting mul-
tiple nominations in the hope of splitting the vote and throwing the election
into the House of Representatives. At about the same time Webster was
nominated by the Massachusetts legislature, Hugh Lawson White was
nominated in Alabama. White was a strong states' rights man who had
defected from the Jacksonians. As a popular Tennessee senator, he would
presumably take votes away from Van Buren both in the South and West.
So much for the politics of Union. Webster would work with Lawson or
any other states' righter who might help make him president.[23]

Whig leaders in the East and Northwest, where Webster would have to
find almost all of his support, could not unite around Webster. They respected him personally as a great senator and party spokesman, but doubted
his ability to win. William Seward, the young Whig leader in New York,
where the Whigs had taken a beating in the elections of 1834, said, "It is the
height of madness to run Webster as a candidate." Seward was a Webster admirer but feared his candidacy would "fix upon the Whigs the perpetual
stigma of federalism." This fear, which Clay and his friends helped to cultivate, finally resulted in a third Whig nomination when General William
Henry Harrison, a sixty-three-year-old hero and former governor of the
Indiana territory was named at a public meeting in Pennsylvania. Harrison
was still an obscure figure with no record on controversial issues. He was
nicknamed "Old Tippecanoe" because of his victorious part in the Indian
Wars, and it was hoped that he might take Western votes away from Van
Buren.[24]

Webster correctly perceived that Pennsylvania would be the key state in
the election. The anti-Masons were stronger than the Whigs in Pennsylvania, and Webster made every effort to get their support. In the election of
1832, he had shied away from the party on the grounds that Masonry was
not a central political issue. Since that time he had discovered that the Whigs
in Massachusetts needed anti-Masonic support, and had approved the passage of a Massachusetts law abolishing secret oaths. Webster was not a
Mason himself and claimed that his father had always suspected the order.

He had no qualms, therefore, about appealing directly to anti-Masonic leaders in Pennsylvania. "The only hope of rescuing the country and preserving the Constitution and the Union," he wrote, "rests in the patriotism and zeal of the anti-masons of Pennsylvania. As they have saved a state, they may save a nation . . . they are well entitled to take the lead, in the great political movements of the time." This was a direct appeal for a nomination from Pennsylvania anti-Masons, and Webster asked Everett to work out the necessary details. The genteel Everett had to negotiate with Thaddeus Stevens, a tough, hard-driving anti-Masonic leader in Lancaster. Stevens tried to play Harrison and Webster off against each other by asking their opinions about Masonry. Harrison refused to commit herself, maintaining that it was an issue to be settled by public opinion rather than by government action. Webster was ready to say whatever Stevens wanted, and it looked very much as if the Pennsylvania anti-Masons would nominate him when he was embarrassed by a revolt among the anti-Masons in Massachusetts caused by his earlier endorsement of John Davis over John Quincy Adams for a Senate seat. Everett was able to explain this away, and on November 11, the anti-Masons of Allegheny County pledged themselves to work for Webster at the state nominating convention in Harrisburg. They asked Webster for a letter expressing his views on Masonry. He replied with a statement supporting anti-Masonic principles, and readily agreed to changes in wording suggested by one of the local anti-Masonic leaders. Meanwhile another group of anti-Masons in Pennsylvania kept working on Harrison, whom they thought to be a potentially stronger candidate. They finally managed to get a few anti-Masonic words out of the old general, and when the convention finally met on December 14, Harrison was named by a substantial majority.[25]

With the failure in Pennsylvania, Webster's campaign collapsed outside of Massachusetts. Even there, the Whigs were forced to witness the departure of local anti-Masons into the Democratic fold. Webster reluctantly stayed in the race, but so far as he was concerned, the results were already in. When the votes were counted in the winter of 1836, Van Buren had 761,000 popular votes and carried 15 states with 170 electoral votes; Harrison had 549,000 popular and 73 electoral votes; White had 145,000 popular and 26 electoral votes; Daniel Webster had Massachusetts—47,000 popular and 14 electoral votes.

As a party, the Whigs did not fare badly. Van Buren's popular majority was only 25,000 out of more than 1.5 million votes, and the Whigs had carried 485 counties to the Democrats 557. A shift of 2,100 Pennsylvania votes from Van Buren to Harrison would have thrown the election in the House of Representatives.

The Whigs came close but Webster did not. It was one thing to lose an election, but Webster had lost more than that. Although his standing in the country depended on his image as guardian of great national principles, he had allowed himself to become identified as a spokesman for the moneyed interests of the country. Ideologically committed to policies which were supposed to be above party interests, he had tried his hand at the most divisive kind of factional politics. He had sought to unify and "save" the country by exploiting local prejudice and he had let the petty demagogues of anti-Masonry put words in his mouth. He had not lost his great talents, and he would continue to render great service to his country—but he had wanted the Presidency too much. It would happen again.

12

THE GODLIKE MAN LEARNS
HOW TO WIN—IN A COONSKIN CAP

Daniel Webster was fifty-four years old in 1836, and had begun to take on the appearance of a venerable statesman. The Webster paunch now was as noticeable as the famous dome and fierce brows. His step was heavier, his manner even more deliberate, and in his customary dress, the black, long-tailed coat with gold buttons and buff-colored vest and pantaloons, he moved through the streets of Washington and Boston like a revolutionary frigate under full sail.

Unlike Clay, whose feelings were always close to the surface and who was addicted to profane tantrums in times of stress and disappointment, Webster was sanguine, almost glacial, in his ability to accept temporary defeat. Even before Van Buren's inauguration, he had begun to plan for 1840. In a remarkably candid letter to Hiram Ketchum, one of his strongest supporters in New York, he outlined his strategy for the next four years. He would leave the Senate for two years. During this period he would travel, keep himself before the public, and at the same time get his personal finances in order so that upon his return to formal political life he would not have to divide his efforts between the Senate and the courts. Meanwhile, Van Buren would have revealed enough of the vulnerability of administrative policies to be effectively attacked. Whig strength, Webster believed, would have to be based "in the great central states & in the North." New York and Pennsylvania would be key states. Harrison would be early in the field again, and those who sought a stronger candidate should act promptly. Webster closed the letter by suggesting that Ketchum get in touch with Whig leaders in

Pennsylvania to prevent any "premature" (Clay) presidential nomination there.[1]

By the spring of 1837 there was abundant reason for Webster and the other Whig leaders to believe that 1840 would be their year. The booming economy which had blessed Andrew Jackson's final year in office had suddenly collapsed. Van Buren's inauguration was greeted by widespread unemployment and suffering in eastern cities. Food riots and demonstrations began to flare up, and on May 10, the banks of New York, followed closely by banks of other leading cities, refused to redeem paper currency in specie.

Economic disaster is rarely the fault of a particular party, but there is no better time to be in opposition than in periods of depression. Although Van Buren would be haunted by other perplexing problems of foreign and domestic policy, it was the Panic of 1837 that sealed his fate. In retrospect, a Whig victory in 1840 seemed almost inevitable. What was not inevitable was the shape that victory would take and the role Daniel Webster would play in it—not the role he sought as the candidate prepared to save the country, but once again in a supporting role, the voice but not the standard-bearer of the Whigs.

Despite his advice to Ketchum that the main political base for the Whigs lay in the populous and commercial Northeast, Webster knew that he had to extend his own political base by attracting substantial western support. Thus, in the spring of 1837 he set off on an extended tour beyond the Alleghenies, accompanied by his wife, his daughter Julia, and the son of an old college chum, William Pitt Fessenden. The Webster party followed an exhausting schedule which took them from Pittsburgh to Wheeling, through Kentucky and Ohio, on to St. Louis and Chicago. Webster was treated like a great public figure and gave dozens of speeches. He was escorted by marching bands, saluted by the artillery of local militia, and hugged by Indian chiefs. In the distance, across the Alleghenies, his audiences could hear the echoes of the giant banks of the East crashing into silence.

Webster was ambivalent about the panic. On the one hand, as a speculator in western land unable to get his hands on hard money (he had been forced to borrow three thousand dollars from Rufus Choate to make the trip), it was hurting him personally. But the political breezes stirred by the panic all seemed to be blowing in his favor. "That bubble, which so many of us have all along regarded as the offspring of conceit, presumption and political quackery, has burst," he announced in Wheeling, recalling that he had met with some political friends from there five years earlier and predicted what would happen. He repeated this theme in all of his speeches, arguing that if his ideas about a federally controlled currency had prevailed the country would still enjoy prosperity. The point Webster was trying to get across to western audiences was that his political ideas and loyalties were as relevant to the needs of western farmers as they were to eastern bankers and merchants. He was entitled to try and make the point, because his record in Congress had consistently favored western interests, especially in the area of internal improvements. But sometimes it must have seemed to some of his listeners that he was protesting too much. In St. Louis, for example, with Clay on the platform beside him, Webster was almost embarrassing in insisting on his own rusticity.

What I am my fellow countrymen you all know: I am a plain man. I never set up for anything: whatever else you may accuse me of, it can never be said I have set myself up for anything. I am a farmer and on the yellow sands of the east, many a time I have tilled my father's field and followed my father's plough. The farmer's patrimony is the true patrimony of the American system. . . . . Give me acres. . . .

Later on in the speech Webster clapped a nearby Missourite on the shoulder and exclaimed, "This honest man, God bless him! is as truly my friend as though I clasped his hand as the descendent of John Hancock."[2]

One wonders what Clay thought about such contrived comradery. Jupiter in a coonskin cap was still Jupiter and Webster did not yet show much talent for the rough-and-ready stump oratory of the West. For all his talk about being just another simple citizen, he found it hard to unbend with the local Whig leaders. The Webster ladies made a great impression on their local hosts, young Fessenden reported, but "Mr. Webster would never gain popularity by personal intercourse—to strangers he appeared repellent." From a political point of view, Fessenden sadly noted, the great man might just as well have stayed home "and left his fame and public service to speak for him."[3]

By midsummer of 1837, Webster had returned East and resumed his more familiar role defending the interests of merchants and manufacturers in Boston, New York, and Philadelphia, who had prevailed upon him not to resign his seat in the Senate. He claimed that his goal in Congress was "to resist new theories, new schemes, new and dangerous projects, until time could be gained for their consideration by the people." Much of Webster's opposition to Van Buren's program was based on principles which he had already clearly articulated. Van Buren advocated a hard-money currency and a subtreasury system which would completely divorce the government from all banks. He opposed government interference with natural economic processes. Webster believed that to impose a specie currency on a great commercial nation in the nineteenth-century was reactionary—a return to medieval bullionism. He argued that Van Buren's subtreasury scheme conjured up visions of vaults, cells, and cloistering. "From commerce & credit it returns to hoarding & hiding." The Democrats sought to reduce the Treasury, which Hamilton had made so glorious, to a sterile depository—a thing of mere bricks and mortar. They refused to recognize that the constitutional power of the federal government to regulate commerce implied federal regulation of the currency, which in turn implied some kind of formal relationship between the government and the banking structure of the country. Without a well-regulated system of paper money there could be no credit, and it was credit that had built American roads, canals, and factories and transformed wilderness into cities. "He who decries the use of credit," Webster said, "reviles the history of the whole country."[4]

He was comfortable attacking the Democratic fiscal policies because what was right in principle made for good politics. But slavery was a different matter. Boston had been a center of radical abolitionist agitation ever since William Lloyd Garrison had founded the *Liberator* there in 1831, and now the slavery issue was being heated to the boiling point in Congress by the controversy over recognizing the new republic of Texas.

There is no question about Webster's personal dislike for slavery. He employed black servants in his own household and was as free of racial prejudice as most white Bostonians, including abolitionists. He had little sympathy with Washington neighbors who complained about their slaves, and he willingly contributed funds to help free Negroes redeem members of their family still enslaved. Publicly Webster had gone on record as opposing slavery in his Plymouth oration, in favoring the Missouri Compromise, and in the Hayne debate.

At the same time Webster disapproved of radical abolitionists just as he disapproved of other radicals. He would not have recognized Garrison if he tripped over him crossing the Common, and would have dismissed his demand for immediate emancipation as incendiary nonsense. As an experienced northern politician anxious to build a national base, he instinctively recoiled from pursuing a divisive issue like slavery. Realizing that slavery had been an unspoken agenda during the nullification debates and had led intelligent southerners to believe that a federal government powerful enough to enforce tariffs could also legislate against slavery, Webster tried to treat the Texas issue in a way which would satisfy the North without irritating or frightening the South.

When the possibility of annexing Texas was first discussed in 1836, Webster quickly opposed it on grounds that it would extend the area of slavery. On March 15, 1837, in a well-publicized political speech before a large Whig audience in New York, he spoke candidly about the problems involved in a political confrontation over slavery. Since slavery was "a great moral, social and political evil," nothing should be done "to favor or encourage its further extension." But since slavery was recognized in the Constitution and, therefore, "beyond the reach of Congress," Webster would not support legislation which in any way interfered with or threatened the authority of slave-holding states over their own slaves. He warned that the anti-slavery sentiment had "arrested the religious feeling of the country" and "taken strong hold of the consciences of men." It could not be trifled with. On the other hand, he believed that abolitionism was still a rational political force comparable in many ways to other interest groups in the country. "It may be reasoned with, it may be made willing, I believe it is entirely willing, to fulfill all existing engagements and all existing duties to uphold and defend the Constitution as it is established."[5]

Although events would show that Webster badly overestimated the abolitionists' ability to behave like other ordinary, law-abiding citizens, he was certainly correct in predicting that suppression would only make the movement stronger. Harassment of anti-slavery lecturers and editors in the early 1830s, including the near-lynching of Garrison by a Boston mob in 1835 and the murder of Elijah Lovejoy in Alton, Missouri, two years later, led many people in the North to sympathize with the abolitionists as martyrs to the cause of free speech.

Meanwhile the Congress was thrown into an uproar over the problem of receiving petitions for the abolition of slavery and the slave trade in the District of Columbia. In more benign days, these petitions had been referred to the standing committee in the District of Columbia without comment. By 1836, however, alarmed southern congressmen and senators had begun a determined drive to keep the petitions from being received. This attack on the traditional Anglo-Saxon right of petition brought many new friends to anti-slavery ranks, especially in Massachusetts, and John Quincy Adams battled furiously and eloquently in the House of Representatives against the gagging of his constituents. Webster's course in the Senate was more circumspect than Adams's, as befitted a potential presidential candidate, but there could be no mistaking where he stood on the issue. When Calhoun introduced a series of resolutions in December, 1837, reaffirming the compact theory of the Union and denouncing abolitionist propaganda and the attempt to abolish slavery in the District of Columbia, Clay and Webster were forced to put themselves on record. Clay tried to fudge the issue with an amendment which declared that agitation of the slavery issue for the District violated the spirit of the agreements by which slaveholder states had originally ceded the territory to establish it. Webster could not swallow this. Congress had a clear constitutional right to legislate over the District; American citizens had a constitutional right of petition, and nothing could explain it away. On the other hand, Webster agreed that it would be unwise for Congress to lead in agitating the slavery issue. Privately, he told Ketchum that Clay and Calhoun were putting their heads together as they had in 1833 and would make a new Constitution if they could get away with it.[6]

Henry Clay was more and more on Webster's mind by early 1838. Clay supporters in several states were already moving for his nomination and there were indications that Clay was gaining powerful friends in Massachusetts like Abbot Lawrence. Webster responded by pointedly reminding influential Whigs in Boston and New York that Clay could not be trusted to support a protective tariff, and that all Whigs did not take their signals from him. In Congress he tried to steer his own course, joining with Clay to unsuccessfully oppose Van Buren's subtreasury bill, but splitting with him by opposing recharter of the Bank of the United States, and supporting a generous pre-emption bill which gave settlers on public lands the right to purchase their land at prevailing prices. The two Whig chieftains remained publicly cordial, but privately they were constantly maneuvering for advantage. Sometimes they almost resembled jealous schoolboys competing for attention, and once Webster complained to Biddle that Clay was being praised for introducing legislation which Webster himself had originally conceived. In the spring of 1838, after Clay had introduced another bill for the establishment of a national bank, Webster fired off another confidential note to Biddle.

The Bank project is a project *to get* New York. Our illustrious friend seeks his great object, by connecting himself with some great idea.
In 1823 that idea was the *establishment of* an American system
In 1833 the idea was *to bargain away that system*
In 1838 it is to make a Bank of U.S. in certain principles (principles!). . . .
This project is an article for the N.Y. market. *I doubt whether it will sell.*

Webster ended by asking for an interview with Biddle. It was time, he said, "to come to some definite object."[7]

But that object, his own nomination for president remained as elusive as ever. Back in 1835 the *Richmond Whig* had written, "It seems really incredible that any men of intelligence . . . can persuade themselves for a moment that [Webster] has even a possible chance of election." Now the traditional objections to Webster's Federalist record were bolstered by the suspicion that he could not be trusted on slavery. One southern admirer predicted that he would never get the southern Whig vote because his statements on Texas would "like Banquo's ghost stare him in the face and shake their gory or rather *sable* locks at him throughout the contest." Webster continued to hope that if Massachusetts and New York refused to nominate any Whig candidate until the fall of 1839, the Democrats would move toward southern leadership, thus making the candidacy of a northern unionist like himself more viable. He had made the same prediction to Thurlow Weed in 1833, and Weed had responded by telling a friend that Webster was "infatuated with the notion" that the country would divide politically into unionists and nonunionists. "My standing objection to the whole of it," Weed said, "is that it eventually looks to Webster's being a candidate for the next presidency which, notwithstanding my warm attachment to the man and exalted estimate of his talents, I regard as utterly unwise and helpless." Five years later that judgment still stood.[8]

It was some consolation to know that Weed rated Clay's chances as poorly as his own, and Webster did what he could to see that his rival's opportunities for the nomination did not improve. In June, 1838, he politely declined a personal appeal from Clay to drop out of the race, ignoring the advice of Massachusetts Whigs like Appleton, Otis, and even his friend Story. Meanwhile, Whigs elsewhere were turning to Harrison. In Webster's eyes, Harrison was more acceptable than Clay although he was still bewildered by the old general's appeal. In September, 1838, the *Boston Atlas* came out for Harrison with Webster's tacit approval. When the Whig convention met in Harrisburg early in December, Webster stayed home, but New England delegates loyal to him helped give Harrison the nomination. By this time he had lost interest and was thinking of his trip to England.[9]

Webster had been wanting to visit England for more than ten years. He had tried hard to secure the ambassadorship during Adams's administration only to find that he was politically unacceptable. Early in 1839 he cherished a faint hope that he might get to England as head of a mission to negotiate a settlement of the rapidly heating boundary dispute between Maine and Canada. Congressional delegations in Maine and Massachusetts recommended that Webster be given the assignment, and there was even some support for him in Van Buren's cabinet. Webster was tempted. He prepared a detailed memorandum indicating the shape which negotiations might take and assured Joel Poinsett, Van Buren's secretary of war, that his approach to the problem would be entirely consistent with administration policy. But politics again prevented the appointment. Van Buren had no reason to give one of his leading adversaries an opportunity to reap additional glory, and he could hardly have forgotten that only a few years before, Webster had joined with other Whig leaders in refusing to confirm his own appointment to the Court of St. James. Still, Webster was eager to turn his back on presidential politicking for a while, and his recent re-election to the Senate had secured his political base at home for another six years. The long congressional recess during the spring and summer months seemed the appropriate time for such a trip and happened to coincide with his daughter's wishes. She had recently become engaged to Samuel A. Appleton, a Boston merchant, born and educated in England, and she longed for a London marriage. Against the substantial cost of such an extended visit, Webster weighed the possibility of his being able to sell some of his heavy and increasingly burdensome holdings in western lands (worth about two hundred thousand dollars by his calculation) to English investors.

Backed with substantial assistance from his father-in-law and from those wealthy Whigs in Boston and New York who were regularly called upon to shore up his solvency, Webster sailed for London on May 18, accompanied by his wife and daughter and Grace Webster's sister-in-law, Harriet Story Paige. After a tranquil voyage, during which Webster fought off the ennui of cabin life by studying navigation with the first mate, the Webster party reached Liverpool on June 2 and was in London a few days later.[10]

The British image of America in 1839 was not a flattering one. British investors were apprehensive because American state bonds were declining in value at the same time that the high price of American cotton was forcing idleness on British mills. Meanwhile, the accounts of American life written by travelers abroad like Mrs. Trollope and Captain Marryat tended to emphasize the violence, vulgarity, and confusion of American civilization. These sources of prejudice and friction were intensified by the smoldering dispute over the Canadian border line. It was in such unpropitious circumstances that the pride of New England chose to introduce himself to the scrutiny of friends and critics in Old England.

When he reached London, Webster discovered that his fame had preceded him. It must have gratified him to know that even though he traveled as a private citizen, he was received as an ambassador. An old-time friend and correspondent, John Denison, a leader in the House of Commons, gave the Webster party the use of his coach, horses, and servants. Webster was still in the process of getting settled in his quarters at Hanover Square when he was taken off to a "literary" breakfast to meet Wordsworth, John Kenyon, and Richard Monckton Milnes. Later, he dined with Sydney Smith, Macauley and Dickens, visited the courts and Parliament, and met most of the great public figures in England, including Lord Melbourne, Lord Palmerston, the Duke of Wellington, Disraeli, Daniel O'Connell, and Sir Robert Peel.

The ladies in the Webster party were quite overcome with the attention they received. Within a few days they found their social calendar filled from breakfast to midnight for weeks ahead. Caroline Webster found that her experience in the drawing rooms in Boston, New York, and Washington had poorly prepared her for the pace and style of English society. She complained of the constant "round of dissipation," and the extravagance of English society ("The Marchioness of Londonderry was positively covered with them [diamonds], in truth I never saw such a display—there were too many—a perfect load of them"). Like other American innocents abroad she found herself drawn into a guilty fascination for royalty. After being presented to Queen Victoria at a royal ball she wrote in her diary, "All the Nobility of Europe I should think were present—it was a most imposing scene. The supper superb, and the gold on the side board of every device and enough to dazzle one. I ate and drank as if I had been among my friends, but confess in other respects felt very insignificant. I never care to witness such a pageant again . . . 4 o'clock in the morning—never kept such hours before."[11]

Daniel Webster had no such anxieties. For about a quarter of a century one of the most publicized men in America, Webster was not easily awe-struck. Remarking on the extraordinary number of invitations which he and his companions found awaiting them in London, Webster wrote to Edward Curtis that "Our heads are rather turned at present but we hope to get right." Webster obviously was flattered by the attention he received from England's great men. He enjoyed being able to meet with them and at the same time to enjoy the anonymity of strolling alone through the streets and squares of London.

Fully aware of the fact that anything he said in public would be instantly picked up by the press of both countries, he kept a fastidious silence on political matters. He spoke but once in public, and then limited himself to a few noncomittal remarks at a meeting of the Royal Agricultural Society in Oxford. Some of his American friends, perhaps still unconvinced that Webster's chances for the presidential nomination were extinguished, urged him to find a platform in England from which he could reach the American people, but he declined. For the moment, at least, he was content with his role as private citizen and distinguished guest of Great Britain.[12]

His hosts, deprived of the opportunity of observing the public Webster in action, were forced to evaluate him on the basis of what they saw of him in personal and social situations. Like most Americans who had the opportunity of meeting Webster in similar situations they were impressed by his physical magnetism and by the image of dignity and authority which he projected. Carlyle, in what has perhaps been the most often-quoted single description of Webster, called him a "Parlimentary Hercules" and wrote

. . . one would incline to back him at first glance against all the extant world, the tanned complexion; that amorphous crag-like face; the dull black eyes under their precipice of brows, like dull anthracite furnaces needing only to be blown; the mastiff mouth, accurately closed:—I have not traced so much of silent Berserkir rage that I remember of, in any other man.

Henry Crabb Robinson noted in his diary that Webster, "far from being a Republican in the modern sense, had an air of Imperial strength, such as Caesar might have had." In more gossipy moments the British referred to Webster as "The Great Western" and a *"spiritual* Yankee." That Webster was an authentically American product, no one doubted. Disraeli called him "a complete Brother Jonathan" and noticed "a remarkable twang" in his speech. It was the contradictory combination of qualities—the Roman senator in Yankee dress—that most fascinated Webster's English hosts.[13]

Although Webster did full justice to the constant round of dissipation, which periodically immobilized his wife, he also kept his eyes open. Like other American visitors before him, he marveled over the gardenlike quality of the British countryside and the antiquity and grandeur of British architecture. But he did not consider himself a tourist. "I do not follow sightseeing," he wrote to Curtis, "what comes in the way I look at, but have no time to hunt after pictures." In company with the ladies in his party, Webster visited the customary places—the Tower of London, Westminster Abbey, and Windsor Castle, but he was more interested in trying to compare political and social systems than in visiting monuments. With a lawyer's sense for the value of detail, he made a list of English food prices and wrote a memorandum on the use of drainage tiles in agriculture. He noted the businesslike atmosphere in Parliment—the lack of emphasis on oratory—and attributed this to the fact that Parliament did not share legislative responsibility with the states. "Where there is much to be *done,*" he wrote to Crittenden, "it is indispensable that there is less to be said." So far as English parties were concerned, Webster found the Whigs to "know more and think better of America than the Tories," and yet he was drawn to the Tories as much as the Whigs and professed surprise at the relative lack of exclusiveness among the members of the aristocracy. His attitude toward the recent reform bill was characteristically conservative. He could see that movement toward greater political equality was overdue, but he feared that social friction would result from legislating political equality without changing economic and social inequality.[14]

Early in August, the Webster party set out for an extended tour of England and Scotland. Caroline Webster, who frequently commented on the money they were spending for clothes and hotels (one hundred dollars for a two-night stay at an inn in Oxford), did not calculate the cost of this journey, but her companion, Harriet Paige, noted that they were traveling "en prince" in a carriage with "four post horses, with two postillions in blue jackets, and yellow topped boots, the horses changed every ten miles, our maid, and manservant Hamilton and Holton in the 'rumble' behind. Mr. Webster, from preference, occupied the coach box, and the ladies the carriage proper. . . ." The *Washington Globe* and other Democratic papers back home would have paid a good price for this picture of Daniel Webster, the agent of merchant princes at home, traveling like an old-world prince abroad.

In Stratford-on-Avon, Webster was shown the room in which Shakespeare was born, and was prevailed upon to add his signature on the wall to those of Schiller, Scott, Washington Irving, and hundreds of other pilgrims. Later, at Shakespeare's church, where the pew he had occupied was being torn down, Webster took a fragment of wood as a souvenir. And then, perhaps somewhat self-conscious at such unabashed tourist behavior, he went off to visit the local needle factory.[15]

From Stratford, the Webster party went to Wales and then north through the lake country into Scotland. Webster grumbled about the hordes of tourists and the rain but not about the magnificent hospitality he and his companions received at such great estates of the nobility as Lowther Castle, Belvoir Castle, and Dalmahoy. After visiting the Earl of Derby's twenty-thousand-acre estate, supported by a yearly income of one hundred thousand pounds, he wrote to Curtis that "everything is in a state of grandeur which strikes one, acquainted with more moderate habits of life, with astonishment." He reacted to this grandeur with some ambivalence. He was too much of a Yankee not to deplore the idleness of the rich and the foolish display of wealth (as, for example, in a medieval tournament staged by Lord Eglinton at the cost of about thirty thousand pounds). At the same time, in England as in America he was drawn to men of wealth and power, and although he retained an American sense of scale (he called Lowther Castle, with its quarter-mile-long terrace and its forty-six servants, "a comfortable shelter against the weather"), he found it congenial to emulate the grand style and shot and rode to the hounds with his aristocratic hosts as if he had been bred to the life.[16]

While Webster dallied with the aristocrats, Edwin Chadwick and Friedrich Engels were preparing their monumental studies of the conditions of the British working class. The England they brought to life was an England of slums teeming with prostitutes, pickpockets, and disease, of factories tended by girl-mothers kept at the machine until the last week of pregnancy, of children mutilated in mine accidents and deformed from sweeping chimneys, of displaced, starving weavers and half-starved farm laborers. The England where men, women, and children paid for modern progress in flesh, blood, and despair. In the elegant society which entertained Webster, this side of the Industrial Revolution did not appear; and in England, as so often in America, he was content to learn there. Not all Bostonians responded this way. A young Beacon Hill lawyer by the name of Wendell Phillips was visiting England at the same time. While the Websters were being feted by royalty, Phillips and his wife were meeting English abolitionists. Two years later, Phillips would give up his "melancholy tour" with "the painful contrasts . . . wealth beyond that of fairy tales, and poverty all bare and starved by its side," and return to the United States to become as famous an orator for radical abolitionism as Webster was for conservatism and the Union.[17]

The independence of the landed nobility attracted Webster. The independence of a man like the Duke of Wellington married to a strong sense of public responsibility could produce the perfect statesman. Webster admired Wellington more than any other British leader. He was an English Washington, "admitted to have no personal motives, to desire no office, and to seek no power. The epithet which all agree to apply to his conduct is 'straightforward'. If he were now to die, he would depart life in the possession of as much of the confidence and veneration of the British people as any man ever possessed." Wellington was the one British leader to whom Webster would have shown special deference, but their acquaintance was limited to one or two formal exchanges.[18]

Webster's son Edward, and his prospective son-in-law Samuel A. Appleton joined the party in Glasgow. Together they journeyed to London where Julia was married on September 20. A week later the newlyweds, with Caroline Webster and Harriet Paige, set off for a short European tour. Webster remained in London in a fruitless attempt to dispose of his property. In October he joined his family in Paris where Ambassador Lewis Cass decked him out in a rented military costume and presented him to King Louis Philippe.

In late November the Webster party set sail for America, arriving in New York on December 29 after a long and stormy passage. Webster had been gone for seven months, his first and only experience outside his own country. He had met the leaders of two great nations and had sharpened his sense of the uniqueness of the American political and social system. But he returned as he had departed—not like a Wellington, spurning the power he might have had—but as a defeated candidate, heavily in debt.

Webster came home to greet the opening of another presidential election year, and although he expected the Whigs to win he was still bleak about the future. "We shall have bad times," he wrote to Everett on February 16, 1840, "whoever may be in or out. The people have been cajoled and humbugged. All parties have played off so many poor popular contrivances against each other, that I am afraid the public mind has become in a lamentable degree warped from correct principles." There were many reasons for Webster to have been disappointed with politics in 1840. In supporting Harrison's nomination, he had done no more than tip the scales against Clay. He knew that Harrison lacked the qualifications traditionally associated with a presidential candidate and was alienated by the choice he had helped to make. Somehow the kind of politics he had grown up with was going out of style. Journalists and party managers like Thurlow Weed were making the kinds of decisions that statesmen used to make, and they preferred to puff up a man like Harrison, with no political past, rather than support an experienced public figure like himself. At fifty-eight, so encumbered with debt that he could no longer afford a house in Washington, Webster found the prospect of retirement more attractive than ever.[19]

As usual, the retirement plans were short-lived. Once Webster began to sense the depth to which Harrison's nomination had struck the popular imagination, his interests in politics began to pick up. "General Harrison's nomination runs through the country most astonishingly," he wrote to a London correspondent on March 29. "This hopeful state of things gives quite a new aspect to our politics." When the Whigs held their great celebration in Baltimore on May 4 with all the attendant pageantry of log cabins, hard cider, and torchlight parades—the kind of political hoopla that he would have dismissed as humbuggery a little earlier, Webster was there to play a leading role—not in a sour and disgruntled mood like Clay, but as the prophet of a new order. "Every breeze says change," he shouted. "Every interest in the country demands it. . . . Let us give ourselves entirely to this new revolution."[20]

What was it that made Webster discard his gloomy prophecies and become a passionate believer in the Whigs of 1840? It was the exhilaration of being on a winning team, of finally being able to march to the people's music. As a Federalist, an Adams Republican, and an opponent of Jackson, Webster had been fighting the dominant political current in America for a quarter of a century. Unable to turn his triumphs over the nullifiers to long-term political advantage, he knew that his unionism kept him unpopular in the South. Now he sensed a general change in political sentiment sweeping across the country. No matter that the official standard-bearer of the Whigs lacked all distinction. Victory was in the wind and those who helped to bring it off could expect to play a major role in reshaping public policy over the next four years.

There were really two Websters in the campaign of 1840. The first was the familiar Webster—the grave and learned defender of the Constitution, the Union, and a sound fiscal system. This was the Webster who reassured bankers, merchants, and other substantial people that despite the carnival atmosphere of the campaign, property would be safe with the Whigs. It was also the side of Webster that the Whigs showed to the South. Early in October a nervous Daniel Webster descended on the party faithful in Richmond. "You see what a stir my visit is likely to produce," he wrote to Edward Curtis in New York. "I wish I had something to say to the Virginians when I get there." But he knew well enough what Virginians and other southerners expected to hear from the Whigs. Claiming that he too was a "states' righter" and would uphold both the rights of Congress and the rights of the states, Webster went on to give the necessary assurances about slavery. "Tell it to all your friends," he told the cheering crowd, "that standing here, in the capital of Virginia, beneath an October sun, in the midst of this assemblage, before the entire country, and upon all the responsibility which belongs to me, I say that there is no power, direct or indirect, in Congress or the general government, to interfere in the slightest degree with the institutions of the South."

This speech would make Massachusetts abolitionists despair, and they would throw it up to Webster a hundred times in the years ahead, but it was the kind of solemn, constitutional doctrine that audiences expected to hear from him.[21]

No one questioned Webster's mastery of the lofty political approach, but many felt that once outside New England he lost the common touch. John Crittenden remembered how incongruous Webster had looked at his first frontier barbecue in Kentucky, perched on a high stump in his blue coat and buff vest overlooking a boisterous crowd and a kettle of squirrel stew. But now, in the "coonskin saturnalia" of 1840, Webster was changing his style. Finding himself competing with such bizarre political entertainers as John Bear, the "Buckeye Blacksmith" who demolished Van Buren on the platform with anvil, sledge, and tongs, Webster concentrated on "getting down to the people." Appearing before a crowd of ten thousand in a pine grove in Syracuse, he momentarily disappeared as the speaker's platform collapsed. Emerging from the wreckage, he announced that "the great Whig platform" still stood, and after being hoisted to the narrow top of a peddler's wagon, he harangued the crowd for more than two hours with a speech that combined a serious lecture on fiscal policy with an appeal to popular prejudice. In an unguarded moment, a Democratic editor had dismissed Harrison as a man more suited for life in a log cabin with a barrel of hard cider by his side than for the White House. Quick to take advantage of the opening, Webster accused the Democrats of sneering "at whatever savors of humble life"—of sneering at Harrison because "a log cabin with plenty of hard cider is good enough for him." This incident together with Webster's following assurances that there had been a log cabin in his own faimly background, have frequently been quoted as an example of political fakery. It is only fair to point out that Webster also said, "No man of sense, supposes certainly, that having lived in a log cabin is any further qualification for the Presidency than as it suggests moral qualities in a person rising from humble beginnings." The real significance of this anecdote is that it shows how skillfully Webster could use the new demagogic rhetoric to turn the ridicule of the Democrats back on themselves by insisting that the Whigs were proud to put a log-cabin candidate in the White House.[22]

Having long since conceded the inviolability of Andrew Jackson's reputation, Webster was careful in his speeches to separate the Van Buren administration from Jackson. He lamented the fact that the Old Hero had been followed by "very ordinary men." Concentrating on the restoration theme which Jackson had used so effectively in 1828 and 1832, Webster said, "We need an administration full of the spirit of former times." The government must be "brought back to its ancient purity, wisdom and dignity."[23]

By the end of June, Webster was convinced that Harrison would win, and he implied to friends that he would be offered a cabinet position. Meanwhile he was under constant pressure to appear at Whig rallies. "I am pressed so hard to show myself in important and doubtful places," he wrote to a friend who tried to entice him away for a few days of recreation, "that I am obliged to give a strict account, almost upon oath, of my engagements every day for the next six weeks. And if I said that I intended four days for a hunt . . . they might shoot me. That they would follow me there and bring me away is certain. You never saw such a commotion hereabouts. Here come a committee from Utica, 250 miles, and as N. Jersey would not quit their hold on me, they snatched up Fletcher, and carried him off in an instant."

Obviously Webster was not running or trying to run Harrison's campaign. Although he occasionally grumbled at monster rallies, where it was impossible to be heard, most of the time he was content to be caught up in the excitement of the moment and do what he was told. After speaking at a great camp meeting in the Green Mountains of Vermont, he said, "We are either on the high road to the accomplishment of the greatest civil revolution ever yet achieved in this country, or else we are on enchanted ground, surrounded by fairies, fancies, phantoms and dreams."[24]

On one occasion Webster let the heat of the campaign destroy his composure. Hoping to blunt his effectiveness, the Democrats put Silas Wright, the hard-drinking, hard-talking senator from New York, on Webster's trail. Wright would appear in the same communities a day or two after Webster and attempt to refute him. Invariably the emphasis would be on Webster's connections with the "moneyed aristocrats" of the Northeast. An old charge, but it rankled, perhaps because Webster was just back from England, where he had seen how real aristocrats lived. On September 22 at Patchogue, Long Island, Webster turned on Wright with a brag-and-bluster speech which delighted his audience but would hardly have been allowed in Marshall's court. Emphasizing his own frontier background, Webster claimed that if he had wanted to put politics above duty he would have allowed Jackson to be crushed during the nullification crisis. ("I could have done it in a single hour.") Then he turned the thunder that had saved Jackson on Wright. "The man that says I am an aristocrat is a liar. . . . But the man that will not meet me fairly with argument, and uses idle and abusive declamation instead—and then will not come within reach of my arm, is not only a liar, but a coward." The people would know where to find the leading American aristocrat. He opposed tariffs in order to keep wages low along with imported luxuries like silk and wine, and he lived in the White House. James Gordon Bennett of the *New York Herald* sold 65,000 copies of Webster's Patchogue speech within the space of a few days.[25]

At election time Webster was exhausted. His health finally gave out after a tour through New Hampshire in an open, rain-drenched carriage, and he was forced to spend a few days recuperating at the ancestral farm in Franklin. The decisive Whig victory showed that his instincts had been sound and his energies put to a good purpose. Harrison began to form his cabinet. Henry Clay, a reluctant dragon throughout the campaign, refused a position, and on December 11, the president-elect asked Webster to be secretary of state.

13

BENEATH THE COONSKIN CAP
A Conservative Philosophy for Americans

Webster's apparent capitulation to the mindless Whiggery of 1840 is a colorful episode to relate, but what are we to make of it in terms of his credibility as a statesman and serious political thinker? How can we reconcile the venerator of Washington and guardian of the people with the stump politician who helped the whooping, hollering Whigs put a nonleader like Harrison into the White House?

Some historians have accepted the Webster of 1840 at face value and have treated him as an example of the way in which the "neo-Federalism," which originally gave shape and substance to the Whigs, was replaced by a political philosophy based "not on ideas but on subterfuges and sentimentalities." From this perspective, Webster emerges as "the greatest intellectual casualty of the new Whig line," a kind of worn-out political hack whose ideas, embellished with "huge gobs of senatorial rhetoric," are useless for the understanding of society.[1]

It is tempting to subscribe to this point of view. There is a lot about Webster's public and private life that is not attractive and cannot be explained away simply by the fact that, like other politicians, he frequently found himself forced to do one thing while saying something else. Still, we do not get far in understanding Webster by dismissing him as an intellectual fake. The truth is that the man who took his place in Harrison's cabinet in 1841 had clearly qualified himself for high public office, not only on the basis of his practical experience in Congress, but also as the most articulate spokesman for a peculiarly American kind of conservatism.

Webster's conservatism must be distinguished at the outset from other types of mid-nineteenth-century conservatism. The conservatism of southern political thinkers like Calhoun, based on the defense of slavery, was essentially reactionary like the conservatism of European intellectuals who defended the old order against the encroachments of democracy and capitalism. Those thinkers sought to turn back the dominant thrust of the age, while Webster, like the great majority of his countrymen, embraced it by assuming that constitutional self-government and private property lay at the heart of the American system.

Webster was not a political philosopher in the classic sense. He disliked abstractions and speculation about ideal systems. Neither was he a profound scholar. He knew the American past as well as any public man of his time and was familiar with English constitutional history, but his temperament and his training in the courtroom and in Congress encouraged him to look at the big questions of man and society from a practical point of view. He sought always to ground his thinking in the realities of American experience. At the risk, therefore, of making his thoughts appear more systematic than they actually were, the following discussion will examine Webster's conservatism in terms of nationalism, traditionalism, and his conception of the "parental" state.

Webster's belief in the indivisibility of Liberty and Union was part of a nationalist faith which came naturally to him. Coming from that generation of Americans who actually grew up with the Constitution and venerated the work of early Federalists, he always perceived it as a living document, designed to preserve the inheritance of the Revolution for a nation composed of diverse and growing states. Webster liked to recall that the first copy of the Constitution he ever read was printed on a bandana which he got from the village store in Salisbury, and it is obvious that his convictions about the surpassing value of the Constitution and the Union which it created were developed early in his life. As a Dartmouth student he said the writing and ratification of the Constitution represented "the greatest approximation towards human perfection the political world ever yet experienced," and resulted in advantages to "the citizens of the Union" which were "utterly incalculable."[2]

As a politician and experienced constitutional lawyer, Webster found rational arguments to support the basic convictions of his youth. The simplest and the most appealing to ordinary people was the argument from expediency. "It is to that Union," he said in the Hayne debate, "we owe our safety at home and our consideration and dignity abroad. It is to that Union that we are chiefly indebted for whatever makes us most proud of our country." Living through a period of unparalleled economic growth, Webster took every occasion to lecture his audiences that the prosperities they enjoyed were the "fruits of a united government, and one general, common commercial system." Visiting Buffalo in 1833, for example, after an eight-year absence during which the population of the city had grown four times, he reminded his listeners that "the place could hardly have hoped to be more than a respectable frontier post" under a system of separate state economies. In America, unlike the rest of the world, ordinary people could pursue their own economic self-interest with the reasonable expectation that the future would be better than the past—but only because a single government united under one Constitution made it possible.[3]

On a more theoretical level, Webster argued for the permanence of the Union by appealing to history and legal principle. He maintained that in accepting the Constitution the people had rejected a confederation of sovereign states for a federal system of government which divided power between the states and the federal government. The Constitution was the contract which created a new nation—the seal and symbol of Liberty with Union. Although the work of some recent historians of the Revolution tends to support Webster's contention, it is fair to say that the weight of historical judgment over the years has been on Calhoun's side. Most scholars have been unable to find evidence that Americans thought they were creating one nation out of thirteen states in 1787. However, it is not what happened in 1787, but his intuitive sense of what happened since that time that makes Webster's achievement impressive. Modern students of nationalism agree that nationhood must be based on something more than a legal document—that it is more a process than an event. It develops when a people become independent and socially cohesive, with an "internally legitimate" political organization. When these requirements are satisfied, the people connect their support of the government and membership in the nation "with broader beliefs about the universe and about their own nature . . . so that support for the nation even in times of adversity is likely." Webster intuitively understood that fifty years of experience which included a war, the development of a national system of communications, and the transfer of power between political parties had made an American nation. He was able to evoke the American *"consciousness of belonging together"* that is the life blood of nationalism by pointing to the Constitution as the enduring symbol of nationhood. His history may have been shaky, but his judgment about the symbolic value of the Constitution is confirmed by modern scholars of nationalism, one of whom has written:

For the American Constitution is unlike any other; it represents the lifeblood of the American nation, its supreme symbol and manifestation. It is so intimately welded with the national existence itself that the two have become inseparable. . . . It draws its lasting strength not from what it says but what it is: the embodiment of the idea by which the United States was constituted . . . to become an American has always meant to identify oneself with the idea.[4]

Nationalism is not, of course, inherently conservative. It often provides the fuel to fire the fanatic. But Webster's nationalism was conservative. He insisted that the political power of the nation through the federal government was limited and repeatedly emphasized the role of local institutions for "local purposes and general institutions for general purposes." His ambivalence toward Jackson, apart from the political considerations involved, was consistent with this position. When Jackson supported the power of the federal government, Webster defended him. When he appeared to violate "constitutional restraints on political power" by taking upon himself the power of constitutional interpretation, Webster thought Jackson was "so wild, so disorganizing" as to be almost as subversive as the nullifiers. A popular government, according to Webster, was "still a limited, a restricted, a severely guarded government," and when Jackson extended executive power by removing federal deposits from the Bank, which Congress had declared a safe custodian, Webster accused him of transgressing the constitutional limits of his office and endangering the people's liberty. Finally, as we will see in detail somewhat later, Webster refused to let his nationalism take him down the road of manifest destiny. During an age when many politicians sought to extend American power everywhere in the Western Hemisphere, he took the conservative position that a nation based on constitutional principles could not continually absorb new cultures and territories without threatening its unity.[5]

Like other conservatives, Webster put a high value on tradition. There was always something reminiscent of the revolutionary era in his dress and manner, and like Edmund Burke, he believed that society had a dimension in time as well as space. It was natural, he said at the bicentennial celebration in Plymouth, "to consider ourselves as interested and connected with our whole race, through all time, allied to our ancestors; allied to our posterity; closely compacted on all sides with others, ourselves being but links in the great chain of being, which begins with the origin of our race, runs onward through its successive generations, bending together the past, the present and the future, and terminating at last, with the consummation of all things earthly at the throne of God."[6]

Webster's traditionalism did not inhibit his political pragmatism. When Federalism lost its power as a party, he joined the National Republicans; and when the manufacturing interest emerged as a powerful interest group in his constituency, he gave up his old ideas on free trade and championed the tariff. His basic conception of the nature of the American political system, however, did not change. He revered the work of the founding fathers not because they had created something new, but because they had built so wisely on the old. The American Constitution and the political system derived from it were not new discoveries, but represented the "full development of principles" of government and forms of society going back two centuries in English and American history. In contrasting the English colonies in the New World with the Spanish, Webster said, "England transplanted liberty to America; Spain transplanted power." When the British came to America they brought with them a rich cultural tradition and the most liberal part of their political tradition and left the rest behind.

The distinctive characteristic of their settlement is the introduction of the civilization of Europe into a wilderness, without bringing with it the political institutions of Europe. The arts, sciences and literature of England came over with the settlers. That great portion of the common law which regulates the social and personal relations and conduct of men, came also. The jury came; the *habeas corpus* came; the testamentary power came. . . . But the monarchy did not come, nor the aristocracy, nor the church, as an estate of the realm . . . a general social equality prevailed among the settlers and an equality of political rights seemed the natural, if not the necessary, consequence.[7]

Along with Tocqueville and modern historians of the American liberal tradition, Webster believed that Americans had been "born free."[8] He also believed that the wilderness condition which had nourished the transplanted tradition of British liberty encouraged the growth of popular government by providing for relative equality among the people.

In the absence of military power, the nature of government must essentially depend on the manner in which property is holden and distributed and there is a natural influence belonging to property whether it exists in many hands or a few; and it is on the rights of property that both despotism and unrestrained popular violence ordinarily commence their attacks. Our ancestors began their system of government here under a condition of comparative equality in regard to wealth, and then early laws were of a nature to favor and continue this equality.[9]

Webster drew this principle partly from his reading of the seventeenth-century English political philosopher, James Harrington, and partly from his own knowledge of the American experience. In 1820 he had based his opposition to the abolition of property qualifications for Massachusetts state senators on this reasoning, and although he later backed away from a position which seemed to oppose the extension of popular suffrage, he never surrendered the fundamental point that the preservation of liberty depended on the widespread distribution of property which had characterized the American experience from the beginning. Thus American unity was supported not only by national sentiment, but also by the fact that most citizens found it to their personal interest to support the system.

Webster admitted that popular government would be threatened if property accumulated in a few hands leaving the masses penniless and dependent, but he denied the existence of such a tendency in America. This conviction

of the essential justice of the American system coupled with his respect for
tradition reinforced his conservatism and led him to take positions which
seemed to defy the democratic spirit of the age. In 1842, when "Dorr's
Rebellion" broke out in Rhode Island, Webster was secretary of state. The
crisis came about when the Dorrites, refusing to recognize the state constitution which through property restrictions denied the suffrage to more than
half the adult white population in Rhode Island, drew up their own constitution and established their own government. With Rhode Island under dual
government and civil war imminent, both parties appealed to President John
Tyler for help. Webster advised the president against intervention. He believed that although the existing government was legitimate, its leaders
should pursue a conciliatory approach to the rebels and propose liberalizing
amendments to the Constitution. [10]

The rebellion soon crumbled and its leader, Thomas Dorr, was sent to
prison, but the legality of what the Dorrites had attempted remained an issue
long after Webster left the cabinet, and he came to grips with it in one of his
most celebrated Supreme Court cases in 1848. Retained by Luther Borden,
who had been an agent of the established state government during the rebellion, Webster based his argument on a historical analysis of the revolution.
American liberty had not been created in 1776, he said, but had a pedigree
which went deep into British history. After reaping the benefits of other
Englishmen in the revolution of 1688, the colonists revolted to take over
their own government, but they did not reject everything that had gone
before. "Where the form of government was already well enough," Webster said, "they let it alone. Where the reform was necessary, they reformed
it." From 1776 on, "the whole progress of this American system was
marked by a peculiar conservatism." Webster agreed that the people provide
the "source of all power in America" but argued that they could only act
through their legislatures. Although suffrage was a basic principle in the
American representative system, it was also true "that the people often *limit
themselves.*" Thus in the United States a simple majority could not amend
the Constitution and separate states varied in the qualifications they set for
electors. Rhode Island had been an established state government which had
joined the Confederation in 1778 and the United States in 1790. This established Rhode Island's validity as a republican form of government and
placed the citizens of the state under the constitutional responsibility of
working through the established political structure if they desired to change
it. "The will of the people must prevail, when it is ascertained," Webster
said, "but there must be some legal and authentic mode of ascertaining that
will . . . the whole system of American institutions do not contemplate a
case in which resort will be necessary to proceedings outside of the law and
the Constitution, for the purpose of amending the frame of government."

Perhaps the leaders in Rhode Island had been wrong in not providing for
an amendment to their constitution earlier. This was an error that prudent

men might make, but it did not alter the fact that Rhode Island had operated under the old constitution for more than half a century while the "contemptible sham" that Dorr and his followers fabricated had lasted just two days. Here was no great re-enactment of the Revolution, but a petty local rebellion, which, under the Constitution, could have been legitimately put down by federal force.[11]

Webster's traditionalism can also be seen in his ideas about society and religion. Conventionally religious in his own life, he believed in the existence of God and the importance of moral principle, and serenely accepted death as an introduction to heaven. But he was never grasped by religious experience. Lacking the agonized conscience of the Puritan as well as the rapture of the saint, he took his religion coolly, like Benjamin Franklin, and refused to be heated up by the successive waves of revivalism which rolled over New England during his life. "I confess that natural religion—that conviction of the existence and perfection of the Deity, which the contemplation of natural objects produces," he wrote to an old college friend in 1828, "grows daily more impressive in my mind."[12]

Unlike Franklin, however, Webster believed that organized religion was "the foundation of civil society," and when Stephen Girard, a wealthy Philadelphia merchant, left his inheritance for the purpose of founding an orphanage which would have excluded religious instruction, Webster, acting as counsel, undertook to break the will. He argued that an alleged charity which excluded religious teaching tended "to destroy the very foundation and framework of society" and could, therefore, not be considered philanthropic. In his conclusion Webster took on a decided Burkean tone in conjuring up a vision of a school full of godless little Tom Paines. There was no room for such a school in America, where Christianity was the law of the land.

Everything declared it. The massive cathedral of the Catholic; the Episcopalian church, with its lofty spire pointing heavenward; the plain temple of the Quaker; the log church of the hardy pioneer of the wilderness; the mementoes and memorials around and about us; the consecrated graveyards, their tombstones and epitaphs, their silent vaults, their mouldering contents; all attest it. The dead prove it as well as the living. The generations that are gone before speak to it, and pronounce it from the tomb. We feel it. All, all, proclaim that Christianity, general, tolerant Christianity, Christianity independent of sects and parties, that Christianity to which the sword and fagot are unknown, general tolerant Christianity, is the law of the land.

The justices were not convinced by this extravagant rhetoric, and even his close friend Story felt that Webster had ended more with "an address to the prejudices of the clergy" than with an argument to the Court.[13]

The old textbook cliché that the Whigs had no program except to defeat Jackson has been shown to be misleading. We know now that for all their imitation of Democratic tactics and propaganda, and despite difficulties in reconciling their own internal differences, the Whigs offered an intelligent, often-progressive alternative to the policies of the democrats. Webster made the Whig case more articulately than any of his colleagues, and his analysis of the parental role of government in a developing nation sounds surprisingly modern today.

Like most other Americans of his generation, Webster was impressed by the accelerating rate of change in the first half of the nineteenth century. Attributing this phenomenon to the "unprecendented augmentation of general wealth" in the Western world since the 1780s, he found the basic cause to be "the successful application of science to art." By this he meant the growth of technology during the Industrial Revolution. The application of steam and water power had created "millions of automatic laborers, all diligently employed for the benefit of man. . . . It multiplies laborers without multiplying consumers." Webster saw that the increased productivity of labor presupposed increased participation in the market by all classes of society. "It requires that the great mass of society should be able to buy and consume. The improved condition of all classes, more ability to buy food and raiment, better modes of living, and increased comforts of every kind are exactly what is necessary and indispensable in order that capital invested in automatic operations should be productive to the owners."

Webster believed that the Industrial Revolution was thrust forward in the United States because everyone benefited from it. Unlike European workers, Americans welcomed capitalists and machines because they were free to become capitalists themselves. Attacking the "specious fallacy" that there is one interest for the rich, and another interest for the poor, he claimed that the position of labor in America had been "constantly rising" with the general increase in wealth and had never been higher than it was in the mid 1830s.

In a revealing phrase, Webster described how American economic growth and prosperity developed under "the broad banner of free institutions, of mild laws, and parental government." The parental image takes us to the heart of his conception of the positive state. The government had a constitutional right and a moral responsibility to aid in economic development. Thus Webster advocated tariffs, a federally funded system of internal improvements, and a sound federal fiscal system. He wanted the government to work as a partner with the people in promoting orderly growth, and he thought the laissez-faire alternative of the Democrats was an abdication of political leadership.[14]

Few things exasperated Webster more than the prejudice many Democrats held toward credit as a device for rewarding the unscrupulous at the expense of the poor. It was true that American capitalists tended to operate with borrowed money, but this, Webster argued, was the genius of the American system. In England, capitalists invested in public stocks and lived off the interest, but in America they played a dynamic role in the development of the country by investing in banks, insurance companies, railroads, manufacturing corporations. Such investment was stimulated by credit, which allowed ordinary men of ambition, intelligence, and character but no capital to become "active men of business" and get on with the great challenge of developing America's vast resources. In America, where every worker was an emergent capitalist, credit was the great equalizer.

The declaration so often quoted that "all who trade on borrowed capital ought to break" is the most aristocratic sentiment ever uttered in this country. It is a sentiment, which, if carried out by political arrangement, would condemn the great majority of mankind to the perpetuate condition of mere day laborers. It tends to take away from them all that solace and hope which arise from possessing something which they can call their own.[15]

It is not easy to separate Webster's political rhetoric during this period from his political philosophy. Like other Whigs, he was quick to blame the depressions of the period on Democratic attacks on the Bank and the inability of Jackson and Van Buren to maintain a sound currency system. Recent studies dispute the importance of government fiscal policies on the boom-and-bust syndrome of the period and point up the importance of changing patterns in foreign investments in America. Webster's image of an American working class of "emerging capitalists" has fared somewhat better at the hands of modern scholars. Although his explanation for the development of liberal political institutions is consistent with that offered by many historians today, Webster probably overemphasized equality as a condition of American life. He was no more aware of life in the slums of Boston, Philadelphia, and New York than he had been aware of the slums of London and Birmingham, and he does not seem to have realized, unlike some Democrats, that more and more of the wealth in America's large cities was concentrating in fewer and fewer hands. Taken as a whole, however, Webster's analysis of American economic development and his plea for positive government policies to stimulate and guide economic growth lift his speeches far above the level of ordinary political dialogue during the period. As one modern scholar has noted, Webster was almost "pro-Keynsian" in his thinking about government and the economy.[16]

Along with his nationalism and his traditionalism, Webster's ideas about the role of the positive state were entirely relevant to the needs of the young, diverse, rapidly growing American nation. But they were not the ideas that Americans had most in mind when they sent Harrison to the White House. The election of 1840 represented a triumph for Whig politics, not for Whig principles, and Webster soon discovered that he would have to rely more on politics than principles to survive in the years just ahead.

14

SECRETARY WEBSTER
SURVIVES THE WHIG BLOOD BATH

No party ever paid a greater price for victory than the Whigs in 1840 when they elected a president without agreeing on a leader. Harrison, a synthetic creation of Whig publicists, was expected to be an obedient White House ornament while Clay remained in the Senate in almost absolute control over the Whig majority in Congress, and Webster, stronger in ability and reputation than in party power, commanded the top post in the cabinet. Webster's friends assumed that he would dominate the government from inside. "The coming administration will be in fact your administration," wrote Biddle in December, 1840, "it is expected that you shall take the lead." But the Clay Whigs shrugged off this possibility with a smile. Webster had tried to stray in the past but had always come back to the party; he might grumble and sulk but he would follow the party leader. Judge Rowan of Kentucky put the matter neatly when he said, "If the two should go duck hunting together, Mr. Clay would expect Mr. Webster to assume the office of spaniel, to bring out the birds, and the latter would not perceive that there was any degradation in his assumption of such an office." Despite the ability of their leaders, the validity of their program, and the magnitude of their victory, the Whigs were still more prepared to fight each other than to govern the country. The period from 1840 to 1844 was one of the stormiest passages in Webster's career. That he not only survived it, but also accomplished something of enduring value to his country is a tribute to his courage, his ability, and his guile.[1]

The political skirmishing began long before Harrison's inauguration. Although Clay was able to put his men in all the other cabinet posts, Webster, as secretary of state, controlled the most important patronage jobs. During the campaign the Jacksonians' abuse of patronage had been a favorite target for Webster, but he did not allow that to inhibit him now. He told Biddle, who wanted a diplomatic post in Vienna, that "nothing could be better for the country" but unfortunately some "tobacco men" had the same idea. It was important for the administration, he believed, to be liberal with southern appointments in the interest of "distribution." At the same time he was careful to see that other good friends would be properly rewarded, including Edward Everett, who became ambassador to England, and Edward Curtis, who took over the duties of collector of the Port of New York. The Curtis appointment, made over the raging objections of Clay, proved that Webster had a strong position with Harrison. Curtis was one of Webster's most important supporters in New York and had played a key role in defeating Clay at the Harrisburg convention. His job, which involved supervision of a five-hundred-man payroll and a budget of about half a million dollars a year could conceivably control the vote in the state. Clay's constant personal intervention with Harrison over this and other matters in the early days of the administration so angered the president that he refused to see Clay personally and insisted that the latter communicate with him through an intermediary.[2]

We will never know whether Harrison would have been his own man in the White House or the weak ornamental president envisaged by the Whigs. Just a month after his inaugural address, an innocuous affair, tidied up and made literate for public consumption by Webster, in which he seemed to defer to congressional leadership, the old general died and John Tyler was called from his home in Virginia to become the first vice-president in American history to succeed to the presidency.

When Harrison was elected, John Quincy Adams noted in his diary that the new president had come in like a hurricane, and he hoped that he would not go out like a shipwreck. Harrison's death at the outset of his administration precluded any such eventuality, but the possibilities of shipwreck seemed even more likely for the Whigs when Tyler took office. Philip Hone had said of the Whig slogan "Tippecanoe and Tyler Too" that "There was rhyme but no reason to it." This was not exactly true. The Whigs could be divided into three groups: the Clay or "ultra" Whigs, who were still committed to rechartering the Bank of the United States; the Webster Whigs, who were more interested in a tariff than a Bank; and a group of states' rights Whigs, with special strength in Virginia. Tyler was given the vice-presidential nomination because he supported Clay at Harrisburg and represented the southern Whigs. His opposition to tariffs, banks, and internal improvements was well known, and he had backed into the Whig party after break-

ing with Democrats over the one Jackson measure that Webster supported—
the Force bill. During the campaign, nobody bothered about Tyler's ideas,
and the Whig song writers disposed of him by writing:

> And we'll vote for Tyler, therefore
> Without a why or wherefore.

Once Tyler became president, the Whigs suddenly woke up to the fact
that a few whys and wherefores might have been in order after all. An aristocratic planter and slaveholder with a pedigree of family leadership in Virginia
going back to the Revolution, Tyler, who had been offended by the "backwoods democracy" side of Jackson, had nothing in common with the log-
cabin-and-cider candidate the Whigs had elected. Rather slight in stature and
without the gifts of a Clay or Webster, he was nevertheless accustomed to
exercising authority and knew his own mind. When Webster told him that
Harrison's policy had been to have matters decided by a majority vote of the
cabinet, President Tyler made it clear that he was only interested in advice.
He would make the decisions himself.[3]

Clay, who had found it difficult to give much respect to Harrison, was
even more impatient with Tyler, who was soon nicknamed "His Ac-
cidency." Despite Tyler's known objections to it, the Kentucky senator introduced a bill to recharter the Bank. Webster urged the president to support
a compromise measure designed to overcome his constitutional scruples by
requiring the consent of individual states for certain operations of the Bank.
In the ensuing Senate debate in which Webster's successor, Rufus Choate,
was brutally handled by Clay, the compromise failed, and Tyler vetoed the
bill early in August.

Once the struggle between Tyler and Clay flared up in the open, Webster
had to decide where he would stand. He got along with Tyler well enough
personally, hoped that Tyler would support most of the Whig program, and
backed the Bank bill that Tyler favored as a sensible compromise. He reminded his Whig friends that Tyler's position on the Bank was well known
when he was nominated, and that a divided party would only help the
"reckless adversary—heading in upon our ranks—union, decision, and energy are all indispensable. But Union is first. If we will but UNITE, we can
form decisive purposes and summon up our energies."[4]

Consistent with this position, Webster did what he could to restore unity
to the party and convinced a special meeting of congressional Whigs after the
first Bank veto to try a second time. But by this time, the breach between
Clay and Tyler had grown too wide for any bridge, and the president vetoed
the second bill as he had the first. On September 11, the day after the second
Bank veto, every cabinet officer except Webster resigned.

Webster's discomfort at this point was acute. In vetoing the Bank, Tyler had repeated the actions of Jackson ten years earlier which had really brought the Whigs into being. The outrage felt by most Whigs at this "betrayal" of the revolution of 1840 was symbolized by the savage attacks on Tyler in the Whig press, and he was even burned in effigy on the White House lawn. If Webster were to stay with Tyler, he would not only be accused of abetting the betrayal, but would also be forced to work with a cabinet of Tyler's appointees—states' rights and anti-tariff men—with whom he had nothing in common.

On the other hand, if he left the cabinet, he could be accused of plotting with Clay to ovethrow Tyler and of being faithless to his responsibilities as counselor to the president, in which role he might continue to work for national unity. There were other reasons for staying in the cabinet. He liked his job as secretary of state and was reluctant to leave it until his projected negotiations with England were complete. He was sixty years old and had just purchased an expensive house on Lafayette Square. He did not relish quitting his post and returning to a neglected law practice to scratch out his living. Finally, and this was the decisive factor, he was not willing to take orders from Henry Clay.

After keeping his own counsel and getting the endorsement of the Massachusetts Whigs in Congress, Webster told Tyler that he would stay in the cabinet if he was wanted there. The president, despite the advice of some southern congressmen who preferred to dispose of Webster by shipping him off as ambassador to London, accepted Webster's offer. "Give me your hand on that," Tyler is supposed to have said, "and now I will say to you that Henry Clay is a doomed man."[5]

Webster's decision to remain in the cabinet was announced in a letter to the *National Intelligencer* dated September 13. Webster said that he still believed in the necessity of establishing a national fiscal agency and the willingness of the president to work with Congress to that end. "It is to the union of the Whig Party," Webster wrote, "by which I mean the whole party, the Whig President, the Whig Congress, and the Whig People, that I look for realization of our wishes. I can look nowhere else."[6]

Unfortunately for Webster, what unity there was left among the Whigs was more prepared to rally around Clay than around Webster and Tyler. The same day that Webster sent his letter to the *Intelligencer,* about sixty Whigs in Congress agreed on a manifesto which read Tyler out of the party. Meanwhile, Tyler began to fill up his cabinet with men whom he called "original Jackson men"—that is, men who were acceptable to neither Whigs nor Democrats. Webster was cut off from the mainstream of his party. He had loyal friends like Biddle, who applauded his action, and the Whigs in Massachusetts, although uneasy about what he had done, were unwilling to openly challenge him. Still, it was an unhappy situation for a man committed to conciliation and unity who had not yet ruled out the presidency. To survive he would have to identify his position in the cabinet with loftier goals than service to an unpopular president.

By experience, intellect, and temperament, Webster was admirably qualified to serve as secretary of state in 1841. His long experience in the Senate had given him a lively sense of the political dimension to diplomacy, and his years of practice before the Supreme Court had helped him to understand the limits of constitutional power. His reputation, personal style, and disposition to reconcile differences and oppose confrontations were suited to the delicate personal negotiations which would be required if America was to protect her natural interests and avoid war with England.

One of the reasons that Webster looked so concerned and troubled in the fall of 1841 was that he was trying to ward off two wars at the same time— the civil war among the Whigs at home—and a potentially bloodier conflict between England and America. The points of conflict between the two countries went back to the Revolution and involved thousands of square miles between New Brunswick and Maine. This long-standing dispute was aggravated by a series of border incidents stemming from the support which Anglophobic American organizations provided Canadian insurrectionists. In 1837 these clandestine operations had resulted in a violent reprisal when a force of Canadian militia crossed to the American side of the Niagara River, and in the course of burning the steamboat *Caroline,* which had been used to supply the Canadian rebels, killed an American citizen. Van Buren's attempts to maintain neutrality were hindered by the British government's support of the action and by the persistence of secret American organizations along the frontier designed to aid revolution in Canada. About the same time that Harrison was elected, a Canadian by the name of McLeod was arrested for murder in New York State after having boasted that he had shot an American on board the *Caroline.* One of Webster's first problems as secretary of state was to consider the demand of the British Foreign Office for McLeod's release, a request which he took with great seriousness because he had been told on good authority when he was in London that England was prepared to go to war over the case. The matter was complicated not only by the militance of Americans in the border states, but also by the fact that Governor Seward of New York was extremely sensitive about federal intervention in the case. Unable to get Seward to intervene for McLeod, Webster assigned a United States district attorney to represent him and sent General Winfield Scott to Utica to protect him from the possibility of mob action. Early in October, 1841, McLeod was acquitted and taken across the border under armed guard.[7]

The settlement of the *McLeod* case helped to create a more cordial relationship between London and Washington and prepared the way for more serious negotiations. Upon taking office, Webster revealed his interest in reaching an agreement about the Canadian boundary line. The new Melbourne ministry, which came into power in the fall of 1841, was receptive to the idea, and in January, 1842, Webster learned that England would send a special mission under Lord Ashburton to negotiate a settlement.

If it had not been for the frantic divisiveness among the Whigs, the diplomatic situation would have been ideal for Webster. His able and loyal friend, Edward Everett, was at the Court of St. James's, and Ashburton, head of the famous Baring Brothers banking house, had been a good friend since Webster's visit to England. Meanwhile, Webster had the total support of the president, who desperately sought for constructive accomplishments in foreign policy to balance out the inevitable domestic disasters of his administration. Ashburton arrived in Washington and rented a mansion in Lafayette Square close to Webster's, which had already become famous for its elegant dinners and receptions. During the spring and summer of 1842 the two men met frequently in a congenial atmosphere ideally suited for the accomplishment of important goals through personal diplomacy.

Although Webster and Ashburton dominated the talks, a special body of commissioners from Maine and New Hampshire represented a vital third party in the negotiations. Ashburton was instructed to hold out for a line east of the St. Lawrence, which would provide the possibility of a military route from Quebec to New Brunswick. The War of 1812 had not yet been forgotten and Maine was ardently opposed to such a concession. Webster solved this problem with the help of the Harvard scholar, Jared Sparks, who had discovered a map in the French archives on which Benjamin Franklin had supposedly drawn the boundary line as the American government understood it in 1782. Franklin's map gave the British more in 1782 than they were asking in 1842, and after Webster showed a copy of the map to the Maine commissioners, they agreed to modify their demands. Meanwhile, Webster wrote to Everett, no stranger to scholarly research himself, asking him to "forbear to press the search after maps in England or elsewhere." This request, well taken in light of the later discovery of maps which appeared to validate the original American demands, was typical of Webster's approach to the negotiations. When he asked Everett to impress on the British Foreign Office the importance of their giving up a strip of land to compensate for American concessions, he emphasized, "The great object is to show mutual concession and granting of what may be regarded *in the light of equivalents*. The absolute value of the thing is not the point of interest." Webster was more interested in agreement than in precisely weighing the opposing claims of the two nations. Like Edmund Burke, when he was forced to choose between peace and truth, he preferred peace.

The agreement was finally concluded when Webster and Ashburton divided the territory in question, giving the United States a little more than half. Additional matters of tension between the two nations involving the extradition of criminals and cooperation over the suppression of the slave trade were covered in formal correspondence but not in the treaty itself, which Webster and Ashburton signed on August 9.

Webster's next problem was to get public support and Senate ratification for the treaty. He relied on his map to convince the senators, and although the Clay Whigs and the Democrats were not anxious to put their seal on an important Webster-Tyler achievement (Silas Wright complained that Webster had been "more English" in the matter than Lord Ashburton), they consented to the treaty on August 20, 1842, by a large majority. Clay's friends dismissed the matter by saying they were content to let Webster "heal his character a little by making peace."

If the senators had realized then how Webster had engineered public support for his treaty, they might well have acted differently. Taking advantage of a seventeen-thousand-dollar secret service fund, Webster hired a journalist by the name of F. O. J. "Fog" Smith to act as his public-relations agent with the Maine press. Soon after Smith got to work, several Maine papers, especially the influential Portland *Eastern Argus,* suddenly found that they had overcome their objections to the treaty. Meanwhile, Webster planted his own anonymous editorials in support of the treaty in the friendly columns of the *National Intelligencer.* To those of us familiar with the "selling of the Pentagon," Webster's actions seemed innocuous enough, but they were extraordinary for the time and suggest the lengths he was prepared to go to accomplish his objective.[8]

Despite his success as a peacemaker, the world of the Whigs, where Webster's political future lay, was just as blood-soaked as ever. His substantial diplomatic achievements took place during the spring and summer of 1842 when he was becoming more politically isolated. Once he had decided to throw in his lot with Tyler, he had no choice but to go all the way. He not only supervised the Department of State but advised the president in matters of general government policy and surreptitiously defended him with anonymous articles planted in the administration's newspaper, *The Madisonian.* Early in April, 1842, Calhoun wrote to a friend that "Webster is regarded as the controlling spirit and he has become almost universally odious. There is no confidence in him. His integrity is questioned by almost all of any party." The South Carolinian who had been the butt of Webster's sarcasm often enough in the past, was hardly an objective observer, but there is no doubt that Webster was in trouble with his own party. He accused Clay's friends of trying to drive him out of the cabinet by planting rumors about his disloyalty to the president. At the same time, he had to allay the suspicions of loyal supporters like Robert Winthrop, who feared that he had permanently deserted the Whigs for Tyler. The Massachusetts Whigs had never wholeheartedly supported Webster's decision to stay in the cabinet. Abbot Lawrence, one of Webster's most enthusiastic supporters in times past and a man who had helped to replenish his purse on more than one occasion, was decidedly cool to Webster now. Lawrence and his brother, Amos, had not forgotten the way Webster deserted Clay in 1840 and they had not been happy about his joining Harrison's cabinet. Amos spoke for both Lawrences when he wrote in the summer of 1840

Webster I suppose will be looking out with a wishful eye for the chair, after Harrison quits it, but I should think it better fortune for Webster's fame, if he was to *die* as soon as Harrison is elected. . . . He can add nothing to his fame by accepting office and may show some of his weak points.

By the summer of 1842, in the eyes of the Lawrence brothers at least,the weak points had been fully disclosed, and Abbot Lawrence was talking about a Massachusetts *"groundswell"* in Clay's favor.[9]

Many Webster Whigs felt that the importance of making peace with England justified Webster's decision to stay in the cabinet, but that rationale disappeared when the treaty was ratified. By then the animus against Tyler had even infected such old and trusted advisors as Story, who urged Webster to write his resignation with the same pen he had used to seal the agreement with Ashburton. "Your best friends here think there is an insuperable difficulty in your continuing any longer in President Tyler's cabinet," Jeremiah Mason wrote on August 28. "I presume you are aware of the estimation in which the President is held in this region. By the Whigs he is almost universally detested. This detestation is as deep and thorough as their contempt for his weakness and folly will permit it to be. I use strong language but not stronger than truth justifies. Your friends doubt whether you can with safety to your own character and honor act under or with such a man."

Webster felt the force of this advice. He told Everett that he was being attacked by the Whigs "with a degree of venom and abuse such as we only used to look for in the Globe." He continued to get along well with Tyler but knew his influence on the president would diminish as he turned more and more to the Democrats. He knew he would have to get out sometime—but when—and for what? Biddle, who had just been through his own dark night of the soul with the failure of the United States Bank and who never had gotten the diplomatic appointment that he sought, agreed that Webster should go his own way "without seeking to conciliate or perpetrate any party," but he warned his old friend that whatever course he took "decides all your future political relations . . . weigh the matter well."[10]

In September, 1842, two things happened to force Webster into decisive action. At a public dinner in New York City, the influential Whigs in attendance pointedly ignored a toast to their own president while honoring Lord Ashburton. Two weeks later, the Massachusetts Whig convention met in Boston to nominate Henry Clay for president and to declare their "full and final separation" from the Tyler administration. Webster could delay no longer. When he was invited by the Whig elite in Massachusetts, including

Abbot Lawrence, who had masterminded the Clay nomination, to a dinner to honor his diplomatic achievements and presumably to receive the announcement of his resignation, he asked for a public meeting in Faneuil Hall instead.

On September 30, the old auditorium, which had offered a triumphant platform to Webster in the past, was jammed with friends and critics and out-of-town reporters anxious to hear how he would respond to the first open challenge to his supremacy in Massachusetts. In introducing Webster, Boston's Mayor Jonathan Chapman pointedly contrasted the conduct of the State Department with the rest of the Tyler administration. But Webster refused to take the hint. He agreed on the importance of his work in preserving peace with England and stated bluntly that "the value of the shipping interest of this city, and of every other interest connected with the commerce of the country" would have been cut in half in a matter of hours if the general public had realized the imminence of war in 1841. And in almost the same breath he acknowledged with pleasure the support he had received from Tyler in making the treaty.

Webster then spoke directly to the implication which had been made in the mayor's opening remarks—that since Webster had taken care of the nation's honor, it was now time to take care of his own.

I am exactly of his opinion. I am quite of the opinion that on a question touching my own honor and character, as I am to bear the consequences of the decision, I had a great deal better be trusted to make it . . . on a question so delicate and important as that, I like to choose myself the friends who are to give me advice; and upon this subject, Gentlemen, I shall leave you as enlightened as I found you.

After twenty years of "not altogether undistinguished service in the Whig cause," Webster had now become an object of Whig wrath, but he refused to be coaxed or driven out of office. Taking on the style of a prosecuting attorney, Webster attacked the recent Whig convention, which had undertaken to separate all Massachusetts Whigs from the Tyler administration. Webster demanded to know what this meant. Did it mean that Massachusetts Whigs were determined to oppose all Tyler legislation, good and bad (including perhaps a tariff bill), over the next three years? Did it mean that every Whig in a patronage job was supposed to get out? What was supposed to happen to Everett—to Webster himself? "Generally, when a divorce takes place, the parties divide the children," Webster said. "I am anxious to know where, in the case of this divorce, I shall fall."

Reminding his audience of the mixed ingredients that had made up the Whig party in the beginning, states' righters, unionists, tariff supporters, and free traders, Webster asked, "What could be expected of such a party, unless animated by a spirit of conciliation and harmony?" He insisted that such a spirit had helped bring victory in 1840 and, if restored, could still accomplish great things for the party and the country. There had been four great issues before the country in 1840. The first, involving the danger of war with England, was solved. Another, involving the proper role of government in the nation's fiscal affairs, was still in dispute. Webster argued that the best course for the Whig Congress was to bow to administration leadership and hold the president responsible for whatever was done rather than to insist on a Bank whose time had past. Executive tyranny had been a third issue. Webster regretted Tyler's use of the veto and had counseled against it, but the Tyler vetoes hardly justified the kind of Whig hysteria that had followed. Finally, there was the tariff issue. In March, 1842, a bill had been passed increasing duties for the first time since 1832. All the new tariff bill did was to "repair the consequences" of Clay's compromise tariff of 1832, the most painful legislation, Webster said, that he ever lived through. "The principle was bad, the measure was bad, the consequences were bad." Webster did not have to mention Clay by name. The message was clear enough. Massachusetts would do well to remember who her real friends had been. Meanwhile, Webster would work with anyone willing to put national interest over party pettiness.

I am ready to act with men who are free from that great danger which surrounds all men of all parties—the danger that patriotism itself, warmed and heated in party contests will run into partisanship. I believe that, among the sober men of this country, there is a growing desire for more moderation of party feeling, more predominance of purely public considerations, more honest and general union of well-meaning men of all sides to uphold the institutions of the country and carry them forward.[11]

The audience heard him out, but the usual cheers were conspicuously absent. The skeptical Charles Sumner wrote that Webster had "looked like Coriolanus" and "seemed to scorn while he addressed the people." John Quincy Adams, always straining to believe the worst about Webster, called the speech "boastful, cunning, jesuitical, fawning and insolent." It was "bitter as wormwood" to the Whigs and calculated to split them in order "to make a Tyler party." The more perceptive Harrison Gray Otis felt that Webster had been betrayed by his emotions. "He was full of black choler on account of Clay, and of his treatment by part of the Whig press and so boiled over." The result, Otis believed, was to offend some of his closest friends and jeopardize Whig chances in the next election. Upon reflection, however, despite his "indiscreet tirade" Otis still thought Webster 'a very great man and I believe true patriot—we may all, I believe, thank God that he remained in the Cabinet."[12]

The Whig papers were less judicious in the weighing of Webster's speech, and Webster accepted their criticism stoically. He had been determined "to do the President justice and myself justice," he wrote to Fletcher, and was prepared to accept the consequences. Temporarily, at least, the Faneuil Hall confrontation brought him peace of mind, and he and Caroline went off to the family homestead in New Hampshire to look at his cows and speculate about an early retirement at Marshfield or on the shores of the Merrimack.

Retirement, however, would mean defeat, and because he was not ready for that he remained defiantly in Tyler's cabinet until the following May. He seems to have felt that Clay was leading the Whigs into oblivion and that a new party composed of dissident Whigs and Democrats might rally around Tyler and himself. Whig reverses, including the loss of the Massachusetts governorship in the fall of 1842, strengthened his confidence in this analysis. "Blight and mildew afford the same auspices for good crops," he wrote to Everett on November 28, "as Mr. Clay's name does for political success. I suppose the Whig Party may be regarded as broken up. The name may remain, but without entirely new leaders, the members of the party can never again be rallied. A vast portion of the moderate and disinterested will join in support of the President and there is reason to think some portion of the other party, composed of persons of like character, will take a similar course. . . . He has two years yet in which to show his management of public affairs and I cannot but think he will gain in the public confidence."[13]

At the same time he found his position as secretary of state increasingly difficult. As Whig fury over his defection began to be matched by Tyler's embarrassment over his presence, Webster began to cast about for a safe passage out of the cabinet. He and Tyler tried to get up a special diplomatic mission to England, which he might lead to deal with problems of mutual concern in Mexico and Oregon, but the necessary appropriation failed in Congress. He had always wanted to be ambassador to England and had pointedly reminded Everett of that fact when he was appointed, but Ambassador Everett was not prepared to suddenly shift to Paris for his benefactor's convenience. Finally, Webster succeeded in getting the Congress to appropriate forty thousand dollars for the purpose of sending a trade mission to China. He secured Everett's appointment to head the mission and wrote to disabuse him of the notion that he himself was after Everett's post. "If it were vacant now, or should be vacated by you, there is not one chance in a thousand that I should fill it." Everett may or may not have been reassured, but he refused the appointment, which then went to another Webster protégé, Caleb Cushing.

Most of Webster's critics saw the attempted juggling of diplomatic appointments as another example of Webster's deceptive self-serving maneuvers. But Biddle saw a great man in distress and wrote to Tyler on March 4, 1843, urging that Webster be kept on as secretary of state. "He has no political party, no body of political adherents. All these he has left for you. He has therefore no political aspirations." The letter was disingenuous. Webster was still full of political aspiration and Biddle knew it, because a few weeks later he was advising Webster to "make a brilliant retreat" and rejoin the Whigs.[14]

By this time, Tyler's involvment with the Locofoco Democrats, whom Webster despised, and his clear desire to add another slave state to the Union with the annexation of Texas, had made Webster's position untenable. He resigned on May 1, 1843. The parting with the president was friendly and gracious, but there were no crowds to throw roses in his path when he returned home. A reception in Faneuil Hall was poorly attended and a formerly friendly paper wrote that if Webster wanted Whig support he would have to support the Whigs—it belonged to him "to make the first move."[15]

The key to understanding Webster's political feelings over the next few months can be found in a letter which he had written to Governor John Letcher of Kentucky in February about the difficulty of getting constructive legislation to improve the nation's fiscal condition. The problem cried out for a political solution, but the insistence of the Whigs on a Bank and the insistence of the Democrats for a subtreasury system allowed little room to maneuver. "I think we must show some enterprise," Webster wrote. "We must make an attempt to adjust old principles to new forms and this we could do if there were among us any union of purpose.[16]

Webster began to show what he meant by enterprise almost as soon as he quit the cabinet, but he did it by talking about tariff rather than banking policy. After a meeting in Boston which left the merchants smiling and the manufacturers scowling, Webster went off to address a group of Baltimore businessmen on May 18. Maintaining that the commercial interests of the great cities supplied the fountain of American economic growth, Webster began to talk about regulating commerce between nations through trade treaties. He speculated over the advantages of this for the United States. If England, for example, would lower duties on tobacco, corn, cotton, and rice, the advantages to the South and West would be enormous. Obviously, such advantages would have to be balanced by some "modification of the tariff," and Webster announced his conviction that *"if by any great operation that should unite the interests and opinions of all parts of the country, we can place American industry and American labor on a permanent foundation,* that is a much more important consideration than the degree to which protection should be extended."[17]

Even the most hardened critic of Webster would have to admit that he was showing enterprise. No American political leader was more closely identified with the tariff. He had spent a decade attacking Clay for his betrayal of the principle in 1832, and had even played on that theme in the Faneuil Hall speech. How are we to explain the sudden reversal? Had he undergone some kind of religious conversion to the principles of free trade and reciprocity, or was he taking a calculated gamble in attempting to build a new political base?

In some ways, Webster's position was not as inconsistent with his earlier career as it appeared. He had shifted from free trade to protection many years before to represent a changing constituency, and he had built an elaborate argument for the tariff as a policy designed to promote the welfare of all sections and classes. Now that Abbot Lawrence was leading Massachusetts manufacturers into the Clay camp, Webster felt his obligation to them was finished, and he was prepared to appeal for a new constituency by arguing for the unifying influence of lower tariffs. As a basic principle, Union had always been more important to Webster than the tariff. This was the "old principle" he had mentioned to Letcher; more liberal tariffs were the "new forms."

Actually, what Webster had in mind when he proposed a new look at American tariff policy was far more ambitious and imaginative than most people realized. He hoped that a new tariff would rally support for a treaty between Mexico, the United States, and England, which would resolve the Oregon boundary dispute potentially even more explosive than the controversy over the northeastern boundary. Mexico owned San Francisco but owed United States citizens more than six million dollars. If Mexico would cede the port of San Francisco and northern California to the United States in exchange for American assumption of these debts, the United States could afford to make concessions to England on the Oregon boundary. A reciprocal tariff would lower duties on British exports to the United States and encourage England to influence Mexico to come to terms. It would also lower duties on agricultural exports to England and thus attract support in the South and West. With Tyler's concurrence, Webster had spent his last months as secretary of state trying to get England to send a commission to America to negotiate such a treaty. Now, after his resignation, he still hoped the British would agree to the idea. Webster, of course, would lead that American commission. A treaty of such magnitude successfully negotiated might alienate some industrialists, but their disaffection would be more than balanced by merchant and shipping interests in the East and by farmers and planters in the West and South. It might even form the basis for a new party.

A bold idea which failed. Tyler was too intent on annexing Texas to make any kind of treaty with Mexico feasible. The British government would not make the necessary overtures. And southern Democrats, always more comfortable in an adversary relationship with Webster, refused to rally to the plan. Meanwhile, many Whigs in Massachusetts shook their heads in amazement and anger at his behavior on the tariff. Winthrop, who had come into political life as a Webster satellite, wondered if he would ever be able to "fathom Mr. W's real ends." Abbot Lawrence thought he knew. The great Daniel Webster had "lent himself to southern folly" and was *"politically doomed."*[18]

By the middle of September, 1843, all of Webster's attempts to build a political base independent of Clay and the Whigs had failed. Seward found him in Boston "talking about his farm with composure," but noted sadly, "He is referred to now as a man of immense talent, but not particularly, etc. etc. So it is to be eclipsed." A week later, the two men were together again for the state fair at Rochester. Eclipsed or not, Webster could still draw crowds and, according to Seward, "all Western New York turned out to hear him." But Webster was "disquieted, moody and morose" during the day, and Seward substituted for him at a banquet. That night, however, Webster gave "one of his great and overpowering speeches."

The performance, which Seward marveled at, was one in which Webster recited good Whig doctrine in the grand style. "The agriculture of this country is the great matter which demands protection," Webster said. Protected home markets for agriculture and manufacture would "make us a happy and strong people," but the South, through some "strange infatuation," could not see the wisdom in such a policy. If people had understood Webster to have said in Baltimore that the president could enter into foreign agreements to supersede the power of Congress over trade, they were mistaken. Webster wanted "to give up nothing, nothing, nothing, essential to the protection of our industry. . . ." The moroseness which Seward had detected in Webster earlier in the day was understandable. The first step back into orthodox Whiggery under Henry Clay was bound to be painful.[19]

It was not a smooth road back. Webster still had his uncritical admirers like Biddle, who despaired at watching such "a colossal statue with no pedestal," but Clay, who had taken over that pedestal for the Whigs, was not sure that he needed his rival's help and told friends that Webster had even become powerless in Massachusetts. This was wishful thinking. Most of the Massachusetts Whigs who blamed Webster for the Democratic victory in the last state election still sought his aid and were thankful when he gave a major address at Andover in November, reaffirming his belief in basic Whig principles without apologizing for anything in the past. "I am a Whig, a Massachusetts Whig, a Faneuil Hall Whig and none shall have the power now or hereafter, to deprive me of the position in which that character places me." He also endorsed George Briggs for governor over Abbot Lawrence. The Clay Whigs might be able to nominate a president, but they would take the governor Daniel Webster wanted for Massachusetts.[20]

By December, although Webster continued to disparage Clay's chances in private, he let it be known through intermediaries that he would work with the Kentuckian. There was even talk of putting Webster on the ticket as vice-president, but Clay would have none of that. Meanwhile, Webster returned to his law practice and early in January went to Washington to argue the *Girard* case and dispose of some of the furnishings he and Caroline had needed when they were living in power and luxury on Lafayette Square. "I have seen the President twice," he wrote to a friend rather wistfully, "but he said not a word on any political subject." The Whigs shut him out also and he felt isolated and lonely. The moment for reconciliation was at hand and Rufus Choate arranged a small dinner party for Webster and a group of influential congressional Whigs. It was a cold affair at first, but as the bottle circulated, Webster charmed his way back into the good graces of his former colleagues. Later, he called on Clay's close friend, Crittenden. "We talked of the approaching presidential election as a *common concern,*" Crittenden wrote to Governor Letcher. "He identifies himself with us and says *we* ought to do *this that* and *the other* and he has decided on his course and will go with us in support of the Baltimore nomination, and he knows well what that will be." The next day, Webster wrote Everett saying that Clay's good chances for the presidency "cannot be denied."[21]

In the spring of 1844, Webster finally broke openly with Tyler by coming out strongly against the annexation of Texas. He wrote to warn Everett that despite rumors that the administration might retaliate "by inflicting blows on my friends, he would "continue to oppose annexation, though I should be the means of breaking all your necks."

Having privately made peace with the Whigs and publicly broken with the administration, Webster was in a position to attend the Whig convention in Maryland on May 2 and endorse Clay's nomination. Admitting past differences over "questions of practical administration," Webster assured the convention that there was "no great interest of the country . . . in which there is any difference between the distinguished leader of the Whig party and myself."

Back in Boston again, Webster found the Whigs in Faneuil Hall responding to him with their old enthusiasm as he gave his "entire and hearty approbation" to Clay's nomination. He said he came neither "to bury Caesar nor to praise him," but perceptive listeners may have caught a note of warning in his words when he referred to the damage Jackson had done in trying to lift the presidency above the Constitution. The implication was clear. If Clay wanted to play Caesar in the White House, Daniel Webster was prepared to act as tribune for the people.

Webster had expected the Democrats to nominate Van Buren and was surprised when James Polk, former Speaker of the House and governor of Tennessee, was chosen. It irritated him to learn that a man like Polk could so easily get the ultimate honor. "Did any of you ever know that there was such a man as James K. Polk?" he said scornfully in a speech late in the campaign. "He may be a respectable person in the class of second or third rate men; but . . . it was his position and not his character that made him a candidate." By contrast he listed the past presidents, Washington, Jefferson, the two Adamses, Madison, Monroe, Jackson, and even Van Buren. Now the presidency was in danger of going to an unknown! He said nothing about Harrison or Tyler.

That was about as foolish as Webster got in the campaign of 1844. For the most part, he talked in favor of the tariff and against the annexation of Texas, saying as little as possible about Henry Clay. When Clay stumbled badly with the publication of his famous Alabama letters, which seemed to countenance the annexation of Texas, Webster dropped any mention of the issue for a while and in a speech in New York almost seemed to apologize for the Whigs, saying, "In the circumstances of the country, they could make no other nomination."

Considering the possibilities for irreversible disaster, Webster had good reason to feel satisfied with his performance during the Harrison-Tyler years. What had begun with a heady initiation into coonskin politics had ended in a Whig bloodbath, but Webster had survived. No public figure in the country was more famous, and with Clay's defeat there was no likelier opposition candidate for the presidency in 1848. That was how he must have seen it himself. He would remember the achievements of the period, and how they might be exploited for the future.

But Clay was not the only loser in 1844. The years of brawling among the Whigs had left their mark on Webster also, and the ugly scars would encourage even some of the faithful to look more searchingly at his Godlike image in the future.[22]

15

BLACK DAN IN DEPTH

According to the story which Samuel Griswold Goodrich heard, Webster attended a private party in Washington for the Mississippi Whig leader S. S. Prentiss around 1840. Late in the evening, after the wine had been flowing freely, William Preston of South Carolina stood up and proposed a toast to "Daniel Webster—a Northern man with Southern principles." Webster hesitated, then struggled to his feet and replied saying, "Well sir, I was born in New Hampshire and therefore I am a Northern man. And if what other people say of us be true, it is equally true that I am a man of Southern principles. Sir, do I ever leave a heel-tap in my glass? Do I ever pay my debts? Don't I always prefer challenging a man who won't fight?" After developing the theme at length he sat down to the laughter and applause of the rest of the party.[1]

It is highly probable that this incident or something quite like it happened as reported. Webster was famous for his ability to make and respond to toasts in off-the-record gatherings among friends, and the negative side of his reputation which he was trying to burlesque at the party was developed in eleborate detail long before the abolitionists put the finishing touches to it after 1850. The prolonged and rancorous controversies of the Tyler years had so inflamed the rhetoric of his enemies and intensified public prejudice against him, that by 1845 Webster could no longer laugh them away in private. Everybody had heard about the accomplishments of the "Godlike man." From now on they would hear more and more about the alleged exploits of "Black Dan."

190

However controversial he had become as a national figure, Massachusetts still looked to Webster for leadership in Washington, and the legislature elected him to the Senate by an overwhelming margin in January, 1845. Upon taking his seat that spring Senator Webster, as befitted a retired secretary of state, paid close attention to the continuing debate over foreign policy. The two big issues were Texas and Oregon, and Webster was opposed to the expansionist policies of the administration in both cases. In February and March of 1846, his confidence in the reasonableness of British intentions strengthened by a private letter from Lord Ashburton, he participated in a long, acrimonious debate about Oregon and came out strongly for a peaceful resolution of the difficulty. In the course of the debate he was accused by war-hungry Democrats of wanting to do for the Northwest what he had already accomplished for the Northeast—to give away valuable American rights to England. Thus Webster was forced into an extended defense of the Ashburton treaty and an ugly confrontation with Senator Daniel Dickinson from New York and Congressman Charles I. Ingersoll, chairman of the House Committee on Foreign Affairs. Dickinson and Ingersoll were enthusiastic expansionists and Anglophiles. The trouble began when Dickinson quoted from a speech of Ingersoll's, then widely circulated in New York, which accused Webster of having tried to pressure Governor Seward into releasing McLeod.

Shortly before Webster replied to his accusers, Robert Winthrop was overheard telling a friend in the House that the "scarifying process" was about to begin. What he meant was that Webster would turn his heavy guns on the impertinent New Yorkers. The scarifying does not appear in the speech as printed in Webster's collected works, but it is fully reported in the *Congressional Globe*. The flavor and style of the former secretary's reply is suggested by the following remarks:

I would thank God to know that such an ebullition had never been made out of a barroom anywhere, and that's a theatre quite too high for it . . . a series of distinct, unalloyed falsehoods—absolute, unqualified, entire—never appeared in any paper in Christendom. . . . this is stated by a man or a thing that has a seat in one of the houses of Congress . . . what can account for the apparent maliciousness of his statements? . . . I think it proceeds from moral obtuseness—a naive want of perception between truth and falsehood. . . . I say the mind of the man seems to be grotesque—*bizarre*. . . . In this case the screws are loose all over . . . the ebullition which I have been commenting upon . . . is as black and foul as ever was ejected from anything standing on two legs.[2]

Why such a display of abusive rhetoric? Everyone knew that the expansionists in Congress had disliked the Ashburton treaty and that Governor Seward had earlier disagreed with the administration over the handling of the *McLeod* case. Perhaps Webster, who at sixty-four had been through a "scarifying process" himself during the Tyler years, now felt free of the restraint that had plagued him in the cabinet. Perhaps he sensed that Ingersoll was after bigger game than could be snared by raking up the *McLeod* business and wanted to destroy him before he could mount a further assault. In any event, the angry, sarcastic, personal attack on Ingersoll was counterproductive. It tumbled Webster from the high ground of the lofty statesman into dirty, back-alley politics, where at this point in his career, he would appear to least advantage.

Taking advantage of the publicity aroused by Webster's philippic, Ingersoll replied by charging that the former secretary of state had not settled his public account when he left office and had used public funds to "corrupt" party presses. Robert Withrop and George Hillard, both pillars of the Whig establishment in Boston, rose to defend Webster with fatuous speeches emphasizing his great world reputation. This brought Yancey of Alabama to his feet. Yancey demanded to know if it was true that Massachusetts manufacturers had raised a one-hundred-thousand-dollar annuity for Webster. Such information, he said, might be useful to have before the debate on the tariff began. When Hillard persisted in a Beacon Hill line of defense by likening Webster's reputation to that of Washington, less genteel congressmen hissed. Yancey would not let the matter of the "pension" drop. "If he is paid, what is it for?" Yancey demanded. "Is it that he may adorn the public counsels merely, without any view to private and personal interests? . . . that is not human nature. . . . No sir, he is bound hand and foot." Yancey reviewed Webster's whole career, including the vote against supplying American troops during the last war and his chronic dependency on bankers and wealthy merchants. He concluded that the Massachusetts senator had "two characters which, Proteus-like, he can assume as his interests or necessities demand—the 'God-like' and the 'Hell-like'—the 'God-like Daniel' and *Black Dan!* . . . For myself I acknowledge the power of his intellect; but I do not award my respect to great men for mere intellect. And when a great intellectual name is not associated with public integrity, I will leave his praise to the hangers on of courts and the sycophants of the palace. Such names are unworthy of commendation from the lips of a virtuous American."[3]

Webster, who had retorted to the much milder attack of Ingersoll with such fury, kept his silence now. It was true, as Yancey had implied, that he had agreed to return to the Senate with the understanding that a fund would be raised to make it possible. He apparently received the money in two ways. The first was in the form of a lump sum of indeterminate amount (paid sometime in the spring and summer of 1845) to cover debts. Correspondence between Webster and his son during this period suggests that the delay in getting up the money and securing agreement on its purpose made Webster threaten to quit his place in Congress. The matter was finally arranged with the help of Samuel Jaudon, an old friend with years of experience in the complications and delicacy of Webster financing. On October 12, 1845, Webster appears to have closed out the first phase of his negotiations with his benefactors in a letter to Jaudon in which he apologized for having caused "so much trouble." "I begin to feel a sense if not of humiliation," Webster wrote, "yet of regrets & awkwardness, at what has occurred within the last six or eight months, & am determined neither to write or talk any more on the subject."[4]

On March 21, 1846, David Sears wrote to Webster from Boston telling him that a thirty-seven-thousand-dollar annuity had been established in his account at the Massachusetts Hospital Life Insurance Company on the behalf of forty Boston subscribers. "This fund has been created freely and cheerfully by your friends," Sears wrote, "in evidence of their grateful sense of the valuable services you have rendered to your whole country. They have done it without your sanction or knowledge, and with some reason to imagine that their purpose might not be entirely acceptable to you." In accepting the gift, which was hardly a surprise, Webster acknowledged the "no small neglect of my profession, and prejudice of my private affairs" which had resulted from his years in public service. Although the exchange was not intended for publication, Webster gave no indication elsewhere in his correspondence of being embarrassed when the matter came up in Congress. He did not mention it himself and was apparently satisfied with Robert Winthrop's defense of the matter in the House as a private transaction between Webster and his friends. That the public might interpret such a transaction as evidence of the corruption of an elected representative of the people seems not to have occurred to him.[5]

The Ingersoll accusations could not be ignored. Here, the charge of corruption was explicit. A House committee was appointed to decide whether or not Secretary of State Webster had (1) made unauthorized use of the Secret Service Fund; (2) used public funds to bribe the press; (3) left office without accounting for public expenditures. Withrop said that he had never seen his friend more upset, and he understood why. Webster was afraid of a vendetta—afraid that a majority of the committee might decide against him despite the evidence. When John Tyler testified that all of the funds in question (seventeen thousand dollars in total) had been authorized by him to finance secret activities in support of the negotiations over the Maine boundary, the case against Webster collapsed. At this point, Webster confided to his friend Curtis that Ingersoll was willing to quit the field on grounds that he had been misinformed, but Webster refused to let him off. "He wants first some soft words from me to begin with. Now this he can never have. . . . I *will not* begin any pacific declaration. Thats flat."[6]

In June, 1846, by a majority of 4 to 1, the investigating committee cleared the former secretary on all counts. The result was something less than a triumphant vindication, however, for the evidence showed that Webster had technically been a defaulter when he left the cabinet and that he had been forced to square his accounts by paying about one thousand dollars out of his own pocket before Tyler left the White House. Of far greater significance was the revelation that while not actually buying newspaper support for their treaty, Webster and Tyler had used public funds to manipulate public opinion among their own citizens. What had been touted as a triumph for enlightened democratic statesmanship now became suspect—a treaty fashioned more in the devious style of old-world diplomacy than in the open democratic style which Americans expected from their government. [7]

The Ingersoll investigation represented the final spasm in the bitter political infighting that had dogged Webster ever since he made the fateful decision to stick with Tyler. It also dramatized the extraordinary vulnerability of his reputation. All public figures are subject to villification, and every political hero shows a dark side to the opposition. Therefore, in politics as in prize fighting, a tough skin is a great blessing. Webster was as tough-skinned as most politicians, but he was more vulnerable to abuse because of his great exposure and the extravagant esteem in which he was held by his most enthusiastic supporters. Even the Democratic press recognized that Webster, despite his failures to gain the highest political office, was the most celebrated man in American public life. "Mr. Webster is undoubtedly *the* lion of the country," wrote the *Baltimore Post and Transcript* in 1839, "The others move in a secondary orbit. Every movement of *the* lion is chronicled with the greatest accuracy. He sells his estate and the news goes to every corner of the country. He goes to England and it is proclaimed from the housetops that he goes out to harmonize the excited feelings of England and America. Wherever he moves, partizans try to make someting out of it." To be so constantly exposed would have been hazardous for the reputation of any public man. For the Godlike man, to be so exposed was frequently fatal. [8]

Much of the ambivalence that became attached to Webster's name can be explained by the fact that he tried to operate on two separate levels at the same time. As a symbolic leader, guardian of the people during a period of tumultuous change, he was perceived as patriotic, disinterested, statesmanlike. This perception inevitably clashed with the role of Webster the ambitious politician, and the Democrats never tired of contrasting the defender of the Union to the narrowly partisan Federalist congressman who had tried to frustrate the war effort during Madison's administration. Twenty years after the war, Democratic papers still quoted from Webster's anti-war speeches and managed to discover New Hampshire Democrats willing to "recall" that Webster had supported the Hartford convention. Webster's friends would reply to these charges by trying to put the quotations in context, by emphasizing that other distinguished men (like Calhoun) had opposed some aspects of the war, and that the only New Hampshire delegates to the Hartford convention had lived one hundred miles away from Webster's home in Portsmouth. Webster, himself, falsely claimed that he had known about the convention in advance and advised against it. At the same time, he was never able to condemn it with proper Democratic vehemence, because many men he respected had participated in it. So persistent were the attempts to discredit Webster on grounds of his alleged Federalist treachery that he finally felt obliged to discuss the matter in the Senate. Claiming that Democratic agents had been employed for over a decade to ransack the journals and examine his private correspondence to see if "I had ever said anything which an enemy might make use of," he said, "my former residence has been searched, as with a lighted candle. New Hampshire has been explored, from the mouth of the Merrimack to the White Hills."[9]

Webster repeatedly challenged his opponents to document the charges that he had conspired with the Hartford convention Federalists, but they found all the documentation they needed in his anti-war speeches, and this hurt him outside New England. John Tyler confessed that for years he, along with most people in the South, had been prejudiced against Webster for his role during the War of 1812. Many papers in the South and West professed regret that a political leader with Webster's gifts should be blocked from high national office by his Federalist past. In reporting his western trip in 1837, for example, the *New Orleans Bee* wrote that people in his audiences had not forgotten "that he refused supplies of food and clothing to their sons and brothers wounded and frozen" during the war.[10]

It is significant that Webster should have been so frequently criticized for what John Quincy Adams called his "ravenous" ambition. Obviously Webster was no more ambitious than competitors like Clay and Calhoun, and it has been repeatedly demonstrated in our political history that a consuming ambition is one of the greatest assets a politician can have. Webster's problem was that his positive image as guardian was constantly at odds with his role as a practical politician forced to try one expedient after another to broaden his political base. Daniel Webster, as defender of the Constitution and Union, always seemed to stand on the same solid ground—the same reassuring themes permeated all his patriotic orations. But in politics, Webster was accused of being Black Dan in disguise. "Feed attorney of the capitalists, a reckless speculator himself . . . the advocate of hard money and paper money—the defender of tariff and anti-tariff policy . . . the supporter of abolitionists . . . yet the defender of the constitutional rights of the south—endowed with great intellectual power and very elastic moral principles, which contract and expand like his paper currency. . . . There is no actor in the theatre of public life in this country who has played so many parts as MR. DANIEL WEBSTER."[11]

A good example of the ambivalence of the Godlike–Black Dan image can be seen on the famous occasion of the completion of the Bunker Hill monument on June 17, 1843. Webster, who had presided over the laying of the cornerstone eighteen years before, was again asked to make the address. The occasion was much as it had been before, with great crowds around the base of the monument and a gathering of about one hundred Revolutionary war veterans directly in front of the platform. The reviled President John Tyler sat on the platform, and early in his address Webster forcefully acknowledged his former chief's presence by saying

Woe betide the man who brings to this day's worship feelings less than wholly American; woe betide the man who can stand here with fires of local resentment burning, or the purpose of fermenting local jealousies and the strifes of local interests festering and rambling in his heart . . . this column stands on Union. I know not that it might not keep its position, if the American Union, in the mad conflict of human passions, and in the strife of parties and faction, should be broken up and destroyed.

With passages like this and with the famous peroration concluding with the words "thank God I—I also—AM AN AMERICAN," Webster carried away many in his audience just as he had done eighteen years before. To the youthful George William Curtis, he looked like a king, displaying "the restless grandeur of a Titan storming heaven." And Emerson, who had already begun to criticize his former idol, wrote "There was the Monument, and here was Webster . . . and the whole occasion was answered by his presence."[12]

But there were others at Bunker Hill that day who were Massachusetts Whigs as well as patriotic Americans and could not reconcile the events of recent months with Webster's patriotic oratory. They could not forget that Webster had also been a schemer for John Tyler and only a few weeks earlier had apparently been willing to bargain away one of the most cherished parts of their political program (the tariff) for his own advantage. John Quincy Adams spoke for them by staying home and writing in his diary that Webster had turned Bunker Hill into "a gull trap for popularity, both for himself and for Tyler, by which he hopes to whistle back his Whig friends, whom he had cast off, as a huntsman his pack." The "spouting" Godlike man was "a heartless traitor to the cause of human freedom," trying to shore himself up by supporting a "slave monger" president.[13]

Thoughtful writers frequently remarked that people were more willing to give Webster their respect and admiration than to trust him with their votes. Their reluctance, prompted in part by his Federalist history and an erratic political course which seemed to contradict the image which he sought to project, was also influenced by Webster's personal style. He had been born in the eighteenth century, when it was still proper to believe that constitutional self-government was best served by entrusting political leadership to the hands of a talented and virtuous elite. His scornful dismissal of the Jacksonians as men "not known till yesterday, and having little chance of being

Webster the guardian at Bunker Hill in 1843.

remembered beyond tomorrow" was frequently thrown up to him, and although Webster played the coonskin game in 1840, he was never able to divest himself of a certain inbred haughtiness and reserve. This served him well in his role of the Godlike defender and helped to account for the awe with which many regarded him, but it was a formidable handicap to him as a political man in a country which came increasingly to expect its leaders to show a common democratic style. As Gamaliel Bradford said, "self was too big an object in Webster's universe to be dissolved under any circumstances," and this hurt him politically. Recalling how difficult it was to introduce a stranger to Webster on the floor of the Senate, one of his colleagues wrote:

Webster evidently felt such introductions to be an intolerable bore, and seldom took the trouble to conceal his annoyance. Usually his manner on such occasions was freezingly indifferent. . . . Sometimes he did not even look at the person introduced, but mechanically extended his hand, and permitted the stranger to shake it if he had the courage to do so. I have seen members of Congress turn crimson with indignation at Webster's ungracious reception of their constituents.[14]

The Democratic propagandists who tried to turn a self-made country boy from the backwoods of New Hampshire into an inaccessible, old-world aristocrat were more effective than truthful, but Webster knew he was vulnerable on this score, repeatedly talked about his simple family background, and tried to present himself as a man of the soil, as much at home standing in his own onion patch or strolling among his oxen at Marshfield as in the Congress. The opposition disposed of this as a typical bit of Black Dan trickiness. *"Himself* a farmer," snorted the *Globe.* "It is true that he owns a farm in Massachusetts, and that he has speculated largely in western lands; but his attempt to gull that portion of the community into the idea that he is one of them is altogether too feeble."[15]

At his most effective, Daniel Webster was a great symbol of national unity. Through his speeches, Americans could periodically transcend the boundaries of time and space and feel that they were a common people with a common history, but they could not believe that he was really one of them. The shrewd Democratic journalist Francis Grund put the matter well when he wrote, "Though respected and admired throughout the country, he is not beloved—no, not even by his own partisans. Mr. Webster knows the laws of his country; but he is less acquainted with the men who are to be governed by them, and possesses none of those conciliatory and engaging qualities which insure personal popularity. This accounts for his position in Congress, where . . . he stands alone—*the terrible Senator from Massachusetts.*"[16]

There was a deviousness about Webster's personal style that tended to undermine his credibility. He was always advising correspondents to burn his letters. Most of these had to do with political matters and seem to have reflected a morbid anxiety about the omnipresence of political spies. There must be hundreds of such letters in manuscript collections around the country. An unimportant mannerism perhaps, but a man of Webster's position could not constantly advise people to burn his letters without suggesting that he had something to hide.

In getting friends to do him favors, Webster could be masterfully disingenuous. When Edward Everett threatened to upstage his own Bunker Hill oration by appearing with Lafayette a few weeks earlier at Concord, Webster had blandly suggested that his protégé was in danger of overexposing himself. When Congress passed an appropriation to reimburse Americans with claims against Spain, Webster diffidently suggested to Boston merchants that they might want to use his legal services. "If however, any the least doubt, difficulty or impropriety occurs to you," he wrote, "I beg you to forbear pressing the matter. . . . I do not remember that I ever before sought any employment with a view to pecuniary profit—no doubt I may make an awkward figure of it now." Then toward the end of the letter he casually disclosed, "it has been suggested to me from a pretty high source, that the persons interested in the North might have some influence in regard to the nomination of one or more of the Commrs." Webster made about sixty thousand dollars on the claims.[17]

There is a thin line between disingenuousness and dishonesty. Webster was made chairman of a committee to study the problem of American merchants who had suffered losses through French attacks on American commerce before 1800. His committee would recommend whether or not the American government should assume responsibility for the payment of the claims. On January 11, 1834, he wrote the following letter to his Boston law partner Henry Kinsman:

I wish to write you a letter in confidence for your own eyes & Mr. Brooks.

The subject is the French claims before 1800. I moved on that subject early in the session.—had a committee appointed—myself at the head of it & we have reported a Bill. By proper pains this Bill *will assuredly pass the Senate.* . . .

It is time, therefore, I think, to move in the matter of the agency. If the Gentlemen in interest, in our quarter, desire my aid I wish them to settle that point before a host of other persons apply. Will you therefore show this letter to Mr. Brooks & if necessary to Mr. Edward Brooks—it need go no further & if Mr Brooks thinks proper, let him draw up an agreement substantially like that in the case of the Spanish treaty; let him sign it himself and ask others to sign it. If this can be done to such an extent as to make it an object you may say to Mr Brooks that it is my intention very much to relinquish other professional employment & give my strictest personal attention to this business

Subsequent correspondence between Webster and Kinsman shows that Peter Chardon Brooks and other wealthy New England merchants were willing to let Webster handle their claims. In January, 1835, Daniel Webster spoke in the Senate to support the legislation which would make this possible. He began by saying that published reports of his own personal interest in the French claims were "wholly and entirely false and malicious. I have not the slightest interest in these claims, or any one of them. I have never been conferred with or retained by anyone, or spoken to as counsel, for any of them, in the course of my life. No member of the senate is more entirely free from any personal connection with the claims than I am."[18]

Webster's humorous reference to the heel tap in his glass acknowledged his reputation as a drinker. His relish and capacity for good food and drink were well known. In 1830 the beverage inventory of his Summer Street house in Boston showed an upstairs closet of 3,200 bottles of wine plus a cellar with hundreds of other bottles of port, Madeira, sherry, claret, brandy, whiskey, rum, and champagne. He could say with confidence "it is not often that good wine is under any roof where I am without my knowing it." As he grew older, friends felt that he had begun to show the effects of overindulgence. Chancellor Kent wrote in his *Diary* after dining with Webster in 1840, "He is 57 years old and looks worn and furrowed; his belly becomes protuberant, and his eyes deep in his head. I sympathize with his condition. He has been too free a liver. He ate but little and drank wine freely." A senator's daughter remembered going to tea with the Websters and then on to the opera. Webster had drunk a lot but seemed normal enough until in the midst of the performance he suddenly leaped to his feet and belted out a few bars of "Hail Columbia, Happy Land" before his wife could grab his coattails and pull him back down again. The anecdote of Webster at one of Jenny Lind's concerts, and how he insisted on standing up in the front row and taking every bow with her was another favorite around Washington. At Webster's death, the rumors about his drinking had become so numerous that his physician and many friends and acquaintances felt called upon to testify that they had never seen him drunk. What most of these statements really say is that Webster could hold his liquor. We must remember, of course, that Webster grew up at a time when wine and whiskey were almost universally approved and even taken liberally by ministers. Other politicians of his generation, like Silas Wright and Henry Clay, were famous drinkers, and at a cold-water banquet in Boston after Webster's second Bunker Hill address, President John Tyler frequently ducked under the table to consult a flask of brandy.[19]

The conventions of the day allowed Webster to do in public what no modern presidential aspirant would dare to do. But no amount of drinking ever seemed to interfere with his ability to keep up with a heavy work load, and his lifelong habit of beginning work long before dawn and generally serene disposition hardly square with the life style of a drunkard. If his reputation suffered in this connection, it was less because of what he did than because of what he encouraged people to expect from him. The real significance of Webster's drinking is that it revealed a strong streak of self-indulgence which clashed with the myth of the Godlike man.

The dimension of the Black Dan image, which was particularly offensive to people in Webster's lifetime but which has receded with the years, involves his relations with women. In the winter of 1842 Webster was bitterly attacked by many Whig papers for staying in Tyler's cabinet and for conspiring with the president to deny printing contracts to papers supporting Henry Clay. On January 19, the ardently pro-Clay *Louisville Journal* announced that Webster was "about to be brought to a full knowledge of the tremendous, fatal blunder he has committed." A week later the paper reported that Webster had tried to seduce a lady visitor in one of the offices in the Department of State. According to the story, the secretary was visited by the wife of one of his clerks who wanted to be employed herself as a copyist. Webster asked her to step into a back room and show him a specimen of her handwriting. When they were alone together he allegedly "threw his brawny arms around the lady's waist, exclaiming, 'This my dear is one of the prerogatives of my office.' " The lady screamed; the other clerks rushed into the office, and "the old debauchee" rushed out.[20]

The story was reprinted across the country. Webster haters claimed the incident was part of a pattern. They discussed "the notorious profligacy of his scarcely concealed amours" and accused him of behaving as if he were beyond the reach of ordinary morality. Pro-Webster papers were properly horrified at the "slander," and even more horrified by the fact that intelligent people seemed ready to believe it. The source of the story turned out to be a Mr. George May, the son of a Washington physician, who published a statement saying that he had repeated it in front of others during a visit to Louisville as "mere rumor" and never intended it for publication. When Webster and the clerks in his office made out affidavits denying the story as "a naked, wilful and base falsehood," the *Louisville Journal* published the affidavits and retracted the story. Readers were left with the definite impression, however, that although the secretary had acquitted himself of "specific charges as printed," his reputation for sexual promiscuity had become a matter of common gossip in Washington.[21]

The story in the *Journal* conjures up intriguing images of an elephantine, satyrlike pursuit around the desk of the secretary of state, but it is hard to take seriously on face value let alone without hard evidence. The editor of the *Journal* was a close friend of Clay, and the political motivations behind the story were obvious. Once Webster left the cabinet and took up arms again with Clay and the Whigs the *Journal* began to praise him as a great statesman.[22] If this were an isolated event in Webster's career, it would hardly be worth mentioning, but the fact is that his sexual conduct was periodically questioned during his life, and after his death even sympathetic historians assumed that the stories about his philandering were grounded in truth.

During the period between his two marriages there was gossip about Webster and Mrs. John Agg. Mr. Agg was a political journalist. The Aggs had been close friends of Daniel and Grace Webster in Washington, and Daniel lived with them in a boarding house for a while after his first wife's death. Webster's copious correspondence with the Aggs has been preserved and shows that he was fond of them both, sometimes corresponded with her separately, and occasionally visited her alone or took her for a drive in his carriage. There is no reason to believe it was a covert relationship, and he and Caroline continued to be friendly with the Aggs after his second marriage. In fact, Webster's correspondence with Mrs. Agg is similar to his correspondence with many other women during his life. He liked to write bantering, affectionate, even flirtatious letters to the wives of his friends. Although such letters were frequently quite personal, he was never secretive about them, and often suggested that they be shown to mutual friends as was the custom with social correspondence at this time.[23]

A reading of Webster's correspondence as a whole suggests that he liked women and was admired by them but may not have been cut out for clandestine affairs. His letters are barren of sexual innuendo, and his friends recalled that even in masculine company, he would not listen to off-color stories. He was shocked by Moore's life of Byron and called the poet "an incarnation of demonism" who "boasted of infidelity" and was properly driven out of England. There is no reason to believe that Webster's prudery was not genuine. When his wife told him that the wife of a good friend had been unfaithful to her husband, Webster was shocked. "I rec'd yr letter, night befor last, giving the awful account of poor Mrs. M's conduct. It has made my heart bleed. . . . I declare I have had no happiness since I rec'd yr letter. The only consolation is the woman must be crazy. She cannot be so wicked as to do such things in her right mind. Poor Mr. M, I fear, will go crazy himself."[24]

Of course this was the nineteenth century—the age of the great double standard when one gentleman might threaten another for imaginary offenses against his wife's virtue and then trot off to the local brothel with a clear conscience. There were plenty of brothels in Washington and New York, and Webster, like most men in Congress, was separated from his family a great deal. Was this what was meant by Webster's alleged licentiousness? Was that what Webster's good friend Charles Stetson, the proprietor of the Astor House, meant when he said, "It is true that he sometimes commits crimes, but without any guilt"?[25]

The problem of Webster's alleged sexual indiscretions will emerge again in connection with the abolitionist assault upon him. At this point in his life the real question to answer is why, on the basis of so little proof, the Black

Dan image came to include Webster's moral as well as his political character. To answer this question it will be necessary to penetrate the Byzantine maze of his money problems.

When Daniel was a boy, he went to the county fair with his brother, Zeke. After they got home, his mother asked him what he had done with the quarter she had given him. Daniel said that he spent it. She asked Zeke about his quarter, and he said he had loaned it to Daniel. The story illustrates a governing principle in Webster's life. He was always using someone else's quarter, as those proud to claim a relationship to Webster through blood or marriage usually discovered. Herman LeRoy, the father of his second wife, paid a handsome dowry for the privilege of being Webster's father-in-law and then found himself forced into the legion of other frustrated Webster creditors. Herman's sons found that visiting Washington could easily involve helping their brother-in-law out of some "temporary" financial embarrassment. As Webster grew older and his affairs became more tangled, the net grew wider. Needing ten thousand dollars in a hurry, Webster persuaded a cousin in Maine to let him draw on his credit. When the note fell due, the cousin wrote the bank that he gave it "expressly for the *accommodation* of Daniel Webster and have his promise that I should not be troubled as to the payment of it." The letter found its way to the *Globe* where it was published at the same time Webster was being touted by the Whigs as the national expert in fiscal policy.[26]

Anyone who works with Webster's papers must be astounded at the enormous number of letters concerning his need to borrow and his inability to pay. He lived in a quicksand of financial distress, and almost everyone who came close to him was sucked in sooner or later. Sarah Goodrich, a talented miniaturist, was commissioned to paint Webster and his family in the late 1820s. Webster promptly borrowed a substantial sum from her. A few years later, she wrote asking for payment, and Webster replied in what became almost a form letter, "I am very poor today but I will let you have some money—a little—in the early part of next week. In 1851, a year before his death, Webster still owed Miss Goodrich two thousand dollars, which he was promising to arrange for "pretty soon."[27]

It was also expensive to be one of Webster's political lieutenants. In the spring of 1837, Webster needed three thousand dollars to purchase land in Illinois. Before leaving on a political tour of the West, he sent Caleb Cushing the certificate of the land and left him to raise the money "by your own means" or by explaining to friends "that I have an interest which would be much promoted by a loan of the money till my return." When he returned, Cushing, who thought he could help make Webster president, congratulated him on his "brilliant tour" and told him he had raised the money by putting up $1,000 for himself and taking a note for the rest. This was the beginning of a long-term investment which Choate ultimately figured at

$16,900. Webster made occasional small payments but the interest on the debt continued to mount. He tried to satisfy the obligation by turning over some western land which turned out to have already been sold for taxes. Webster never denied owing the money and signed a statement in 1848, repudiating any rights under the Statute of Limitations, but he never paid the debt. Finally, in 1852, Cushing, needing money badly, wrote a letter which showed his frustration and bewilderment and made the point that Webster's two vast country estates did not square with his inability to liquidate the debt. Webster's brief reply included a note for twenty-five hundred dollars payable in six months, "if I live."[28] The note was written September 30, 1852, less than a month before he died.

It is possible that Webster felt that he had satisfied his obligation to Cushing in political coin by securing his appointment to head the trade mission to China. For Cushing, obviously, there had been no such understanding, but one gets the impression that many of Webster's creditors were wealthy men who never expected to be paid and who treated their loans in much the same way that we think of party or campaign contributions. Roswell Colt was probably such a man. A confidential business agent to Biddle, Colt loaned Webster five thousand dollars in the mid-1820s, and Webster's letters show that he continued to postpone payments over a period of several years. Colt may never have been paid, but he continued to befriend Webster by sending him gifts of wine, livestock, and evergreen trees. For Colt, as for many others, it was perhaps enough to know that he was always welcome at Marshfield and could always get the ear of the powerful senator from Massachusetts.[29]

Whatever Webster borrowed was in addition to what he earned, and he earned a great deal. During the 1820s, when he began to collect high fees, his income seems to have averaged between fifteen and twenty thousand dollars a year. In addition he made more than sixty thousand dollars representing northern merchants in claims against Spain. Although he complained that Senate duties forced him to neglect his law practice after 1830, his receipt books for 1834–1835 show a total income of $15,183 and for the following year $21,793. If we assume that the dollar then was worth about seven times the dollar today, and remember how small taxes were and the comparative cheapness of luxuries, it is obvious that Webster earned enough to be considered a very wealthy man by any ordinary standards.[30]

The mid-thirties represent the high point in Webster's financial condition. Momentarily solvent, he worried about the future and the problems of maintaining two large farms plus establishments in Boston and Washington at a time when he was trying to curtail his law practice. He, therefore, took advantage of the easy credit terms available, borrowed to the hilt, and invested heavily in western lands, including another large farm in Illinois.

Webster approached his western investments naïvely, thinking that farm land near rivers or projected canal lines was bound to produce handsome returns. When a speculator by the name of Kinney bragged that he had bought land for himself for $1.25 an acre and watched it go up to $30 in less than a year, Webster paid attention. He made Kinney his agent, gave him money to invest, and was soon gratified to hear that land Kinney purchased for him in Illinois had almost immediately doubled in value. Kinney advised Webster to wait before selling. The price would go up another 500 percent within a year. This was in June, 1836. Two years later, when Webster was trying to sell this land, he sent Fletcher and his Marshfield neighbor Henry Thomas to inspect his acquisitions. Fletcher reported that the titles to many of his purchases were imperfect, and Thomas found that his lots near St. Joseph were two feet under water. Meanwhile Kinney slipped off to Texas and left Webster holding a ten-thousand-dollar note. Webster's timing was even more damaging than his choice of agents. With the Panic of 1837, credit dried up and the sale of public lands dropped from twenty to three million acres a year. By his own estimate Webster owned over two hundred thousand dollars worth of land which he could not sell.[31]

Unable to find buyers for his land either in America or England, Webster found himself in the embarrassing position of owing the Bank of the United States over $100,000 just as he was about to assume his duties as secretary of state. Anxious to rid himself of this obligation before being sworn into the cabinet, he persuaded the directors of the Bank to take some of his land in payment. These negotiations continued through March, 1841, and when the bank held out for a $93,000 instead of a $114,000 settlement, Webster bluntly told the directors through an intermediary, that he considered the arrangements to liquidate the larger sum "as *final,* and that he has very good reasons, which he could give you if his time permitted, *why* it is *certainly* for the interest of the Bank that it should be so regarded by the Committee. . . ." And so the matter was closed, except for the fact that a few months later the Bank began to question the titles on the land which Webster had transferred to them. A year later, the Bank closed its doors.[32]

So ended Daniel Webster's controversial association with the Bank of the United States. Biddle, who seemed even closer to Webster in 1841 than he had been during the furious days of the Bank war, did what he could to influence the directors in Webster's favor, but Biddle's most recent biographer finds nothing improper in the way Webster's debt was settled. The alternative would have been for Webster to default and suffer disgrace just as he was taking his most important office, and Biddle was not prepared to see an old friend, whom he considered to be the most distinguished man in American public life, suffer such a fate. This may be the literal truth of the matter, but we must weigh against it the fact that in the same letter which Biddle wrote to Webster recommending that he have his agent "write a decided & specific letter which will place you at your ease as to your affairs with the Bank," he also included a list of specific, strongly worded patronage suggestions.[33]

Webster did not need to be subsidized by the Bank of the United States as long as he could tap his wealthy constituents. It is not possible to reconstruct this story in full detail, but Webster was brought to Boston in the first place by a group of Federalists, including Harrison Gray Otis, who agreed to help him pay his debts in Portsmouth. In 1834, as we saw earlier, Edward Everett solicited funds from wealthy Whigs in Boston and New York to enable Webster to continue his fight in the Senate "for the intelligence and property of the country." Everett apparently scaled the first formal Webster fund down from one hundred thousand to fifty thousand dollars, enough, presumably, to help Webster get out of debt. Peter Brooks, Everett's wealthy father-in-law, said at that time that everyone knew how Webster was with money, that his habits would not change, and that from a business point of view there was no solution to his problem. Brooks was proved correct, when a few years later Webster's friends again got up a purse (represented in the Democratic press as a "loan") to help finance his trip to England. But neither this nor the subsequent negotiations liquidating Webster's debt to the Bank of the United States was enough to get him established as secretary of state. He needed fifteen thousand to purchase a house in Washington and wrote a letter "absolutely and strictly confidential" to the wealthy Philadelphian Whig, J. R. Jackson, for help. Jackson at first pleaded a lack of funds but later agreed to supply two thousand dollars. Webster sent him an unsigned note on March 19, 1841, asking for a check "drawn not by you, but by some cashier, payable to bearer," and telling Jackson to come to Washington as soon as possible. Mr. Jackson was made charge d'affaires at the Court of Denmark, while the secretary of state moved into a mansion on Lafayette Square.[34]

After Webster quit the cabinet he again took up his law practice and agreed to return to the Senate only with the understanding that his friends would make up the difference between what he could make in the law practice and what he would make as a senator. Wealthy Boston Whigs were now accustomed to the Webster fund-raising ritual, and Harrison Gray Otis noted with amusement that thousands were still raised for Webster from men who held his notes for other thousands and who condemned his extravagance. "This affair of W's reminds me of George Selwyn's remark when a subscription was raised for George Fox," wrote Otis, "somebody adverting to the delicacy of the subject expressed his wonder how Fox would *take it*—'Take it', said Selwyn, 'quarterly to be sure.' "[35]

What drew smiles from the sophisticated Otis drew harsh accusations from William Yancey on the floor of Congress. What, he demanded, was Webster being paid for? "That he may adorn the public councils . . . with-

out any view to private and personal interests. That is not human nature."
Congress never investigated the Webster subsidies, but the questions about
his "public integrity," which the Democrats had been asking for years,
remained. "A man who runs down periodically like a clock, and requires to
be from time to time wound up, is the instrument of him who holds the
key," wrote the *Providence Journal* in 1839. "How can . . . the pensioner of a
few great capitalists . . . be called the servant of the *people*?"[36]

It is easy to show that Webster spent most of his life on the edge of financial chaos and disgrace and how this harmed his reputation and career. It is
something else to explain why he behaved this way. It is not enough to say
that he was careless and extravagant and unlucky and that he gave up his professional income for public service. All of this is at least partially true, and it
is certainly true that Webster felt that he could not continue in politics
without financial help from his constituents. But why was it that a man who
boasted that he never forgot an important point of law could never remember to pay a debt? How was it that a man who consciously sought to
emulate Washington—to put his public career above every petty interest—
persistently made himself dependent on the bounty of others? If we can answer this question we can get close to the heart of the Godlike man—Black
Dan paradox.

In some ways Webster fits the psychological profile for the compulsive
spender. Although one could not argue that he was the kind of person who
had been denied money and love as a child and, therefore, spent to give himself "something akin to love," he did seem to be emotionally comfortable
only when he was free to spend. Some compulsive spenders "maintain a reliable economic relationship with a member of their family or with a friend,
who will come to their financial rescue when overtaxed." Webster certainly
fits this description, and to understand how he came to depend on supportive economic relationships with a host of other people throughout his life,
it is necessary to return to his relationship with his father.[37]

It is useful to recall that Webster picked up the Black Dan nickname as a
boy because he looked like his father who, as General Stark once said, "had a
complexion like burnt gunpowder." Ebenezer Webster was the dominant
influence in Daniel's life. Farmer, veteran of the Revolution, guardian of the
local community, he was the George Washington of the Webster family. He
had picked Daniel out of all his sons and given him the opportunity to build
the public career he would have liked for himself. If we are to understand
Webster's ambition—his refusal to give up the presidency long after he had
been honored far beyond most presidents—we must go back to that day at
Dartmouth when Ebenezer reminded Daniel in front of his roommate that
with an education "he could have done anything he chose." Like many sons
driven to satisfy the ambitions of their fathers, Webster could never overcome his dependency on Ebenezer, who, despite his towering stature as a fa-

ther, had been a dissatisfied local politician and an unsuccessful, debt-ridden farmer. When his brother Ezekiel died, Daniel took over the modest family farm in New Hampshire and at considerable expense turned it into a handsome thousand-acre stock farm. He would periodically return to refresh himself at the Elms, where his overseer, John Taylor, always referred to him as Squire Webster. Old friends and neighbors would come from miles around to catch a glimpse of Ebenezer's famous son.

But it was not enough for Webster to turn the family homestead, where his father was buried, into a show place. He needed to have his own farm closer to Boston. In 1832 he purchased John Thomas's 160-acre farm in Marshfield and proceeded to turn it into one of the most famous estates in the country. Thomas had been a Revolutionary patriot and, like Ebenezer Webster, had retained the title of captain. Like Webster's father, Captain Thomas had also fallen into debt. Webster not only rescued him from debt by purchasing the farm; he insisted that Thomas and his wife continue to live at Mansfield after the purchase. They became an extension of his own family and acted like godparents to his children. From Washington Webster would send the old captain examples of Julia's sketching ability, or a fragment from one of Fletcher's letters. He also sent back reports of his own political triumphs; the captain delighted in them all and took special pleasure in reading the famous speech Webster made in reply to Hayne. Webster also advised Captain Thomas about matters of farm management, reminding him about the watering of newly planted trees, or instructing him about the use of a special kind of fertilizer.

Ebenezer Webster had died a poor man when Daniel was just starting out on his own career. Now that he was famous, the son was doing for Captain Thomas what he would have done to gain his own father's approval if he had lived. He made him financially secure, gave him the opportunity to vicariously experience political success on a national scale and transformed his farm into something more lavish than anyone in Salisbury could ever have imagined. Eventually Marshfield would become a complex of thirty buildings spread over 1,400 acres with a staff of twenty-five men and some of the most exotic livestock in the country, including a herd of llamas from Peru. All of which cost money. Claude Fuess estimated that Webster spent $90,000 in improving Marshfield, and his own records show that at one point in the 1840s he was borrowing about $2,500 a month and spending about the same amount in expenditures at Marshfield.

Caleb Cushing was wrong when he said that Webster did not need his two luxurious farms. He needed them just as much as he needed political success. He spent and borrowed compulsively and continued to campaign for the presidency up to the last year of his life because he needed to show the trappings of economic and political success to earn the approval of his dead father. He could depend on other people's money with a reasonably clear conscience because he had never really given up depending on his father, the most powerful influence on his own life, and a man of unquestioned integrity, who had lived and died in debt himself.[38]

Not long after the alleged sexual scandal in the office of the secretary of state, the *Globe* referred to Webster as "one who is more degraded in public and private estimation than any man who has held exalted station in this country." No one took this kind of assassination rhetoric very seriously. Webster was a dominant figure in American public life when this was written in 1842, and he was a dominant figure when he died ten years later. But even close friends and supporters were troubled by weaknesses in his character. Edward Curtis was afraid that Webster's money problems might lead him "into the indulgence of habits which . . . would prove ruinous to him." Thomas Wren Ward, the American agent for the Barings, who believed Webster was "by far the greatest man we have," warned his employers against trusting him with anything that had to do with money. "I regret with you that we cannot give Mr. Webster our full confidence," Ward wrote as Webster was preparing to leave the cabinet. "Nevertheless he must be kept as nearly right as possible to prevent the evil which might come from such a mighty intellect acting on the wrong side. He has no regard to his pecuniary engagements and his tastes are for those who will flatter him and not oppose him, and who will contribute to his gratification." Yet, when it was time to send him back to the Senate, Ward contributed to the Webster fund and considered the money well spent. "He will save the country," Ward wrote. "There is no man in the United States capable of speaking to the Nation and the World as he does." And Edward Curtis never stopped trying to make Webster president.[39]

Yancey was right. Webster did have a double character. As a symbol of Constitution, Union, and the patriotic virtue of the age of Washington, he was far more than an ordinary politician. Consequently, minor vices stemming from appetite and ambition seemed more important in Webster than in a lesser figure, and the basic dependency in his personality appeared to give the lie to his Godlike reputation and undermined his private as well as his political character.

To many Americans, especially to those of Webster's generation from New England, he would always be the Godlike man. To a younger generation, growing up with Jacksonian Democracy, he would pose the Godlike man–Black Dan paradox. And to still a younger generation of Americans, who identified themselves with the cause of the slave, he would become the Prince of Darkness himself.

16

THE "TERRIBLE SENATOR
FROM MASSACHUSETTS"—AT HOME

Celebrities usually treasure their privacy and show themselves to friends and family in a way the world never sees. Francis Grund could write about "the terrible Senator from Massachusetts," but Priscilla Tyler, the president's coquettish daughter-in-law, remembered the "enchanting nonsense" of Webster's dinner conversation and how, after she fainted at her first White House banquet, Webster tried to carry her away from the table while the president poured ice water over them both. Departing from that table in soggy disarray, he continued to be one of the most sought-after dinner guests in Washington, as celebrated for his gossip and his knowledge of good food and wine as for his solemn pronouncements about statecraft.

Despite his reputation for being cold and haughty to strangers, Webster was naturally gregarious and always enjoyed himself in good society. John Kenyon, the intimate of almost every major literary figure in England and a masterful host, remembered Webster "because the man was so genial, so social, so affectionate, so much disposed to talk about prose or verse or fishing or shooting or fine greensward, or great trees, or to enter into common chat about daily things."

Although at ease with the powerful and wealthy on either side of the ocean, he did not forget old friends whose lives had turned out less successfully than his own. A Mrs. Fuller, who had known Webster in her youth, wrote that her family had fallen on hard times after her husband was caught embezzling funds in a Boston bank. The senator gave Mr. Fuller a stern lecture but at the same time wrote a friend to help the Fullers get a new start in New York.[1]

Close friends like Edward Everett remembered how unaffected Webster was in private, how willing to admit his limitations and to play the role of student. For example, when it came to answering an invitation in French. He was instinctively gracious in little things. A lady spent an evening with the Websters and departed in the rain with a rain hood over her head, leaving her bonnet behind. The next morning the former secretary of state left the bonnet at her door with the following note.

> I have demanded parlance with your bonnet; have asked it how many tender looks it has noticed to be directed under it; what soft words it has heard, close to its side; in what instances an air of triumph has caused it to be tossed; and whether, ever, and when, it has quivered from trembling emotions proceeding from below. But it has proved itself a faithful keeper of secrets, and would answer none of my questions. It only remained for me to attempt to surprise it into confession, by pronouncing sundry names one after another. It seemed quite unmoved by most of these, but at the apparently unexpected mention of one, I thought its ribbands decidedly fluttered! I gave it my parting good wishes, hoping that it might never cover an aching head, and that the eyes which it protects from the rays of the sun, may know no tears but of joy and affection.[2]

Some people with driving ambition have no time for personal relationships. Webster continued to correspond with old college chums until the end of his life. His respect and admiration for close personal associates like Mason and Story was almost boundless, and as he grew older he leaned more and more heavily on the advice and assistance of younger men like Everett and Edward Curtis. Perhaps the best evidence that Webster took friendship seriously is to be found in his relationship to Henry and Ray Thomas, the sons of Captain John Thomas of Marshfield. To the older son, Henry, Webster acted almost like a brother. He used Henry as his agent in building up the Marshfield estate, regularly sent him large sums of money, and confided in him with absolute confidence. Henry was one of the very few people to learn the depths of Webster's financial distress in the winter of 1837, when he actually considered selling Marshfield, and he was always one of Webster's favorite correspondents. "I must say that even your slightest letters afford me pleasure," he wrote. "Anything is welcome which calls my thoughts back to Marshfield, though it be only to be told which way the wind blows." Webster treated the younger Ray Thomas as one of his own sons and sent him to Illinois to manage the big farm which he purchased there in the 1830s. In March of 1840, while visiting Washington, Ray was stricken with a raging fever and Webster quit the Senate for ten days to stay at his bedside day and night until he died.[3]

The Thomases were farmers, and Webster found his mind turning more

Marshfield.

The Marshfield farmer.

and more to farming as he tried to stay afloat through the political storms of the forties. Although his Illinois farms turned out disastrously, he continued to pay close attention to his New England estates. John Taylor ran the Elms on shares and Porter Wright was Webster's head farmer at Marshfield. Webster insisted on weekly reports from his farmers in New Hampshire and Massachusetts and his voluminous correspondence with them was a source of great refreshment to him. To talk about crops and animals, especially those rooted most closely to the soil, like oxen, pigs, and sheep, was a welcome change from the uncertainties of politics. He was less interested in horses. "I cannot lay out one dollar on horseflesh," he reminded Taylor in the summer of 1851, "and the rule is, you know, to have no trading in horses. . . . Never mention the word horse to me." Horse trading was too much like politics. When Taylor brought up the latter in a letter in March, 1852, Webster said, "You and I are farmers, we never talk politics; our talk is of oxen. . . . John Taylor!. never write me another word upon politics."[4]

When Webster was in residence at Elms Farm, he presided with an air of rustic hospitality over the visitors who came to see him. He might prepare a chowder for a large delegation of friends, and was known to appear at the door before unexpected guests in his dressing gown and straw hat and sweep them off for a visit to the pig pen. On occasion he would slip away by himself to coax a trout out of Punch Brook or from the clear waters of nearby Lake Como where he always kept a boat. In New Hampshire it was the combination of mountains, fresh streams, and lakes and the well-groomed fields and gardens of his parents that refreshed and comforted Webster.

If Elms Farm was something to be preserved, Marshfield was Webster's own creation. Beginning with a modest family farm Webster spent more than eighty-seven thousand dollars to build a 1,400-acre estate that became the rural showplace of New England. Here is how he described Marshfield at its best.

I never saw Marshfield look so well as it does now; the crops are heavy, the lawns and pastures perfectly green, and the trees remarkably bright and glossy. There are several hundred thousands of trees here, which I have raised myself from the seeds; they are all arranged in avenues, copses, groves, long rows by the roads and fences, and some of them make beautiful and impenetrable thickets on hills which were mere sand hills when I came here. The herds and flocks are in fine order. Llamas from Peru feed in the pastures with the sheep. We have a little fresh-water lake, which is frequented not only by the ordinary ducks and geese, but by beautiful Canada geese or wild geese, which breed in retired places, but will always join their kindred in their emigrations, spring and fall, unless their wings are kept cropped. We have also China geese, India geese, and in short, the same birds from almost every quarter of the world. As to the poultry yard, there is no end to the varieties which my man has collected. I do not keep the run of half the names and breeds.

The situation of this place is rather peculiar. Back of us, inland, rises a large forest, in which one may hide himself, and find as odorous an atmosphere as among the pines of Maine. In front of us, a mile distant, is the sea, every mast visible over the beach bank, and all vessels visible, hulls as well as masts, from the chambers of the house. A drive of one mile and a half, almost entirely over my own farm, brings us to what is called Duxbury beach, a breadth of clean, white, hard sand, seven miles long, which forms at low water a favorite ride or drive in hot weather.

These, my dear Sir, are all trifles, and of course without much interest to any one but myself; but, I confess, that to me Marshfield is a charming place; perhaps one reason is that so many things about it which now appear handsome, are the result of my own attention. I sometimes try to read here, but can never get on, from a desire to be out of doors.[5]

The mansion house at Marshfield was a spacious frame building in the Gothic style, with broad verandas from which the "squire" was accustomed to address his neighbors. The first floor of the house held a series of connected drawing rooms and a large library. Murals, portraits of Webster and his family, and the prized moments of a long and varied career were prominently displayed, including a model of Bunker Hill monument, Webster's personal collection of George Washington's congressional medals, and a spectacular arrangement of mounted butterflies presented by a South American diplomat.

Webster liked to show off Marshfield and offer his guests a variety of entertainment and expeditions. For the gentlemen there was the possibility of fishing with Seth Peterson, who took charge of the boathouse at Green Harbor, or of hunting for birds in the great marshes. For the ladies there was the possibility of an exhilarating ride on the beach or a trip to Webster's own pine groves overlooking the sea. Whatever the activity, the master of Marshfield was the perfect host, at home in fishing boots and hunting jacket or in the formal dress he demanded for the dining room.

Webster confessed that he loved Marshfield because he had made it himself. He had also created the role of the "Farmer of Marshfield," a role which involved a good deal more than playing the ordinary New England farmer. He had created a great spectacle at Marshfield, and he presided over it with appropriate ceremony. There are hundreds of stories about him at Marshfield, some of them true, some of them apocryphal, but they all seem to reflect the kind of image he sought to project as the Farmer of Marshfield. Webster was depicted as a man who loved great beasts, who named his favorite ram Goliath, who upon reaching Marshfield after long absence would go straight to the barn and give each of his oxen an ear of corn, who insisted that his horses be buried standing upright with their shoes and halters on, who could pitch more hay in an hour than any hired hand and pull in more cod than any fisherman, who knew the secrets of the earth and was the first in the region to fertilize with kelp, who loved simple things like pigs and onion beds, but put an acre of his land into flowers and decorated his estate with peacocks from India and llamas from Peru.[6]

When the Famer of Marshfield stood beside the great lawyer, statesman, orator, and guardian of America's past, it seemed to many people that there was too much of Daniel Webster for one man. Whatever else he lost in the last decade of his life, Webster never lost his reputation as a giant almost too big for life. Granted that he played the part more naturally than lesser men, we must believe he also deliberately cultivated the image. Once, while being interviewed in the garden at Marshfield, Webster was asked about great men. "Whoever is a great man, viewed in the greatest number of lights," he replied, "must be regarded as the greatest of men."[7]

Webster had always been an attentive husband and father, and as he grew older he became more dependent on his family. Caroline proved to be a durable, affectionate companion and good stepmother for his children, and apart from its childlessness, there is no reason to believe that his second marriage was any less happy than his first. Unlike Grace Webster, Caroline was not awed by her famous husband. Having circulated in the best New York society since childhood, she was used to expensive dresses, elegant parties, and the company of famous people. Like Grace, however, she found it hard to keep up with her husband. A few years after her marriage, her father was writing to remind her of the "nervous" condition which ran in their family and to advise her to stay on a diet. "From the accounts you give me of the numerous parties you are attending," Herman LeRoy wrote, it "astonishes me that you continue as well as you are."[8]

Only a few of Caroline Webster's letters survive, and she was not the kind of person to give herself away in those. Unhappy at not having a child of her own, she tried unsuccessfully to adopt one of her brother's, but neither this disappointment nor any other kind of strong personal feeling shows up in her letters. Nevertheless, it is obvious that she had a mind of her own. In a footnote to a letter to Daniel she wrote, "Don't criticize my servants." When her husband refused to confide in her about their English itinerary, and then accepted a last-minute invitation for which she was unprepared, Caroline pouted but acquiesced. She was much firmer, on their return to this country, when it came to going to Washington with Webster for the long congressional sessions. Caroline was a good hostess, and her "tall, majestic figure" next to Webster was a familiar sight in Washington drawing-rooms, but she had begun to tire of Washington life and encouraged her husband to quit politics. In the spring of 1840 she stayed in New York with her father, planning to join Webster in Washington later. When she failed to appear as scheduled, he wrote a series of anxious inquiries, culminating in the following outburst on March 7.

You say not one word about coming here or not coming here, if you had wished to mortify me you could not have taken a better course. I care nothing about the things about which you write. *Are you coming here or are you not?*

Caroline LeRoy Webster

My Dear Wife what possesses you to act as you do? Why do you not tell me what you mean?

I am disappointed—ashamed—mortified—For Heavens sake, tell me what you mean. I say to everybody that I am looking for you every day—*This must be explained*

The frustration and exasperation revealed in this letter were probably intensified by the fact that Webster was then alone with the mortally ill Ray Thomas. The next day he wrote a more chastened, half-apologetic letter to Caroline, and when her letters to him finally arrived explaining that she chose to stay in New York until he returned to Boston, he gave in gracefully enough.[9]

Webster's ideas about marriage were predictably conservative. He believed that divorce laws had contributed to the fall of Rome and that the sanctity of the marriage bond had been a principal cause in the advancement of Christian nations. He was thus very sensitive to anything which might lead people to question the stability of his own marriage, and must have been distressed by the gossip about Caroline and himself which cropped up in the fall of 1841. According to Willie Mangum's New York correspondent, there was "a breach between the LeRoy family and Mr. W.—Mrs. W. has been in this city upwards of two months in her father's family, holding meanwhile no intercourse with her husband, whose quarters while here was at 'the Astor' and failing for the first time to accompany him to Marshfield— It is understood that Mrs. W. is about to separate from Mr. W. . . ." The cause of the trouble was said to be a provision in Herman LeRoy's will which left Caroline "A large slice of property secured upon her and in no case to revert to her husband."[10]

What Magnum said about Herman LeRoy's will was correct. The will called for Caroline's share of his estate to be invested by his executors, the income to be paid to her twice a year for the rest of her life, "to her separate use and on her own receipts for the same whether married or single." Mr. LeRoy had contributed substantially to keep Webster solvent during his lifetime, and he was obviously anxious to keep the family money out of Webster's hands after his death.

Webster may not have been pleased by this arrangement, but there is no evidence of displeasure in his correspondence. He and Caroline were separated for some time during the summer and fall of 1841, when his wife left Washington while their new house on Lafayette Square was being decorated. Newly installed as secretary of state, Webster stayed in the capital working furiously to solve the McLeod crisis and avert the breakup of Tyler's cabinet. He was in no mood to cope with a distracted wife, and when Caroline began to fret about where she should go after visiting her family in New York, he wrote:

What can I do?—I really feel embarrassed, & distressed.—It is impossible for me to leave Washington at present. Congress sits longer than was expected—we are in the midst of most important matters—& my leav'g here for some time to come, is out of all question. I am perplexed. Between your uneasiness where you are, & your indecision where to go, & the critical & harrassing state of th'gs here—I find noth'g to solace me.[11]

Webster's correspondence shows clearly that Caroline visited Julia in Boston in early September, and that Webster went to Marshfield by way of New York in early October and stayed there several weeks. Whether or not Caroline joined him at that time is difficult to say, but if their marriage was temporarily threatened, the danger passed. The Websters moved into their Washington mansion together and turned it into one of the most hospitable houses in the capital while Webster remained secretary of state.[12]

After Webster resigned as secretary, he disposed of the expensive Lafayette Square house, and when he returned to the Senate in 1846 he and Caroline moved into a modest furnished house "about as big as two pigeon boxes." Caroline continued to divide her time between Washington, New York, and Massachusetts. When they were separated Webster wrote to her regularly, and the tone of his letters, his solicitude for her health, and his easy way of writing to her about political matters as well as domestic details reflect the kind of comfortable, mutually supportive, and affectionate relationship which helped to sustain him for the rest of his life.[13]

At various times both Grace and Caroline Webster felt the strain of being married to a great man. Without exceptional ability or ambition, they were always willing to put domestic fulfillment over public duty. Webster's children felt the same pressure in different ways, but it was Fletcher, his oldest son, who felt it the most.

When Fletcher was serving in the Massachusetts legislature, he was once heard to say that a person "could but come to little unless he was of good size and appearance." His photograph, taken in 1861, shows a doleful, bearded man of average size with his officer's cap pushed forward and cocked over one eye in a vain attempt at dramatic effect. He looked like any other Union officer. That was Fletcher's trouble. He was not much different from anyone else—except in being Daniel Webster's son.[14]

When Daniel Fletcher Webster was twelve, he wrote to his father saying, "I hope that I shall always be a good boy and realize your wishes, and when you are old I shall be a comfort to you in your old age." Although he named his first son after himself, Webster always called him Fletcher, and there is no reason to believe that he consciously put him under special pressure. The father expressed his most "affectionate anxiety" upon the boy's progress, did not insist that he be top scholar at the Boston Latin School, and congratulated him for the reports of "respectable progress" in his class. Nevertheless Fletcher labored under a heavy load as he prepared for Harvard, a condition which persisted throughout his college years. He wrote to his father about problems with his eyes and his difficulty in concentrating, but his real problem was in trying to live up to the Webster image.

> I hope that there is more in me than has yet appeared, for I have done nothing heretofore, and should be very sorry to think that a son of yours was wholly good for nothing; but I fear that people think there is more in me than there really is.

Such gratuitous self-deprecation must have seemed incredible to Webster, but when he suggested that the solution lay in greater effort, Fletcher emphatically disagreed. "It is on my word impossible for me to become first scholar," he wrote. "The fact is that we have some very capable men in the class, much older than I, and with minds much more matured. . . . I am at a loss to know where you had the idea I had neglected anything." Fletcher Webster's self-consciousness at Harvard was acute, and it was not just academic attainment that worried him. "If there should be a rebellion and it should extend to our class I should take out my name and go into town until I had orders from you," he told his father. "I should not like to be the most conspicuous leader or the most conspicuous 'holder back' in the class; for one would ruin me with the Government, and the other in the opinion of my fellow students."[15]

Webster approved of Fletcher's conservative instincts and did what he could to buoy up his confidence. "It gives me great delight to hear that you have learned how to sit still & read a book. If you have really accomplished that, you have certainly made your future." He advised Fletcher to focus his studies on law and politics, as he himself had done, but to save time for liberal knowledge which could be used later if only for effect—"an honest quackery" which he had practiced himself "and sometimes with success."[16]

After Fletcher was admitted to the bar, he married the daughter of Stephen White, a successful Massachusetts merchant and old friend of the family, and started out on his own by looking after his father's farms and land investments in the West. The rugged, outdoor life that he found in Illinois, Michigan, and Wisconsin appealed to him, and he boasted to his father in the summer of 1836 that he could "drink whiskey of a morning, steer across the prairie by a compass, follow an Indian trail in the woods & sleep on the floor of a log cabin with my saddle as a pillow." He opened a law office in Peru, Illinois, and installed his wife on his father's farm in the nearby village of Salisbury, where their first two children were born. Webster had purchased his Illinois land near the projected site of a canal, with the expectation that the canal would quickly build up the local population and raise land values. The panics during Van Buren's administration halted work on the canal and put a damper on the extravagant aspirations of both Daniel and his son. Fletcher had originally "resolved not to go East until I go there *rich* & can go as I please." By early 1840 he was complaining about his unpromising law practice and suggesting that his father find him a place in New York or Washington "which would give me a start at once & which you might by your countenance and influence make a desirable one to the other party." Meanwhile, although he had repeatedly borrowed from his father, his family was without money, and the trip back home "of such length and at such expense terrifies us."[17]

When Harrison was elected, Webster took Fletcher to Washington with him as chief clerk in the Department of State. It was Fletcher Webster who was sent to Virginia to inform John Tyler that he had succeeded to the presidency, and when his father vacationed at Marshfield, Fletcher stayed behind as acting secretary of state. Before quitting the cabinet, Webster saw to it that his son was made secretary to the China trade mission under Caleb Cushing. The trip took him around the world and resulted in a commercial treaty favorable to American interests, but did little to expand Fletcher's intellectual and cultural horizons. "I look upon Chinese language and literature as beyond contempt," he wrote to his father. When the commission was stalled in Macao waiting to receive emissaries from the government in Peking, he said, "They still try to be *Celestial* and I doubt if anything short of a complete thrashing can bring them to their senses."[18]

Despite his advantages and experience, Fletcher never attained the self-assurance that he sought. He was status conscious and complained when his widowed father-in-law married the widow of a steamboat captain. As a son, however, he served his father well and lived up to his promise to be a help to him in his old age. The dominant tone in all the letters between Daniel and Fletcher is one of mutual love and respect. The older he became, the more Daniel Webster relied on his oldest son.[19]

Although Webster relied the most on Fletcher, he gave his heart to his younger son, Edward, and to his daughter, Julia. Only nine years old when his mother died, "Neddy" was the pet of the Webster family, and, like most pets, he was spoiled. After Grace Webster died, Daniel asked his children to write him every day in Washington, and he carefully preserved the childish scrawls of his youngest son communicating important messages about his new sled and his progress in school. "We find it a pretty hard task to write to you every day," the boy wrote on one occasion, and then as a happy afterthought, "We all get on very well in freanch." Unlike Fletcher, who seems to have inherited his mother's sense of inadequacy, Edward was a free spirit. On one occasion, when he was at the Boston Latin School, Caroline Webster reported to her husband that the boy had received "23 marks for misdemeanors." Webster sent Edward to Exeter in Fletcher's charge with specific instructions to help him get started on the right foot. He was to stress "the importance of exact and steady habits" and the need for "personal cleanliness." He would also give Edward some pocket money, make arrangements for a regular allowance, and stay with him a few days until he became adjusted to his new environment. Webster obviously did not want Edward to be as traumatized by Exeter as he had been almost half a century earlier.[20]

From Exeter, Edward went on to Dartmouth. If he felt overwhelmed at the prospect of trying to follow in his famous father's footsteps, he did not admit it. It was Daniel who was worried. From the beginning, Edward did not write home enough, and the letters which did come were disconcerting. "I am sorry to hear you were wounded by a sword," the puzzled father wrote, "but what had you to do with swords? You would have been safe from this accident, I presume, if you had been about your proper business. . . . You are to have nothing to do with horses, dogs or guns." When Edward wrote asking for money, his father marked it up and sent it back to him, saying, "There are misspellings; there is no totally correct punctuation; there are instances in which sentences, after periods, are begun with small letters; and words which should be begun with large letters are begun with small ones. Write me immediately a more careful & a better letter."[21]

Webster's apprehensions about his youngest son were not entirely without cause. In September, 1838, Edward wrote a long, agonized letter to his father explaining that he owed $225. The debts were contracted during his freshman year and he had been unable to pay them out of his regular allowance. Ignoring his father's advice, he had allowed himself "to be led astray by silly boys and willy [sic] storekeepers," and now, "like the Prodigal son of old," he asked his father's forgiveness. The letter stunned Webster. Edward had repeatedly told him that he owed nothing that could not be taken care of with his allowance. Was his son turning into a gambler, a drunkard—or worse? He waited a few days, and then dispatched a stern letter demanding the truth. "I would not expose you to public reproach, nor cast you off, for slight cause; but with all my affection, I will not excuse misconduct, and especially, I will not put up with any degree or particle of misrepresentation, or concealment of the truth." Edward responded by saying that he had never gambled "a cent in my life." He had borrowed most of the money from upperclassmen and spent it on "nuts & raisins, crockery, cigars, candy, pantaloons, chip men, backgammon boards, knifes [sic] and some *wine* a very little of which I can say with a clear conscience I drank myself, riding on horseback and other ways of pleasure."[22]

What went on in Webster's head when he received this letter? Did he remember the bills he had run up himself at Lang's store in Hanover? Did he consider the possibility that Edward, for all his outward aplomb, was terrified by the prospect of competing against the Webster legend and sought to buy the esteem of his fellow students? Was he haunted, in some dark, half-conscious corner of his mind, by the fear that his own weaknesses were being repeated in his son? Whatever the confusion of emotions, Webster chose to trust him. Although hard put to find cash himself, he sent Edward the money "to clear off your embarrassments—& to give you a fair opportunity to retrieve whatever may have been amiss & to resume your studies"—and said no more about the matter.[23]

For all his indiscretions Edward remained the family favorite. Webster brought him to England for Julia's wedding, sent him to study in Switzerland and from there to live for a while with Edward Everett and his family in Florence. Upon his return to the United States he studied law and, like his older brother, cashed in on Harrison's election by being named secretary to the commission to establish the northeast boundary line. Always the most adventurous of Webster's children, he resigned this commission soon after the Mexican War broke out to become a captain with the First Massachusetts Volunteers. The rest of the Webster family was unhappy with Edward's decision and Daniel, especially, was fearful of what the Mexican climate might do to his son. At the same time, he was ambitious for both Fletcher and Edward and troubled that their careers were not developing more rapidly. Perhaps the war would give Edward an opportunity to get his name before the public. Soon Webster was writing to commanders in the field, urging a major assignment where his son could "make useful acquaintances" and suggesting "that his advancement would not be disagreeable."[24]

Of all Webster's children, his daughter Julia was the most sensitive and the most beloved. A dark-haired beauty who looked like her father, Julia inherited the Puritan conscience of her mother. Always conscious of family responsibilities, she was quick to rebuke her brother for not writing and treating the rest of the family "like a parcel of strangers." "Of all the defects of character," she told Edward, "I think the want of gratitude & affection is the greatest." Because she was his only surviving daughter and reminded him of his first wife, Julia enjoyed a particularly intimate relationship with her father, and was not afraid to speak her mind to him. Although a woman of society, married into the wealthy Appleton family, Julia retained her mother's sense of proportion, disapproved of her father's tendency to live beyond his means, and once confided to her diary that she was the only one in the family with "the least grain of prudence." More than anyone else close to him Julia seems to have understood the perils which Webster faced by remaining in politics. "Surely you have done enough for your country," she wrote at the end of the campaign of 1840, "to be considered the best and noblest among the noble sons of America. Has not the fame of your greatness, your goodness, extended to the uttermost parts of the earth? It can not be increased; and do not, dearest father, wear yourself out for the good of a country ungrateful at best. What is the whole country to your family when weighed in the balance with one hour of sickness or anxiety which it causes you? I am no great patriot: I do not love Rome better than Caesar; the advancement of party better than my own dear father. . . . Don't you think you would be happy to live at home once more with your old friends? Do come back to us dear father, and do not be persuaded to stay in Washington by persons who may not be altogether disinterested in their motives. . . . I am not naturally suspicious, but I do distrust some of your friends. I hope I am wrong."[25]

Although he did not follow Julia's advice, Webster must have been moved by her letter, and despite the distractions of political life he was never closer to his wife and children than during the last ten years of his life. As with other solidly based families it was not just common joy but common sorrow that bound the Websters together. When his granddaughter Grace lay dying in Boston during Fletcher's long absence in the Orient, Webster wrote consolingly to his distraught daughter-in-law "to unite our tears with yours and give you what consolation we might." Death had become increasingly familiar to him. Not just the death of parents, brothers, sisters, wife, and friends—but the death of children—and the worst was yet to come. On February 23, 1848, Webster paid his last respects to John Quincy Adams, who lay senseless and at the point of death where he had fallen in the House of Representatives. Later the same day he heard from the War Department that Edward had died in Mexico. He sent the mournful news on to his "Dear and Only Son" Fletcher, who communicated it to the rest of the family. Julia would not be consoled. "Oh, my Father," she wrote, "Sam has just told me that My dear brother is lost to us forever. I do not realize it, yet it seems a troubled dream! & yet when Edward left us for that accursed land, I felt I had looked my last upon him. . . . He went forth to a wicked and cruel war, & there he has died; like many before him; without one friend to smooth his dying pillow. Oh that I had been with him! . . . I feel nothing but that my brother in the honor of his youth was a useless sacrifice—to what?— ambition, vain-glory—? May God in his mercy, sanctify this great affliction to us all."[26]

Weighted down by his own grief, Webster was still alarmed by the rebellious tone in his daughter's letter and sought to reconcile her to the mysterious ways of Providence. Beneath their solemn dialogue over the meaning of death was the unstated awareness that her time had also come. Along with Grace Webster's conscience and devotion to her family Julia had inherited a fatal tendency toward consumption. She died at the end of April and was buried in Boston on the first of May, the same day that Edward's coffin arrived from Mexico.

After the funeral Webster went to Marshfield where he planted two weeping willow trees which he called "Brother and Sister." He was sixty-eight years old, tired, heartsick, and terribly aware of his own fragile mortality. Politics had never seemed more distant or more trivial. Yet the planting of the trees was symbolic. Surrounded by death, he would still believe in life.[27]

17

WEBSTER AND THE
"CONSCIENCE WHIGS"

Late in the winter of 1848, a group of admiring young Whigs visited Webster in Boston. They had come to be instructed and inspired, to be reassured that the leadership of their party would not fall into the hands of Zachary Taylor, the victorious general of the Mexican War, who was being touted for the presidency with the same frenzy that had accompanied the Harrison boom eight years earlier. At first they were let down. Glum and noncommitive, Webster muttered that "the day for eminent men seems to have gone by." Of course, the young Whigs protested, and as the protests mounted, he began to thaw out, and finally gave them what they wanted—a rousing political speech in which he promised never to support "a swearing, fighting, frontier colonel" as a Whig candidate for president.

Daniel Webster was proud of his own eminence in public life, but during the six years between 1844 and 1850 his determination to continue in politics wavered many times. The generation of distinguished men who had helped to shape his own career—men like Story, Mason, Clay, Calhoun, and Adams—was dying off while honor and power were passing into the hands of smaller men. "It mortifies my pride of country," Webster had said after Polk's victory, "to see how the great affair of the President may be disposed off." Although not a melancholy man by temperament, he felt the sense of isolation that is the price old men pay for their longevity in a rapidly changing society—a sense cruelly intensifed by the death of two of his children in the winter and spring of 1848. The serenity of Marshfield beckoned as never before, but he stayed on in Washington to devote his final years in the Senate

224

to those causes on which his eminence rested—the protection of New England and the preservation of the Union. As these two issues became increasingly involved with slavery the nation might yet recognize the need for a guardian in the White House. If the grand assignment came, Webster would be ready.[1]

When Webster took his seat in the Senate in March, 1845, he must have felt that his political career had slipped back ten years. Jackson was gone in person but a belligerent younger disciple was in firm control of the White House and the Congress. The prospects for a sensible tariff or fiscal policy were dim, and the truculent posture of Polk toward England over Oregon threatened to undo the great work of conciliation which Webster had fashioned so patiently with Ashburton. Moreover, in 1845 unlike 1835, the dreary prospects in Washington were not brightened by the knowledge that he had the unanimous support of his party at home. The other Massachusetts senator, Isaac Bates, a steady, independent-minded Whig from Northampton, died late in March, and the legislature chose John Davis, a former Whig governor who, according to the gloating Abbot Lawrence, had not been on speaking terms with Webster for three years.[2]

Despite the scars of battle and all the muffled grumbling among former admirers, Webster was still the most powerful single man in New England and one of the three or four most famous Americans in the world. What political future was left to him at the age of sixty-four would depend on his ability to continue to represent the conscience and the interests of Massachusetts in a way that would keep alive his chances for the presidency. Heretofore, the Whigs had been able to express the conscience of the state with strong union and moderate anti-slavery sentiments which were perfectly consistent with their interest in a protective tariff. Webster's ability to hold conscience and interest together had been tested by the Texas issue during the recent campaign, and he had reason to feel that he managed the matter with some success. There was no mistaking where he stood on Texas. He was against annexation because it meant the extension of slavery. True American sentiment and the conscience of the civilized world opposed slavery; to abolish it "by the efforts of philanthropy and true policy acting in cooperation with each other" would represent "a new era in the history of human liberty." When Clay had temporized on the Texas issue in the famous "Alabama letters," Webster, along with most of the other northern Whig leaders, was furious. For a short while afterward he omitted any mention of Texas in his political speeches, but soon returned to the theme again as vigorously as ever. When Clay lost, Webster attributed a good part of his defeat to vacillation over Texas.[3]

Even in Massachusetts, Texas was a problem. The dispute over annexation had widened the generation gap within Massachusetts Whiggery far enough to allow a group of "Young Whigs" to emerge and begin acting as a bloc. The Young Whigs were determined to put anti-slavery principles above ordinary party interest. They were led by experienced local Whig politicians like the Salem businessman, Stephen Phillips, and the Worcester judge, Charles Allen, and by talented political newcomers like Charles Francis Adams and Charles Sumner. Adams, the former president's son, was not only a famous name, but a hard-hitting political writer who would soon turn the *Boston Whig* into a Young Whig mouthpiece. And the handsome Sumner, a close friend of the abolitionist orator Wendell Phillips, but still a welcome ornament in the most elite Beacon Hill drawing rooms, had the kind of mind and bearing that reminded people of Webster himself.

Although he emerged from the election as the leader of the anti-Texas crusade in Massachusetts, Webster soon found this position to be a mixed blessing. He was gratified to find himself the favorite of Young Whigs like Stephen Phillips and Charles Allen, who clearly preferred his leadership to that of Lawrence, and after the election, when it appeared likely that Congress would take Texas into the Union by joint resolution, he supported their plan for an anti-Texas convention in Faneuil Hall. On the other hand, he saw no future on splitting the party over Texas and during the campaign he had repeatedly warned against the danger of third-party actions. Thus when the Lawrence Whigs refused to support the meeting and his New York supporters warned that continued agitation over Texas might cement an alliance between northern and southern Democrats, Webster found it convenient to be out of town on legal business when the meeting took place. After having dictated the first part of the statement devoted solely to the constitutional issue of annexation, he left the rest of it—the tough anti-slavery part—to his younger friends.[4]

The Faneuil Hall meeting on Texas took place in January, but by the time Webster had taken his place in the Senate in March, annexation had become a fact. He took the defeat philosophically and urged his supporters to concentrate their efforts on causes where they might still be effective, like the tariff. For the rest of the spring and the following summer, he said nothing about Texas. At the annual Whig convention in Boston that fall, he was pointedly severe in blaming the recent Whig defeat on divisions within the party. Putting the abolitionist Liberty party on the same moral plane with the anti-immigrant Native American party, Webster argued that each of the minor parties had hurt its cause by deserting the Whigs. He even went so far as to blame annexation on the political abolitionists who, by withholding votes from Clay, had in effect given votes to Polk.

I think it must stand in the pages of history as the recorded judgment of mankind, that those among us who have asserted themselves to be in a peculiar and marked degree, friends of universal liberty, have by their own deliberate act, fastened the chains of slavery on a great portion of the black race. It is to me the most mournful and most awful reflection

A month later, at the final reading of the bill for Texas statehood, Webster stood in the Senate and made his final judgment on annexation.

I agree with the unanimous opinion of the legislature of Massachusetts; I agree with the great mass of her people; I reaffirm what I have said and written during the last eight years, at various times, against this annexation. I here record my own dissent and opposition: and I here express and place on record, also, the dissent and protest of the State of Massachusetts.

The message should have been clear to Whigs, young and old, North and South—Webster would never support the extension of slavery; neither would he encourage his party to break up over the issue.[5]

Although Mexico had terminated diplomatic relations with the United States after the annexation with Texas, the real threat to peace in the summer and fall of 1845 seemed to come from problems connected with the northwest border. The Democrats had campaigned on a platform which claimed all of Oregon (occupied jointly by British and American settlers since the convention of 1818) for America, a claim which Polk reiterated in his message to Congress in December and which many congressmen and senators were prepared to support by any means including war.

We know now that Polk never envisaged war with England. His belligerent demands were designed to draw concessions from a powerful rival rather than to provoke hostilities. Unlike many other Whigs, Webster seems to have understood this from the start. He knew from personal experience that the disingenuous approach was often a necessary part of diplomacy. He was distressed, however, to hear how easily the representatives of the new western states could talk about war "as a pleasant excitement or recreation," and he hoped that the interest in the South in selling cotton abroad and the interest of the North in maintaining trade would force sanity in the government. Before returning to Washington for the winter session of Congress, he gave a speech in Faneuil Hall condemning the recklessness of American extremists and expressing the hope that Oregon would eventually become an independent nation.[6]

Webster's role in the congressional debates over Oregon in February and March of 1846 led directly to the Ingersoll investigation which occupied most of his energy until June. Although officially exonerated, he emerged from that contest badly bruised and needed to identify himself with some new positive achievement in the public mind. It would have been a great thing for him, therefore, to have managed the defeat of the administration's tariff bill late that summer. Such a victory, on an issue so vital to Whig principles and to the interests of his own constituents, would have gone far to demonstrate his dominant position in the party. But it was not to be. The bill, which abolished specific duties and thus represented an almost complete abandonment of the protective principle, passed the House early in July and moved on to the Senate where Webster did everything he could to defeat it. He gave an interminable lecture on the blessings of protection in the Senate. He buttonholed colleagues in the corridors. He wrote editorials for the *National Intelligencer*. Finally, he contrived an amendment to the House bill which preserved specific duties at reduced rates and urged his colleagues to vote for the compromise. If it passed the Senate and the House they would have a better protective bill than ever before. If it passed the Senate and was killed in the House, the Protective Tariff of 1842 would remain in effect. He failed to get the necessary support for his amendment, and on July 28, the original bill passed the Senate by the margin of a single vote. Webster attributed his defeat to the fact that the Whigs were more interested in keeping the tariff alive as a political issue for the future than in supporting a reasonable and safe settlement with an administration label on it. That was a partial explanation at best. The truth was that even on matters of Whig orthodoxy, Webster could no longer automatically expect to lead his party in Congress.[7]

The reason he had been so eager to rally the Whigs behind him on the tariff was that, in theory at least, it offered an opportunity for him to emerge a clear-cut political winner. The other big issues which he confronted did not. His dogged resistance to the war hawks over Oregon had helped in the peaceful settlement of that dispute (by treaty on June 15), but Polk would get the credit for that, while Webster was left to cope with the squalid aftermath of the Ingersoll affair. Meanwhile, Polk had declared war on Mexico and thus forced the issue which would ultimately be fatal to Webster's political future.

The real causes of the war with Mexico went back to American expansionism and the annexation of Texas. The immediate cause was the outbreak of fighting between Mexican and American troops in disputed territory along the Rio Grande River. Polk claimed that Mexico had shed American blood on American soil and the Congress overwhelmingly supported his call for war. One of the two senators voting against war was John Davis of Massachusetts. Webster was not recorded, since he was in Boston attending Edward Everett's inauguration as president of Harvard. Would Webster have joined his colleague in a protest vote against the war? The question is hard to answer. Opposition to the war was intense in Massachusetts, where it was viewed as one more attempt to add slavery territory to the Union. On the other hand, Webster had never been allowed to forget the mistake he made in opposing the War of 1812. Although there is no reason to believe that he deliberately ducked the war vote on Mexico, he must have been relieved at not having to decide whether to line up in splendid isolation beside Davis or not. Certainly his first reactions to the war were cautious. On May 20, while still under investigation by the House committee, Webster had advised Fletcher to recommend "guarded" resolutions to an anti-war protest meeting in Boston. The war should be condemned as an instrument to get new territory but supported as a measure of national defense. And in the closing days of the congressional session in August, throughout a raging debate over the propriety of the war, and in the face of David Wilmot's proposal to prohibit slavery in territory acquired from Mexico, a proposal identical with own sentiments, Webster kept silent. Whatever misgivings his own constituents may have had about the war, he knew that most Americans were cheering for it in the South and West. It would be hard enough to deal with the war issue when he got back home. Clearly, prudence was the best policy in Washington at the moment.

But it was not easy to stay cool in the face of so many frustrations and disappointments. The president, who had sneaked into the White House when the people weren't looking, was besting him at every turn. Webster had managed to help Polk get what he wanted in Oregon while hurting himself. He had lost on the tariff, been unable to prevent the re-establishment of a subtreasury system (a victory for Van Buren in absentia), and had looked on in helpless fury while Polk vetoed a major bill for internal improvements. The final indignity came two days before adjournment on August 8. Twelve years earlier, Webster had failed to get the government to assume responsibility for claims of American merchants against France in the 1790s. He was still trying and had helped push a five-million-dollar indemnity bill through the Senate which he hoped would bolster his son's faltering law practice. "Beyond all expectation, the Bill for the Old French claims will probably pass the House today," he wrote to Fletcher on August 4. "Give notice, immediately that you propose to act as agent for claimants. . . . I will help you do the business—&so you may say—though not publicly—stir quick." The bill passed, and on the evening of August 8, Polk carried it back to Congress with his veto. As the president sat sedately in an anteroom to the legislative chambers, the first session of the Twenty-ninth Congress roared on to a tumultuous climax. "Several members," Polk noted in his diary, "were much excited by drink. Among other I was informed that Senators Webster and Barrow were quite drunk."[8]

As Webster set off for New England in the late summer of 1846, he knew that his immediate sense of frustration would soon be eased by the amenities at Marshfield. The sound and sight of the sea, the taste of a good chowder, an exhilarating tramp through his own carefully tended fields would set him right again; to commune with his own cattle, poultry, swine, and sheep would be infinitely more satisfying than to wrangle with stubborn, wrongheaded congressmen. Marshfield would be good therapy; it always was. But Webster needed more than therapy to remain a significant political force nationally and at home. His basic political strategy, which he felt was consistent with principle and self-interest, had been worked out during his earlier stay in Boston and during the congressional session. It was simply to espouse traditional Whig principles—to fight for a sound tariff and fiscal and internal improvement policy and to oppose both reckless territorial expansion and the extension of slavery. The secret was to keep a proper balance—not to be stampeded by anti-war or anti-slavery sentiment into driving away the southern Whigs or splitting the Whigs at home.

Webster provided a stunning example of what he meant by political balance at the Whig convention in Faneuil Hall on September 23. The Young Whigs were determined to force a confrontation at any cost, and what was customarily a ritualistic exercise in the expression of consensus turned into a moralistic brawl. Charles Sumner commandeered the platform from Robert Winthrop, demanded that the party raise its banner to the constitutional abolition of slavery, and asked Webster to lead the Whigs under that banner. Winthrop, already badly mauled by a series of newspaper attacks from Sumner because of his congressional vote to support the war, tried to divert the delegates by appealing to the traditional Whig pieties of tariff and fiscal policy, but he could not prevent the introduction of a resolution requiring Whig candidates to openly support abolition by "all Constitutional measures." At this point, Webster, who had purposely arrived late, walked into the hall with Abbot Lawrence on his arm. In the noise and confusion of the ensuing ovation, the strong anti-slavery resolution was voted down and Webster came to the platform. He had already made one statement by appearing with Lawrence and he added little to this in his formal remarks. There were some issues of the day in which gentlemen of mutual respect would differ, he said, but he preferred to inhale the "ordor of liberty" which Whig meetings always exuded, and to put his faith in the "intelligent, patriotic, *united* Whig party of the United States." No one but Daniel Webster could have proclaimed the "general unanimity" of the Whigs that day and gotten away with it. By slipping Abbot Lawrence's arm into his own he had helped to tip the balance of power against the Young Whigs without appearing to take up arms against them.[9]

Webster wanted the middle ground for himself. He would not openly oppose the Young Whigs; neither would he become their standard bearer. If there were those so impatient with old-fashioned Whiggery as to think of straying from the party, let them remember how the Liberty party had helped put Polk in the White House and bring on war with Mexico. Webster made this point in a second Faneuil Hall appearance on November 6, at which time he also mildly rebuked the Young Whigs for their attacks on Winthrop.[10]

Believing that his own position helped produce Whig gains in the congressional and state elections in the fall of 1846, Webster advised Thurlow Weed that "prudence, moderation and discretion" were the keys to a brighter political future. By early December, he had begun to sound like a presidential candidate again. He gave a long political speech in Philadelphia in which he compared Polk unfavorably with Jackson and Van Buren. It was pretty much a standard performance in the old-fashioned Whig manner, loaded with detail on tariffs and internal improvements, with a few tearful references to the widows and orphans (to say nothing to Webster's creditors) who would suffer because of the French claims bill veto. Circumspect about the war, he was careful to separate his criticism of Polk's unconstitutional actions from the war itself. He could find "no sympathy" with a military despotism like Mexico, and likened the gallantry of American soldiers at Monterey to the courage of the patriots of Bunker Hill.[11]

After Congress reconvened in December, 1846, Webster was forced to take a more explicit position on the war. The issue was drawn over the administration's Three Million bill, which provided funds for military support and the acquisition of Mexican territory, and the Wilmot Proviso, which amended that bill by prohibiting slavery from any territory acquired through the war. In the first three months of 1847 nine northern states endorsed the proviso and directed their senators to support it. Calhoun led the southern response by introducing resolutions into the Senate specifying that territories were held jointly by the states and that any slaveholder had a right to emigrate to any territory with slaves.

Webster wanted to prevent the creation of more slave states without unnecessarily offending the South. The only way to do that was to get the Congress to declare its intent to acquire no new territory through the war, and he supported such an amendment. When it failed, he supported the Wilmot Proviso, which also failed. Finally he was forced to vote with the Whig minority against the Three Million bill itself. His final remarks after this dreary succession of defeats were filled with foreboding. If new territories were insisted upon, he could see nothing ahead but "contention, strife and agitation." The nation appeared "to be rushing upon perils headlong, and with our eyes wide open." But in the end, he put his faith "in Providence, and in that good sense and patriotism of the people, which will yet, I hope, be awakened before it is too late."[12]

Webster had lost too many battles to be panicked by temporary defeat, and he rejected the politics of extremism on principle. Thus in explaining to Fletcher the limits to which opponents of the war were entitled to go, he said,

We should oppose the policy and counsels which prevaila in the Country, instead of attempting to resist that state of things, and that state of *law* and of duty, which those counsels have produced. . . . And snarling and grumbling, and all attempts to sever oneself from what the country has decided upon, are but the effusions of narrow feelings.

He rejected extremism on practical grounds also. It simply was not a winning game. Neither Calhoun in the South nor the anti-slavery party in the

North could ever build a national constituency. To call for immediate abolition or the unlimited extension of slavery was not in the common interest. Peace, prosperity, and unity were in the common interest and might still carry him to the presidency. This hope at least was still alive as Webster set out for the South at the end of April, 1847.[13]

His original plan was to travel through the coastal states to Savannah and to return by way of New Orleans and the Mississippi River. He had several reasons for wanting to make the trip, not the least of which was that he had never seen that part of the country which had been so painfully important to his career. He enjoyed playing the role of the Great Man on tour and looked forward to savoring southern hospitality. And, of course, he wanted to know how he stood politically in the South.

In addition to Webster, the party included his wife, two servants, and Josephine Seaton, daughter of one of the editors of the *National Intelligencer*. Passing from Washington to Richmond and then south through Raleigh and Wilmington, North Carolina, Webster refrained from formal speech making. He was content to let his reputation as defender of the Constitution and distinguished statesman speak for him. In South Carolina, he went to great lengths to be gracious. "Where in this continent," he said in Charleston, "is there a higher freedom of social enjoyment, or a more ready extension of the relations of private friendship, than in this city and state?" The abolitionists at home would groan when they read this, but as Webster pointed out in a letter to his son, "The people are all kind and civil, and I get along with the nullifiers, without making any sharp points." In South Carolina, he was less interested in being known as the senator of an anti-slavery state than as the former secretary of state who "paid just regard to the protection of Southern interests."[14]

Webster made his most significant speech in Savannah where he spoke from a platform at the base of the Green and Pulaski Monument. The setting evoked memories of an earlier day when all states had united in a great common cause and provided a good sounding board for his appeal to a higher loyalty which might once again unite Americans. "Others may value this union of confederated states as a convenience or arrangement or compromise of interests," Webster said, "but I desire to see an attachment to the Union existing among the people, not as a deduction of political economy, nor as a result of philosophical reasoning, but cherished as a heartfelt sentiment." This was something more than an appeal to traditional Whiggery, which had always emphasized the commonality of sectional interests. It was an echo of the famous peroration to the Hayne debate, when Webster had dreamed that patriotic sentiment might overwhelm local interests and sweep him into the White House. It had not happened then and it would not happen now. Webster knew as much, himself, for he concluded his speech by specifically pledging himself to work for "the completion of a southwestern railroad from Savannah to Pensacola."[15]

A few days after the Savannah speech, the party sailed directly to New York. The change in plans which prevented them from reaching New Orleans was caused in part by Webster's poor health. Another reason was that he had already accomplished the major goal of his trip. He had discovered that although southern Whigs would turn out in great numbers to listen to him, they were planning to vote for someone else. While Webster was making his dignified procession through the coastal states, the reputation of Zachary Taylor was sweeping across the nation "like a gigantic tidal wave out of the Gulf of Mexico." In the South, newspapers of both parties were coming out for Taylor in wholesale numbers and by midsummer he would have nominations from state conventions in Maryland and Georgia. His appeal was easy enough to explain. He had become a national hero after the Battle of Buena Vista, he had no embarrassing political record, and he was a Mississippi slaveholder. The *New Orleans Bee* underlined the importance of the last point by saying, "When it is considered that both the great parties of the North court the anti-slavery faction; that both are opposed to the extension of slavery . . . the importance of placing at the head of the Govt one who from birth, association and conviction, is identified with the South and will uphold her rights and guard her from oppression cannot fail to strike every candid mind." "Old Zach" was a godsend to the Southern Whigs. Against such heaven-sent competition Webster could only offer thirty years of distinguished public service and a tarnished Godlike image. It was not nearly enough.[16]

Webster's southern venture in the spring of 1847 not only tells us why he could not build a strong political base there; it also suggests why he would encounter increasing difficulties at home. As a traveler, he was an extraordinarily careful observer, and as he moved through the South, he sent meticulous reports of his observations of southern life and agriculture to friends in Massachusetts. He discussed how the trees were notched to start the turpentine making process in North Carolina, described the rice fields outside Charleston as "a beautiful soft, light green, like the color of a Gosling's wing," and explained how cotton seed was "sown in rows of drills, three feet apart, in common light lands, and four or four and a half in land of richer quality." He wrote about the topography of the piedmont and alligator swamps on the coast and how young cotton plants looked like beans in the color and shape of their leaves. All this and more he recorded in detail. But it is what he failed to record that is most significant. Although he traveled through some of the blackest country in America and visited some of the biggest plantations, Webster never used the word slavery. He noticed that the huts in the "settlement" or "negro quarter" of a plantation varied from hovels to "decent" houses "according to the ability or pleasure of the proprietor," and he devoted a few sentences to describing how the slaves picked cotton. His characteristic style was objective and dispassionate. "In general, the proportion of labor to land, is one hand to six or seven acres, and one mule to three hands." It was as if Webster put turpentine, cotton, and slave labor all on the same moral level. He did not, of course, but it is significant that at no time during his trip or thereafter did he say anything more about slavery. It was almost as if he had been studying the process of southern agriculture without seeing the peculiar labor system that made it work. One could argue that he was afraid his letters would get into unfriendly hands and was properly discreet or that he had seen enough of slavery in Washington so that it seemed too familiar to remark about in South Carolina. All this may be true, but it is also true that in 1847, for Webster to attempt to walk with equanimity through the cotton fields in South Carolina while still claiming the united loyalty of Massachusetts Whigs had become impossible. He could as easily have tried to walk on water.[17]

Back home again at Marshfield, where his reputation and wisdom were still uncontested, Webster contemplated the future. The alternatives before him were singularly unpromising. He was too poor and too ambitious, even at sixty-five, to retire; he had too much of a sense of his own worth to jump on the Taylor bandwagon; and it was morally impossible for him to put the slavery cause above the value of union. The latter point is crucial to our understanding of him during the grim months ahead. Ever since the 1820s he had played a symbolic role as guardian of the Union, defender of the Constitution. Now the symbol and the man had fused. Daniel Webster had become the guardian. Abolitionism was no more plausible an alternative for him than it would have been for Garrison to shoulder a rifle and march off to Mexico. If we are to judge Webster fairly during this period, it must be within the narrow limitations of his situation. The view from Marshfield in 1847 was not expansive. It was a soothing experience for Webster to tramp across his own elegant fields and to mingle with the sleek, fat livestock in which he took such pride, Marshfield would restore his vigor but it could not provide him with a grand new strategy for the future. What future there was would be determined by the past.

Ever since 1840, Webster had been fighting to maintain his eminence in Massachusetts as well as in Washington. The next phase in that struggle took place at the state Whig convention in Springfield on September 29, 1847. The Whigs were divided between the Webster men, who took their orders from trusted lieutenants like Everett, Winthrop, and Choate; the Lawrence men, who wanted to divide the spoils of victory with Zachary Taylor; and the Young Whigs, who sought to replace the tradtional priorities of the party with "conscience" by making an explicit, uncompromising commitment to the anti-slavery position as enunciated in the Wilmot Proviso. The one thing the Lawrence and conscience factions had in common was an interest in blocking Webster's nomination by the convention. A resolution declaring it inexpedient for the convention to make any presidential nomination failed by a mere ten votes, and Webster gave the keynote address while the nominating committee was still in session. According to the later recollection of the conscience Whigs, this was the speech in which Webster emphasized his anti-slavery convictions in stronger and stronger language the longer the nominating committee remained out of the hall. It was this situation, according to the Young Whigs, that made him claim the Wilmot Proviso as his own "thunder." The story is consistent with the general image that the abolitionists sought to convey of Webster, an image of the opportunistic politician living off the capital of his past but unwilling to make a genuine commitment to the central moral issue of the day. A reading of the speech, however, does not support this view. Webster was simply restating what he had been saying for years. The war was unjust, even "vicious," and should be opposed rationally under the Constitution. "Violent counsels" were always "weak counsels." Webster's public opposition to the extension of slavery went back to 1838. Thus the Wilmot Proviso enthusiasts were johnnies-come-lately in comparison. On the other hand, Webster refused to waste his energy moralizing about slavery. It was sufficient for him that to extend the institution would increase the "inequality of free and slave representation, so wholly inconsistent with the fundamental principles of self-government." He reiterated his opposition to the acquisition of new territory with or without slavery, distinguished between slavery as a moral and as a political problem, and insisted that he would resist attacks on slavery under the Constitution with the same firmness that he resisted the extension of slavery. What was past "must stand. We cannot go back."[18]

When it was all over, Webster had the nomination he wanted by acclamation. He was the biggest monument to the Whig past in Massachusetts and he still stood in first place. But the future lay elsewhere. In the short run, it lay with Lawrence and the Taylor Whigs; in the long run it lay with the angry young idealists who would soon quit their party altogether.

Meanwhile, Webster played his traditional role. In November he went to New Hampshire to preside over the ceremony opening the Northern Railroad, whose tracks now cut through the family homestead in Franklin. Recalling the extraordinary progress of the period—that steam and iron rails now vaulted across rivers that he had forded as a boy—he refused to speculate on the future. That was known "only to Omniscience."[19]

Still Webster was inclined to help Omniscience along. He arranged with Everett to have an editon of his diplomatic papers published—an obvious attempt to keep his name before the public as an experienced and accomplished statesman. At the same time he made it clear to his political friends in New York that he opposed any premature endorsement for Taylor. This would only serve to drive many Whigs back to Clay, who was already actively in the field again.[20]

On January 8, 1848, the president's emissary to Mexico, Nicholas Trist, signed a treaty with Mexico ceding New Mexico and California to the United States. The treaty was submitted to the Senate on February 23 and on the same day, Daniel Webster learned that his son, Edward, had died in Mexico of typhoid fever. Few men in public life had suffered more from the war than Webster, and after the treaty was passed over his opposition, he gave his final judgment on the war and its effect on the nation. The opportunity came in debate over a bill calling for additional troops to enforce provisions of the treaty. Webster spoke in opposition, as usual. American blood and treasure had been expended to force Mexico to give up territory through a dishonorable peace. What had been gained was not worth the price. "Forty nine fiftieths, at least, of the whole of New Mexico" was "a barren waste." The people were composed of "coarse landholders and miserable peons," a point Webster tried to document with long passages from travelers' accounts of the cringing, lying, thieving ways of the people who lived in the territory.

It was a brutal speech, and it did Webster little credit until at the end he came back to fundamental conservative principles. He opposed new territory because he was convinced that new territory meant continued agitation of the slavery issue. But he would have opposed it even without slavery because he believed that American growth should be a gradual and essentially organic process.

> . . . it has long been my purpose to maintain the people of the United States, what the Constitution designed to make them, *one people,* one in interest, one in character, and one in political feeling. If we depart from that, we break it all up. . . . Arbitrary governments may have territories & distant possessions, because arbitrary governments may rule them by different laws and different systems. Russia may rule in the Ukraine and the provinces of the Caucasus and Kamatschatka by different codes, ordinances or Ukases. We can do no such thing. They must be of us, *part* of us, or else strangers.[21]

There is a note of resignation about this speech. Webster, after all, was an old hand at campaigning. He had been a star performer in the huckstering of 1840. He knew what would sell on the American political market and what would not, and the expansionists were obviously carrying the day in the public mind. He persisted in lecturing to a majority who was not listening because, without having completely given up his ambitions for the immediate future, he had more at stake in preserving his guardian image than in trying for short-run political victories. Indeed, political victory did not seem to be worth much in the spring of 1848, when the death of his two children made the gloomy political picture even more dismal.

The nomination of Lewis Cass by the Democrats at the end of May was consistent with Webster's vision of a deteriorating political system. Cass was "the most likely man in the country" to bring on more war, he confided to Everett. Now, he said, was the time for the Whigs in the South to propose "a Northern candidate." But when the Whigs met in Philadelphia, Webster's showing was pitifully small, and Taylor won on the fourth ballot. Anticipating the worst, he had stayed away and communicated to the convention through Fletcher. Even so, he was humiliated by the results, especially by the "utter indifference" of the northern delegates to the possibility of supporting a northern candidate. "Nobody has shown any pluck except Massachusetts," he announced in a sharp letter to Ketchum. "How can she stand alone? How is it to be shown that the South is to be blamed for what the North did not demand?"[22]

For all his disgruntlement and reluctance, Webster seems to have felt from the beginning that he had no alternative but to support Taylor. "I can see no way but acquiescence on Taylor's nomination," he wrote to Fletcher a week after the convention, "not enthusiastic support, nor zealous approbation; but acquiescence."[23] There were other alternatives open to him in theory, but none of them seemed viable. He could have supported Taylor enthusiastically and hoped for a share of the spoils. This would have been demeaning. He could have kept absolutely silent. This would have meant giving up his party influence when he had already emphasized the grave necessity of defeating the Democrats. Or, he could have followed the conscience Whigs into the Free-Soil party.

When Taylor was nominated, a substantial number of anti-slavery Whigs walked out of the convention and pledged to work against his nomination. At the same time, anti-slavery Democrats were moving to choose a candidate of their own in preference to Lewis Cass. Late in June, the dissident Whigs held separate conventions in Columbus, Ohio, and Worcester, Massachusetts, while their counterparts among the Democrats, called Barnburners, met in Utica, New York. These conventions led to the call for a coalition, and a national convention for the Free-Soil party was called at Buffalo for August 9. Even before the convention in Philadelphia, some of Webster's younger admirers among the conscience Whigs had told him they would leave the party if Taylor was nominated and would need "a great Man" for their leader. Webster did not offer at the bait, but when the conscience convention was held at Worcester, his son Fletcher was in attendance thus keeping the possibility alive that the father might still be available.[24]

After the Free-Soil convention in Buffalo nominated Van Buren for president and gave second place on the ticket to Charles Francis Adams, E. Rockwood Hoar, a converted Free-Soiler still loyal to Webster, wrote to his old hero asking him to endorse the Buffalo nominations. "I know that you are the natural leader of the great movement which is now going on," he wrote, "and I believe in my conscience, that one word from you would blow out of existence this Taylor faction, throughout New England, and throughout the North, in twenty-four hours." Webster was not convinced. If he had to choose between a bona-fide Whig candidate and a man like Van Buren, who had been on the wrong side of every important issue in national politics for more than fifteen years, he felt his duty was clear. "It is utterly impossible for me to support the Buffalo nomination," he wrote to Hoar. "I have no confidence in Mr. Van Buren, not the slightest."[25]

On September 1, Webster broke his public silence about the election and before a group of Marshfield neighbors made a statement intended for the nation. He set up three criteria for the next president. He should be a leader who could keep the peace, prevent the expansion of slavery, and support sound fiscal and tariff policy. Cass was a war candidate. Van Buren had been wrong about banks and tariffs for years, and his public record on slavery was well known. He had opposed abolition in the District of Columbia, had supported censorship of anti-slavery literature through the public mails, and had supported the annexation of Texas. Given such sorry circumstances, Taylor, "a military man merely," was the best practical candidate because he could be trusted to support traditional Whig principles.[26]

It was a cold endorsement and many Whigs would have been happier if Webster had said nothing. But he was satisfied, to have spoken his mind and unwilling to do much more. When he was asked to give a campaign speech in Philadelphia, he refused. He did speak in Faneuil Hall on the eve of the election—a lackluster performance filled with data about subtreasury systems and tariffs, the kind of speech which was increasingly turning the younger Whigs away. Now that the lines had been drawn between tyranny and liberty, the man who for so long had been the voice and conscience of New England was droning on and on about the dangers of imported mackerel.[27]

One is tempted to think that Daniel Webster in Faneuil Hall that October was a man who had lost his place in time. He wanted to go back to the 1830s. The real issues, then, he said, were the real issues now. They were not, of course, and never had been. The real issue had always been how to reconcile slavery with a free society, but politicians had preferred to argue less divisive questions. Now it was becoming more and more difficult to avoid headlong conflict over slavery. Webster said he found it utterly impossible to support Free-Soil because everything he had stood for in public life, his whole history, was opposed to Van Buren's history. That was only one reason. The other was that Webster had always identified himself with Union and could not now identify with a party which based itself exclusively upon a platform which threatened Union. In this sense, Webster was perfectly sincere when he insisted on concentrating on the doctrines of old Whiggery. It was better to talk about mackerel than to blunder into civil war.

Shortly after the election, Webster attended a dinner in Boston. Lawrence was there, and in the course of the evening he eulogized Taylor by likening him to Washington. Webster felt the insult and in a remarkable outburst referred to his own public accomplishments. "I say here and now that I am quite aware that I am a man of considerable importance, not only within the boundaries of Massachusetts, but without her boundaries and throughout the length and breadth of this continent."[28]

One mark of a man's greatness is in not having to insist upon it himself, but none of the other Whigs around the table had the temerity to mention that. Neither did they smile as they might have at a lesser man. For after all, Webster was only reminding them of the truth. He had played a giant's role outside the party and within, while Taylor was just another political windfall. The pathos in the incident derives not from Webster's vanity but from his lack of moral vision. He could lament the passing of great men and the waning of national sentiment as a personal loss, but he would never feel with equal intensity the terrible internal contradictions of a free society committed to the constitutional preservation of slavery. And yet, because he loved the Union more and felt the burden of national sin less, there was still a major role left for him to play in the American political future.

18

THE GREAT COMPROMISE

According to the story, Daniel Webster never slept more than four hours a night after he spoke out in favor of the fugitive slave law. "His face showed it; he began to die that day and he *knew* it."[1]

This was what the abolitionist imagination would do to Webster's image. Perhaps a good way to begin as we approach this last great drama in his public life is to remind ourselves that the man who would soon be likened to a fallen god, who would inspire some of the most eloquent denunciations in the history of American literature, was even in these final years a remarkably vigorous, zestful, and versatile person.

During the months following Taylor's election, Webster does not seem to have taken any great interest in politics. He did not expect to be invited into Taylor's cabinet, and told friends that he would probably not serve if asked. As the tempo of his political life slowed down, his law practice increased. "I am overwhelmed with labor," he wrote in February, 1849, "obliged to study from 5 to eleven AM; be in court from eleven to three; and all the rest of the day in the senate till ten o'clock." This extraordinary work load was caused by a rush of clients making claims against the government for damages incurred during the recent war. As usual, he could not afford to turn them away.[2]

The issue which engrossed Webster during the spring of 1849 involved not policy but patronage. He wanted a lucrative appointment for Fletcher, preferably the post of United States district attorney in Boston. The job, however, had been promised to George Lunt, a Lawrence supporter. Webster did everything in his power to discredit Lunt and get the appointment for his son. He solicited help from leading Massachusetts lawyers, sought the intercession of influential senators like William Seward, insisted on personal interviews with cabinet members and even with the president himself—but to no avail. Fletcher ultimately had to content himself with a much less prestigious appointment as surveyor to the Port of Boston.[3]

There is something puzzling about this episode. Usually filled with a sense of his own dignity as a statesman, Webster was now playing the role of petitioner and petty spokesman. He was worried about money, of course, and wanted some kind of sinecure for a son who had not been conspiciously successful in supporting himself. The other part of the story may be related to his outburst at the dinner party with Abbot Lawrence. Lawrence had backed the winner in 1848 and would soon be sent to the Court of St. James's a post which Webster had coveted many times earlier in his career. Having chosen to play an independent role in 1848, Webster expected to pay a certain political price as far as the Whigs were concerned, but he would not be outmuscled on his own territory by a second-rater like Lawrence—at least not without a fight.

The crushing work load and the tenacious struggle for Fletcher's appointment attest to Webster's continued vigor. He was aging like a lion, still the center of attraction in whatever environment he occupied. Despite political defeats and a profound sense of personal loss over the death of his children, he was not a bitter or unhappy man. Prolonged brooding was simply not in his nature. Webster was one of those healthy minded souls whom William James would later describe as the "once born." Like Emerson, a man whom he resembled in no other way, Webster might have said of himself, "Though defeated every day, yet to victory am I born." His healthy mindedness derived in no small measure from a continued interest in the practical details of everyday life. He insisted on proper style in the smallest matters, was full of advice on how to catch a halibut, how to boil potatoes for the table, how to cure an ailing ox. Always up before the sun, he took pride in noting the time as well as the date in the upper-right-hand corner of his private letters. Prodigiously energetic at times, he was not a compulsive worker and took his leisure seriously. "Like you I am disposed to ramble," he wrote to Richard Blatchford in August from Boston, "I have no urgent professional business on hand, and am disposed to play." Two days later he led a party of eight into the inn at Edgartown in Martha's Vineyard. Webster described the trip in detail to Blatchford and made it clear that in this spot of unspoiled Yankeedom, his name had lost none of its magic.

I thought I knew nobody here, but the hotel was soon full of friends, some of whom I well recollected, all tendering boats, men, tackle, &c., for fishing; guns and company for the plover plains; and carriages, with attendants, for the ladies. All sorts of expeditions were planned before we parted at ten o'clock. Among others these, namely; to-day blue fish; to-morrow, shooting on the plains; next day sword fish; the next a party to Gay Head, and so on. The ladies are delighted. I am looking round and meditating about locality, climate, ocean scenery, &c., that is, I have meditated in bed, and am now looking round by daylight.

The next day, Webster caught twenty-five bluefish. The following day, he went plover hunting with less success. "My eye is hardly quick enough to see the birds in the grass, and I am a little too much out of play to be sure of them when they rise." The experience reminded him of an earlier hunting experience on the Sandwich downs. He was in a chaise with Fletcher and Julia on his lap "and holding them both, and also the reins in one hand, and shooting a plover on the wing, holding the gun in the other." There was nothing melancholy about the reminiscence—he simply assumed the plover would fall another day. Meanwhile, there would be swordfish tomorrow! When Daniel Webster decided to play, he assumed that the rest of creation would cooperate.[4]

As the summer of 1849 came to an end, Webster sent a short note to Edward Curtis. Remarking on his own advancing age and the length of their acquaintance, he wrote, "My feelings at the present moment are made up of a thousand recollections of thankfulness to Providence for so much of a good life of an acquiescence in and a good portion of enjoyment of the things of the present hour & of some hopes of the future." We do well to take this self-evaluation at face value. Webster was still the greatest public man in New England, and he continued to play his ceremonial role with relish. In late September at a cattle show in Dedham, he lectured an audience on the virtues of the turnip. At Boston a few weeks later, he presided over a large formal dinner honoring New Hampshire natives like himself who had made good in Massachusetts. This was the kind of occasion he enjoyed most— recalling the old New Hampshire frontier and telling stories of the valor of New Hampshire men in the French and Indian Wars and the Revolution. No politics here, except perhaps to remind his listeners that the American mission had nothing to do with territorial aggrandizement. "Our great destiny on earth," he told the sons of New Hampshire, "is to exhibit the practicability of good, safe, secure, popular governments."[5]

The serene exterior which Webster presented to the world as the winter of 1849–1850 approached would be severely tested by developments in Washington over the next several months. The stage was set for one of the great dramas in the history of the Congress. The conflict was provided by free and slave states contending for western territory. In the Senate, the star players were all old men in familiar roles: Clay, back again as genial and assertive as ever; Calhoun, emaciated and intense, almost burned out but still uncompromising; the patriarchal Benton, ancient but still able to roar like a frontier brawler; Cass, the defeated presidential candidate, with more folds to his face than a beagle, still on the scent of the White House. These were the big names, but there were other veterans too—loyal Southern Whigs whom Webster respected—men like John Berrien of Georgia and Bell of Tennessee.

Although the old stars continued to blaze, new stars were beginning to take over more of the sky. Half the members of the Senate in 1849 were under fifty. Some of them, like the Mississippians Jefferson Davis and Henry Foote, were prepared to follow Calhoun. Others like Seward of New York, John Hale of New Hampshire and Salmon Chase of Ohio represented the new breed of practical-minded anti-slavery politicians. Finally, there was the remarkable Stephen A. Douglas from Illinois, the "little Giant" who was determined to let the West decide the slavery issue on its own terms.

Although the Whigs occupied the White House, Democrats controlled both houses of Congress, but were as badly split as the Whigs over the slavery issue. The House, always more boisterous than the Senate, opened in chaos on December 3, 1849. Sixty-three ballots were required before Robert Winthrop, the incumbent speaker, was finally defeated by the young Georgia Democrat Howell Cobb. It was perhaps just as well for Winthrop. He would hardly have been comfortable presiding over the kind of session in which one member's threat to strangle another passed for debate. Even after a speaker was chosen, the wrangling persisted. It took twenty votes for the House to elect a clerk, three for a chaplain, eight for a sergeant at arms, and after fourteen votes there was still no doorkeeper.

As representatives and senators struggled among themselves to put the nation's legislative machinery into some kind of order, the word *disunion* was heard more and more frequently on the floor of Congress. The presence of outspoken abolitionists in both houses of Congress infuriated southern legislators, who began to liken the former more and more to "incendiaries" and "assassins" thirsting for the blood of southern women and children. Much of this Webster would have dismissed as extreme and irresponsible rhetoric. He would have listened more carefully, however, to an old friend like John Berrien speak for the "wronged and insulted" South. "If you seriously believe that slavery is a stain upon the land where it exists—that it will pollute the soil—that you cannot dwell among slaveholders—if this be your real belief," Berrien challenged his anti-slavery colleagues, "make a partition of the country."[6]

Webster would have felt the force of this challenge, and although he does not mention Berrien's speech, he was stimulated by it, along with W. H. Furness's letter, to carefully review his own position on slavery at this time. Furness was an abolitionist and a leading Unitarian minister in Philadelphia. He wrote to Webster on January 9, 1850, asking him to make a supreme contribution to the nation by concentrating his powers on slavery and *"stat-*

ing the great case, so that it would be argued once for all and forever." Webster took more than a month to reply. He confessed to having been "a good deal moved" by Furness's letter and proceeded to make a specific statement of his own anti-slavery convictions.

From my earliest youth, I have regarded slavery as a great moral and political evil. I think it unjust, repugnant to the natural equality of mankind, founded only in superior power; a standing and permanent conquest by the stronger over the weaker. All pretence of defending it on the ground of different races, I have ever condemned. I have even said that if the black race is weaker, that is a reason against, not for, its subjection and oppression. In a religious point of view, I have ever regarded it, and ever spoken of it, not as subject to any express denunciation, either in the Old Testament or the New, but as opposed to the whole spirit of the Gospel and to the teaching of Jesus Christ.

But, Webster continued, it was one thing to have convictions and something else to have the power to implement them. "What can be done by me," he asked Furness, "who have no power over the subject of slavery as it exists in the states of the Union? I do what I can to restrain it; to prevent its spread and diffusion. But I cannot disregard the oracles which instruct me not to do evil that good may come. I cannot cooperate in breaking up social and political systems, on the warmth, rather than the strength, of a hope that, in such convulsions, the cause of emancipation may be promoted." Webster reminded Furness that "the effect of moral causes, though sure, is slow," and "in regard to the final abolition of human slavery; while we give to it our fervent prayers, and aid it by . . . all justifiable influences . . . we must leave both the progress and the results in His hands who sees the end from the beginning, and in whose sight a thousand years are but as a single day."[7]

Webster's anti-slavery convictions were only part of a conservative view of the world which gave social and political stability a higher value than the eradication of evil. In this sense his position was diametrically opposed to that of the radical abolitionists. They would destroy slavery at any cost and leave the Union to Providence. Webster would preserve the Union at any cost and leave abolition to Providence.

In writing to Furness, Webster was rehearsing arguments he would use in the Senate a few weeks later. The Great Debate had already begun. It was touched off by Taylor's message to the Congress. Seeking to avoid a continuation of the controversy over slavery in the territories, the president had recommended that California be admitted to the Union immediately and that New Mexico be kept under military rule until she satisfied requirements for statehood. Taylor's message was a nationalistic document which strongly condemned sectional politics. Webster liked it, but he was in the minority.[8] Everyone knew that Californians had agreed on a constitution prohibiting slavery, and the general expectation was that New Mexico would do the same. This prospect infuriated southern Whigs and Democrats because it threatened to permanently alter the even split between free and slave states. Thus while northern legislatures, prodded by organized anti-slavery sentiment, began to pass resolutions demanding statehood for California and New Mexico without slavery, slaveholding states began to plan for a sectional convention to defend southern rights. The possibility of disunion seemed closer than ever before.

The situation cried out for compromise, and Henry Clay was the first to try and move the country in that direction. On January 29, Clay laid a series of eight proposals before the Senate. He would appease the North by admitting California as a free state and prohibiting the slave trade in the District of Columbia, and appease the South by passing an effective fugitive slave law and pledging no interference with the interstate slave trade and with slavery in the District of Columbia. Additional proposals called for the organization of New Mexican territory without restriction on slavery, adjustments of the Texas–Mexican boundary, and assumption of the Texas debt in exchange for the renunciation of Texas claims on Mexican territory.

Webster had foreknowledge of Clay's plan and generally approved it. Before Clay addressed the Senate on February 5 and 6, the two old rivals spent an evening together huddled before the fire in Webster's library to talk matters out. After more than a generation of jealous political maneuvering, they were finally able to put common cause over personal advantage. Their party had given its highest gift to an outsider and they could no longer call the tune for the Whigs. But they were patriarchs in the party and could command at least as much of a public hearing as the president.

If Clay had expected a groundswell of national approval for his plan, he was disappointed. Northeastern Democrats and southern Whigs supported it with reservations. Abolitionists found it repugnant. Southern extremists were dead set against any plan to admit California as a free state, and a heavy majority of northern Whigs in the Senate continued to support Taylor's plan, which ignored most of the issues covered by Clay's proposals.

During the controversy following Clay's speech, Webster said nothing in public. He had told Clay in private that he was prepared to support his plan. On the other hand, a close political friend like Winthrop believed he would come out for the president's proposal. If Webster seemed to be giving conflicting cues to different people, it was partly because he had difficulty assessing the gravity of the crisis. As late as mid-February, he was telling friends that differences in the Congress were more rhetorical than substantive. On February 23, however, the capital was rocked by reports of a dramatic confrontation between President Taylor and Congressmen Stephens and Toombs from Georgia. The Georgians had reportedly told the president that secession was the only alternative to Clay's compromise. Taylor had responded by promising to hang all "traitors." After talking with some of the southern leaders, Webster came away in despair. "I am nearly broken down with labor and anxiety," he wrote to Fletcher on the twenty-fourth. "I know not how to meet the present emergency, or with what weapons to beat down the Northern and Southern follies, now raging in equal extremes. . . . I have poor spirits and little courage." As usual, however, the depression was only momentary. By early March, Webster felt that extremism was dying down and had begun to plan his own speech.[9]

The classical argument for the South was made in the Senate by Calhoun on March 4. The speech was Calhoun's but the voice was that of James Mason from Virginia. Calhoun, consumed with fever, lingering on the edge of death, sat speechless in his chair. This was his final effort. He argued that the compromise of 1787 which had created the Union had been fatally violated. Northern majorities had passed preferential tariff legislation which supported northern industry. This attracted immigrants further swelling the northern majority, which was becoming increasingly hostile to slavery. The only alternative to secession was to prohibit abolitionism, insure free access to slavery in new territory, and guarantee the South's right to self-protection by constitutional amendment. Calhoun's constitutional solution, not specified in the speech, called for dual executives from the North and South.

On March 7 it was Webster's turn to speak. The Senate was packed with visitors when he began:

Mr. President—I wish to speak today not as a Massachusetts man, nor as a Northern man, but as an American, and a member of the Senate of the United States. . . . I have a part to act, not for my own security or safety, for I am looking out for no fragment upon which to float away from the wreck, if wreck there must be, but for the good of the whole, and the preservation of all. . . . I speak today for the preservation of the Union: "Hear me for my cause."[10]

Webster spoke for more than three hours from a sheaf of manuscript notes. The published speech comes to forty-two pages in the standard edition of his works. It can be best summarized here by discussing four related arguments. Webster was attempting to defend the Union by showing

(1)   that the slavery controversy was more a matter of historical circumstance than fundamental moral principle;

(2)   that the issue of slavery in the territories was already settled by human and natural law;

(3)   that both North and South harbored legitimate grievances against each other, some of which were redeemable by law;

(4)   that peaceable secession was impossible.

Everyone knew that the immediate cause of the crisis was the Mexican War. Webster invited his listeners to go beyond this and examine slavery in the long sweep of history. Slavery had been a fact in the ancient world; it had been inherited by the Christian world; and it had only recently come under general disapprobation in Western civilization. In America, slavery had been a fact of life when the Constitution was framed. The founders had agreed that it should be protected where it already existed, but their willingness to abolish the slave trade and keep slavery out of the Northwest Territory showed they did not want it to expand. The general expectation had been that it would gradually be extinguished. As the nineteenth century proceeded, this expectation was changed by "the rapid growth and sudden extension of the cotton plantations of the south." More and more southerners became concerned that their prosperity, even their survival, depended on slave labor. Webster described this change as "natural. It has followed those causes which always influence the human mind and operate upon it."

The situation in the North was quite different. Having few slaves in the beginning and no economic incentive to expand their number, northerners continued to hope and work for the abolition of slavery. Thus religious sentiment in the North began to support an anti-slavery movement at the same time that southerners, just as religious as their nothern countrymen, were finding slavery to be an essential part of their way of life not only in the present but for the foreseeable future.

The unspoken premise upon which Webster based this historical analysis was that social changes take place slowly and are determined more by the mysterious hand of Providence than by individual effort. Therefore, he was more sympathetic with conscientious shareholders whose place in history tied them to slavery than to the passionate northern philanthropists who sought to make the role of Providence their own.

They deal with morals as with mathematics; and they think what is right may be distinguished from what is wrong with the precision of an algebraic equation. . . . They are impatient men; too impatient always to give heed to St. Paul, that we are not to "do evil that good may come"; too impatient to wait for the slow progress of moral causes in the improvement of mankind.[11]

The next point that Webster sought to make was that the question of slavery in the territories was already settled by law. The Northwest Territory had been reserved for freedom in 1787 with unanimous southern support. Slavery had been excluded from territory in the Louisiana Purchase north of the line 36°30′ with southern acquiescence in 1820, and the Oregon Bill had provided for the organization of that territory without slavery. In the South, new slave states had been added out of Florida, the Louisiana Territory, and Texas. Webster said that Texas had "pretty much closed the whole chapter

. . . settled the whole account." While admitting his own opposition to annexation, he pointed out that it had been supported by northern votes—had been a national act. Now that the agreement was made, slavery in Texas had the same absolute protection that it enjoyed in other southern states. Not only that, but in accordance with the annexation agreement, Texas could be divided into four separate slave states, should the inhabitants desire it. Thus federal law had settled the question of slavery in all territory east of New Mexico.

In California and New Mexico the slavery issue was also settled, not by positive law, but by "the law of nature, of physical geography. The law of the formation of the earth." Nature herself outlawed slavery in these areas. The California constitution prohibiting slavery simply institutionalized this natural fact, which was even more apparent in New Mexico where climate and terrain made anything but small-scale irrigation farming impossible. Given the natural conditions of the climate and the land, it was foolish to argue over something like the Wilmot Proviso for New Mexico. Because such a provision tended to offend southern feelings without actually preventing slavery, Webster announced that "if a proposition were now here to establish a government for New Mexico, and it was moved to insert a provision for a prohibition of slavery, I would not vote for it."

Having demonstrated, as he hoped, the fruitlessness of further debate about slavery in the territories, Webster turned his attention to legitimate grievances between North and South. In this, the most delicate part of the speech, he spoke bluntly. The South had a right to expect northerners to obey their constitutional obligations and return fugitive slaves. In Webster's eyes state legislators who supported a personal-liberty law designed to obstruct the return of fugitives were to be condemned just as much as the abolitionist on the Underground Railroad. "I put it to all the sober and sound minds of the North as a question of morals and a question of conscience," Webster said. "What right have they, in their legislative capacity or any other capacity, to endeavor to get round this Constitution, or to embarass the free exercise of the rights secured by the Constitution to the persons whose slaves escape from them? None at all; none at all. Neither in the forum of conscience, nor before the face of the Constitution. . . ."[12]

Webster admitted that it was reasonable for southerners to be offended by anti-slavery petitions sent to the Congress by northern legislatures; and he announced that he, for one, would be unwilling to receive instructions from the Massachusetts legislature directed at slavery within the states. He dismissed the abolitionists with a paragraph. For twenty years they had agitated and "produced nothing good or valuable." Their one accomplishment had been to create a great counterreaction and thus "not to set free, but to bind faster, the slave population of the South."

Of all the grievances of the South against the North, only one was redressable by law, and Webster pledged himself to support that—a new fugitive slave law with teeth in it.

Webster devoted five pages to southern grievances against the North but less than two pages to northern grievances against the South. His essential point was that people in the North had accepted the Constitution with the understanding that slavery was a necessary evil "which all hoped would be extinguished gradually." They now confronted and were offended by southern insistence that slavery was "an institution to be cherished, and preserved, and extended." They were particularly offended to hear pro-slavery enthusiasts argue that slaves in the South were happier and more comfortable than laborers in the North. In his published speech, Webster added a brief paragraph protesting the "oppressive" treatment of free black seamen on northern vessels in southern ports. He called for no specific legislation because "all that we can do is to endeavor to allay the agitation, and cultivate a better feeling and more fraternal sentiments between the South and the North." So much for northern grievances against the South.

Webster directed his final remarks at what he considered to be pure fantasy—the idea of a peaceable secession by dissatisfied states.

Secession! Peaceable secession! Sir your eyes and mine are never destined to see that miracle. The dismemberment of this vast country without convulsion! The breaking up of the fountains of the great deep without ruffling the surface! . . . There can be no such thing as a peaceable secession. Peaceable secession is an utter impossibility. . . . I see that it must produce war, and such a war as I will not describe, *in its twofold character*. [13]

The last phrase implied not just a civil war but a bloody, servile insurrection as well. And where, Webster asked, was "the line to be drawn"? Who would stay in the Union? What would remain American? What would become of the great Mississippi Valley? Webster had come back now to the brink of the precipice he had occupied in his debate with Hayne. He had refused to peer into the pit then, and he would not do it now. "Let us come out into the light of day," he said as he began his peroration, "let us enjoy the fresh air of Liberty and Union. . . . let our comprehension be as broad as the country for which we act, our aspiration as high as its certain destiny; let us not be pigmies in a case that calls for men." [14]

Webster would later say that he felt he was acting absolutely alone when he addressed the Senate on March 7, and the immediate response to his speech in Congress confirms that estimate. Administration Whigs continued to support Taylor's plan, which was less comprehensive and less generous toward the South than what Webster proposed; southern extremists continued to shun compromises of any kind; while Free-Soilers and anti-slavery Whigs were more impressed by William Seward's speech about the "higher law" than they were by Webster's more familiar pleading for constitutional responsibility. Throughout most of his career, Webster had been able to count on the almost unanimous support of New England Whigs, but the Taylorites and Free-Soilers had demolished that base, and the kind of support he was able to attract now from moderates of both major parties outside New England was far short of a legislative majority.[15]

On the other hand, no performance of Webster's since his debate with Hayne, had so dominated the public mind. "The clamor for speeches So. & West is incredible, " he wrote to Fletcher on March 21. "Two hundred thousand will not supply the demand." His own exhilaration over the tone and vigor of the national response to his address was in striking contrast to the reaction of customary supporters like Everett and Winthrop, who knew that at least half the Whig press in Massachusetts opposed it. Winthrop claimed that Webster's speech "would have killed any Northern man except himself & we shall all have hard work to sustain ourselves under it." Everett, who had made a career out of championing Webster's causes, found parts of the speech morally objectionable and refused to sign a public letter applauding it.[16]

Confronted with a critical response at home, a divided Congress, and the possibility of burgeoning national support, Webster devised a strategy that was at once conciliatory and aggressive. He would not insist on the letter of the Clay compromise but would support similar legislation either in the form of a single bill or as separate laws. At the same time he pledged himself to "take the stump in every village in New England," if necessary, to "put the disorganizers down" at home.[17]

Meanwhile, the greatest "disorganizer" of them all, who had never been put down by mortal eloquence, was dying. Calhoun died March 31, and Webster delivered a short eulogy to the Senate the following day. He and Calhoun were the same age and had served together in the Congress more or less continuously since 1813. In his tribute to Calhoun, Webster emphasized the logical qualities of his mind, his intensity, and his strict adherence to basic principles. Whatever his differences from others, Webster said, Calhoun had served long enough and honorably enough "to connect himself for all time with the records of his country. He is now an historical character." Calhoun's death reminded Webster of his own mortality and the little time that was left to complete his own record in history. Everything that he would write or say in public or in private from this point on suggests that he was determined to finish the course as Calhoun had done by sticking to the principles and policies with which he had been closely identified for more than a quarter of a century.[18]

This is not to say that Webster had reached the point where he consciously decided to put principle over politics. It would be more accurate to say that he felt devotion to principle required a new kind of politics. New doors were open to him in the South at the same time that new enemies were rising in the North. Webster weighed the possible advantages and disadvantages of accompanying Calhoun's body to South Carolina and finally concluded against the trip. "It might be thought I was carrying my Southern courtesy too far," he wrote to Fletcher, "considering my age and station."[19]

The situation in Massachusetts called for more than southern courtesy. A Faneuil Hall meeting, which Webster had hoped would be a testimonial for his March 7 effort, was commandeered by radical abolitionists like Wendell Phillips, who said that Webster's speech reminded him of what might have happened during the Revolution if Sam Adams "had gone over to the British or John Hancock had ratted." Anxious to show that this was not true Boston sentiment, Webster had some of his friends get up a laudatory public letter with about one thousand signatures on it. "The letter is admirable; too good, too good," he replied upon seeing a draft copy. "I don't deserve the one hundreth part of what it says. Let it come immediately." By encouraging the writing of public letters of support, Webster assured himself newspaper space for public letters of reply, in which he could restate the argument of his original speech.[20]

At the end of April, Webster entered Boston for the first time since March 7. His friends Edward Curtis and Peter Harvey had arranged for a "spontaneous" public reception at Bowdoin Square. The senator was defiant. "The proper business of the country" (every solid Boston Whig knew that this referred to a good tariff bill) would not proceed until the public controversy over slavery was put to rest. "Take that truth home with you and take it as truth!" He contrasted the patriot's devotion to a "union of brotherly regard" to the "unreal ghostly abstractions" of the abolitionist and asked Massachusetts to "conquer her own prejudices" and return fugitive slaves as the law required.[21]

By mid-May, Webster was back in Washington, working for satisfactory compromise legislation in the Senate, continuing his barrage of public letters, writing editorials for friendly papers, and using what political pressure he had to discipline the Boston Atlas, one of the leading Whig papers at home that had turned against him. Despite rumors that Taylor might try to curry southern support by taking Webster into his cabinet, he remained what he had been when the Taylor administration was formed—an independent Whig leader outside the fold. "I shall support cordially the President's measures whenever I can," he advised a friend on May 18, "but I have been in public life some time longer than the President, or any of his advisors, and suppose I shall not be much blamed, if on great public questions, I feel as much confidence in my own judgment as I do in theirs."[22]

Two months later, Webster found that his own judgment and the judgment of the administration had become identical. Zachary Taylor's sudden death on July 9 brought Vice-President Millard Fillmore to the presidency.

Fillmore, a New York Whig out of sympathy with the administration and omitted almost entirely from its highest counsels, was a strong compromise advocate and a warm admirer of Webster. Suddenly assuming the presidency at a time of unprecedented crisis, he needed an experienced secretary of state. There were only two Whigs who qualified—Clay and Webster—and Clay supported Webster's appointment.

Webster did not agonize over the decision to accept. The work load ahead and especially the summers to be spent in Washington and not in Marshfield distressed him, but the advantages of the change were obvious. He would free himself from the embarrassment of a divided Massachusetts constituency and at the same time acquire a national platform along with the political leverage of the executive office.

On July 17, Webster gave his farewell address to the Senate. It was a plain-spoken but graceful appeal for compromise. Pointing out that the abolitionists and secessionists were also enemies of each other, Webster tried to make a case for reason. Neither North nor South could reasonably insist on legislation which fundamentally injured the other. If the North wanted California in the Union as a free state, she must be willing to give up the Wilmot Proviso and return fugitive slaves. If the South wanted to feel secure about slavery she must accept the fact that the vast territory in California and new Mexico would not be open to slaves. In these matters, reflective, sober-minded citizens would find that patriotism and self-interest led to the same conclusion. "If we mean to live together," Webster said, "common prudence should teach us to treat each other with respect."[23]

As the president's chief advisor, Webster was now in a position to throw the weight of the administration behind the compromise. The New Mexico boundary situation provided an opportunity. Taking advantage of the threats of Governor Bell of Texas to use state militia to occupy disputed territory in New Mexico, Webster drafted a special message to Congress for the president. The message asserted that the government would meet force with force in Texas and that the new administration favored a speedy adjustment of all the controversies at hand relating to the territories. Spurred by this kind of prodding from the White House, and under the brilliant maneuvering of Stephen A. Douglas in the Senate, the legislation finally went forward. Three days after the special message, a Texas–New Mexico boundary bill passed the Senate. By September 20, bills had been signed by the president providing for the statehood of California, the organization of territories in New Mexico and Utah, abolition of the slave trade in the District of Columbia, and a new fugitive slave law.

As the end approached, Washington celebrated. Public buildings were illuminated, and crowds gathered around bonfires and formed torchlight processions which paraded through the city calling out the more famous political figures for speeches. On one such evening, when the Fugitive Slave Law

had passed, a procession of unionists called out, "Webster." The secretary of
state appared on the doorstep in his dressing gown supported by two
friends. His legs were unsteady but his tongue was ready, and after one false
start, he began by quoting Shakespeare. "Now is the winter of our discontent made glorious summer by this Son of York." A few days later, in a less
exalted mood, he said simply to his friend Harvey, "It is over. My part is
acted, and I am satisfied."[24]

He was wrong. It was true that he had given a great speech and had helped
to resolve a momentous crisis. He had a right to be proud of that. But it was
not over. A new image of Daniel Webster was just beginning to emerge. It
would be a dramatic and highly controversial part of his own "historical
character" forever.

19

BLACK DAN AND THE
LEGACY OF MARCH 7, 1850

The implications of what Webster liked to call the "settlement" of 1850 for his career and reputation are suggested by three separate events which took place on May 2, 1850, when Edward Everett heard Webster tell friends at a Boston dinner party that he would support a strong fugitive slave law. After the senator retired, "everyone at the table agreed that it would be madness for Mr. W. to support the bill referred to," but no one had the courage to tell him so. The same day a brilliant young Georgia Whig, Alexander Stephens, wrote to his brother that Webster was standing "up to the rod" in Massachusetts and would be a strong presidential possibility in 1852. Sometime also on May 2, the *National Era* printed Whittier's "Ichabod," which Robert Penn Warren has described as "one of the most telling poems of personal attack in English." Taking its title from the Biblical passage "And she named the child Ichabod, saying the glory is departed from Israel," Whittier's poem included these stanzas:

> *Of all we loved and honored, naught*
> *Save power remains;*
> *A fallen angel's pride of thought,*
> *Still strong in chains*
>
> *All else is gone; from those great eyes*
> *The soul has fled:*
> *When faith is lost, when honor dies*
> *The man is dead!*[1]

As Everett noted, Webster never really understood the depth of anxiety which his March speech had aroused even among staunch supporters at home. He was prepared for the attacks of someone like Horace Mann, an abolitionist dressed up in Whig clothing who had somehow appropriated John Quincy Adams's seat in Congress. When Mann published a long letter accusing Webster of speaking "for the South and slavery" rather than "for the North and freedom," Webster dismissed it as "wandering and vagrant" philanthropy and said that arguing with Mann would be like "attacking a feather bed with a sledge hammer." "Puff him off, by a breath," he advised Ticknor, "if you can bestow a few idle hours upon such a person."[2]

The problem which Webster refused to face was that almost all the influential Massachusetts Whigs were worried about supporting him. Only two Whig congressmen had backed the compromise without qualification, and the Whig state convention in October had openly defied Webster by declaring the Fugitive Slave Law unacceptable without changes. Even Everett was offended by Webster's concessions to the South, and Winthrop, who had taken Webster's place in the Senate and was a Taylor as well as a Webster Whig, failed to understand why Webster had never supported the administration's plan for California. He confessed to Everett that he felt himself to be "halfway between Webster and Horace Mann," and when it came to the crunch, like Mann, he refused to support fugitive slave legislation or to vote for the organization of the Utah and New Mexican Territory without a specific prohibition against slavery.[3]

As long as he remained in the Senate, there was not much Webster could do about the disruption in his customarily loyal ranks at home. He warned that southerners would hardly support a sound tariff bill while Massachusetts fought the compromise. He replied to the *Boston Atlas* through the columns of the still loyal *Courier,* suggested to Winthrop that if he couldn't vote right on the compromise, he might avoid the issue by being "called away for a fortnight or so," and made it clear to Abbot Lawrence's friends that if the prospective minister to the Court of St. James's expected prompt Senate action on his nomination, he would get the *Atlas* to change its tune.[4]

The truth of the matter, however, as Congressman Stephens recognized, was that Webster was shifting his power base. He would always retain a hard core of support in Massachusetts, but in committing himself completely to the compromise, he was taking on a new set of allies. It had been southern Whigs and northern Democrats who had made the compromise possible, and it was to them that he would look for support in the months ahead. To hold on to this support, it would be necessary to make the "settlement" (he seems to have intuitively rejected the negative implications of "compromise") work. As the top man in Fillmore's cabinet, Webster would do everything in his power to enforce the agreements of 1850.

During the Senate debates, Webster had impressed southern Whigs with his determination to satisfy legitimate southern interests. Without forgetting that he had once claimed the Wilmot Proviso as his own, they admitted that in the debates of 1850 he had gone "further than any Northern man dare go." They were delighted to have him leading the cabinet. After observing the way Webster was taking hold of the Fillmore administration in late August, Secretary of the Navy W. A. Graham wrote his brother that "light is dawning in Congress after an Arctic winter of chaos and dissension, . . . in ten days more tranquility will prevail everywhere except among Abolitionists and disunionists." Graham had just attended an informal cabinet meeting at Webster's and was impressed by the fact that Webster had sounded like a southern man in wanting to kill the Wilmot Proviso and pass a strong fugitive slave law. Warmed by his new supporters in the South, Webster spoke menacingly about the dissidents at home. "Winthrop is a good man—he means well but wants moral courage, but d—n John Davis—we'll whip him in."[5]

Certainly by the fall of 1850, Webster found his life in the cabinet much more pleasant than he would have found continuing in the Senate. He liked the perquisites and ceremonial duties that went with being secretary of state and enjoyed the company of three talented young aides who were always at his call to help research his speeches, handle his correspondence, or accompany him for an occasional early morning fishing jaunt on the banks of the Potomac. He was easily the dominant figure in the cabinet. Like Fillmore, himself, Webster's fellow cabinet officers were all lawyers and experienced Whig politicians of the second rank. The two possible exceptions were John J. Crittenden, Clay's long-time champion from Kentucky whose public career was almost as long as Webster's and who had served with Webster in Harrison's cabinet ten years earlier, and Thomas Corwin, more celebrated for his eloquent denunciation of the Mexican War than for his qualifications as secretary of the treasury. W. A. Graham, secretary of the navy, Charles M. Conrad, secretary of war, and Alexander H. H. Stuart, secretary of the interior, were all Union-minded southern Whigs with legislative experience in state and federal government. N. K. Hall, Fillmore's choice for postmaster general, was a New Yorker and the president's former law partner.

Webster was sixty-eight, Crittenden sixty-three, Corwin fifty-six, Conrad and Graham forty-six, Stuart forty-six, and Hall forty. In age, experience, and reputation, Webster towered over the rest of the cabinet and overshadowed the president. After dining with the full cabinet in mid-August, Edward Curtis said that "Mr. Webster appears among them like a father teaching his listening children." However much this may be overdrawn, it is clear that the administration deferred to him far more than the divided Whigs back home. Webster welcomed the change. "The President is a first rate business man," he wrote to Frank Haven, "& the Heads of

Departments, of different characters and abilities, are yet agreeable, sensible & industrious gentlemen. So that the inside of the Administration is quite pleasant."[6]

Webster's problem was to find some way to make the political world outside the government as harmonious as the world inside—to make the kinds of policies he favored acceptable to a constituency large enough to keep his own career afloat. In this connection, he recognized the importance of northern Democrats in securing the compromise and told Harvey that he would never feel the same about old adversaries like Cass and Daniel Dickinson. Perhaps a new Union party would emerge out of their combined efforts. He and Dickinson had clashed bitterly during the Ingersoll affair, but Webster now wrote to praise the New York Democrat ("You have stood where others have fallen") and to advise Fillmore that he preferred "respectable" Democrats in Congress to Free-Soilers masquerading as Whigs.[7]

At the same time that he made overtures to the Democrats, Webster worked to whip the Whigs back into line. Heretofore, men had called themselves Whigs and differed emphatically over how to deal with the slave issue. From now on that question was to be considered as settled. The test of Whig orthodoxy would be support of the compromise, he told Harvey, and those who continued "to talk about Wilmot Provisos, & to resist, or seek to repeal the Fugitive Slave Bill, or use any other means to disturb the quiet of the Country will have no right to consider themselves either as Whigs, or as friends of the Administration. Because there is one thing that is fixed & settled & that is, that the present Administration will not recognize one set of Whig Principles for the North, & another for the South."[8]

It was easier to talk about orthodoxy than to enforce it. Webster kept a close eye on patronage in Massachusetts and tried to withhold favors from the *Atlas* and reward those Whigs sound "on pending questions." At the same time he urged Everett to address the Whig convention in Massachusetts and reprimand the state committee for its "miserable" involvement in abolitionism and *"other issues."* The most divisive issue involved the Fugitive Slave Law. Webster put agitation against the return of fugitive slaves on the same moral level with threats of secession. By the fall of 1850 it had become agitation to break the law, and he could not understand how rational, patriotic citizens could countenance it. From the beginning, Webster's thinking on this subject was political and legalistic. He was convinced that there could be no settlement of the slavery question until slaveholders knew their property was protected by federal law. His confidence in the constitutionality of such a law was apparently influenced by *Prigg* v. *Pennsylvania,* in which his friend Story had emphatically confirmed the constitutionality of the Fugitive Slave Law of 1793. If Story was right, the personal liberty laws passed in many northern states to circumvent the return of escaped slaves were wrong, and Webster explicitly condemned them. So convinced was he of the necessity for a strong fugitive slave law that he declared for the original bill, proposed by Senator Mason of Virginia, even before he read it. a fact which astounded the conservative Everett. During the debates, Webster backed down from his wholesale endorsement of Mason's bill and, on June 3, offered an amendment which would would have allowed the alleged fugitive a jury trial. The amendment was voted down and he accepted the final bill essentially as it had stood in the beginning.[9]

Webster's great error was in misjudging moral sentiment in the North. The law which Charles Francis Adams said was designed to gauge how far Americans would go "to pledge themselves to uphold a system they abhorred" was loaded against anyone accused of being a fugitive. It provided for commissioners, subject to removal by the courts without notice, who were to decide whether a person was to be returned to slavery or not. The commissioners were to be paid for their work at differential rates, receiving a greater sum for returning a person than for declaring him free. The alleged fugitive was denied a jury trial and could not testify on his own behalf. The evidence against him was to be accepted without question even though sworn to a southern judge in another state. Harboring a fugitive or obstructing the law in other ways was punishable by fine and imprisonment.[10]

Such a law posed a genuine threat to any black person living in a free state. Acquiescience to it by the white majority in the North simply showed that northern whites, who in many states had their own "black laws," did not like black people. Webster did not comprehend this. Although one looks in vain for any trace of racial prejudice in his own writing or behavior and remembers that he purchased the freedom of black servants and was solicitous to see that their rights were not violated when they traveled between Washington and Massachusetts, the fact remains that he could never fathom the horror with which morally sensitive but ordinarily law-abiding Americans regarded a law so prejudicial to the freedom of other human beings.[11]

In late October, Webster spent two weeks at Elms Farm, the longest visit to his ancestral home in years. Inspecting fields his father had tilled, and roaming the hills where he had played as a boy, his thoughts went back to childhood days. He dictated a memorandum recalling how at the age of eight he had visited the country store and bought a cotton handkerchief with the Constitution printed on its two sides. He also searched for and found a pair of steel spectacles that Ebenezer Webster had worn at the end of his life.[12]

These reveries of an older, simpler day, when piety for the founding fathers was taken for granted and the clear, untutored vision of men like his father was respected in the quiet village of his birth took place at the very time that people in Boston, including a number of his own former enthusiastic supporters, were organizing to break the law. Rumors of slave catchers in the vicinity sparked a giant Faneuil Hall meeting. Charles Francis Adams presided and Frederick Douglass, the most eloquent and celebrated of all the escaped slaves, gave a speech. Although Douglass had now purchased his own freedom, he told how the Fugitive Slave Law threatened him and other free blacks in the North. Any commissioner might discover some question about his "free papers" and return him to bondage. The audience of 3,500 passed a resolution.

Resolved, that we cannot believe that any citizen can be found in this city or vicinity, so destitute of love for his country and his race, and so devoid of all sense of justice as to take part in returning a fugitive slave under the law.

A vigilance committee was formed, 200 strong, with a special subcommittee to supply legal aid and find other ways of helping fugitives. When two agents of a Georgia slaveholder showed up in Boston looking for William and Ellen Craft, who had been living there since 1848, they found themselves accompanied on the street by a group of well-dressed men who shouted, "Slave hunters, slave hunters, there go the slave hunters!" One of the Georgians called William Craft a thief and was arrested for slander. After Theodore Parker, the abolitionist minister who had helped to organize the vigilance committee made a pastoral visit to warn the slave catchers that they were in physical danger, they quietly left town.[13]

The Crafts affair was one in a long list of embarrassments that plagued Webster in Massachusetts after the summer of 1850. He had been repudiated by the Whig state convention; the sniping in the columns of the *Atlas* had continued, and now the first attempt to enforce the law in Boston had been made to look both futile and ridiculous. The secretary was angry. At a dinner in Boston to honor a visiting Turkish disgnitary, he departed long enough from his ceremonial role to condemn the "crazy and mischievious men," the moral meddlers, who were disrupting nationary harmony. New England had no more to do with slavery in the South, he solemnly declared, "than she has to do with the municipal government or city on the island of Cuba." When Fillmore wrote to ask whether or not the federal government should use troops to enforce the law, Webster was emphatically affirmative. "There must be no flinching, nor doubt, nor hesitation. The thing must be done as mildly & quietly as possible, but it must be done."[14]

A mild, quiet, efficient, and democratic way of enforcing a law on an unwilling community is something politicians dream about but rarely find. Webster assured the president that there were "thousands" of young men in Massachusetts ready to help enforce fugitive slave warrants "at a moment's warning," but after spending two days investigating the Crafts affair, he was forced into a more sober assessment. The United States district attorney for Boston was George Lunt, the candidate who had been preferred over Fletcher Webster. Not only was Lunt inadequate, but his chief assistant was an active Free-Solier who had apparently notified the Crafts that they were being pursued. In addition to this, the United States marshal was a fumbler, and "the *general weight*" of most federal office holders in the district was against executing the law.[15]

It is well to remember at this point, that the first sputtering attempts to enforce the Fugitive Slave Law came at a time when the response of the South to the compromise was still uncertain. Southern radicals argued that the law was the only concession made to their region, and they insisted on vigorous enforcement. The radicals, especially in South Carolina and Mississippi, remained active and promised to rally all their strength at a convention in the fall of 1850. In addition, Fillmore and Webster had secret information leading them to believe that hotheads in South Carolina were planning to seize the federal forts in Charleston as a beginning move toward secession.[16]

Webster was frustrated by his inability to set matters right. He could hardly expect moderation in South Carolina if he was unable to break the hold of fanaticism on Boston. What he could do was to withdraw patronage from offending Whigs, write exasperated letters to Everett, and scatter public letters to presses throughout the country invoking the virtues of conciliation and Union. The last was threating to become a tired song; old rhetoric did not make new converts.

What Webster needed was to attach himself to a larger issue which would inflame the national imagination and put partisan bickering in the shade. He had been in a similar situation more than a quarter of a century earlier. As a young congressman, dragged down by the incubus of his anti-war record, he had been able to identify himself with the surging nationalism of the 1820s by urging the American government to lend its moral support to the revolutionaries in Greece. His speech in the House in 1824 had gone a long way toward changing his image from a sectional leader to a national statesman.

Now, as secretary of state, he saw a similar opportunity to ride the wave of patriotic sentiment in a direction which might favor both his own and the public interest. Recognizing the sympathy with which Americans viewed the European revolutions of 1848, particularly the attempt of Hungarians to secure independence from Austria, President Taylor had sent a special agent, A. Dudley Mann, to Austria to study the situation there and advise Washington on the wisdom of recognizing Hungary. After observing the hopelessness of the Hungarian cause, Mann advised John Clayton, Taylor's Secretary of state, against recognition. Sometime later, the Mann mission was discussed in Congress and the Austrian minister in Washington, Chevalier J. G. Hulsemann, who had complained verbally about the matter to Clayton, sent a formal note to Webster protesting American involvement in Austrian internal affairs.

Webster began work on a reply to Hulsemann at the same time antislavery vigilantes were routing the slave catchers in Boston and secessionists were breathing fire in Charleston. From an objective point of view, he knew there was much to be said for Hulsemann's position. His conservative instincts had always been offended by the kind of Manifest Destiny demagoguery that had made his negotiations with Ashburton so difficult and had actually helped to take the nation to war against Mexico. But now his political instincts prevailed. After securing Fillmore's approval, Webster dispatched a flag-waving, sword-rattling reply to the Austrian minister.

Hulsemann had warned the United States that agents like Mann could be considered spies, and that by meddling in Austrian affairs the United States opened itself to "acts of retaliation, and to certain inconveniences which could not fail to affect the commerce and the industry of the two nations." The latter was a delicate reminder that Austrians bought cotton. Webster replied by haughtily contrasting the power and vastness of America to the House of Hapsburg—a mere "patch on the earth's surface." He warned that treating Mann as a spy would have meant war, and said that Americans were proud to provide a model for the rest of the world because they believed their principles to be "the only principles of government which meet the demands of the present enlightened age."[17]

The famous "Hulsemann letter" was written in late December, 1850. It was widely praised in all sections of the country and reinforced Webster's reputation as the dominant voice of the administration. It also created problems by helping to set the tone for the reception which the defeated Hungarian Revolutionary, Lajos Kossuth, received when he visited America a year later. As a senator, Webster had joined others in asking the United States to provide asylum for Kossuth. As secretary of state, he arranged for Kossuth's release from Turkey, where he was being held in internment with other Austrian refugees, and for his transportation to the United States by the American Navy. Webster made these arrangements in February, 1851. During the rest of the year, pro-Hungarian sentiment continued to build, and Kossuth's journey by way of London was lavishly reported in the press. Hulsemann believed that he had oral assurances from Webster that Kossuth would be received not as a political leader but as a private person and would not receive an official cannon salute in New York harbor. In view of the avalanche of favorable publicity Kossuth was getting in the press, Hulsemann doubted that the secretary would stick to this position. He knew that Americans were seeing only one side of Kossuth, that there were official letters and documents showing that the imperious hero had already insulted his American benefactors, and he fruitlessly urged Webster to make these documents public. When his private interviews with the secretary began to appear in the press in a garbled form highly unfavorable to Austria and to himself, Hulsemann protested to Fillmore. He suspected, with good reason, that Webster was leaking information to the journalist Francis Grund, thus continuing to identify himself with the strong tide of pro-Kossuth sentiment.[18]

The real possibility of a formal break in diplomatic relations between Austria and the United States seems to have worried Webster less than having to decide how to treat Kossuth once he arrived. Despite his assurances to Hulsemann, the cannons roared when Kossuth sailed into New York Harbor in December, 1851, and that roar unmistakably expressed the American majority. Kossuth was feted at huge rallies, where he exploited his impressive oratorical talents to raise money and encourage federal support for another Hungarian struggle for independence. Some northern conservatives and a large number of southerners demurred, but many Americans believed Kossuth was offering Europe what Washington and Jefferson had already given the United States. Webster, who had done more than his share to promote the excitement, was alarmed. He wrote to Abbot Lawrence in London that New York seemed to have gone "crazy" over Kossuth, and that reckless interventionists in the Democratic party would certainly use him to their advantage.[19]

Since Congress had invited Kossuth to Washington, there was no way that Webster could avoid meeting him. He debated with himself on how to handle the situation. He could not afford to ignore Kossuth's popularity, yet he had no intention of getting the United States involved in European wars. He assured friends he intended to steer clear of extremes and would be as deaf as an adder if Kossuth approached him about "intervention." Some members of the cabinet and a good many senators and congressmen thought it wise to duck the banquet. Webster told Fillmore he would go because he did not want the administration to be accused of boycotting a reception given by Congress for the nation's guest. "In the present state of the country," he wrote, "especially in the interior, where Kossuth is going, I should not like unnecessarily to provoke popular attack."[20]

According to one account of the Kossuth dinner written many years after the event, Webster observed great discretion in his official remarks, and then, after the champagne, gave "what appeared to be his impromptu, individual opinions, but unluckily dropped at his seat a slip of paper on which his gushing sentences had been carefully written out." Whether this actually happened or not, it is obvious that the speech which Webster wanted the country to hear had been conceived as a sequel to the Hulsemann letter. "Let it go out," he said, "let it be pronounced in thunder tones, let it open the ears of the deaf; let it open the eyes of the blind; and let it be everywhere proclaimed what we of this great republic think of the principle of human liberty, and of that oppression which we all abhor." Reminding his audience that he had been the one largely responsible for getting Kossuth out of exile, Webster made a brief for Hungarian nationality and closed with a toast *"Hungarian Independence*—Hungarian control for her own destinies; and Hungary as a distinct nationality among the nations of Europe."

When George Ticknor had asked Webster about the rhetoric in the Hulsemann letter, he said that he had purposely made a statement which would reflect "the unparalleled growth of this country" and "touch the national pride, and make a man feel *sheepish* and look *silly,* who should speak of disunion." In explaining the Kossuth speech to another friend, he said that he had wanted to "act a conservative part" in a way that would be consistent with his opposition to European autocracy and at the same time politically useful. Obviously the last consideration weighed most heavily in his mind. Although he justified his speech to the frustrated Hulsemann by insisting that his remarks had been made as a private citizen and not as secretary of state, the *New York Herald* was closer to the truth when it noted that Kossuth was a trump card which might take a skillfull player all the way to the White House.[21]

In the short run, Webster appeared to be playing that game as well as anyone in 1850 and 1851, but some of his former admirers would never forgive him for the way he played it. Webster must have been relieved when Kossuth left for England empty-handed in the summer of 1852. Webster had always been more interested in what Hungary could do for him than in what America could do for Hungary, and his maneuvering over Kossuth in the first half of 1851 can only be understood within the context of the political and moral legacy of the compromise. Early in January, about two weeks after the Hulsemann letter, Secretary of the Navy Graham decided that the compromise was working in the sense that party feeling had cooled. Cass and the expansionist Democrats were pleased with the way Webster was treating Austria, and southerners believed that "the firm course of the administration in the execution of the Fugitive Slave Law has given a new lease to slavery, and property of that kind has not been so secure for the last 25 years." As one of the southerners in the cabinet, Graham was acutely aware of the importance of enforcing the Fugitive Slave Law, and his letters from constituents in early February, 1851, clearly show that he and his colleagues were expected to make Massachusetts toe the line. The administration could not afford another Craft affair.[22]

Cooperation in Boston, however, was not easily come by. On February 15 a mob of blacks, some of them fugitives themselves, swept in and out of the Boston Court House taking with them the prisoner "Shadrach," whose case was then being heard by Webster's friend, Commissioner George T. Curtis. That was the last Boston ever saw of Shadrach. Once again the abolitionists hooted, southerners raged, and Webster burned. These rescues challenged his authority not just because they occurred in his own state but also because the secretary of state at this time rather than the attorney general administered the federal courts. Webster telegraphed Boston. "Was it by collusion or absolute force?" he demanded. "Did the Marshall do his duty?" He insisted that leaders of the rescue party be arrested, tried to recruit the best legal talent in Boston to prosecute the cases, and repeatedly warned District

Attorney Lunt that he was expected to bring in convictions. "These causes are of the utmost importance," he said. "You must be fully aware of the consequences if just decisions should fail to be attained through any want of skill on the part of those who manage the trials." Although the cases were never successfully prosecuted, Lunt later complained that Webster tried to take them "into his own hands" and turn them into "political trials."[23]

The last fugitive slave case to be tried in Boston during Webster's lifetime came in April with the arrest of Thomas Sims, a young mulatto claimed by a man in Chatham, Georgia. Sims was held in the Court House, which was surrounded by an iron chain and guarded by three hundred policemen with a pack of bloodhounds held in readiness nearby. For the first time, the vigilance committee was thwarted. They failed in their attempts to free Sims on legal grounds and could not agree on any plan of confronting the overwhelming show of force put up by the government.

Meanwhile, Webster had come to Boston in person to make sure that for once the law would be executed. He assured Fillmore on April 9 that although the commissioner had not yet made his decision, the fugitive was safe. "The proofs are clear; & the Marshal will move south with him on Friday." Webster's prediction was borne out on April 13 when a company of policemen took Sims from the Court House and marched him through the square and across the spot of the Boston Massacre to the wharf where he boarded a ship bound for Savannah.

The same day, Webster wrote Fillmore. "On this occasion all Boston people are said to have behaved well," he reported, except for a small number of "insane" abolitionists and Free-Soilers. It only remained to convict and punish the rescuers of Shadrach. Then it would be "no more difficult to arrest a fugitive slave in Boston, than to arrest any other person." To cap it all off, Webster would say a few words at "a meeting of congratulation at Faneuil Hall."

Not exactly. The fanatics turned out to have friends on the board of aldermen who refused the use of the historic hall to honor Daniel Webster for sending Sims back to Georgia. Instead, the meeting was held outdoors in Bowdoin Square, three days after Sims had been publicly whipped in Savannah. "Gentlemen," Webster said, "a long and violent convulsion of the elements has just passed away, and the heavens, the skies, smile again upon us. . . . Let me congratulate you and ask you to congratulate me, that the events of the last year or two have placed us under better auspices; we see clearer and breathe freer. . . . Every citizen feels that he is a man."[24]

Webster never departed from that position. In speeches made later in the spring, his tone became more aggressive. He ridiculed those who felt their "honor" required them to break the law, flatly labeled abolitionists traitors, and boasted that the law would be executed "in all the great cities," even in Syracuse, where the next anti-slavery convention was to be held. "If the occasion shall arise then," he thundered, "we shall see what becomes of their lives and their sacred honor." Later, at Capon Springs, Virginia, he disposed of the Higher Law. How high was it he demanded—as high as the Blue Ridge—as high as the Alleghenies? And he contrasted the "fanatical and factious abolitionists of the north" with southern secessionists, who, though wrong in principle, were "learned and eloquent . . . animated and full of spirit . . . highminded and chivalrous."[25]

Daniel Webster was astride the last peak of his career. He was probably correct in thinking that the big interests in the country, the merchants and manufacturers in the North, the planters in the South, and a majority of the people in all sections, wanted the laws obeyed and agitation ended. He had perhaps done more than any other man in public life to bring this temporary situation about, and, in the process, he reinforced among many of his followers the image of the Godlike man. But for others, Webster had fallen like Lucifer. One of the greatest men God ever sent, Wendell Phillips said, to "let the devil buy."[26]

The denunciation of Daniel Webster by New England reformers and intellectuals in 1850 and 1851, which continued long after his death, has been noted in varying degrees of detail by Webster's biographers and other historians of the period. What has not been satisfactorily explained is why the attacks were so intensive, and why they made such a lasting impact on Webster's reputation. The secnd part of the question can be answered by simply observing that the most famous Webster denigrators, men like Emerson, Parker, Lowell, Whittier, and Wendell Phillips, were among the most eloquent Americans of their time. No matter how savage and extreme, their rhetoric would endure.

To understand why these men reacted so violently to Webster after March, 1850, we must recall the source of the power he had wielded over the American mind, especially in New England, for thirty years. The leading abolitionists, Free-Soilers, and Transcendentalists in New England in 1850 had been young men when Webster was coming into his prime, and he had been their guardian. "Did men honor Daniel Webster?" Parker asked in Webster's funeral oration. "So did I. I was a boy ten years old when he stood at Plymouth Rock and never shall I forget how his clarion words rang in my boyish heart." Whittier had thought Webster a giant ever since the Hayne speech and had compared the political attacks of the Jacksonians against him to a tomcat challenging an eagle or "the nibble of a mouse at the heel of an elephant." Lowell remembered what Webster had meant to the young intellectuals of his time by describing him as one "the massive simplicity of whose language, and the unvarying force of whose argument, flashing into eloquent flame as it heated, recalled to those who listened and saw before them one of the most august shapes manhood ever put on, no inadequate image of Pericles." Wendell Phillips, the eloquently abusive abolitionist orator, had written in Webster's Harvard class book in 1831, "I love the Puritans, honor Cromewell, idolize Chatham & Hurrah for Webster." And Emerson, whose detailed analysis of Webster in letters, journals, and lectures lasted more than three decades, regularly compared him with the greatest figures in history.[27]

It was not simply as a guardian that the young intellectuals saw Webster. They also perceived him as the great American statesman who would carry the nation out of mediocrity to realize her proper destiny. To understand the special position which Webster occupied in the minds of these men, it will be helpful to follow Emerson's perceptions more closely. On July 3, 1822, Emerson wrote to John Boynton Hill, a friend and former classmate living in the South, "I think we Yankees have marched since the Revolution to strength, to honors and at last to ennui. . . . I shall expend my patriotism in banqueting on Mother Nature." Emerson was lamenting the lack of distinction, especially the lack of great men, in the new democracy. Two months later, Boston elected Webster to Congress, an event which Emerson thought significant enough to note in his journal while musing over the "Genius of America." He wrote to Hill saying, "We are sending our Giant down among you false Southerners . . . anticipating the triumph of a Northern interest to be begun to be achieved by Mr. Webster." Later, he advised Hill to study law in the north "where Webster fought his way up,"[28]

Webster captured Emerson's imagination by appearing as the man of principle and genius in American politics. Ordinary politicians were constantly shifting course in an attempt to represent the public will, but Webster was the self-reliant statesman. "This is one that is not blown about by every wind of opinion," Emerson wrote after reading the reply to Hayne, "but has mind great enough to see the majesty of moral nature and to apply himself in all his length & breadth to it." Later, equating moral achievement with greatness, Emerson wrote, "This has been done by the Pitts & Burkes & Websters & is second only to the praise of Godliness."[29]

The general tone of Emerson's remarks about Webster remained the same throughout the thirties and forties. As long as he continued to champion the principles of 1776 and 1787 and oppose the extension of slavery, the senator appeared to be a living vindication of American institutions. "Who as rich in the room where Socrates sits but he," Emerson wrote in 1834. "Whilst Webster speaks to the Senate who is formidable but he?" During Webster's visit to England in 1839, Emerson wrote to Carlyle:

I cannot tell you how glad I am that you have seen my brave Senator and seen him as I see him. All my days I have wished that he should go to England & never more than when I listened two or three times to debates [in] the House of Commons. We send out usually mean persons as public agents, mere partisans, for whom I can only hope that no man with eyes will meet them, and now those thirsty eyes, those portrait-

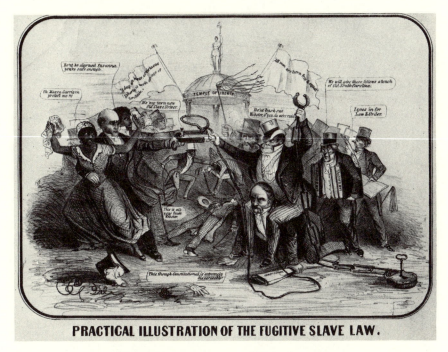

PRACTICAL ILLUSTRATION OF THE FUGITIVE SLAVE LAW.

A typical representation of Webster in the
abolitionist press.

eating, portrait-painting eyes of thine, those fatal perceptions have fallen full on the
great forehead which I followed about, all my young days, from court house to
senate chamber, from caucus to street.[30]

Webster's well-publicized weaknesses were not lost on Emerson. He
knew about the senator's prodigal ways, told Carlyle that he had drunk the
"rum of party" so long "that his head is soaked sometimes," and would
have agreed with Lowell that he should "leave Banks and Tariffs to more
slender fingers," because "If ever a man was intended for a shepherd of the
people Daniel Webster is." When the great man came to Concord to try a
case, Emerson entertained him at his home, filled his journals with adulatory
remarks such as Elizabeth Hoar's saying "that in Mr. W's case, modesty
ceased to be a virtue," and noted that it was senseless "to quarrel with
Webster because he has not this or that fine evangelical property. . . . His
expansiveness seems to be necessary to him. Were he too prudent a Yankee
it would be a sad deduction from his magnificence. I only wish that he
would never truckle, I do not care how much he spends."[31]

Even after the fateful truckling in 1850, Emerson acted reluctantly. He had
never liked the abolitionists, and as late as 1850 was able to dismiss Garrison

by saying, "He cannot understand anything you say, and neighs like a horse when you suggest a new consideration." It was not simply what Webster said on March 7 that made Emerson add his voice to the abolitionists' attacks upon him; it was his entire role then and afterward in corrupting public opinion. When Bostonians sent a memorial of congratulation to Webster, Emerson called it one of the most "painful" events in the city's history and wrote "the badness of the times is making death attractive." The public yelped with delight at the Hulsemann letter. Emerson saw only the falseness of Webster's position in pandering to jingoism with one hand while he tried to clamp a muzzle on the abolitionist and a halter on the slave with the other. Webster talked like Jefferson but, like Metternich, "He would dragoon the Hungarians for all his fine words." The word "liberty" in Webster's mouth now sounded like "love" in the mouth of a whore.[32]

Emerson expected ordinary politicians to surrender their principles, but the great man of conscience was charged to represent the great idea of the age. In 1850 that idea was freedom, expressed in America by "the idea of emancipation." This was the course of the future, and Webster could not represent it because for all his natural gifts he was content to be just another political manager. Sorrowfully, Emerson delivered the judgment:

I have as much charity for Mr. Webster, I think, as any one has. I need not say how much I have enjoyed his fame. . . . Mr. Webster, perhaps, is only following the laws of his blood and constitution. I suppose his pledges were not quite natural to him. Mr. Webster is a man who lives by his memory, a man of the past, not a man of faith or hope. He obeys his powerful animal nature;—and his finely developed understanding only works truly and with all its force when it stands for animal good; that is for property. . . . He looks at the Union as an estate, a large farm, and is excellent in the completeness of his defence of it so far. He adheres to the letter. Happily he was born late. . . . What he finds already written he will defend. Lucky that so much had got well written when he came. . . . A present Adams & Jefferson he would denounce. . . . So with the eulogies of liberty in his writing—they are sentimentalism & youthful rhetoric . . . it means as much from him as from Metternich or Talleyrand. This is all inevitable from his constitution. All the drops of his blood have eyes that look downward.[33]

When the gods fail, the faithful turn upon them with greater scorn and fury than that directed at mortal enemies because they have lost part of their own identity. Emerson grieved over Webster's fall because he believed that the man who once promised to represent the transcendent American idea had in fact come to represent "the American people just as they are, with their vast material interests, materialized intellect and low morals. Heretofore their great men. . . . have been better than they, as Washington, Hamilton & Madison. But Webster's absence of moral faculty is degrading to the country."[34]

Emerson's judgment was repeated over and over again in the anti-slavery literature. "The people are fast awaking to great principles," Lowell had written some years earlier. "What they want is a great man to concentrate and intensify their enthusiasm," a popular leader like Webster "to gather the scattered electricity into one huge thunderbolt and let it fall like the messenger of an angry god among the triflers in the Capitol." Phillips said that in Webster "we looked to find the King of Men, one who should be the voice of the Spirit of the Age." But Webster fell. Great men had fallen in the past, said Parker, "But it was nothing to the fall of Webster. The Anglo-Saxon race never knew such a terrible and calamitous ruin. His downfall shook the continent. Truth fell prostrate in the street."[35]

These are not the cries of self-righteous moralists delighted to see the mighty topple. To many sensitive, intelligent New Englanders of principle, the last years of Webster's life were an agony to watch. Whittier said he wrote 'Ichabod' in one of the saddest moments of my life." "O Webster! Webster!" Parker mourned, "would God that I had died for thee!" The lament was not limited to radicals like Parker. "We have all mourned for him," the more conservative Richard Henry Dana wrote in 1851 "because we felt that when he fell we fell with him." And Amos Lawrence, the very personification of respectable Massachusetts Whiggery, who had made Webster a gift of silver plate in 1831, wrote "I never wish to look *upon his face again* until I can see some token of that high toned principle, he did so much to instill among us." In 1867, fifteen years after Webster's death, George Hillard, a former friend and ally, said a majority of people in Massachusetts were still "actually ashamed" of his memory.[36]

20

THE LAST TIME AROUND

Although abolitionists were not worth worrying about, Webster took his troubles with the Whigs seriously. He made a clear distinction in his own mind between the "eminent man" and the "man in the most eminent position." Calhoun had been an eminent man; Clay was an eminent man, and so was Webster. But the Whig presidents all fell in the second category. Like Harrison and Taylor, they were carried into office on the wave of military glory, or like Tyler and Fillmore, fell into it by accident. Webster's last great ambition and the final major effort of his public life was to reverse this trend.[1]

Fallen irretrieveably in the eyes of the New England abolitionists, Daniel Webster was still a major power to most Americans. Easily the best-known and most experienced presidential possibility in the country, he was able to enhance his visibility by carrying out the duties of secretary of state. At the same time, he had left the Senate and did not need to act on traditionally partisan issues like the tariff. He was prominently identified with the compromise, which majority sentiment in all sections favored, and he could probably count on Fillmore's support.

Although he knew he needed strong Whig support, Webster no longer thought or acted along strict party lines. Ever since the Massachusetts election of 1850, which gave a narrow plurality to the Whigs and tipped the balance of power to a coalition of Free-Soilers and Democrats, his strategy had been to let the state fend for itself, Ordinarily, this would have meant keeping hands off in the fight for his own Senate seat between Winthrop, whom he had practically created, and the radical Charles Sumner. But since Winthrop had refused to support the Fugitive Slave Law, Webster now dropped the word that he would not object to a union-minded Democrat in his old place.

Sumner was finally elected in late April, 1851, about the same time that the Boston aldermen (Whigs to a man) kept Webster out of Faneuil Hall. The split between Webster and the Whig establishment had now become irreconcilable, and Webster wrote to Harvey explaining why he and his friends should find a broader base for their support. The truth was that on the big question of keeping the compromise, sound Whigs in other states, especially in the South, believed there was little to choose from between a Winthrop and a Sumner and preferred Massachusetts Democrats over Massachusetts Whigs. Besides, Webster went on, there was a growing belief that Union-minded Whigs and Democrats all over the country were ready to break off old loyalties and form a new national party.[2]

Webster had been waiting twenty years to lead a new party based on principles of constitutionalism and union. Now, perhaps, there was more to the idea than wishful thinking. He had letters from old Democratic adversaries predicting the same thing. David Henshaw, for example, who only a few years earlier had been swapping insults with Webster through the party presses in Massachusetts, now insisted that Boston Democrats cared more for the Union than the Whig aldermen who had snubbed him. "The old issues that long divided parties have mostly passed away," wrote Henshaw, and "new ones have arisen under new combinations." Perhaps the new combinations were already coming into power. Perhaps the influential new coalition of Union Whigs and Democrats in Georgia would be a model for other states. Webster hoped so and thought he saw encouraging signs of the possibility in Mississippi, Connecticut, and Pennsylvania.[3]

Meanwhile, as the new party lay aborning, the immediate problem was to get his own campaign launched. His preference, expressed in the spring of 1851, had been for a "meeting of Union men of all parties" to be held in Massachusetts. An endorsement from such a meeting at home could set an example for Webster supporters elsewhere. However, the candidate's thinking was more advanced than that of his managers. Close friends like Everett, Choate, Harvey, and Haven felt that Webster's name should be put forward at the Whig state convention, but in a way that would be outside the regular party leadership. This meant a statewide petition campaign, which took time. It also meant a closer identification with the Whigs than Webster desired, and when it became clear that Winthrop was to be the Whig candidate for governor, Webster flatly refused to have anything to do with the Whig convention, which met in Springfield in September. Having recently assured a Virginia audience that if the North deliberately refused to obey the

Fugitive Slave Law "the South would no longer be bound to observe the compact," he could hardly afford to have his name associated with a convention which wanted to make an opponent of that law governor.[4]

After Winthrop was beaten in the fall elections, Webster's friends staged their own meeting at Faneuil Hall. Everett wrote the address which was everything that Webster wanted. He was given the credit for saving the country in 1850 and put forward as one behind whom "good citizens of both parties, and in both of the great sections of the country, may cordially and consistently unite." After reading the statement in a Washington paper, Webster wrote to Frank Haven that he was "affected and overwhelmed by the sentiments and efforts of such ardent friends. . . . Whatever may happen hereafter, I am satisfied."[5]

It was good that Webster was so satisfied with the beginning of the campaign, because there would be little to take pleasure in thereafter. The road from Faneuil Hall in November, 1851, to Baltimore in June, 1852, was all downhill and ended in defeat and humiliation. The first thing to go wrong was that party lines, although severely strained by the compromise, refused to break. Webster's vision of a new party had always been idiosyncratic, and some of his closest supporters, like Everett, had taken pains to disassociate themselves from it. Moreover, what Webster could do to bring about the desired result was very limited. If the compromise was working, why should there be a new party? If it was not working, how could Webster get credit for it? When he received the Faneuil Hall endorsement, Webster was "certain that there can be no *entire Whig ticket* nominated for President & Vice President." Consequently, he said little about the Whigs, and constantly invoked the blessings of Union in his speeches. The crowds continued to come, perhaps as much to get one last glimpse of the man as to hear the message. In New York where he spoke in February on "the Dignity and Importance of History," people paid fifty dollars apiece for tickets. As usual, he stressed the golden age in American history, the age of Washington. He wanted the audience to see that the man and the message were one, that Washington had returned. But for this to happen, the generation of '52 would have to behave like the generation of '89, and that was implausible even to Webster's reading of history. "The character of man varies so much from age to age, both in his individual and collective capacity," he said, "and so many new and powerful motives spring up in his mind, that the conduct of men in one age . . . is no sure and precise indication of what will be their conduct, when times and circumstances alter." In 1852 most Whigs and Democrats were inclined to take the Union as a matter of course and to stay with familiar political roles. In March when it appeared that the Democratic party would officially support the compromise, Webster finally saw the light. "I have to say that in my opinion," he wrote to Everett, "if we have any good in store for us, it will be through the *Whig Convention*."[6]

The trouble with this alternative was that the Whigs still threatened to put secondrate men into "the most eminent position." Two other Whig contenders were Fillmore and Winfield Scott, the perennial Whig general who had gotten the support of powerful anti-compromise Whigs like Seward. Webster does not seem to have worried too much about Scott, but Fillmore was a problem. When he joined the cabinet, Webster believed that Fillmore would not run for a second term. That was Fillmore's understanding, too, although he and Webster made no formal commitments to each other beyond pledging to keep their hands off patronage for personal political gain. By late 1851, however, Fillmore's modest intentions had begun to conflict with the ambitions of many Whig leaders who felt he would be the strongest candidate. Just as northern anti-slavery Whigs had fastened on Scott, the southern Whigs began to group around Fillmore. They preferred him to Webster because he had proven himself under fire in the White House and did not have to live down his past as a New England man. Not that Fillmore's support was limited to the South. His standing was also high in many areas of the North and West—so much so that Edward Everett felt obliged to explain that although bound by filial ties to support Webster's initial thrust for the presidency, he stood ready to work for Fillmore if the latter were nominated. Everett thought he could say the same for most of Webster's friends. The upshot of all this was that without formally acknowledging the fact, Fillmore allowed his name to be kept in the contest. He apparently still favored Webster and felt that he would be able to transfer his strength to him at the convention.[7]

In late January, 1852, an administration paper in Washington quashed the rumor that Fillmore would withdraw. That night, one of the secretary of state's dinner guests remarked, "Mr. Webster was not in a very genial mood." Later Webster's friends accused Fillmore of violating his pledge not to run. The story was probably false, but there was nothing contrived about Webster's distress. He simply could not believe that serious Union-minded Whigs in the South or anywhere else would put Fillmore's candidacy above his own. On the other hand, the president and the secretary of state remained on good personal terms and continued to work well with each other. Webster's resignation, much talked about in Washington, never came to pass.[8]

Perhaps no public man in America was more politically experienced than Webster. He had lived with the uncertainties of politics through four decades. He knew how capriciously elections were decided, how frequently the larger prize went to the lesser man. If he had been toughened by defeat, that did not show up. Psychologists tell us that age has a way of bringing out a person's real character. As a younger man, Webster had tried to conceal his ambition. Now, the last time around, he wore his

heart on his sleeve. He told a New York audience that the whole purpose of his life had been to serve his country and win the "approbation
and regard" of his countrymen. In response to the fulsome remarks made
on his behalf at a reception by the New Jersey legislature, Webster ejected
the customary modest rejoinder, to say that "nothing more than justice
has been awarded." And in Faneuil Hall on May 22, where he had been
rejected a year earlier, he told a cheering audience that he proposed "no
platform but the platform of my life and character . . . no assurance . . .
but the assurance of my reputation."[9]

Unconsciously, perhaps he knew this would not be enough. He admitted that as a practical matter his chances depended on getting Fillmore's
support, and complained about the futility of his friends' efforts. "Nobody
does anything on our side," he wrote to Fletcher in May, "I have had eno.
of cheer'g prospects & sicken'g results." A carriage accident which occurred about the same time while he was driving near Marshfield added physical to psychological anguish. Thrown to the ground, spraining both
wrists, he was more or less immobilized for days, could not tip his hat or
lift a cup of tea, and could barely sign his name. He was still suffering
from the effects of the accident as he returned to Washington to sit out the
convention which opened in Baltimore on June 16.[10]

During the four hot, humid days it took to make a nomination, Webster
and Fillmore remained in Washington, out of touch with each other until
the end. The areas of strength of the three candidates were clearly staked
out at the beginning. Fillmore was solid in the South with a smattering of
strength in the North and West. Scott held the West, most of the North
outside New England, and hoped for support in the upper South. Webster, who claimed to speak for the nation, was sure only of New England.

In early skirmishing over the platform, Websterites and Fillmorites
worked together and managed to force agreement on a strong statement
endorsing the compromise. Then the balloting began. On the firrst ballot
Fillmore had 133, Scott 131, and Webster 29. A combined Fillmore-
Webster vote would produce a nomination. George Babcock, a Fillmore
delegate, reread the president's instructions, asking to have his name withdrawn from the contest "whenever you may deem it proper." He con-
sulted his fellow delegates but found they had no intention of giving up on
Fillmore.[11]

Between Friday evening when the balloting began, and Saturday night,
when the convention was adjourned, forty-six ballots were taken with
only slight shifts in the positions of the three candidates. On Sunday the
Webster and Fillmore managers tried fruitlessly to come to terms.
Humiliated by his poor showing, Webster denounced both Fillmore and
the faithless southerners for his disgrace, and refused to release his delegates.

In the end reason won out. Concerned that Scott would win unless he acted, Webster reluctantly advised his supporters to switch their votes to Fillmore on Monday morning. The instructions came too late or were ignored, and as the balloting began again, the Webster delegates stubbornly held on. Finally, on the fifty third ballot, enough Fillmore votes shifted to give Scott the nomination. Once more the Whigs had passed over the statesman for the general.[12]

Immediately after Scott's monination, Edward Curtis and Fletcher Webster took the train to Washington. They found Webster calm but grim, and that night, when, according to custom, the Whigs came by his window for a speech, he once again played out his role as the graceful loser. But the labored serenity of the public man belied a private agony. Daniel Webster was hurt, and hurt badly by what he called the "folly" and "infidelity" at Baltimore.[13]

At the risk of using too strong a word, one could say that the whole "Webster organization" had a share in the folly. There had been precious little organization and no real national effort in his behalf. Influential friends like Peter Harvey, Frank Haven, and Edward Everett in Boston and Edward Curtis and Charles March in New York had planned rallies, collected petitions, and distributed speeches, but there was no systematic attempt made to line up delegates in other states. Everyone seemed to believe that winning the nomination would simply be a matter of presenting the great statesman's accomplishments and cashing in his reputation for votes.

Nor did Webster himself seem to be interested in reaching out for new friends in order to broaden his political base. Judge Key, for example, a popular young Whig from Cincinnati, had gone to Washington to meet Webster before the convention only to find himself treated like a minor diplomatic functionary. "A half a dozen kind words from Mr. Webster," complained the judge's friend to Fletcher, "would have made him his champion."[14]

Despite his antics for Harrison in 1840, Webster had never really cultivated the new democratic style. He had always been a weighty orator and his heavy, reserved manner in private conversation was better suited to the patriarch than to the politician on the make. In one way this made Webster an attractive figure, but it was not an attraction easily turned into votes. The contrast between his manner and the new political style was captured by a reporter who traveled with Webster and Stephen A. Douglas in the presidential car which went through New York in 1851 to celebrate the completion of the Erie Railroad.

... a Senator of great ability and fame, sits curled up on a seat, smoking his friendly cigar, chatting with everyone about everything—having no separate atmosphere of dignity, and wishing to be among the first intellectually, by no other right than he would claim the place physically—that is by actual superiority. As a gentleman very happily said, "Mr. Douglas has plenty of loose change—Mr. Webster has nothing but 50 (pound) notes."[15]

It was folly to think that those fifty pound notes would be worth as much to Americans in the fifties as they had been to the generations which grew up under the shadow of Washington and Jefferson. Whether there had been "infidelity" or not is a harder question to answer, but there is some reason to believe that not all of Webster's followers shared his distaste for Scott. One of Fillmore's confidants reported that several of them were "Scott men at heart," an observation which is supported by evidence among the Websterites themselves. A few weeks before the convention opened, Edward Curtis wrote to Harvey explaining why "Northern men who want to see Mr. Webster's Presidency but who prefer Scott to Fillmore" should *"hold on for Webster without flinching."* Curtis predicted that if Webster delegates held their ground, the South would shift to Webster because Fillmore could never get a majority. "If there were any danger of having Fillmore hoisted on us by adhering to Mr. Webster," Curtis said, "the case w'd be very different."[16]

The Curtis letter may help to explain why Webster's supporters never carried out his instructions. They were northern politicians, after all, and their future lay with the North. Perhaps some of them had begun to doubt the political vision of their great man, had begun to realize that the question of Union was a secondary issue after all, and that if one wanted a political future in the North, he had better be right about slavery.

On April 19, 1850, a Philadelphia correspondent to the *New York Herald Tribune* reported that he had just traveled on the same train with "the remains of Daniel Webster" and was struck by the fallen statesman's ravaged appearance. "His face was sallow and shrunken, and his eyes languid and glazed. . . . His steps faltered even to tottering; and his whole person seemed the emblem of infirmity." If we would believe his critics and enemies, Webster died in pieces, losing first his soul (March 7, 1850), then his hope (the Baltimore convention), and finally his life—when the ruins passed into dust at Marshfield on October 24, 1852.[17]

This melancholy interpretation of Webster's last years assumes that the aging Webster sought the presidency above all else and failed. The ambition, failure, and disappointment are all there in the record, certainly, and Webster never tried to conceal them. Yet for all its plausibility and obvious attraction to moralists and dramatists, the picture of a defeated giant expiring in disgrace and anguish needs to be redrawn. As he approached the end, Webster continued to work hard and productively, to play when he was able, and

A daguerreotype taken in 1850.

to prepare for a death-bed scene that would be played just once—but according to his own direction.

Although, Webster was not above tailoring American foreign policy to suit personal political needs, it would not do to let his handling of Hulsemann and Kossuth speak for his entire career as secretary of state under Fillmore. The objectives of American foreign policy at this time were essentially Whiggish—to express American sympathy for liberal causes elsewhere and to defend American economic interests abroad while avoiding foreign entanglements and the acquisition of new territory—all this in the face of an opposition party which identified itself with Manifest Destiny. Whatever his other goals, Webster's treatment of Austria was consistent with these objectives, and during his tenure in the Department of State he was forced to confront many other problems which a potential presidential candidate might have wanted to avoid.

Webster and Fillmore inherited the Clayton-Bulwer Treaty from the Taylor administration. This treaty, which pledged England and the United States not to control countries in Central America or monopolize future canal rights there, was filled with ambiguities, one of which exploded when a British brig-of-war fired on an American ship off the coast of Nicaragua. As American Anglophobes swung into action, Webster managed to get the British government to disavow the incident, and at a conference at Marshfield with the British minister he worked out an agreement which temporarily eased the crisis.

Another prickly problem for Webster's department involved the proposed railroad across the Tehuantepec peninsula in Mexico. American investors had secured the rights to this project from France, but Mexico would not let them build. Webster, who had always thought poorly of Mexico, pressed the American case, but ultimately realized that no Mexican government could afford to indulge American interests to this extent so soon after the war. He warned Mexico, however, that the United States would never permit a railroad across the peninsula to fall into the hands of a third power.

American relations with Spain during this period reached crisis proportions over Cuba. Traditional American policy held that Cuba should never be allowed to fall into the hands of a major European power like France or England. Webster had affirmed this position as Tyler's secretary of state when he assured Spain that the United States would help her hold Cuba as a Spanish possession. Since then, the acquisition of Cuba had become a goal of many expansionists, but American attempts to purchase the island had failed. By the time Webster returned to the State Department, an alliance of Cuban revolutionaries and American adventurers had sprung up under the leadership of Narciso López, a kind of Cuban Kossuth. López and his American supporters had already tried two unsuccessful invasions of Cuba before Webster came into office. They were prosecuted by the government in New

Orleans, but local juries refused to convict them. A third attempt was made by the López band in August, 1851. It failed miserably, and López and many of his American followers were executed. When this news reached the United States, it set off a wave of anti-Spanish rioting in New Orleans, wrecking the Spanish consulate there and destroying the property of Spanish nationals. Webster's response to the Spanish minister's letter of protest, in contrast to the inflammatory rhetoric he had employed in dealing with Hulsemann and Kossuth, was a masterly exposition of rational conciliation. Pointing out that occasional mob action is an affliction to be endured in all countries, Webster repudiated the popular violence in New Orleans, assured the Spanish minister that his government would be indemnified for its loss of property, and promised that the returning Spanish consul would be honored with "a national salute to the flag of his ship" in the harbor of New Orleans. At the same time, he urged Spain to release the remaining American prisoners (this was eventually accomplished) and to bear in mind that Americans reacted vigorously to the summary executions in Havana because they could not understand how punishment could be meted out without due process of law.[18]

During Webster's day, the Department of State was still a relatively small organization very much under the supervision of the secretary. He frequently drafted important diplomatic documents with his own hand and sometimes resorted to his own library to do the necessary research. The abolitionists thought he was dead on his feet, but Webster knew better. On a typical day he might spend seven hours in his office, dictating simultaneously to two secretaries on different subjects, and then retreat to his study to work for several more hours. His dispatches were well thought out, clearly written, and generally consistent with his conservative, anti-expansionist philosophy. For example, he read the dispatches from the American representative on the Sandwich Islands with great care and replied with a long, private letter explaining to what lengths the United States was prepared to go to preserve the independence of those islands without encouraging expectations of annexation on the part of Americans living there. When the French republic fell in 1852, Ambassador William Rives was reluctant to appear in public before Napoleon III and wrote to Webster for instructions. In replying, the secretary plunged into a long analysis of why the republic had failed. "The whole political Government of France," he wrote, "was vested in one numerous Assembly and in the President. There was no third power, no check, no mediator. . . ." This was a fatal error because "it is impossible to unite public Liberty with the safety of society & the security of persons & property without guards & balances. . . . Hence the proposition, apparently paradoxical, is strictly true, that Liberty consists in restraint; that is to say, the Liberty of each individual is in proportion to the restraint imposed on other individuals & public bodies who might otherwise have the power as well as the disposition to do him wrong." The fall of republican government in France was a catastrophe leaving our own government as "the only great Republic on earth." Nevertheless it had been a principle ever since Washington's time to recognize "that every nation possesses a right to govern itself according to its own will." Therefore, as long as the new government stood, the United States should recognize it as the legitimate government in France. Webster wrote this memorandum out for his own purposes. Only the latter part involving the instructions to Ambassador Rives actually appeared in the official dispatch. It is an important document because it shows the vigorous intellectual process he went through as he approached important diplomatic problems.[19]

Webster wrote his last important diplomatic paper late in August, 1852, about two months before he died. He was trying to work out an agreement between England and the United States over American fishing rights on the North Atlantic coast when trouble erupted over the obscure Lobos Islands off the coast of Peru. American ships, accustomed to taking guano from these uninhabited rocks, had been suddenly prohibited by Peru's claim to sovereignty over them. Webster's initial reaction was to assume the Americans were right and to back them up with the authority of the Navy. Subsequent investigation led him to doubt the wisdom of this move, and he wrote a long, detailed analysis dealing with American and Peruvian claims to the islands in the perspective of history and international law, and urging that both countries exercise restraint until a final settlement could be reached. This able document, which later became the basis on which the United States recognized Peru's sovereignty over the islands, had unfortunate political implications. The American giant had flashed his power at a weak neighbor to the south and suddenly backed away. This was not the kind of consistent, strong behavior young Americans expected from their leaders, and the Democrats made the most of the matter. But Webster felt he had brought the country back on the course of law and reason, and he was prepared to take the consequences. "My dear sir, you have as I hope a future," he wrote to Fillmore a month before he died, "& if in your fortunes hereafter, it shall be necessary to say that Lobos proceeding was mine, say so and use this letter as my acknowledgment of that truth."[20]

Webster still had other roles to play besides that of the statesman. Even during the last year of his life, it was not uncommon for him to make his early morning promenade through the Washington market. His costume was always the same, blue coat, buff vest, black pants, all sailing majestically along under a broad-brimmed soft felt hat. Frequently he would have a servant in tow with a market basket, ready to pick out a choice shad glistening from the river, a saddle of lamb, or a bunch of fresh asparagus. Solemnly joking with the butchers, grocers, and fish mongers along the way, the secretary would momentarily forget about his troubles with Austria, Cuba,

Mexico, and Boston while he kept his eye out for a likely possum to set on his table stuffed with chestnuts and surrounded by baked yams.

Half a century of impressive eating had left its mark on Webster. He complained occasionally of the gout, but despite his swollen belly the zest and grace of the younger man lingered on. Dining, like practicing law, was an important part of his life, and he rarely forgot an important precedent. In planning a dinner party in Washington, for example, he sent a long personal letter to a friend in Boston recalling a particular dish of tripe. "Unscathed by the frying pan it was white as snow; it was disposed in squares, or in parallel-ograms, of the size of a small sheet of ladies' note paper; it was tender as jelly; beside it stood the tureen of melted butter, a dish of mealy potatoes and the vinegar cruet. Can this spectacle be exhibited in the Vine Cottage, on Louisiana Avenue, in the City of Washington?" In exchange for the recipe he offered an instructive postscript explaining the Greek and Latin origins for *tripe*. [21]

During his first tenure as secretary of state the Webster mansion on La-fayette Square had been renowned for its formal parties and banquets, and Webster's black cook, Monica Carty, was generally thought of as one of the great culinary artists in Washington. Now Webster lived in much more modest quarters, and his hospitality was on a correspondingly more modest scale. Nevertheless, a summons to his table was as highly regarded as ever. How could young Congressman Ashmun of Massachusetts have disregarded a note like the following?

Sat 4 oclock

We have a small party to dine today & one vacancy has suddenly occurred by Death or resignation. My wife abhors a vacant seat at table, as much as nature abhors a vac-uum in the old philosophy. Our party is select & we can think of nobody young, handsome & agreeable enough to supply our loss & who is at the same time on such a footing with us that we venture on an invitation at so late a period as yourself. Therefore & wherefore & for these reasons, I beg of you to present yourself at 5 oclock at the Vine Cottage, Louisiana Avenue. "Now is the time & this the hour" Come on![22]

As a dinner guest, Webster continued to be sought after as much as any-one in the capital. He was noted less for his wit than for his ability to talk in-telligently on almost any subject. This ability was derived in part from his memory, which was almost perfect, and partly from his library, which was large and eclectic. He was said to have spent more than thirty thousand dollars for books on history, biography, geography, travel, literature, agri-culture, and natural philosophy. His favorite writers, like Scott and Shake-speare and the prophets of the Old Testament, he knew almost by heart. Writing to John Latrobe in the summer of 1851, Webster recalled a conversation they had had twenty years before about "whether shoes were made right and left in Shakespeare's time" and how they resolved it by referring to the passage in *King John:*

> *standing on slippers which his nimble feet had falsely*
> *thrust on contrary feet.*

A lifetime spent poring over law books and drawing up legal documents had never cured Webster of his Dartmouth predeliction for bad humorous verse. At a political dinner on December 22, 1851, for example, he offered the following lines in tribute to Henry Foote, senator from Mississippi:

> *Oh thou whatever name delight thine ear*
> *Governor, Senator or Brigadier!*
> *Allow thy friends, who are sincerely thine,*
> *To pledge thy health in bumpers of rich wine,*
> *Although thy name be but thy lower limb*
> *Thy head and heart are always in good trim.*
> *Squadroons of cavalry may be disarmed,*
> *But Mississippians put all foes to route.*
> *Whenever they make gallant fight on Foote.*[23]

Temperamentally generous, Webster found it hard to bear grudges and gracefully acknowledged the apologies of a former clerk in the State Department who had turned secret papers over to the Democrats to help launch the agonizing Ingersoll investigation. One of his black servants, Paul Jennings, whose freedom Webster had purchased from Mrs. Madison some years earlier, remembered that when the former president's wife fell on hard times, Webster told him "whenever I saw anything in the house that I thought she was in need of to take it to her."[24]

Neither age nor ambition curtailed Webster's far-flung curiosity. When he went to Capon Springs, Virginia, for a political speech, he sent Fletcher a long letter saying little about politics but discussing at length and in great detail the history and geography of the place. His interest in practical details never flagged and his oration to the New-York Historical Society, one of the most impressive intellectual efforts of his last few months, called characteristically for "a history of firesides; we want to know when kings and queens exchanged beds of straw for beds of down and ceased to breakfast on beef and beer."[25]

As an old man, Webster was as much in the public eye as ever. Publishers begged for anecdotes about him, and any scrap if information about Marshfield was considered newsworthy. "Everybody writes and prints about me just what he pleases," Webster complained in December, 1851, "& I have tried in vain to stay the current. Friends do as much harm as enemies." Although friends hurt him by their incessant adulation, the gossip associated with Webster during the last two years of his life emphasized his all too human weaknesses. Henry Thoreau picked up some of this gossip in the summer of 1851, when he paused on a walking trip which took him through the village of Marshfield to chat with some of the local farmers about their famous neighbor. Webster "would eat only the produce of the farm during the few weeks he was at home—brown bread and butter and milk—and sent out for a pig's cheek to eat with his greens," Thoreau noted in his journal, "ate only what grew on his farm, but drank more than ran on his farm."[26]

Webster's reputation as a heavy drinker had become so widespread at the time of his death that his physician and close personal friends felt compelled to formally deny it. Dr. Jeffries's assertion that Webster discovered the virtues of temperance during the last months of his life may be taken at face value, but the pious remarks of Edward Everett Hale, who said he had seen Webster thousands of times socially and "never had a ream or thought that he cared anything about wine or liquor," are obvious nonsense. As he grew older, Webster relied on alcohol more and more to help get him through public occasions. He would sip brandy and water while he spoke, and sometimes this practice got him into trouble, as at the ceremony celebrating completion of the Boston-Montreal Railroad. The affair took place in Boston in September, 1851, and the honored guests included President Fillmore and Lord Elgin, governor general of Canada. Using the occasion to sing a hymn of praise to America, Webster so completely ignored Lord Elgin that the latter almost left the platform in anger. Complaining later of the "great rudeness" of the speech, the lord was told that "Webster had taken too much & was not fully himself." Naturally, the opposition press made the most of such incidents and treated their readers to cartoons depicting the Secretary of State as an old toper drinking with the British minister ("Daniel in the Lion's Den") and as a red-nosed bartender mixing a cocktail ("The Great Ornament of the Bar Preparing a 'Smash' For General Scott").[27]

Upon seeing Webster late in life mumble incoherently to a large audience for ten minutes, James Parton concluded "that the man had expended his sincerity and that nothing was real to him except wine and office." But Parton also said that "such were the might and majesty" of Webster's presence "that he seemed to fill and satisfy the people by merely sitting there in an armchair, like Jupiter, in a spacious yellow waistcoat with two bottles of madeira under it." Parton was a careful observer and a good journalist. His recollection cannot be treated frivolously. It is instructive to read further, therfore, and find him saying, "All this gradual, unseen deterioration of mind and character was revealed to the country on the 7th of March 1850, . . . and still exerts perverting power over timid and unformed minds." Like other moralists, Parton assumed that a man who would support the Fugitive Slave Law would debase himself in other ways. Because Webster continued to fascinate the people in spite of his sins, Parton felt obliged to paint him in the darkest color possible.[28]

Other anti-slavery writers wrote about Webster's alleged promiscuity the way Parton wrote about his drunkeness. The basic source for these stories was Jane Swisshelm, abolitionist editor of a Pittsburgh weekly, the *Saturday Visitor*. In a letter to the *Visitor* from Washington in May, 1850, she said, "nearly everyone knows that he sometimes drinks to excess and his friends here say he requires to be excited by wine to make him approachable-civil. His mistresses are generally, if not always, colored women—some of them big black wenches as ugly and vulgar as himself. These will openly run store bills on his account." In his home state, the *Liberator* printed the piece without comment, and the Lowell *American* said, "We have never before heard that Mr. Webster's 'mistresses' were 'colored women', but the fact that he has 'mistresses' of some color is, we suppose, as notorious as any other fact concerning him."

Thirty years later, Jane Swisshelm explained how she came to write her story. Upon reaching Washington she heard stories about "a family of eight mulattos, bearing the image and superscription of the great New England statesman, who paid the rent and grocery bills of their mother as regularly as he did those of his wife." Upon investigating Webster's reputation more closely she discovered "that his whole life was full of rottenness." She wrote her story, showed it to anti-slavery congressmen Joshua Giddings, George Julian, and Gamaliel Bradford, editor of the abolitionist *National Era*. They all agreed that she was correct but urged her to withhold publication for fear of recrimination. Because they confirmed the truth of the story, Jane Swisshelm allowed it to be printed, knowing "where to find the proof if it should be legally called for." The legal challenge never came and the closest she ever came to offering the proof occurred five years later, when she claimed that an article in *Putnam's Monthly* justified her. The article in question merely stated that there were many brothels in Washington patronized by congressmen. It offered no support whatsoever for her specific allegations against Webster.[29]

One of the more intriguing aspects of the Swisshelm charge is that it is similar to an oral tradition still existing in Marshfield to the effect that Webster's black cook, Monica Carty, also served as his mistress. Was Jane Swisshelm referring to this when she mentioned the family of eight mulattoes? We know that Webster was fond enough of Monica Carty to have her portrait painted, that she was sometimes with him alone in Washington when his wife was away, that in some instances she might very well have made purchases on his account. But that is all we know.[30]

There is good reason to distrust the Swisshelm story. She was an abolitionist journalist writing shortly after the March 7 speech and had decided on his moral character long before she went to Washington. She offered no

THE GREAT ORNAMENT OF THE BAR
PREPARING A "SMASH" FOR GENERAL SCOTT.

The great statesman ridiculed as a great tippler just before his death.

Daniel in the Lion's Den.
"THE FISH QUESTION WILL BE SETTLED, AS THE BULWER TREATY WAS, WITH THE BRITISH MINISTER OVER A BOTTLE OF BRANDY."—[*Democratic Review*.

proof, and her detailed explanation of the charges against him was not made until 1880, when it appeared in an unreliable book of reminiscences. But reliable or not, she did permanent harm to Webster's reputation. Serious historians and biographers writing about Webster in the late nineteenth century did not question the allegations of his sexual promiscuity. James Ford Rhodes claimed that Webster "was not scrupulous in observing the seventh commandment" and that it was "generally believed that in his later years he was daily flustered with brandy and that he trod the path of the gross libertine." Henry Cabot Lodge, destined to become a famous Massachusetts senator himself, said that Webster was "a splendid animal as well as a great man, and he had strong passions and appetites, which he indulged at times to the detriment of his health and reputation." Rhodes and Lodge were northern men brought up in the afterglow of the Civil War. Like other Victorians, they believed that a person's character was all of a piece, and that a man who could slip in one part of his moral life would naturally fall short in other ways. They could not believe that high-minded abolitionists would blacken a person's reputation without cause.[31]

W. W. Corcoran, the wealthy New York financier, was so impressed by Webster's March 7 speech that he canceled two of Webster's notes for five thousand dollars. Deciding that this in itself would be a poor show of gratitude—since Webster would probably not have paid the notes anyway—he also wrote a check for one thousand dollars and sent it to the senator. People could differ over the moral implications of Webster's position on the Fugitive Slave Law, but everyone knew his vulnerability when it came to money, and during the last two years of his life money problems continued to plague him and to undermine his credibility as a disinterested statesman.[32]

When the news of Scott's nomination was flashed to Boston, Edmund Quincy said, "Hogarth himself would have broken down" in an attempt to portray the faces of despair on State Street over the political death of the man they had "bought and paid for so many times over." Despite the fact that the Democrats had been accusing Webster of being a paid retainer of banks, merchants, and manufacturers for more than twenty years, he continued to look to the same sources for financial help. The fund set up by friends to enable him to return to the Senate in 1846, which had helped to spark the Ingersoll investigation had not stabilized his financial situation. He certainly felt no qualms about accepting Corcoran's check. Indeed, his correspondence at the time suggests that he probably encouraged it. "Two rather smart showers are now falling on me," he wrote to the Boston banker Frank Haven March 9, 1850, "a shower of praise and a shower of censure. I wish the variety could be farther increased and that there would come in a small shower of Gold. The interest and installments of these old debts keep me in poverty and humiliation & I am afraid I shall not live long enough to see them thru."[33]

When Webster was offered the top position in Fillmore's cabinet, his benefactors were once again called upon to make it possible for him to accept. In addition to a few thousand dollars raised by friends, "to meet the expenses of his table," as George Curtis delicately put it, Webster was to receive twenty thousand dollars, payable in regular installments, from a group of forty New York bankers and businessmen who had agreed to subscribe five hundred dollars each.

In February, 1851, Charles Allen, a Free-Soil congressman from Massachusetts, publicly charged that in return for their gifts Webster had arranged for a syndicate of bankers in Boston, New York, and Washington to handle a three-million-dollar indemnity to Mexico at a preferred rate, which cost the government between thirty and forty thousand dollars. George Ashmun, speaking for Webster in the House, denounced the baselessness of this charge, which never developed into a formal investigation. Officially, Webster was cleared of wrongdoing, but the suspicion lingered on, and Andrew Johnson spoke for many of his colleagues in the Congress when he said the secretary's indebtedness and his dependence on the bounty of others was well known and it was "reasonable to infer that Mr. Webster would like to realize a little percentage in this way."

Theodore Parker said that Webster's last speeches "smell of bribes." All of his serious biographers have disputed this charge, more on the basis of their conviction that Webster was too big a man to be bribed than on the basis of proof. The fact is that the bankers who were given the Mexican indemnity included men who had contributed to the Webster fund, and we know now what was earlier denied, that Webster knew who they were. The circumstances were damaging to his reputation, to say the least.[34]

One might almost feel that it would have been worth it if the largesse which he took from wealthy business interests ever succeeded in making Webster solvent, but it never did. In July, 1851, we find him writing again to Haven, complaining about old debts and asking, "How am I to pay expenses from day to day?" At the same time he was continuing to expand his estates. In the spring of 1852 he spent $879 on 150 additional acres in New Hampshire. On September 29, less than a month before his death, he borrowed $1,000 from Frank Haven to add 50 acres to Marshfield. Borrowing had become a way of life. He needed his great farms. They had become the only world over which his leadership was undisputed, and he would maintain them and continue to expand them at any cost. Somewhere deep in his heart Webster must have known how great the cost had become. Four days before he died, the man who sought comparison to Washington and Wellington dictated a letter to Corcoran & Riggs, asking them to honor a check for which there were no funds. "I must therefore, once more, throw myself on your *kindness,*" he said. "I shall see you as soon as our Whig candidate is elected President." In a postscript he added what were perhaps the last words he ever wrote, "My eyes are weak & inflamed with catarah. D.W."[35]

Anxious to ease Webster's disappointments after the Baltimore convention, Everett wrote assuringly to remind him that he did not depend "upon office, even the highest, for influence or reputation." Poor consolation, perhaps, for a man who felt he deserved the presidency, but it helped. The people of Boston also helped. On July 9, they closed their stores and decorated their streets and brought out their companies of gaily uniformed militia as if for a national holiday to receive Daniel Webster for the last time. Men and women fainted away and one militia man dropped dead from the one-hundred-degree heat, but there were crowds all along the way from Roxbury, where Webster stepped into his carriage, to the platform at the foot of Beacon Hill. It took three and a half hours to complete the procession. No one had seen anything like it in Boston since the reception for Lafayette. On the platform, Webster once again heard himself lauded as "the American" and "Champion of the Union." Once again he lectured his constituents on the lessons of their history. Conjuring up the ghost of old Sam Adams in half-Quaker dress, with his broad-brim hat and gold-headed cane, after all his doubting crying out "Aye" for the Constitution, Webster said Massachusetts had never drawn "a breath that was not a national breath." Thus he was proud to call himself a Massachusetts man, and he assured his listeners, "What I have been, I propose to be."[36]

A few days later with his secretary Charles Lanman, Webster made his last visit to Elm Farm where he found John Taylor laid up from an encounter with a Hungarian bull, which had recently been sent by an admirer in New Jersey. The bull, on its way to becoming a celebrity, had been called St. Stephen, but Webster agreed that he was more like Kossuth and that all creatures out of Hungary, whether on two legs or four, could give trouble to well-meaning Yankees. Except for a noticeable lack of appetite, Webster was in reasonably good health at this time, but he tended to dwell more on the past than on the present or the future. Driving Lanman through the countryside, he pointed out a hill where he had gone sledding as a boy and frozen his feet. He stopped at Boscawen, where he had first practiced law and met Grace Fletcher and went up to Punch Brook where he had caught his first trout. In such an environment, the press of official business seemed unreal. He corresponded with the president about the fisheries and Lobos Islands controversies, but included long, rambling descriptions about his farm and what it had been like during frontier days.[37]

In late July, Webster came back to Boston to prepare for a meeting at Marshfield with the British minister. He was well enough to spend a day with a young friend fishing for tautog near William Paige's summer house at Nahant. Upon getting off the cars at Kingston before the short carriage ride that would take him to Marshfield, Webster found that his neighbors there had planned their own reception. A procession of carriages two miles long followed him all the way home, where he addressed the multitude from a platform on a hill overlooking his home. The speech was short, informal, and apolitical except for one brief crowd-pleasing moment when he promised to protect American fishermen "hook and line, bob and sinker." Marshfield, at least, was secure, and the tears of gratitude which reportedly overtook him when he reached the refuge of his own house were undoubtedly authentic.[38]

What would the future hold? Shortly after Baltimore, Webster had toyed with the idea of becoming minister to England. Fillmore was encouraging, but Webster declined partly because he thought it would mean moving down in status and power and partly because he expected Pierce to win in November and could not trust his future to the Democrats. Reluctantly returning to Washington in the first week of August, Webster found the president cordial and the weather and his health better than he had expected. Plunging into the routine of his department with some of the old Webster gusto, he was able to report to Blatchford that he had his "great halibut hook" in the fishery question and would soon pull it aboard. Webster left Washington for the last time on September 8. Four days later he was back in Marshfield, accompanied by his secretary George Abbot, trying to fight off his annual attack of hay fever. "We talk of everything but law and politics," Webster wrote the president, "and one advantage of my condition is that it excuses me from looking into any newspapers."[39]

What Webster said about the ban on political talk was deceptive. Although he discouraged general conversation on the subject, he had in fact become the object of a political tug of war among his own close friends and supporters. He might think of himself as a nearly retired statesman who had put politics behind him, but he remained a power in the country, and practical men wanted to know how he would use his influence in the coming election. He received plenty of advice by mail, some of it urging him to support Scott as the party's choice, some of it urging him to let his own name be put forward as an independent candidate, thus supporting movements already afoot in Massachusetts and Georgia. Webster chose a third alternative; he would exercise whatever power remained to him by keeping silent about the election. He would not sacrifice his self-respect by endorsing Scott, nor would he support or discountenance any movement on his own behalf. Privately he proclaimed the death of the Whig party and spoke approvingly of the Democratic candidate, Franklin Pierce, an old New Hampshire friend. Many of his closest associates were dismayed. Men like Everett, Harvey, and Edward Curtis felt their future lay with the Whigs, and refused to support separate Webster movements. Not even a formal request from seven of his most stalwart New York supporters, men who had given him both money and votes, could move Webster to come out for Scott. George Abbot was revolted by the attempts to squeeze the last drop of influence out of a dying giant, and referred darkly to a "bribe of twenty pieces of silver each weighing $1000." This may have been a reference to the twenty thousand dollars pledged in New York to Webster when he entered the cabinet, or it may have referred to another source of money. In any event, Webster refused to publicly endorse any candidate, and the election which took place after his death confirmed his prediction that Pierce would win.[40]

Webster's declining interest in politics was influenced by the growing apprehension of his own death. He approached death as he approached life— deliberately and with a sense of the seriousness of the occasion and the role he should bring to it. Who would win the election of 1852 was no longer a matter of any importance. How he, himself, would spend his last days on earth was very important. Webster was not oppressed by the details of death and had already overseen completion of the family tomb on a hill near the sea on land early consecrated by the Pilgrims. "It is quiet and secure against change," he told Fillmore, "and not far from my house. . . . I dwell on these things without pain. I love to see a cheerful old age; but there is nothing I should dread more than a thoughtless, careless, obtuse mind, near the end of life . . . its sobers the mind, I think, and leads us to salutary reflections, to contemplate our last resting place."[41]

Returning to Marshfield from Washington, Webster's major concern was not his hay fever, as he led others to believe, but the debilitating effects of dysentery and other intestinal disorders. He felt soon after his return that he might survive and was thinking about books he would write in his retirement on religion and the life of Washington. After a visit to Dr. Jeffries in Boston on September 20, his hopes diminished. He gave Fillmore regular and candid reports of his condition but preferred the world to understand that he was simply struggling with his annual siege of hay fever. Meanwhile, guests continued to flow in and out of the house. On most mornings Webster was still able to dictate for a few hours, and on good days he might appear pale and shrunken but still impressive, bundled into a great coat and tucked under the familiar broad-brimmed felt hat, to take a carriage around Marshfield and point out its special beauty spots to visitors. He presided at dinner as usual in formal dress, but while others helped themselves from the generous table he contented himself with a little gruel and brandy and water. Every morning he had a conference with Porter Wright and went over the work of the day in detail.

Sometime in late September or early October, Webster was sitting by the fire at Marshfield with a few friends when one of them read an account of the Duke of Wellington's death on September 14 which emphasized that the Duke had expired in Spartan simplicity on a campaign cot in a tiny room at Walner Castle. Webster began to prepare for his own death. On October 10 he dictated a statement of faith, which he corrected five days later, with directions that it be inscribed on his tombstone.

Lord, I believe; help Thou mine unbelief.
Philosophical argument, especially that drawn from the vastness
of the universe in comparison with the apparent insignificance
of this Globe, has sometimes shaken my reason for the faith
that is in me; but my heart has assured, and reassured me, that
the Gospel of Jesus Christ must be a Divine Reality.

The Sermon on the Mount cannot be a merely human production.
This belief enters into the very depth of my conscience. The
whole history of man proves it.

D A N ' L   W E B S T E R [42]

The abolitionists would make much of the "opiated piety" of Webster on his death bed, but he knew what he was doing. Without going through any special kind of spiritual transformation the pre-eminent authority on the American Constitution found it appropriate to say a few final words about religion. God was still worth pronouncing upon even if General Scott was not. He knew that his words would be effective. Soon his eulogists would be reminding the faithful that "Daniel Webster, the most intellectual man of recent history, the profoundest reasoner of modern times, near the end of his days, but while all his faculties were in full vigor, and at a season of the utmost solemnity, gives us deliberate testimony to the truth and reality of religion."[43]

Not all of Webster's final ceremonial acts were solemn. To help him through the increasingly difficult nights he called on one of his boatsmen, Thomas Hatch, for help.

[October 1, 1852]

Mr Hatch,—I have
A Secret to reveal to you
I want you to light a lamp on the home squadron.
"My light shall burn & my flag
shall fly as long as my life lasts."

Do you see to this Mr. Hatch & let nobody know of it, & take them by surprise in the evening by Six o'clock. There is no one here in my room but you & I & William & if he mentions it I will put a brace of balls through him.

D.W.

The home squadron was a small boat moored in a duck pond outside Webster's room. A flag was attached to the mast, and Webster asked Hatch to hang a ship lantern from the mast so that he could look at the boat at night. It is worth noting that he put this request in writing, thus assuring that it would be a part of his papers. At about the same time, he asked that his favorite oxen be brought by the window of his room. To watch them crop the grass, according to Porter Wright was "his last enjoyment."[44]

Webster wrote his final letter to Fillmore on October 18. On the twenty-first, George Abbot informed the president that there was no hope for his recovery. George Curtis had come down from Boston to work out the final details of Webster's will, carrying with him a fat roll of greenbacks from Samuel Appleton in Boston, who was disturbed at reports that the dying statesman could not pay household expenses.

On the morning of October 22 Webster received the plain gold ring which he had ordered two days earlier from a Boston jeweler. He looked at the inscription attentively. It read "D.W. to S.S. Oct. 1852." Then he slipped the ring on the finger of his black nurse Sarah Smith, who had also been Julia's nurse, saying, "Wear it in memory of me and Julia."[45]

The next morning Webster announced that he would die sometime that night. He asked Dr. Jeffries, who had sat up with him the night before, to send to Boston for Dr. Mason Warren to be with him at the end. In the evening he assembled the household, signed his will, and gave a short address dwelling on the certainty of the existence of God and the importance of the hope of immortality. George Curtis, who was there with pencil and paper to take down the words, noted that Webster referred to the "crepuscular twilight." He was still on the platform; he knew Americans would dwell on Daniel Webster's final hours at Marshfield as the world had read about Wellington at Walner Castle. After a fainting spell he revived and asked Dr. Warren to tell him exactly what would happen up to the moment of death, and on one occasion, as he heard the Twenty-third Psalm being recited at his bedside, he muttered "Yes, Thy rod, Thy staff—but the *fact,* the fact I want." As Curtis noted, Webster "seemed to have an intense desire for a consciousness of the act of dying." It was an appropriate way, many thought, for him to die. "Of the millions of the human family who had died, perhaps no one had ever carried any perfect recognition of this final act into the future state," one eulogist would write, "and it is possible that Mr. Webster may have conceived the original and sublime thought of being the bearer of this new knowledge into the pure, intellectual world of which he was so soon to become an inhabitant."[46]

Webster died according to his own schedule at 2:37 A.M., October 24. He had asked for a simple, respectful burial. They laid him out in his blue coat and black trousers in an open coffin on the grass in front of the house at Marshfield, and the mourners filed by in the thousands. No intelligent American could ignore the occasion. "He was a statesman and not the semblance of one," Emerson wrote in his journal. "But Alas! he was the victim of his ambition." Webster would not have understood that remark, but he would have smiled modestly at the neighboring farmer who said as he passed by the coffin, "Daniel Webster, the world without you will be lonesome." The smile would have been real, but not the modesty.[47]

EPILOGUE

After Calhoun died, Webster told the Senate that no matter how controversial his career had been, Calhoun's opinions would "now descend to posterity under the sanction of a great name," for he had lived long enough and performed well enough in public "to connect himself for all time to the records of his country"—he had become "a historical character."

What Webster said about Calhoun can be said with even more confidence about himself. Calhoun had been a great man tied to slavery and sectionalism, ideas that had outlived their time. Webster identified himself with liberalism (liberty) and nationalism (Union) the two dominant tendencies in the nineteenth-century Western world. Whether or not his defense of the Union postponed the war is arguable. What is not arguable is that the war came as he predicted; secession was followed by bloodshed. Webster was spared the agony of peering into the bloody pit of civil war as he had prayed to be. Had he lived, his one consolation would have been that the presidency, which had so often eluded him, was in the hands of a man whose every action after 1860 would be based on a devotion to the same principles Webster had first articulated thirty years before.

Much of American history can be explained by the recurrent tensions between the Movement and the Establishment. The champions of the Movement, our most impressive reformers and radicals, have been dominated by the idealism of the Declaration of Independence, by the vision of America as a city on a hill in which everyone lives together in freedom, justice, and equality. They have found the main theme of American history to have been the corruption of this vision by an Establishment, which has remained

in power through plunder and systematic oppression. To the champions of the Movement, Webster has always appeared as Black Dan—a great talent bought by the Establishment to throw up a rhetorical smoke screen obscuring the real injustices in American life.

The defenders of the Establishment, on the other hand, have been happy to accept Webster as one of their own. Like their radical adversaries, they too have been motivated by an idealistic vision of the American past. But they have been impressed less by the corruption of this vision than by its substantial realization, by the fact that even with all her faults America represented, as Webster said in 1825, "the last hopes of mankind," a sentiment which Lincoln reiterated as "the last best hope of earth" in 1862. To conservative-minded Americans, Daniel Webster at his best represented the Establishment in America with an intelligence, dignity, and eloquence which have rarely been equaled in our history. To thousands of Americans growing up in the new American nation, he performed this function so sublimely that, in James Parton's words, they "reposed to Daniel Webster" as if he were something more than mortal. "He represented to them the majesty and strength of the United States. He gave them a sense of safety. Amid the flighty politics and loud insincerities of Washington, there seemed one solid thing in America as long as he sat in an arm-chair of the Senate-chamber."

The perspective of history encourages us to consider a more mixed judgment. From this perspective, Webster appears as a great man flawed. The flaws cannot be ignored; they are all there in the record and they are the flaws of most of his countrymen. Like other Americans, Webster appeared assertive and self-reliant, but was propelled and held down by unfathomable forces deep within himself. Like them he was too fond of money, power, and the trappings that go with them, and too inclined to overlook the seamy side of American life.

If Webster's flaws were the flaws of his countrymen, his power was all his own. At his best he was exactly as he appeared, the aboriginal patriot, so convinced of the integrity and inviolability of one nation under the Constitution, that he helped multitudes discover their own identities as Americans. When war came nine years after his death. Americans whose sense of nationality had been sharpened by Webster's rhetoric and whose moral sense had been sharpened by the anti-slavery crusade would rally to Lincoln's banner. Because the Movement and the Establishment could join together, victory in the Civil War would mean a victory for liberty and Union. To have contributed mightily to this end would be Daniel Webster's enduring contribution to the world.

NOTES

Although the general literature available on Daniel Webster is enormous, the scholarly literature has been thin until quite recently. When I began this study, George T. Curtis's two-volume authorized biography (1872), Claude Fuess's two-volume biography (1930), and Richard Current's carefully done *Daniel Webster and the Rise of National Conservatism* (1955), the only book-length study of Webster from a modern scholarly point of view, were the most reliable accounts of Webster's life. Since that time, four more specialized studies have appeared and I have profited from them all. Maurice Baxter's *Daniel Webster and the Supreme Court* (1966) deals authoritatively with an aspect of Webster's career that I have chosen to leave largely undeveloped. Norman Brown's *Daniel Webster and the Politics of Availability* (1969) is a useful close analysis of Webster's role in the election of 1832. The scholarly, well-written monographs of Sydney Nathans and Robert Dalzell, *Daniel Webster and Jacksonian Democracy* (1973) and *Daniel Webster and the Trial of American Nationalism* (1972) deal with the middle and latter parts of Webster's political career in much fuller detail than I have been able to do here.

As the notes indicate, all of the books mentioned above along with hundreds of other articles and secondary works relating to Webster have contributed to my own work. At the same time I have tried to base this book as closely as possible on the manuscript record. When I began my research a small fraction of Webster's correspondence was available in Vols. 1, 2, and 16 of *The Writings and Speeches of Daniel Webster* (Boston, 1903) and in C. H. Van Tyne's *The Letters of Daniel Webster* (New York, 1902). Thousands of manuscript letters were scattered in collections across the country. I visited most of these collections with the aid of a Guggenheim Fellowship in 1967 and 1968. Since that time under the general editorship of Charles M. Wiltse the *Microfilm Edition of the Papers of Daniel Webster* has appeared in forty-one rolls along with *The Papers of Daniel Webster: Correspondence,* Vols. 1 and 2, *1798–1824, 1824–1829* (Hanover, N.H., 1974, 1976). For the purposes of simplification in documenting Webster's correspondence I have referred to the new printed edition (referred to as *Papers*) when I could. Other letters or manuscripts are referred to the older printed sources (*Writings* and Van Tyne) when possible. Letters and manuscripts not available in print but in the *Microfilm Edition* are so attributed (*Microfilm*). I have checked all quotations from the printed letters with the microfilm edition.

CHAPTER 1

1. *New York Times,* October 26, 1852. Wendell Phillips, *Speeches and Lectures* (Boston, 1863), p. 615.

2. Henry Cabot Lodge, *A Fighting Frigate and Other Essays and Addresses* (New York, 1907), p. 119.

3. The various editions of Webster's speeches can be followed in Clifford Clapp, *The Speeches of Daniel Webster, A Bibliographic Review,* Papers of the Bibliographic Society of America (1919), Vol. 13. The Printed Cards for the Library of Congress for 1946 list 148 entries under Webster's name as opposed to 119 for Jefferson, 90 for John Quincy Adams, 73 for Clay, 42 for Calhoun, and 20 for Jackson.

4. S. P. Lyman wrote a series of articles for the Boston press in 1849 celebrating Webster's farmer image. They were reprinted in his *The Public and Private Life of Daniel Webster,* 2 vols. (Philadelphia, 1852).

5. George S. Hillard, in S. P. Lyman, *The Public and Private Life . . . ,* vol. 2, p. 217.

6. *Ibid.,* p. 223. Nelson Singer and H. S. Drayton, *Heads and Faces and How to Study Them* (New York, 1892), pp. 47, 52.

7. See for example, Orrin E. Klapp, *Symbolic Leaders: Public Dramas and Public Men* (Chicago, 1964), and Robert C. Tucker, "The Theory of Charismatic Leadership," in *Philosophers and Kings: Studies in Leadership,* ed. Dankwart Rustow (New York, 1970), pp. 69–95.

8. Hugh Duncan, *Symbols in Society* (New York, 1968), p. 96.

9. Marvin Meyer, *The Jacksonian Persuasion* (New York, 1960); William Taylor, *Cavalier and Yankee* (New York, 1957). Fred Somkin, *Memory and Desire in the Idea of American Freedom, 1815–1860* (Ithaca, N.Y., 1967).

10. Ruth M. Elson, *Guardians of Tradition: American Schoolbooks of the Nineteenth Century* (Lincoln, 1964). Daniel Webster, *The Life, Eulogy and Great Orations of Daniel Webster* (Rochester, 1854), p. 6.

11. William Yancey, *Congressional Globe,* April 10, 1846, p. 652.

12. Allan Nevins (ed.), *The Diary of John Quincy Adams* (New York, 1951), p. 531. Charles Binney, *The Life of Horace Binney* (Philadelphia, 1903), pp. 125, 264.

13. Edmund Quincy to Richard Webb, July 14, 1846, Boston Public Library. Theodore Parker, *A Discourse Occasioned by the Death of Daniel Webster* (Boston, 1853), pp. 77, 97.

14. Bliss Perry, *The Heart of Emerson's Journals* (Boston, 1926), pp. 45, 85, 252, 261. Ralph Waldo Emerson, *Journals of Ralph Waldo Emerson* (Boston, 1912), vol. 8, p. 189.

15. Stephen Vincent Benét, *The Devil and Daniel Webster* (New York, 1937), pp. 14, 36.

16. Van Wyck Brooks (ed.), *The Journal of Gamaliel Bradford* (Boston, 1933), pp. 378, 445. Claude Fuess, *Daniel Webster* (Boston, 1930), vol. 2, pp. 398–399.

17. James Parton, *Famous Americans of Recent Times* (Boston, 1873), p. 57.

18. Peter Harvey, *Reminiscences and Anecdotes of Daniel Webster* (Boston, 1855), p. 58. Oliver Dyer, *Great Senators Forty Years Ago* (New York, 1889), p. 289.

CHAPTER 2

1. There is little significant manuscript material on Webster's parentage or his early childhood. The basic printed sources are Webster's brief autobiography, written when he was forty-seven years old, which appears in *Writings,* Vol. 1; George Ticknor Curtis, *Life of Daniel Webster* (New York, 1870); Claude Fuess, *Daniel Webster* (Boston, 1930), and S. P. Lyman, *The Public and Private Life of Daniel Webster* (Philadelphia, 1860). Much of the Lyman book was published in article form before Webster's death when Lyman visited New Hampshire to do a series on Webster's early life.

2. *Writings,* vol. 17, p. 4.

3. Daniel Webster to Millard Fillmore, July 12, 1852, *Writings,* vol. 18, p. 535. Lyman, *Public and Private Life . . . ,* vol. 1, p. 156. Undated clipping from *New York Observer,* Webster Papers, New Hampshire Historical Society.

4. F. B. Sanborn, *Recollections of Seventy Years* (Boston, 1909), vol. 2, p. 582.

5. Fuess, *Daniel Webster,* vol. 1, p. 26.

6. Alice Morse Earle, *Stage Coach and Tavern Days* (New York, 1900), p. 66.

7. Fuess, *Daniel Webster,* vol. 1, pp. 10–11. John J. Dearborn, *History of Salisbury New Hampshire* (Marlboro, N.H., 1890).

8. Fuess, *Daniel Webster,* vol. 1, pp. 23 ff.

9. Lyman, *Public and Private Life . . . ,* vol. 17, p. 195.

10. Daniel Webster to R. M. Blatchford, May 3, 1846, *Writings,* vol. 18, p. 228.

11. *Writings,* vol. 17, p. 9.

12. *Ibid.,* p. 12.

13. Fuess, *Daniel Webster,* vol. 1, p. 49.

14. *Writings,* vol. 17, pp. 53, 55.

15. "Reminiscences of Aaron Loveland," typed copy of Ms., Dartmouth Archives.

16. Copied extract from the Records of the United Fraternity, Brandeis University.

17. Curtis, *Life of Daniel Webster,* vol. 1, pp. 31, 44–46.

18. *Ibid.,* p. 32. *Writings,* vol. 17, pp. 71–72.

19. Curtis, *Life of Daniel Webster,* vol. 1, p. 13. Undated clipping, New Hampshire Historical Society.

20. Dearborn, *A History of Salisbury New Hampshire.* Webster was baptized in the village church as a baby, but did not formally unite with the church until he was twenty-five.

21. *Writings,* vol. 15, pp. 475–484.

22. "Richard Lang's Students Book," Ms., Dartmouth Archives.

23. *The Dartmouth,* Dec., 1872, p. 404.

24. Curtis, *Life of Daniel Webster,* vol. 1, p. 51. Augustus Alden to Daniel Webster, Nov. 5, 1831, *Microfilm,* 9639. Daniel Webster to Jereremy Bingham, Feb. 11 and Dec. 28, 1800, *Writings,* vol. 17, pp. 81, 85. Daniel Webster to George Herbert, Jan. 7, 1801, *Papers,* vol. 1, p. 31. Daniel Webster to Jeremy Bingham, Feb. 5, 1800, *Papers,* vol. 1, p. 28.

25. "Reminiscences of Aaron Loveland."

26. *Microfilm,* 17 ff.

27. *The Dartmouth,* Dec., 1852, p. 21; Sept. 9, 1875, p. 21. Fuess, *Daniel Webster,* vol. 1, pp. 50–51. Daniel Webster to Jeremy Bingham, *Writings,* vol. 17, p. 94.

28. *Writings,* vol. 15, p. 502.

CHAPTER 3

1. Daniel Webster to Jeremy Bingham, Sept. 22, 1801; *Writings,* vol. 17, p. 92, Daniel Webster to N. Coffin, Oct. 3, 1801, *Writings,* vol. 17, p. 94. Daniel Webster to Jeremy Bingham, Oct. 26, 1801, *Papers,* vol. 1, p. 33. Daniel Webster to Jeremy Bingham, Dec. 8, 1801, *Writings,* vol. 1, p. 98.

2. Daniel Webster to Jeremy Bingham, Feb. 25, 1802, *Papers,* vol. 1, p. 36.

3. Daniel Webster to Thomas Merrill, [1802?], *Microfilm,* 88.

4. Daniel Webster to Jeremy Bingham, Feb. 11, 1800, Dec. 28, 1800, June 14, 1801, *Writings,* vol. 1, pp. 80, 84, 90.

5. Daniel Webster to Jeremy Bingham, Jan. 17, 1801, *Writings,* vol. 1, p. 86. Daniel Webster to H. Fuller, Jan. 26, 1801, *Writings,* vol. 1, p. 87.

6. *Writings,* vol. 17, p. 101. C.D. to Daniel Webster, Feb. 25, 1802, *Microfilm,* 114.

7. Daniel Webster to Jeremy Bingham, May 18, 1802, *Papers,* vol. 1, pp. 38–42. *Writings,* vol. 17, p. 113. Daniel Webster to H. Fuller, Aug. 29, 1802, *Writings,* vol. 17, p. 121.

8. Daniel Webster to Ezekiel Webster, Nov. 4, 1802, *Papers,* vol. 1, p. 43.

9. James W. Hurst, *The Growth of American Law: The Law Makers* (Boston, 1950), pp. 253–254. Charles Warren, *A History of the American Bar* (New York, 1966), pp. 216–220.

10. Daniel Webster to John Porter [1802–1803], *Microfilm,* 171.

11. Warren, *A History of the American Bar,* ch. 8. Daniel Webster to Thomas Merrill, Jan. 4, 1803, *Writings,* vol. 17, p. 128.

12. Daniel Webster to Thomas Merrill, March 16, 1804, *Writings,* vol. 17, p. 160.

13. *Microfilm,* 109.

14. Daniel Webster to Thomas Merrill, March 16, 1804, *Writings,* vol. 17, p. 160.

15. Daniel Webster to Jeremy Bingham, May 18, 1803, *Writings,* vol. 17, p. 137. Morton J. Horwitz, "The Emergence of an Instrumental Conception of American Law 1780–1820," in Bernard Bailyn and Donald Fleming (eds.), *Law in American History* (Boston, 1971), pp. 287–329.

16. John Demos, "The American Family in Past Time," *The American Scholar* (Summer, 1974), 431. *Microfilm*, 103 ff. *Writings*, vol. 15, p. 533.

17. Daniel Webster to H. Fuller, Dec. 21, 1802, *Writings*, vol. 17, p. 126. Daniel Webster to Thomas Merrill, Aug. 3, 1803, *Microfilm*, 232. Daniel Webster to Thomas Merrill, Nov. 11, 1803, *Writings*, vol. 17, p. 149. Daniel Webster to Thomas Merrill, Dec., 1803, *Writings*, vol. 17, p. 153.

18. Daniel Webster to Jeremy Bingham, April 3, 1804, *Papers*, vol. 1, p. 50. Ezekiel Webster to Daniel Webster, April 4, 1804, *Papers*, vol. 1, p. 52. Daniel Webster to Ezekiel Webster, May 5, 1804, *Papers*, vol. 1, p. 53.

19. Daniel Webster to Jeremy Bingham, Aug. 4, 1804, *Writings*, vol. 17, p. 185.

20. Dumas Malone (ed.), *Dictionary of American Biography* (New York, 1930), vol. 5, pp. 280–281; vol. 14, pp. 271–273. *Writings*, vol. 17, pp. 183–184.

21. William H. Gilman and others (eds.), *The Journals and Miscellaneous Notebooks of Ralph Waldo Emerson* (Harvard, 1960), vol. 1, p. 9.

22. Daniel Webster to Thomas Merrill, Nov. 30, 1804, *Papers*, vol. 1, p. 65. *Writings*, vol. 17, p. 178.

23. Daniel Webster to Jeremy Bingham, Jan. 2, 1805, *Writings*, vol. 17, p. 198. S. P. Lyman, *Public and Private Life of Daniel Webster* (Philadelphia, 1860), pp. 16–18.

24. Judah Dana to Daniel Webster, Jan. 18, 1805, *Papers*, vol. 1, p. 67. *Manuscripts*, Summer 1959, 33–34. Daniel Webster to Judah Dana, Dec. 29, 1804, *Microfilm*, p. 430.

25. *Writings*, vol. 17, pp. 31–33.

26. Daniel Webster to Jeremy Bingham, May 4, 1805, *Papers*, vol. 1, p. 69.

27. Daniel Webster to Jeremy Bingham, Jan. 19, 1806, *Writings*, vol. 17, p. 219. Sally Webster to Ezekiel Webster, May 25, 1805, *Writings*, vol. 17, p. 210. Daniel Webster to Ezekiel Webster, May 25, 1805, *Papers*, vol. 1, p. 71. Claude Fuess, *Daniel Webster* (Boston, 1930), vol. 1, pp. 85–91.

28. *Writings*, vol. 18, p. 229.

29. P. Thacher to Daniel Webster, May 17, 1805, *Microfilm*, p. 508. Ezekiel Webster to Daniel Webster, May 19, 1805, *Writings*, vol. 17, p. 211.

30. Daniel Webster to Jeremy Bingham, Jan. 19, 1806, *Writings*, vol. 17, p. 219. Daniel Webster to Thomas Merrill, March 8, 1807, *Papers*, vol. 1, p. 92.

31. Charles Jellison, *Fessenden of Maine* (Syracuse, 1962), p. 31.

32. Daniel Webster to Thomas Worcester, Aug. 8, 1807, *Writings*, vol. 16, p. 9.

33. John C. French, "Grace Fletcher," *Manchester Historical Association Collection* (1897), vol. 1, pp. 73–81.

34. Daniel Webster to Grace Fletcher, Sept. 4, 1807, *Papers*, vol. 1, p. 97.

35. Stephen Allen, "Reminiscences of Daniel Webster," clipping, Webster Papers, L.O.C. Microfilm, 15555–6.

CHAPTER 4

1. Claude Fuess, *Daniel Webster* (Boston, 1930), vol. 1, pp. 94 ff.

2. Peter Harvey, *Reminiscences and Anecdotes of Daniel Webster* (Boston, 1877), p. 9.

3. Fuess, *Daniel Webster*, vol. 1, p. 105.

4. George Ticknor Curtis, *Life of Daniel Webster* (New York, 1870), vol. 1, p. 90. *Writings*, vol. 17, p. 24.

5. Samuel Hopkins Adams, *The Godlike Daniel* (New York, 1930), pp. 56 ff.

6. Harvey, *Reminiscences . . .* , pp. 48–50, 71, 96–97.

7. *Writings,* vol. 15, pp. 548, 556.

8. Lewis Simpson, *The Federalist Literary Mind* (Baton Rouge, 1962). P. Thacher to Daniel Webster, April 24, 1807, *Papers,* vol. 1, p. 93.

9. *Writings,* vol. 15, pp. 579–580.

10. Curtis, *Life of Daniel Webster,* vol. 1, p. 96. David Fischer, *The Revolution of American Conservatism* (New York, 1965), p. 17.

11. Mark Kalapanoff, " 'Religion and Righteousness': A Study of Federalist Rhetoric in the Election of 1800," *Historical New Hampshire* (Winter, 1968), 12, 14.

12. *Papers,* vol. 1, p. 25. Daniel Webster to Jeremy Bingham, Dec. 28, 1800, *Writings,* vol. 17, p. 84.

13. Daniel Webster to James McGaw, Dec. 18, 1802, Daniel Webster to Jeremy Bingham, May 18, 1802, *Papers,* vol. 1, pp. 41, 43. *Writings,* vol. 15, pp. 514, 516. Daniel Webster to Moses Davis, Feb. 5, 1804, *Writings,* vol. 17, p. 158.

14. *Writings,* vol. 15, pp. 522–531. Daniel Webster to Jeremy Bingham, Jan. 19, 1806, *Writings,* vol. 17, p. 221. Thomas Thompson to Daniel Webster, Feb. 14, 1806, *Papers,* vol. 1, p. 77.

15. *Writings,* vol. 17, p. 547; vol. 15, pp. 564–574.

16. Daniel Webster to Ezekiel Webster, March 2, 1810, *Papers,* vol. 1, p. 116.

17. *Portsmouth Oracle,* March 14, 1812. *Writings,* vol. 15, p. 596.

18. *Writings,* vol. 15, p. 609.

19. *Writings,* vol. 17, p. 547.

20. Curtis, *Life of Daniel Webster,* vol. 1, p. 86.

21. *Writings,* vol. 17, pp. 546–547.

CHAPTER 5

1. Daniel Webster to S. Bradley, May 28, 1813, *Papers,* vol. 1, p. 140.

2. Charles Warren, *A History of the American Bar* (New York, 1966), p. 254. James Young, *The Washington Community 1800–1828* (New York, 1966), p. 43. Constance M. Green, *Washington Village and Capitol* (Princeton, 1962), p. 41. *Washington National Intelligencer,* June 15 and 21, 1813.

3. Daniel Webster to Timothy Pickering, Dec. 11, 1812, *Papers,* vol. 1, p. 133. Daniel Webster to John Pickering, Dec. 11, April 24, 1813, *Writings,* vol. 16, pp. 12–13. Daniel Webster to E. Cutts, May 26, 1813, *Papers,* vol. 1, p. 138.

4. Young, *The Washington Community,* pp. 87–109.

5. Ezekiel Webster to Daniel Webster, June 5, 1813, *Papers,* vol. 1, p. 144.

6. *Writings,* vol. 14, pp. 3–10. Irving Brant, *James Madison Commander in Chief* (New York, 1961), 186–187. Daniel Webster to C. March, June 21, 1813, *Papers,* vol. 1, p. 151.

7. Daniel Webster to T. Farrar, Dec. 30, 1813, *Microfilm,* 1623.

8. *Writings,* vol. 14, pp. 21–23. *Washington National Intelligencer,* Jan. 17, 1814. *Writings,* vol. 14, pp. 35–46.

9. *Papers,* vol. 1, pp. 169.

10. Daniel Webster to James McGaw, Dec. 31, 1814, *Microfilm,* 1781.

11. Ezekiel Webster to Daniel Webster, Oct. 29, 1814, *Papers,* vol. 1, p. 172.

12. Daniel Webster to "Dear Sir," Feb. 11, 1814, *Papers*, vol. 1, p. 163.

13. *Writings*, vol. 14, p. 49. Daniel Webster to "Dear Sir," Oct. 30, 1814, *Papers*, vol. 1, p. 174.

14. Daniel Webster to William Sullivan, Oct. 17, 1814, *Papers*, vol. 1, p. 170.

15. *Writings*, vol. 14, pp. 68–69.

16. Daniel Webster to M. Kent, Dec. 22, 1814, *Writings*, vol. 16, p. 32. Daniel Webster to Ezekiel Webster, Dec. 22, 1814, *Papers*, vol. 1, p. 178.

17. Daniel Webster to "Reverend Sir," Jan. 11, 1815, *Papers*, vol. 1, p. 100.

18. Daniel Webster to J. Paige, March–April, 1816, *Microfilm*, 1926. *Writings*, vol. 14, pp. 44–45.

19. *Writings*, vol. 14, p. 76.

20. Daniel Webster to William Sullivan, Jan. 2, 1817, *Papers*, vol. 1, p. 205.

21. Daniel Webster to Ezekiel Webster, March 26, 1816, *Papers*, vol. 1, p. 196.

22. *Portsmouth Oracle*, July 3, 1813, Jan. 28, 1815.

23. *New Hampshire Patriot*, Sept. 29, 1812, May 17, 1814, June 21, 1814, July 5, 1814, Aug. 2, 1814, Aug. 9, 1814.

24. Daniel Webster to John Randolph, April 1816, *Papers*, vol. 1, p. 198. On April 30, Webster sent Randolph a polite note asking for a copy of his letter refusing the invitation to dual. Randolph courteously complied the same day. *Papers* vol. 1, p. 198.

25. Daniel Webster to Charles March, May 31, 1814, June 14, 1814, *Papers*, vol. 1, pp. 142, 149.

26. Daniel Webster to E. Cutts, Jan. 27, 1814, *Microfilm*, 1632a.

27. *Writings*, vol. 18, p. 184. *New Hampshire Patriot*, April 25, 1815.

CHAPTER 6

1. Claude Fuess, *Daniel Webster* (Boston, 1930), vol. 1, pp. 210–212. *Writings*, vol. 10, pp. 173–194.

2. Harrison Gray Otis to Mrs. Harrison Gray Otis, Jan. 26, 1819. Massachusetts Historical Society.

3. James McLachlan, *American Boarding Schools: A Historical Study* (New York, 1970), p. 72.

4. Van Wyck Brooks, *The Flowering of New England* (New York, 1941), p. 97.

5. The plight of Massachusetts Federalists at the time Webster went to Boston is well analyzed in James M. Banner, *To the Hartford Convention* (New York, 1970).

6. Daniel Webster to N. Haven, Nov. 9, 1816, *Papers*, vol. 1, p. 20.

7. Boston society during this period is delightfully reconstructed in Samuel Eliot Morison's, *Harrison Gray Otis* (Boston, 1969), pp. 186–217.

8. Peter Harvey, *Reminiscences and Anecdotes of Daniel Webster* (Boston, 1877), pp. 11 ff.

9. Thomas Thompson to Prof. Adams, July 13, 1815, ms. copy, Dartmouth Archives. John Wheelock to Daniel Webster, Aug. 5, 1815, *Papers*, vol. 1, p. 188. *New Hampshire Patriot*, Oct. 3, 1815.

10. *Portsmouth Oracle*, Oct. 14, 1815.

11. *New Hampshire Patriot*, Dec. 30, 1817.

12. Daniel Webster to F. Brown, Nov. 15, 1817, *Microfilm*, 2093.

13. *Writings*, vol. 10, pp. 194–234. Fuess, *Daniel Webster*, vol. 1, p. 231.

14. Daniel Webster to Jeremiah Mason, April 23, 1818, *Papers,* vol. 1, p. 223. Daniel Webster to Joseph Story, Sept. 9, 1818, *Writings,* vol. 17, p. 287. Fuess, *Daniel Webster,* vol. 1, p. 235.

15. Daniel Webster to J. Hopkinson, March 22, 1819, *Papers,* vol. 1, p. 251.

16. *Writings,* vol. 10, pp. 261–268; vol. 11, pp. 3–24.

17. Daniel Webster to T. Farrar, Jr., Feb. 7, 1819, *Papers,* vol. 1, p. 242.

18. *Writings,* vol. 15, pp. 55–74. Glover More, *The Missouri Controversy* (University of Kentucky, 1966), pp. 69, 191.

19. Gerald T. Dunne, *Justice Joseph Story and the Rise of the Supreme Court* (New York, 1970), p. 161.

20. *Ibid.,* pp. 206 ff. *Journal of Debates and Proceedings in the Convention of Delegates, Chosen to Revise the Constitution of Massachusetts* (Boston, 1853), p. 229. *Writings,* vol. 5, pp. 8–26.

21. Daniel Webster to Jeremiah Mason, Jan. 12, 1821, *Papers,* vol. 1, p. 280. Robert Lucid, *The Journal of Richard Henry Dunn, Jr.* (Cambridge, Mass., 1968), vol. 1, p. 164. George Ticknor Curtis, *Life of Daniel Webster* (New York, 1870), vol. 1, p. 181.

22. *Writings,* vol. 15, pp. 21, 41. Daniel Webster to James McGaw, Oct. 11, 1828, *Writings,* vol. 16, p. 184.

23. *Life Letters and Journals of George Ticknor* (Boston, 1876), vol. 1, pp. 328–331.

24. *Writings,* vol. 1, p. 183.

25. *Ibid.,* p. 221.

26. Harrison Gray Otis to Mrs. Harrison Gray Otis, Dec. 30, 1820, Massachusetts Historical Society.

CHAPTER 7

1. Bliss Perry, *Life and Letters of Henry Lee Higginson* (Boston, 1921), p. 15. Joseph Quincy, *Figures of the Past* (Boston, 1883), pp. 138–147.

2. Claude Fuess, *Daniel Webster* (Boston, 1930), vol. 1, p. 208.

3. Grace Webster to Daniel Fletcher Webster, Nov. 12, 1823, Dec. 19, 1823, Jan. 3, 1824. New Hampshire Historical Society.

4. Grace Webster to Daniel Fletcher Webster, Jan. 16, 1824. Grace Webster to J. Paige, Jan. 6, 1824. New Hampshire Historical Society.

5. Grace Webster to J. Paige, Feb. 24, 1824, Massachusetts Historical Society.

6. Grace Webster to Daniel Webster, Dec. 6, 1824, *Microfilm,* 4451. Daniel Webster to Grace Webster, Dec. 1, 1824, *Writings,* vol. 17, p. 355. Grace Webster to Daniel Webster, Dec. 11, 1824, *Microfilm,* 4471.

7. Daniel Webster to Edward Everett, Dec. 31, 1824, *Papers,* vol. 1, p. 380. *Writings,* vol. 17, p. 376.

8. Grace Webster to Daniel Webster, Jan. 7, 1825, Jan. 12, 1825, Van Tyne, pp. 554–555.

9. Grace Webster to Daniel Webster, Jan. 1, 1825, Van Tyne, p. 554.

10. Eliza Buckminster to Grace Webster, Feb. 18, 1823, New Hampshire Historical Society.

11. See Grace Webster's letters to Daniel Webster from Dec. 9, 1824 to March 5, 1825, Van Tyne, pp. 551–564. For the "liege and lord" quotation see Grace Webster to Daniel Webster, Jan. 29, 1827, *Microfilm,* 5912.

12. Daniel Webster to George Ticknor, Dec., 1824, Jan., 1825, *Writings,* vol. 16, pp. 93, 96.

13. Fuess, *Daniel Webster,* vol. 1, p. 345. Daniel Webster to Mrs. George Blake, July 15, 1825, *Writings,* vol. 17, pp. 385–392.

14. Grace Webster to J. Paige, March 30, 1826, New Hampshire Historical Society. Daniel Webster to George Ticknor, Jan. 8, 1826, *Writings,* vol. 16, p. 119. Charles Lanman, *The Private Life of Daniel Webster* (New York, 1852), p. 217. S. P. Lyman, *The Public and Private Life of Daniel Webster* (Philadelphia, 1860), vol. 2, p. 269. Quincy, *Figures of the Past,* pp. 255–256.

15. Grace Webster to Daniel Webster, Jan. 18, 1827, *Microfilm,* 5830. Grace Webster to Daniel Webster, Jan. 21, 1827, Jan. 29, 1827, Feb. 15, 1827, Van Tyne, pp. 566–568.

16. Grace Webster to Daniel Webster, Dec., 1827, *Microfilm,* 6512; Daniel Webster to J. Paige, Dec. 5, 1827, *Writings,* vol. 17, p. 424. E. Buckminster Lee to Grace Webster, Jan. 4, 1828, New Hampshire Historical Society. M. March to Daniel Webster, Jan. 22, 1828, *Microfilm,* 6667.

17. George Ticknor Curtis, *Life of Daniel Webster* (New York, 1870), vol. 1, p. 314. George Ticknor to Joseph Story, Jan. 25, 1828, Massachusetts Historical Society.

18. Daniel Webster to Mrs. Ezekiel Webster, March 2, 1829, *Writings,* vol. 17, p. 472. Daniel Webster to Eliza Buckminster Lee, May 18, 1828, *Writings,* vol. 17, p. 457. Daniel Webster to Daniel Fletcher Webster, Feb. 17, 1828, *Writings,* vol. 17, p. 448. Daniel Fletcher Webster to Daniel Webster, Jan 3, 1831, *Microfilm,* 9123.

19. Daniel Webster to Cyrus Perkins, April 17, 1829, *Writings,* vol. 17, p. 475. Daniel Webster to R. Peters, May 7, 1829, *Microfilm,* 7946.

20. Unidentified correspondent to Daniel Webster, April 13, 1829, *Microfilm,* 7910. Mrs. Edward Everett to Edward Everett, Feb. 6, 1828, Massachusetts Historical Society.

21. Eliza Buckminster Lee to Daniel Webster, March 1, 1829, *Microfilm,* 7846. Mrs. Langdon Elwyn to Daniel Webster, Sept. 12, 1829, *Microfilm,* 08074. William Sullivan to Daniel Webster, Jan. 3, 1829, *Microfilm,* 8282.

22. Daniel Webster to Stephen Van Rensselaer, May 15, 1829, *Microfilm,* 7962. Ward Thorn (ed.), *Letters to Mrs. Henry Adams* (Boston, 1936), p. 432.

23. Fuess, *Daniel Webster,* vol. 1, pp. 358–360. Caroline LeRoy was probably the woman Webster was seen with in Washington in January, 1829. Herman LeRoy to Daniel Webster, Jan. 10, 1829, *Microfilm,* 8301. A note acknowledging receipt of the last $5,000 of the $25,000 dowry signed by Webster July 21, 1830, is in the Boston Public Library. Edward Everett to Mrs. Edward Everett, Jan. 17, 1831, Massachusetts Historical Society. Daniel Webster to James McGaw, Nov. 18, 1829, *Writings,* vol. 16, p. 190.

24. Caroline Webster to E. LeRoy, Jan. 4, 1830, Houghton Library, Harvard University. Caroline Webster to Daniel Webster, May 3, 1830, *Microfilm,* 8772.

CHAPTER 8

1. The United States assumed these claims under the Adams-Onis Treaty of 1819. Beginning in 1822 Webster represented claims totaling approximately a million dollars for a commission of between 5 and 10 percent. By the summer of 1824 he was

able to record receipts of $61,730.39 from this business. *Microfilm,* 4077 ff. My judgment that these fees made Webster a wealthy man is based on the fact that the dollar in 1824 was worth between six and ten times the dollar of 1970. Edward Pessen, *Riches, Class and Power before the Civil War* (Lexington, Mass., 1973), p. 17.

2. Sydney Nathans, *Daniel Webster and Jacksonian Democracy* (Baltimore, 1973), pp. 17–20.

3. Daniel Webster to Joseph Hopkinson, Nov. 13, 1822. *Papers,* vol. 1, p. 317. *Writings,* vol. 17, p. 560.

4. *Writings,* vol. 15, p. 8.

5. Daniel Webster to Jeremiah Mason, Nov. 30, 1823, *Papers,* vol. 1, p. 336. Daniel Webster to Ezekiel Webster. Dec. 4, 1823, *Papers,* vol. 1, p. 337.

6. Daniel Webster to Edward Everett, Nov. 28, Dec. 5, 6, 20, 1823, *Papers,* vol. 1, pp. 335–342.

7. Daniel Webster to Edward Everett, Jan. 2, 1824, *Papers,* vol. 1, p. 344, *Writings,* vol. 5, p. 76.

8. James F. Hopkins (ed.), *The Papers of Henry Clay* (Lexington, Ky, 1963), vol. 3, pp. 603–618.

9. Joseph Hopkinson to Daniel Webster, Feb. 1, 1824, *Writings,* vol. 17, p. 343. Daniel Webster to Edward Everett, Feb. 13, 1824, *Papers,* vol. 1, p. 352. Henry Clay to M. Carey, Mary 2, 1824, *Papers,* vol. 3, p. 745.

10. Daniel Webster to Jeremiah Mason, Feb. 15, 1824, *Papers,* vol. 1, p. 353. Daniel Webster to Ezekiel Webster, Feb. 22, March 14, 1824, *Writings,* vol. 17, pp. 346–347.

11. Charles Francis Adams, *Memoirs of John Quincy Adams* (Philadelphia, 1875), vol. 6, pp. 332, 352.

12. *Writings,* vol. 17, pp. 364–373. Daniel Webster to Gales and Seaton, Dec. 9, 1824, *Papers,* vol. 1, p. 368.

13. Daniel Webster to Ezekiel Webster, Jan. 13, 1825, *Writings,* vol. 17, p. 374. Henry Warfield to Daniel Webster, Feb. 3, 1825, Daniel Webster to Henry Warfield, Feb. 5, 1825, *Writings,* vol. 17, pp. 377–380.

14. *Writings,* vol. 2, p. 8. Daniel Webster to Jeremiah Mason, Feb. 14, 1825, *Writings,* vol. 16, p. 99.

15. Shaw Livermore, *The Twilight of Federalism* (Princeton, 1962), pp. 172–196.

16. *Ibid.,* pp. 197–222.

17. Daniel Webster to Gales and Seaton, June 7, 1827, *Microfilm,* 6196. J. Sprague to Edward Everett, May 25, 1827, Massachusetts Historical Society. Claude Fuess, *Daniel Webster* (Boston, 1930), vol. 1, p. 337. Edward Everett to J. Sprague, June 30, 1827, Massachusetts Historical Society.

18. Adams, *Memoirs of John Quincy Adams,* vol. 7, pp. 430, 468. Although he wanted to go to England Webster seems to have understood the political barriers in the way and to have been worried about the wisdom of such a move if it were possible. Daniel Webster to Jeremiah Mason, March 20, 1828; Daniel Webster to J. Sprague, March 22, 1828, *Microfilm,* 6888, 6894.

19. Daniel Webster to Ezekiel Webster, Feb. 5, 1829, *Writings,* vol. 16, p. 186.

CHAPTER 9

1. Ralph Waldo Emerson to William Emerson, June 24, 1827, Ralph Rusk (ed.), *The Letters of Ralph Waldo Emerson* (New York, 1939), vol. 1, p. 202.

2. Daniel Webster to Edward Everett, Feb. 23, 1825. *Microfilm*, 04864. George Warren, *The History of the Bunker Hill Monument Association* (Boston, 1877).

3. Claude Fuess, *Daniel Webster* (Boston, 1930), vol. 1, p. 295–299.

4. *Writings*, vol. 1, p. 237.

5. *National Intelligencer*, July 17, 1830.

6. Allan Nevins (ed.), *The Diary of John Quincy Adams* (New York, 1951), p. 363. *Writings*, vol. 1, p. 309; vol. 16, p. 298.

7. Theodore Lyman to Daniel Webster, April 12, 1824, *Microfilm*, p. 4096. John W. Whitman, *Report of a Trial in the Supreme Judicial Court Holden at Boston Dec 16th and 17th 1828 of Theodore Lyman, Jr.* (Boston, 1828). Theodore Lyman to Francis Baylies, Nov. 19, 1828, Massachusetts Historical Society. Joseph Benton, *A Notable Libel Case* (Boston, 1904).

8. George Ticknor Curtis, Life of Daniel Webster (New York, 1870), vol. 1, p. 336.

9. Daniel Webster to Mrs. Ezekiel Webster, Feb. 19, 1829, *Writings*, vol. 17, p. 470. Daniel Webster to Mrs. Ezekiel Webster, March 4, 1829, *Writings*, vol. 16, p. 188.

10. William Ward, *Andrew Jackson, Symbol for an Age* (New York, 1962).

11. William W. Freehling, *Prelude to Civil War: The Nullification Controversy in South Carolina* (New York, 1965), pp. 1–177.

12. *Writings*, vol. 5, pp. 248–269.

13. Mrs. Samuel Harrison Smith, *The First Forty Years of Washington Society* (New York, 1906), p. 309. Fuess, *Daniel Webster*, vol. 1, p. 372.

14. *Writings*, vol. 6, p. 22; vol. 14, p. 137.

15. *Writings*, vol. 6, pp. 66, 68, 49, 75.

16. A. M. Hughes to Daniel Webster, April 28, 1830, *Microfilm*, 8722.

17. Amos Lawrence to Daniel Webster March 3, 1830, *Writings*, vol. 17, p. 489. George Ticknor, "Webster's Speeches," *American Quarterly Review* (June, 1831).

18. William Sullivan to Daniel Webster, March 23, 1830, *Writings*, vol. 17, p. 497. Daniel Fletcher Webster to Daniel Webster, March 23, 1830, *Microfilm*, 8592.

19. W. Lloyd Warner, *The Living and the Dead: A Study of the Symbolic Life of Americans* (New Haven, 1959), pp. 90, 97.

CHAPTER 10

1. *Microfilm*, 39757. Claude Fuess, *Daniel Webster* (Boston, 1930), vol. 1, p. 343; vol. 2, p. 324.

2. Caroline LeRoy Webster to E. LeRoy, Jan. 4, 1830, Houghton Library, Harvard University. Daniel Webster to W. Dutton, Jan. 15, 1830, *Writings*, vol. 17, p. 483.

3. Daniel Webster to Mr. Pleasants, March 6, 1830, *Writings*, vol. 17, p. 491. Daniel Webster to Jeremiah Mason, March 10, 1830, *Writings*, vol. 16, p. 194.

4. Daniel Webster to Henry Clay, April 18, 1830, *Writings,* vol. 16, p. 195. Joseph Story to Daniel Webster, April 17, 1830, Van Tyne, p. 153.

5. Daniel Webster to Jeremiah Mason, April 14, 1830, Daniel Webster to Henry Clay, May 29, 1830, *Writings,* vol. 16, pp. 201, 197. Henry Clay to Daniel Webster, June 7, 1830, *Writings,* vol. 17, p. 504.

6. Daniel Webster to James Madison, May 24, 1830, *Microfilm,* 8842. James Madison to Daniel Webster, May 27, 1830, *Microfilm,* 8847. Daniel Webster to James Mason, June 4, 1830, *Writings,* vol. 16, p. 204. The letter from Madison to Webster, March 15, 1830 in *Writings,* vol. 17, p. 496, is misdated and refers to his later debate with Calhoun in 1833.

7. Joseph Story to Daniel Webster, April 7, 1830, Van Tyne, p. 153. *Boston Transcript,* Aug. 28, 1830.

8. Daniel Webster to N. Williams, Dec. 28, 1830, *Microfilm,* 9088. Edward Everett to A. Everett, Dec. 28, 1830, Massachusetts Historical Society. George Ticknor, "Webster's Speeches and Foreinsic Arguments," *American Quarterly Review,* 9 (1831), 420–457. Samuel L. Knapp, *A Memoir of the Life of Daniel Webster* (Boston, 1831). Daniel Webster to Henry Clay, March 4, 1831, *Microfilm,* 9031.

9. Edward Everett to Mrs. Edward Everett, March 24, 1831, Massachusetts Historical Society. George T. Curtis, *Life of Daniel Webster* (New York, 1870), vol. 1, p. 398. Daniel Webster to A. Spencer, Nov. 16, 1831, *Writings,* vol. 16, p. 214. Stephen White to Daniel Webster 1831, Van Tyne, p. 161.

10. Daniel Webster to Henry Clay, April 18, 1830, *Writings,* vol. 16, p. 195. Henry Clay to Daniel Webster, April 29, 1830, Curtis, *Life of Daniel Webster,* vol. 1, p. 374. Henry Clay to Edward Everett, Aug. 30, 1831, Massachusetts Historical Society. *Writings,* vol. 6, p. 96. Glydon G. Van Deusen, *The Jacksonian Era* (New York, 1963), p. 58.

11. Robert Remini, *Andrew Jackson and the Bank War* (New York, 1967), pp. 1–109.

12. Maurice Baxter, *Daniel Webster and the Supreme Court* (Amherst, 1966), pp. 169–195. Daniel Webster to Nicholas Biddle, April 19, 1831, Library of Congress.

13. *Writings,* vol. 6, p. 124–148. Remini, *Andrew Jackson and the Bank War,* pp. 82–83.

14. Remini, *Andrew Jackson and the Bank War,* p. 84. *Washington Globe,* March 12, 1832. John Marshall to Daniel Webster, June 16, 1832, *Writings,* vol. 17, p. 518.

15. Daniel Webster to Joseph Story, July 21, 1832, *Writings,* vol. 16, p. 222. *Writings,* vol. 6, pp. 179–180.

16. Henry Clay to Daniel Webster, Aug. 27, 1832, Van Tyne, p. 176. *Writings,* vol. 2, p. 125.

17. *Washington Globe,* Dec. 11, 1830, Oct. 22, Nov. 2, 5, 1832.

18. Remini, *Andrew Jackson and the Bank War,* pp. 106–107.

CHAPTER 11

1. *Washington Globe,* Nov. 14, 1832, April 29, July 4, 1833, March 11, 1834.

2. George Ticknor Curtis, *Life of Daniel Webster* (New York, 1870), vol. 1, p. 590. Daniel Webster to A. Livermore, Jan. 5, 1833, *Writings,* vol. 16, p. 224. Charles M. Wiltse, *John C. Calhoun (Indianapolis, 1944–*1951), vol. 2, p. 449.

3. Curtis, *Life of Daniel Webster,* vol. 1, p. 442.

4. *Writings,* vol. 6, pp. 181–182, 237.

5. Andrew Jackson to J. Poinsett, Feb. 17, 1833, John S. Bassett (ed.), *Correspondence to Andrew Jackson* (Washington, D.C., 1931), vol. 5, p. 18.

6. Daniel Webster to Hiram Ketchum, Jan. 18, 1838, *Writings,* vol. 16, p. 293. Daniel Webster to Hiram Ketchum, Jan. 20, 1838, *Microfilm,* 14579. Harrison Gray Otis to Daniel Webster, Feb. 18, 1833, *Microfilm,* 10693, Edward Everett to A. Everett, Feb. 13, 1833, Massachusetts Historical Society. Sydney Nathans, *Daniel Webster and Jacksonian Democracy* (Baltimore, 1973), p. 60.

7. Curtis, *Life of Daniel Webster,* vol. 1, p. 464. *Writings,* vol. 15, p. 106.

8. Henry Clay to Nicholas Biddle, April 10, 1833, Reginald McGrane, *The Correspondence of Nicholas Biddle Dealing with National Affairs 1807–1844* (Boston, 1919), p. 202. Nicholas Biddle to Daniel Webster, April 10, 1833, *Microfilm,* 10853.

9. *Writings,* vol. 2, pp. 129–157. *Washington Globe,* July 4, 1833.

10. Curtis, *Life of Daniel Webster,* vol. 1, p. 464.

11. Nathans, *Daniel Webster and Jacksonian Democracy,* p. 64. Norman D. Brown, *Daniel Webster and the Politics of Availability* (Athens, Ga., 1969), pp. 47–50.

12. Rufus Choate to Daniel Webster, Aug. 12, 1833, Van Tyne, p. 184.

13. Daniel Webster to Ezekiel Webster, Jan. 17, 1829, *Writings,* vol. 17, p. 467. Daniel Webster to Ezekiel Webster, Feb. 5, 23, 1829, *Writings,* vol. 16, pp. 186–189. *Writings,* vol. 6, p. 180. *Writings,* vol. 2, p. 143.

14. Daniel Webster to Nicholas Biddle, Dec. 19, 1833, *Microfilm,* 11242. Edward Everett to A. Everett, Dec. 10, 1833, Massachusetts Historical Society. Brown, *Daniel Webster . . . ,* p. 58.

15. Nathans, *Daniel Webster and Jacksonian Democracy,* pp. 69–70. Daniel Webster to Edward Everett, Dec. 13, 1833, *Microfilm,* 11217.

16. Thomas P. Govan, *Nicholas Biddle: Nationalist and Public Banker 1786–1884* (Chicago, 1959), p. 262. Daniel Webster to Nicholas Biddle, Dec. 19, 21, 1833, *Microfilm,* 11242, 11258.

17. *Microfilm,* 11257. Govan, *Nicholas Biddle,* p. 263.

18. *Washington Globe,* Aug. 21, 1834. Daniel Webster to Edward Everett, April 26, 1834. *Writings,* vol. 18, p. 6. Daniel Webster to Samuel Jaudon July 25, Aug. 2, 6, 1834, *Microfilm,* 11821, 11838, 11840. Ralph Catterall, *The Second Bank of the United States* (1904; rpt., Chicago, 1960), p. 254.

19. Nathans, *Daniel Webster and Jacksonian Democracy,* pp. 74–78.

20. Daniel Webster to Caleb Cushing, Feb. 17, 1834, *Microfilm,* 11486.

21. Edward Everett to Thomas Ward, Feb. 8, 1834, Massachusetts Historical Society. Daniel Webster to Edward Everett, Aug. 1, 1834, *Microfilm,* 11834.

22. For recent discussions of conflict of interest which emphasize the difference between modern and nineteenth-century practices, see Association of the Bar of the City New York, *Conflict of Interest and Federal Service* (Cambridge, Mass., 1960), and James C. Kirby, *Congress and the Public Trust* (New York, 1970). The Webster example was brought into a Senate debate in the mid-1960s in defense of Senator Dodd of Connecticut. See 113 Cong. Record, 16,209 and 16,277 (1967).

23. Brown, *Daniel Webster . . . ,* pp. 87–94. *Washington Globe,* Aug. 5, 1834.

24. Brown, *Daniel Webster . . . ,* p. 113. Nicholas Biddle to H. Cope, Aug. 11, 1835, McGrane, *The Correspondence of Nicholas Biddle,* p. 255.

25. Daniel Webster to H. Denny, Nov. 20, 1835, *Microfilm,* 12709. Edward Everett to Thaddeus Stevens, Nov. 2, 1835, Massachusetts Historical Society. Daniel Webster to H. Denny & others, Nov. 20, 1835, *Writings,* vol. 18, p. 12. Brown, *Daniel Webster . . . ,* pp. 124–148.

CHAPTER 12

1. Daniel Webster to Hiram Ketchum, Jan. 28, 1837, *Microfilm,* 13995.

2. *Writings,* vol. 2, p. 235; vol. 13, p. 80–81.

3. Francis Fessenden, *Life and Public Services of William Pitt Fessenden* (Boston, 1970), vol. 1, p. 12.

4. *Writings,* vol. 2, p. 268; vol. 8, p. 148; vol. 13, p. 97.

5. *Writings,* vol. 2, pp. 206–207.

6. *Writings,* vol. 2, pp. 109–114. Daniel Webster to Hiram Ketchum, Jan. 15, 1838, *Writings,* vol. 18, p. 33.

7. Daniel Webster to Nicholas Biddle, May 24, 1838, *Microfilm,* 14943.

8. *Washington Globe,* Aug. 8, 1835. H. Jones to W. Mangum, Dec. 22, 1837, Henry T. Shanks, *Willie Mangum Papers* (Raleigh, 1950), vol. 2, p. 514. Thurlow Weed Barnes, *Memoir of Thurlow Weed* (Boston, 1894), p. 49.

9. Sydney Nathans, *Daniel Webster and Jacksonian Democracy* (Baltimore, 1973), pp. 122–129.

10. Claude Fuess, *Daniel Webster* (Boston, 1930), vol. 2, pp. 714—74. Daniel Webster to Samuel Jaudon, Jan. 12, 1839, *Microfilm,* 15307.

11. Claude Fuess (ed.), *"Mr W & I"* (Binghamton: Ives Washburn, 1942), pp. 1–3, 14, 19, 22.

12. Daniel Webster to Edward Curtis, June 12, 1839, *Writings,* vol., 18, p. 48. Daniel Webster to C. Thomas, June 9, 1839, *Writings,* vol. 16, p. 307.

13. Joseph Slates (ed.), *The Correspondence of Emerson and Carlyle* (New York, 1964), p. 240. Fuess, *Daniel Webster,* vol. 2, p. 75.

14. Daniel Webster to Edward Curtis, July 4, 1839, *Writings,* vol. 18, pp. 55, 60; Van Tyne, p. 647. Daniel Webster to John Crittenden, July 31, 1839, *Writings,* vol. 16, p. 312. Daniel Webster to Hiram Ketchum, July 71–74. 1839, *Writings,* vol. 18, p. 58.

15. Fuess, *"Mr W & I,"* pp. 53, 78–79.

16. Daniel Webster to Edward Curtis, June 3, 1839, Daniel Webster to George Ticknor, Aug. 21, 1839, *Writings,* vol. 18, pp. 48, 63.

17. E. P. Thompson, *The Making of the English Working Class* (New York, 1966). Irving H. Bartlett, *Wendell Phillips, Brahmin Radical* (Boston, 1961), p. 73.

18. Daniel Webster to I. Davis, June 24, 1839, *Writings,* vol. 18, p. 50.

19. Daniel Webster to Edward Everett, Feb. 16, 1840, *Writings,* vol. 18, p. 76.

20. Daniel Webster to Samuel Jaudon, March 29, 1840, *Writings,* vol. 18, p. 79. *Writings,* vol. 13, pp. 108–109.

21. Daniel Webster to Edward Curtis, Oct. 3, 1840, *Writings,* vol. 18, p. 89. *Writings,* vol. 3, p. 94.

22. Robert Gray Gunderson, *The Log Cabin Campaign* (Lexington, Ky., 1957). *Writings,* vol. 3, pp. 28–29.

23. Daniel Webster to gentlemen of Indiana, April 17, 1848, *Writings,* vol. 16, p. 325. *Writings,* vol. 13, p. 113.

24. Daniel Webster to C. Warren, Aug. 15, 1840, July 12, 1840, *Writings,* vol. 16, pp. 334, 330.

25. *Writings,* vol. 13, p. 118.

CHAPTER 13

1. Arthur M. Schlesinger, Jr., *The Age of Jackson* (Boston, 1945), pp. 279–280.

2. *Writings,* vol. 15, p. 480.

3. *Writings,* vol. 6, p. 74; vol. 2, p. 132.

4. Major Wilson, "The Concept of Time and the Political Dialogue in the United States," *New England Quarterly* (Winter, 1967), 619–644. Sydney Nathans, *Daniel Webster and Jacksonian Democracy* (Baltimore, 1973), p. 58. Karl Deutsch and William Foltz (eds.), *Nation Building* (New York, 1963), pp. 1–17, 41. Hans-Kohn, *American Nationalism* (New York, 1957), p. 8.

5. *Writings,* vol. 3, p. 207; vol. 2, pp. 175–186; vol. 6, pp. 239–284.

6. *Writings,* vol. 1, p. 6.

7. *Writings,* vol. 1, pp. 268, 277.

8. See, for example, Louis Hartz, *The Liberal Tradition in America* (New York, 1955).

9. *Writings,* vol. 1, p. 211.

10. Daniel Webster to J. Whipple, May 9, 1842, *Microfilm,* 22416. Daniel Webster to John Tyler, April 18, 1844, *Writings,* vol. 18, 189.

11. *Writings,* vol. 11, pp. 217–247.

12. Daniel Webster to James McGaw, Oct. 11, 1828, *Writings,* vol. 16, p. 184.

13. *Writings,* vol. 11, p. 176. James McClelland, *Joseph Story and the American Constitution* (Norman, Okla., 1971), p. 131.

14. Writings, vol. 13, pp. 63–78.

15. *Writings,* vol. 8, pp. 167–170.

16. Peter Temin, *The Jacksonian Economy* (New York, 1969); Marvin Meyers, *The Jacksonian Persuasion* (New York, 1957); Louis Hartz, *The American Liberal Tradition;* Edward Pessen, *Jacksonian America: Society, Personality and Politics* (Homewood, Ill., 1969), pp. 39–59; Melvin Dubofsky, "Daniel Webster and the Whig Theory of Economic Growth," *New England Quarterly* (Dec., 1969), 551–572.

CHAPTER 14

1. Nicholas Biddle to Daniel Webster, Dec. 13, 1840, *Microfilm,* 17131. George Poage, *Henry Clay and the Whig Party* (Chapel Hill, N.C., 1936), p. 37.

2. Daniel Webster to Nicholas Biddle, Dec. 24, 1840, *Microfilm,* 17150. Daniel Webster to P. Sprague, Dec. 19, 1840, Duxbury Historical Society. P. Porter to Henry Clay, Jan. 28, 1841, Calvin Colton (ed.), *Works of Henry Clay* (New York, 1904), vol. 5, p. 448.

3. Robert Seager, *And Tyler Too* (New York, 1963), pp. 135–149.

4. Sydney Nathans, *Daniel Webster and Jacksonian Democracy* (Baltimore, 1973), pp. 162–171. Daniel Webster to Hiram Ketchum, July 17, 1841. *Writings,* vol. 16, p. 348.

5. "The Diary of Thomas Ewing," *American Historical Review* 18 (Oct., 1912), 97–112. Seager, *And Tyler Too,* p. 116. Lyon G. Tyler, *The Letters and Times of the Tylers* (Richard, 1885), vol. 2, pp. 121–122.

6. Daniel Webster to Gales and Seaton, Sept. 13, 1841, *Writings,* vol. 16, p. 358.

7. Claude Fuess, *Daniel Webster* (Boston, 1930), vol. 2, pp. 100–104.

8. *Ibid.,* vol. 1, pp. 105–112. Daniel Webster to Edward Everett, June 14, 1842, *Writings,* vol. 16, p. 374. Richard Current, "Webster's Propaganda and the Ashburton Treaty," *Mississippi Valley Historical Review* (Sept., 1947), 187–200. Frederick Merk, *Fruits of Propaganda of the Tyler Administration* (Cambridge, Mass., 1971).

9. Gamaliel Bradford, *As God Made Them—Portraits of Some Nineteenth-Century Americans* (Boston, 1929), p. 32. Nathans, *Daniel Webster and Jacksonian Democracy,* pp. 165–167. Daniel Webster to Edward Curtis, Feb. 24, 1842, *Microfilm,* 21681. Sydney Nathans, "Daniel Webster, Massachusetts Man," *New England Quarterly* (June, 1966), 165. Mrs. Chapman Coleman, *The Life of John J. Crittenden* (Philadelphia, 1871), vol. 1, p. 187.

10. Jeremiah Mason to Daniel Webster, Aug. 28, 1842, *Writings,* vol. 18, p. 148. Daniel Webster to Edward Everett, Aug. 25, 1842, *Microfilm,* 23293. Nicholas Biddle to Daniel Webster, Sept. 14, 1842, *Microfilm,* 23414.

11. *Writings,* vol. 3, pp. 109–141.

12. Edward L. Pierce, *Memoirs and Letters of Charles Sumner* (Boston, 1878), vol. 2, p. 226. Charles Francis Adams, *Memoirs of John Quincy Adams* (Philadelphia, 1874–1877), vol. 11, p. 256. Harrison Gray Otis to G. Harrison, Oct. 25, 1842, July 1, 1843, Massachusetts Historical Society.

13. Daniel Webster to Daniel Fletcher Webster, Oct. 5, 1842, *Writings,* vol. 16, p. 384. Daniel Webster to Edward Everett, Nov. 28, 1842, *Microfilm,* 23779.

14. Daniel Webster to Edward Everett, March 10, 1843, *Writings,* vol. 16, p. 398. P. R. Frothingham, *Edward Everett, Orator and Statesman* (Boston, 1925), p. 233. Reginald McGrane, *The Correspondence of Nicholas Biddle Dealing with National Affairs* (Boston, 1919), p. 346.

15. Kinley Brauer, "The Webster-Lawrence Feud: A Study in Politics and Ambitions," *The Historian* (Nov., 1966), 43.

16. Daniel Webster to John Letcher, Feb. 15, 1843, *Microfilm,* 24360.

17. *Writings,* vol. 13, p. 158.

18. Nathans, *Daniel Webster and Jacksonian Democracy,* pp. 201–211.

19. Frederick W. Seward, *Autobiography of William H. Seward* (New York, 1877), pp. 681–682. *Writings,* vol. 13, pp. 182–188.

20. Nicholas Biddle to Daniel Webster, Oct. 9, 1843, *Microfilm,* 25380. Henry Clay to E. Sargent, Sept. 26, 1843, Boston Public Library. *Writings,* vol. 3, p. 185.

21. Daniel Webster to ?, Jan. 11, 1844, New York Public Library. Nathan Sargent, *Public Men and Events* (Philadelphia, 1875), vol. 2, p. 209. R. Winthrop to Edward Everett, Dec. 12, 1843, Massachusetts Historical Society. Coleman, *The Life of John J. Crittenden,* vol. 1, p. 215.

22. Daniel Webster to Edward Everett, April 1, 1844, *Microfilm,* 25764. *Writings,* vol. 13, pp. 198, 201–211, 272, 282, 301–305.

CHAPTER 15

1. Samuel G. Goodrich, *Recollections of a Lifetime* (New York, 1857), vol. 2, p. 417.

2. *Congressional Globe,* April 7, 1846.

3. *Congressional Globe,* April 10, 1846.

4. Daniel Webster to Daniel Fletcher Webster, Jan. 30, 1846, Van Tyne, p. 728. Daniel Webster to Samuel Jaudon, Oct. 12, 1845, *Microfilm,* 26476.

5. David Sears to Daniel Webster, March 21, 1846, Daniel Webster to David Sears, March 26, 1846, *Writings,* vol. 16, p. 445–447.

6. R. Winthrop to Edward Everett, April 16, 1846, Massachusetts Historical Society. Daniel Webster to Edward Curtis, no date, New York Public Library.

7. *Writings,* vol. 16, pp. 448–452.

8. *Washington Globe,* June 26, 1839.

9. *Writings,* vol. 8, p. 241.

10. Lyon G. Tyler, *The Letters and Times of the Tylers* (Richmond, 1884), vol. 2, p. 393. *Washington Globe,* July 29, 1837.

11. *Washington Globe,* Oct. 2, 1840.

12. *Writings,* vol. 1, p. 265. Claude Fuess, *Daniel Webster* (Boston, 1930), vol. 2, p. 133. Ralph Waldo Emerson, *The Writings of Ralph Waldo Emerson* (New York, 1940), 863.

13. Charles Francis Adams, *Memoirs of John Quincy Adams* (Philadelphia, 1874–1877), vol. 11, p. 383.

14. *Writings,* vol. 2, p. 22. *Washington Globe,* March 11, 1837. Gamaliel Bradford, *As God Made Them: Portraits of Some Nineteenth-Century Americans* (Boston, 1929), p. 30. Oliver Dyer, *Great Senators of the United States Forty Years Ago* (New York, 1889), p. 238.

15. *Washington Globe,* Aug. 10, 1837.

16. Francis Grund, *Aristocracy in America* (New York, 1959), p. 170.

17. Daniel Webster to unidentified correspondent, Feb. 24, 1819, *Microfilm,* 2654.

18. Daniel Webster to Henry Kinsman, Jan. 11, 1834, *Writings,* vol. 16, p. 238. Henry Kinsman to Daniel Webster, Jan. 17, 1834, *Microfilm,* 11390. *Writings,* vol. 4, p. 152.

19. *Microfilm,* 9017–9019. Daniel Webster to Stephen White, 1832, *Writings,* vol. 17, p. 524, Van Tyne, p. 744. Henry T. Shanks, *Willie Mangum Papers* (Raleigh, 1950), vol. 5, p. 751. Henry Foote, *A Casket of Reminiscences* (Washington, 1874), p. 10. Mark A. DeWolfe Howe, *Life and Letters of George Bancroft* (New York, 1908), vol. 1, p. 246. Webster once admitted to Harvey that he cometimes overindulged in food and drink. Peter Harvey, *Reminiscences of Daniel Webster* (Boston, 1877), p. 10.

20. *Louisville Journal,* Jan. 8, 11, 19, 25, 1842.

21. The *Louisville Journal* published Webster's affidavit and retracted the story Feb. 14, 1842, but kept the issue alive through March and April by printing the reaction of other anti-administration papers to the alleged assault. Most pro-Webster papers tried to ignore the story but some of them confessed to its damaging effect and insisted on a refutation. *Providence Journal,* Feb. 12, 23, 1842.

22. By the fall of 1842, when Webster had begun to publicly criticize Tyler, the *Louisville Journal* had begun to give him measured praise in an attempt to woo him back into the Clay camp. See, for example, the issue of Oct. 10, 1842.

23. The correspondence with the Aggs can be followed in *Microfilm,* 38159 ff.

24. Daniel Webster to George Ticknor, April 8, 1833, *Writings,* vol. 17, p. 533. Daniel Webster to Caroline Webster, Feb. 12, 1840, Van Tyne, p. 743.

25. Samuel Hopkins Adams, *The Godlike Daniel* (New York, 1930), p. 307.

26. Henry Cabot Lodge, *A Fighting Frigate and Other Essays* (New York, 1902), p. 116. Herman LeRoy, Jr., to Daniel Webster, Jan. 25, 1840, *Microfilm,* 16265. *Washington Globe,* Feb. 2, 1838.

27. Daniel Webster to Sarah Goodrich, May 12, 1834, Jan. 2, 1851, *Microfilm,* 11675, 32013.

28. Daniel Webster to Caleb Cushing, April 29, 1837, Caleb Cushing to Daniel Webster, July 28, 1837, Sept. 11, 1852, Daniel Webster to Caleb Cushing, Sept. 30, 1852, *Microfilm,* 14244, 14340, 37744, 37903. Claude Fuess, *Daniel Webster* (Boston, 1930), vol. 2, pp. 387–389.

29. Daniel Webster to Roswell Colt, May 8, 1838, Jan. 9, Feb. 26, May 1, 1839, *Microfilm,* 14916, 15301, 15379, 15479.

30. Webster Account Books, Brandeis University Library. Edward Pessen, *Riches, Class, and Power before the Civil War* (Lexington, Mass., 1973), pp. 17–18.

31. Daniel Webster to Daniel Fletcher Webster, June 15, 1836, *Writings,* vol. 18, p. 20. H. Kinney to Daniel Webster, May 24, June 20, 1836, *Microfilm,* 13255, 13386. Coleman McCampbell, "H. L. Kinney and Daniel Webster in Illinois in the 1830's," *Journal of the Illinois State Historical Society* 47 (Spring, 1954), 35–44. Magdalen Eichert, "Daniel Webster's Land Investments," *Historical New Hampshire* (Fall, 1971), 29–35. The two-hundred-thousand-dollar figure is taken from a signed document in the Brandeis University Library dated Feb. 12, 1841. The exact figure is $210,089.30.

32. A record of Webster's account with the Bank showing a debt of $111,166 on Dec. 24, 1840 can be found in *Microfilm,* 39835–166. Webster's negotiations with the Bank can be followed in letters from Herman Cope to Daniel Webster, *Microfilm,* 17479, 17520, 17713, 18583, 18728, 20506. Webster's agent in the negotiations was James Doty, sometime judge on the Michigan frontier, congressional delegate for the Wisconsin territory, and a heavy speculator of doubtful reputation in his own right. It was Doty who delivered Webster's ultimatum to the Bank, James Doty to Herman Cope, April 1, 1841, Brandeis University Library.

33. Thomas Govan, *Nicholas Biddle, Nationalist and Public Banker, 1786–1844* (Chicago, 1959), p. 389. Nicholas Biddle to Daniel Webster, April 3, 1841, *Microfilm,* 18720.

34. Peter Brooks to Edward Everett, Aug. 7, 1835, Massachusetts Historical Society. On May 16, 1839, shortly before he left for Europe, Webster borrowed twenty-seven thousand dollars from Samuel Ruggles and Richard Blatchford, *Microfilm,* 39835–301. On May 29, the *Washington Globe* reported that sixty-five thousand dollars had been raised in Boston, New York, and Philadelphia to help Webster pay his debts and travel abroad. Webster's correspondence with Jackson can be followed in *Microfilm,* 17498, 17523, 18345, 18380, 19380.

35. Harrison Gray Otis to G. Harrison, Feb. 7, 1845, Massachusetts Historical Society.

36. *Congressional Globe,* April 10, 1846. *Washington Globe,* May 29, 1839.

37. James A. Knight, *For the Love of Money: Human Behavior and Money* (New York, 1968), pp. 47–51.

38. Fuess, *Daniel Webster,* vol. 1, p. 384; vol. 2, p. 325. Daniel Webster to John Thomas, Feb. 20, 1837, *Microfilm,* 14084. Also two undated letters Daniel Webster to John Thomas, *Microfilm,* 39053, 39055. Webster Marshfield Memorandum Book,

Dec., 1847–April, 1848, Webster Account Book, Nov., 1847–Jan., 1851, Brandeis University Library.

39. *Washington Globe,* March 26, 1842. The Curtis remark was reported to Henry Clay, P. Porter to Henry Clay, Feb. 20, 1841, Calvin Colton, *The Private Correspondence of Henry Clay* (New York, 1855), vol. 5, p. 450. Thomas Ward to Baring Brothers, April 29, 1839, Dartmouth Library. Thomas Ward to J. Bates, Feb. 27, 1843, March 2, 1845, Massachusetts Historical Society.

CHAPTER 16

1. Elizabeth T. Coleman, *Priscilla Cooper Taylor* (University of Alabama, 1955), 88. George T. Curtis, *Life of Daniel Webster* (New York, 1870), vol. 2, p. 22. Mrs. J. Fuller to Daniel Webster, Jan. 1, 1833, *Microfilm,* 10420. Daniel Webster to J. Fuller, Jan. 3, 1833, Van Tyne, p. 742. Daniel Webster to C. Perkins, Jan. 3, 1833, *Microfilm,* 10435.

2. Daniel Webster to Edward Everett, Jan., 1831, *Microfilm,* 09163. Daniel Webster to Miss ——, March 4, 1844, *Writings,* vol. 16, p. 425.

3. Daniel Webster to C. Thomas, Feb. 4, 1837, *Writings,* vol. 16, pp. 283, 316–325.

4. Daniel Webster to John Taylor, July 2, 1851, Writings, vol. 16, p. 598.

5. Daniel Webster to Millard Fillmore, July 23, 1851, *Writings,* vol. 18, p. 452.

6. The journalist who did the most to enhance Webster's image as the "Farmer of Marshfield" was S. P. Lyman, whose articles in the 1840s were later published in *The Public and Private Life of Daniel Webster* (Philadelphia, 1860), vol. 2.

7. *Ibid.,* vol. 2, p. 104.

8. Herman LeRoy to Caroline Webster, Feb. 7, 1837, New Hampshire Historical Society.

9. E. LeRoy to Caroline Webster, Dec. 28, 1842, New York Public Library. Caroline Webster to Daniel Webster, May 14, 1830, *Microfilm,* 8821. Claude Fuess (ed.), *Mr W & I,* (Ives Washburn, 1942), p. 109. W. A. Graham to S. Graham, Jan. 25, 1841, G. De Roulhac Hamilton (ed.), *W. A. Graham Papers* (Raleigh, 1957), vol. 2, p. 148. Daniel Webster to Caroline Webster, March 7, 8, 1840, *Microfilm,* 16432, 16441.

10. *Writings,* vol. 13, p. 566. N. Carroll to Willie Mangum, Oct. 28, 1841, Henry T. Shanks, *Willie Mangum Papers* (Raleigh, 1950), vol. 3, p. 248.

11. The LeRoy will, dated Mar. 28, 1841, is filed in the Surrogates Court for New York County. Daniel Webster to Caroline Webster, Aug. 22, 1841, *Microfilm,* 20005.

12. Daniel Webster to Caroline Webster, Aug. 24, 1841, *Microfilm* 20019. I. P. Davis to Daniel Webster, Sept. 13, 1841, *Microfilm,* 20212.

13. Daniel Webster to George Ticknor, Jan. 24, 1846, *Writings,* vol. 16, p. 442. Daniel Webster to Caroline Webster, May 21, 23, 1842, *Microfilm,* vol. 17, 22510, 22519.

14. George Boutwell, *The Lawyer, the Statesman and the Soldier* (New York, 1887), p. 51.

15. Daniel Fletcher Webster to Daniel Webster, March 29, 1825, *Microfilm,* 4909.

Daniel Webster to Daniel Fletcher Webster, Feb. 17, 1829, *Microfilm*, 7763. Daniel Fletcher Webster to Daniel Webster, Feb. 25, 1832, *Microfilm*, 9879. Daniel Fletcher Webster to Daniel Webster, March 11, 1832, *Microfilm*, 9925.

16. Daniel Webster to Daniel Fletcher Webster, March 14, 1836, *Microfilm*, 13067. Daniel Webster to Daniel Fletcher Webster, Jan. 15, 1836, *Writings*, vol. 18, p. 16.

17. Daniel Fletcher Webster to Daniel Webster, July 1, 1836, *Microfilm*, 13417. Daniel Fletcher Webster to Daniel Webster, Oct. 30, 1839, New Hampshire Historical Society. Daniel Fletcher Webster to Daniel Webster, March 5, 1840, May 26, 1840, *Microfilm*, 16425, 16701.

18. Daniel Fletcher Webster to Daniel Webster, May 30, 1842, *Microfilm*, 25842.

19. Daniel Fletcher Webster to Daniel Webster, Jan. 28, 1838, *Microfilm*, 14596.

20. Edward Webster to Daniel Webster, Jan. 10, 1829, *Microfilm*, 7641. Caroline Webster to Daniel Webster, Dec. 31, 1832, *Microfilm*, 10395. Daniel Webster to Daniel Fletcher Webster, June 5, 1834, *Writings*, vol. 16, p. 236.

21. Daniel Webster to Edward Webster, April 22, 1837, Sept. 16, 1837, *Microfilm*, 14226, 14407.

22. Edward Webster to Daniel Webster, Sept. 2, 1838, *Microfilm*, 15172. Daniel Webster to Edward Webster, Sept. 8, 1838, *Microfilm*, 15190. Edward Webster to Daniel Webster, Sept. 13, 1838, *Microfilm*, 15200.

23. Daniel Webster to Edward Webster, Sept. 21, 1838, *Microfilm*, 15209.

24. Daniel Webster to J. Wool, April 7, 1847, *Microfilm*, 27806. Daniel Webster to Caleb Cushing, April 15, 1847, *Microfilm*, 27822.

25. Julia Webster to Edward Webster, Feb. 4, 1837, *Microfilm*, 14023. Claude Fuess, *Daniel Webster* (Boston, 1930), vol. 2, p. 379. Julia Webster Appleton to Daniel Webster, Dec. 11, 1840, *Microfilm*, 17120.

26. Daniel Webster to C. S. Webster, Feb. 5, 1844, *Microfilm*, 25660. Daniel Webster to Daniel Fletcher Webster, Feb. 23, 1848, *Writings*, vol. 18, p. 271. Julia Webster Appleton to Daniel Webster, Feb. 23, 1848, *Microfilm*, 28426.

27. Julia Webster Appleton to Daniel Webster, Feb. 26, 1848, *Microfilm*, 28442. Fuess, *Daniel Webster*, vol. 2, p. 184.

CHAPTER 17

1. George Hoar, *Autobiography of Seventy Years* (New York, 1903), p. 151. Daniel Webster to Edward Everett, Dec. 15, 1844, *Microfilm*, 26022.

2. Abbot Lawrence to Edward Everett, March 31, 1845, Massachusetts Historical Society.

3. *Writings*, vol. 13, p. 248. Daniel Webster to Edward Everett, Dec. 15, 1844, *Microfilm*, 26022.

4. Robert F. Lucid (ed.), *The Journal of Richard Henry Dana, Jr.* (Cambridge, Mass., 1968), vol. 1, pp. 395–397.

5. *Writings*, vol. 13, p. 322; vol. 9, p. 59.

6. Daniel Webster to D. Sears, Jan. 17, 1846, *Writings*, vol. 18, p. 215. *Writings*, vol. 13, pp. 310–324.

7. Robert Dalzell, *Daniel Webster and the Trial of American Nationalism 1843–1852* (Boston, 1973), pp. 109–113. Daniel Webster to Daniel Fletcher Webster, June 1, 1846, *Writings*, vol. 16, p. 453.

8. Daniel Webster to Daniel Fletcher Webster, May 20, 1846, Van Tyne, p. 326. Daniel Webster to Daniel Fletcher Webster, Aug. 4, 1846, *Writings,* vol. 16, p. 464. Charles Sellers, *James K. Polk Continentalist 1843–1846* (Princeton, 1966), p. 475. Allan Nevins (ed., *The Diary of a President* (New York, 1929), p. 137.

9. Dalzell, *Daniel Webster . . . ,* pp. 118–130. *Writings,* vol. 13, pp. 327–329.

10. *Writings,* vol. 13, pp. 330–341.

11. Daniel Webster to Thurlow Weed, Nov. 16, 1846, *Microfilm,* 27449. *Writings,* vol. 4, pp. 32–33.

12. *Writings,* vol. 9, p. 261.

13. Daniel Webster to Daniel Fletcher Webster, April 24, 1847, *Writings,* vol. 16, p. 473.

14. *Writings,* vol. 4, pp. 73, 80. Daniel Webster to Daniel Fletcher Webster, May 10, 1847, *Writings,* vol. 18, p. 245.

15. *Writings,* vol. 4, pp. 102–103.

16. Joseph G. Rayback, *Free Soil: The Election of 1848* (Lexington, Ky., 1970), pp. 40–42.

17. Daniel Webster to S. Weston, May 10, 1847. Daniel Webster to Mrs. Paige, May 13, 1847, May 15, 1847. *Writings,* vol. 18, p. 246–254.

18. Robert F. Lucid (ed.), *The Journal of Richard Henry Dana, Jr.* (Cambridge, Mass., 1968), vol. 2, p. 486. *Writings,* vol. 13, pp. 347–365.

19. *Writings,* vol. 4, p. 116.

20. Daniel Webster to Edward Everett, Jan. 29, 1848, Van Tyne, p. 361. Daniel Webster to Richard Blatchford, Jan. 30, 1848, *Writings,* vol. 16, p. 491.

21. *Writings,* vol. 10, pp. 23–32.

22. Daniel Webster to Edward Everett, May 29, 1848, *Microfilm,* 28643. Daniel Webster to Hiram Ketchum, June 11, 1848, *Microfilm,* 28692.

23. Daniel Webster to Daniel Fletcher Webster, June 16, 1848, *Writings,* vol. 16, p. 495.

24. H. Wilson to Daniel Webster, May 31, 1848, *Microfilm,* 28652.

25. Daniel Webster to E. Rockwood Hoar, Aug. 23, 1848, *Writings,* vol. 16, p. 498.

26. *Writings,* vol. 4, pp. 123–144.

27. Daniel Webster to ——, Oct. 14, 1848, *Writings,* vol. 16, p. 500. *Writings,* vol. 4, pp. 147–174.

28. Claude Fuess, *Daniel Webster* (Boston, 1930), vol. 2, p. 192.

CHAPTER 18

1. E. P. Smith to H. Carey, Nov. 28, 1856, Historical Society of Pennsylvania.

2. Daniel Webster to Richard Blatchford, Jan. 1, 1849, Feb. 27, 1849, *Writings,* vol. 16, pp. 503, 508.

3. Van Tyne, pp. 374–389.

4. Daniel Webster to Daniel Fletcher Webster, May 2, 1849, May, 1849, *Writings,* vol. 18, pp. 321–322. Daniel Webster to Richard Blatchford, Aug. 5, Aug. 7, Aug. 8, 1849, *Writings,* vol. 18, pp. 330–334.

5. Daniel Webster to Edward Curtis, Sept. 24, 1849, *Microfilm,* 29559. *Writings,* vol. 13, pp. 381–385; vol. 4, p. 208.

6. Holman Hamilton, *Prologue to Conflict: The Crisis and Compromise of 1850* (Lexington, Ky., 1964), pp. 36–64.

7. W. H. Furness to Daniel Webster, Jan. 9, 1850, Van Tyne, p. 389. Daniel Webster to W. H. Furness, Feb. 15, 1850, *Writings,* vol. 18, p. 353.

8. "The message is regarded here as a good Whig Document, written in a plain and simple style." Daniel Webster to F. Haven, Dec. 25, 1849, *Writings,* vol. 16, p. 527.

9. Robert F. Dalzell, Jr., *Daniel Webster and the Trial of American Nationalism* (Boston, 1973), pp. 171–177. Daniel Webster to Peter Harvey, Feb. 14, 1850, *Writings,* vol. 16, p. 533. Daniel Webster to Daniel Fletcher Webster, Feb. 24, 1850, *Writings,* vol. 16, p. 534. Daniel Webster to C. Warren, March 1, 1850, *Writings,* vol. 16, p. 534.

10. *Writings,* vol. 10, p. 57.

11. *Ibid.,* p. 64.

12. *Ibid.,* p. 87.

13. *Ibid.,* p. 93.

14. *Ibid.,* p. 97.

15. Allan Nevins, *Ordeal of the Union* (New York, 1947), pp. 291–296.

16. Daniel Webster to Daniel Fletcher Webster, March 21, 1850, *Writings,* vol. 16, p. 535. Robert Winthrop to Edward Everett, Mrch 17, 1850, Massachusetts Historical society. Everett disagreed with Webster's contention that Texas could constitutionally be divided into two or more slave states, and believed that he had fatally miscalculated New England's moral repugnance to the return of fugitives. Edward Everett Letterbook, Massachusetts Historical Society.

17. Daniel Webster to F. Haven, March 12, 1850, *Writings,* vol. 16, p. 537.

18. *Writings,* vol. 10, p. 102.

19. Daniel Webster to Daniel Fletcher Webster, April 8, 1850, *Writings,* vol. 16, p. 538.

20. Irving H. Bartlett, *Wendell Phillips: Brahmin Radical* (Boston, 1961), p. 142. Daniel Webster to Peter Harvey, March 28, 1850, *Writings,* vol. 18, p. 363.

21. *Writings,* vol. 13, p. 387.

22. Daniel Webster to J. Hall, May 18, 1850, *Writings,* vol. 16, p. 538.

23. *Writings,* vol. 10, p. 161.

24. Claude Fuess, *Daniel Webster* (Boston, 1930), vol. 2, p. 240. Daniel Webster to Peter Harvey, Sept. 10, 1850, *Writings,* vol. 18, p. 385.

CHAPTER 19

1. P. R. Forthingham, *Edward Everett, Orator and Statesman* (Boston, 1925), p. 320. Richard Johnston and William Brown, *Life of Alexander H. Stephens* (Philadelphia, 1878), p. 254. Robert Penn Warren, *John Greenleaf Whittier's Poetry: An Appraisal and a Selection* (Minneapolis, 1971), p. 27.

2. Jonathan Messerli, *Horace Mann: A Biography* (New York, 1972), p. 515. *Writings,* vol. 12, p. 235. Daniel Webster to George Ticknor, June 13, 1850, *Writings,* vol. 16, p. 545.

3. Robert Winthrop to Edward Everett, May 12, 1850, Massachusetts Historical Society.

4. On May 1, 1850, the *Atlas* reported that a simple reading of the Fugitive Slave Law was enough to curdle the blood of any "free Massachusetts man." Robert C. Winthrop, Jr., *A Memoir of Robert C. Winthrop* (Boston, 1897), p. 133. Daniel Webster to S. Eliot, June 14, 1850, *Microfilm,* 30568.

5. DeRoulhac Hamilton (ed.), *W. A. Graham Papers* (Raleigh, 1957), vol. 3, pp. 321, 369.

6. Robert J. Rayback, *Millard Fillmore: Biography of a President* (Buffalo, 1959), pp. 242–246. Edward Curtis to Peter Harvey, Aug. 16, 1850, Van Tyne, p. 426. Daniel Webster to Frank Haven, Dec. 5, 1850, Writings, 16:580.

7. Daniel Webster to Peter Harvey, Oct. 2, 1850, Van Tyne, p. 432. Daniel Webster to S. Dickinson, Sept. 27, 1850, *Writings,* vol. 18, p. 392. Daniel Webster to Millard Fillmore, Sept. 19, 1850, Van Tyne, p. 432.

8. Daniel Webster to Peter Harvey, Oct. 2, 1850, Van Tyne, p. 432.

9. Daniel Webster to Millard Fillmore, Sept. 11, 1850, Van Tyne, p. 430. Daniel Webster to Edward Everett, Sept. 20, 1850, *Microfilm,* 31222. Stanley Campbell, *The Slave Catchers: Enforcement of the Fugitive Slave Law 1850–1860* (Chapel Hill, 1970), ch. 1. Frothingham, *Edward Everett . . . ,* p. 320. *Writings,* vol. 10, pp. 105–107.

10. Adams is quoted in Larry Gara, *The Liberty Line: The Legend of the Underground Railroad* (Lexington, Ky., 1961), p. 128. Campbell, *The Slave Catchers . . . ,* ch. 2.

11. When Webster's servants traveled without him, he gave them a note over his own signature certifying to their status and arranged for hotel keepers along the way to look after them. See, for example, his note of June 12, 1849, regarding Paul Jennings and Monica Carty, Dartmouth Library.

12. *Writings,* vol. 18, pp. 398–400.

13. Harold Schwartz, "Fugitive Slave Days in Boston," *New England Quarterly,* 28 (1954), 191–212.

14. *Writings,* vol. 14, p. 391. Daniel Webster to Millard Fillmore, Oct. 29, 1850, *Microfilm,* 31562.

15. Daniel Webster to Millard Fillmore, Nov. 5, 1850, *Writings,* vol. 18, p. 400. Daniel Webster to Millard Fillmore, Nov. 15, 1850, Van Tyne, p. 440.

16. Allan Nevins, *Ordeal of the Union* (New York, 1947), pp. 358 ff. Rayback, *Millard Fillmore,* p. 274.

17. Merle Curti, *Austria and the United States 1848–1852: A Study in Diplomatic Relations.* Smith Colletge Studies in History, 11 (October 1925), 141–206. *Writings,* vol. 12, pp. 162–178.

18. The Hulsemann-Webster-Fillmore correspondence can be followed in Van Tyne, pp. 487–497.

19. Daniel Webster to Abbot Lawrence, Dec. 29, 1851, Van Tyne, p. 507.

20. Daniel Webster to Richard Blatchford, Dec. 30, 1851, Daniel Webster to Millard Fillmore, Jan. 7, 1852, Van Tyne, pp. 501–503.

21. Washington Reminiscences," *Atlantic Monthly* (April, 1881), 541. *Writings,* vol. 13, p. 454. Daniel Webster to George Ticknor, Jan. 16, 1851, *Writings,* vol. 16, p. 586. Daniel Webster to Richard Blatchford, Jan. 11, 1852, *Writings,* vol. 18, p. 504. Daniel Webster to C. McCurdy, Jan. 15, 1852, *Writings,* vol. 16, p. 589. *New York Herald,* Jan. 15, 1852.

22. *W. A. Graham Papers,* vol. 4, pp. 3, 25.

23. Daniel Webster to Peter Harvey, Feb. 17, 1851, Daniel Webster to G. Lunt,

April 4, 1851, Van Tyne, pp. 457, 467. Robert F. Lucid, *The Journal of Richard Henry Dana, Jr.* (Cambridge, Mass., 1968), vol. 2, p. 531.

24. Irving H. Bartlett, *Wendell Phillips, Brahmin Radical* (Boston, 1964), pp. 155–157. Daniel Webster to Millard Fillmore, April 9, 1851, April 13, 1851, *Writings,* vol. 16, pp. 604–606. *Writings,* vol. 13, pp. 405–406.

25. *Writings,* vol. 13, pp. 420, 435.

26. Campbell, *The Slave Catchers . . . ,* p. 75. Wendell Phillips, *Speeches and Lectures* (Boston, 1863), p. 45.

27. Theodore Parker, *A Discourse Occasioned by the Death of Daniel Webster* (Boston, 1853), p. 75. John Pollard, *John Greenleaf Whittier: Friend of Man* (Boston, 1949), p. 88. Horace E. Sudder, *James Russell Lowell* (Boston, 1901), vol. 2, p. 365, Bartlett, *Wendell Phillips . . . ,* p. 31.

28. Ralph Rusk, *The Letters of Ralph Waldo Emerson* (New York, 1939), vol. 1, pp. 120, 121, 123, 129.

29. William Gilman and Alfred Ferguson, *The Journals and Miscellaneous Notebooks of Ralph Waldo Emerson* (Cambridge, Mass., 1963), vol. 2, pp. 184, 224.

30. Alfred Ferguson, *Journals . . . of Emerson,* vol. 4, p. 321, Joseph Slater, *The Correspondence of Emerson and Carlyle* (New York, 1964), p. 244.

31. *Ibid.* Scudder, *James Rusell Lowell,* vol. 2, p. 223. William H. Gilman and J. E. Parsons, *Journals . . . of Emerson* (Cambridge, Mass., 1970), vol. 8, p. 361.

32. A. W. Plumstead and William H. Gilman, *Journals . . . of Emerson* (Cambridge, Mass., 1975), vol. 11, pp. 231, 249, 250, 348, 346.

33. *Complete Works of Ralph Waldo Emerson,* Centenary ed. (Boston and New York, 1911), vol. 11, pp. 202–204.

34. Plumstead and Gilman, *Journals . . . of Emerson,* vol. 11, p. 385.

35. Scudder, *James Russell Lowell,* vol. 2, p. 223. *Liberator,* Dec. 24, 1852. Parker, *A Discourse . . . . ,* 74.

36. Parker, *A Discourse . . . ,* p. 77. Bliss and Perry, *John Greenleaf Whittier,* (Boston, 1907), p. 89. Sanuel Shapiro, *Richard Henry Dana, Jr.* (East Lansing, 1961), p. 65. Amos Lawrence Ms., Sept. 23, 1850, Massachusetts. Historical Society. George Hillard to J. F. Fisher, Feb. 19, 1867, Historical Society of Pennsylvania.

CHAPTER 20

1. *Writings,* vol. 10, p. 143.

2. Daniel Webster to Peter Harvey, May 4, 1851, *Writings,* vol. 16, p. 610.

3. David Henshaw to Daniel Webster, April 21, 1851, *Writings,* vol. 18, p. 433. Daniel Webster to T. Curtis, Jan. 24, 1851, *Microfilm,* 32245.

4. Robert Dalzell, *Daniel Webster and the Trial of American Nationalism 1843–1852* (Boston, 1973), pp. 230–233. Webster made his remark about the South and the compact in his speech at Capon Springs, *Writings,* vol. 13, p. 439.

5. George T. Curtis, *Life of Daniel Webster* (New York, 1870), vol. 2, p. 581. Daniel Webster to Frank Haven, Nov. 27, 1851, *Writings,* vol. 18, p. 490.

6. Everett wrote the address, but did not attend the Faneuil Hall meeting. Dalzell, *Daniel Webster . . . ,* p. 241. Daniel Webster to Frank Haven, Nov. 30, 1851, *Writings,* vol. 16, p. 629. *Writings,* vol. 13, p. 466. Daniel Webster to Edward Everett, March 13, 1852, *Microfilm,* 36215.

7. Robert Rayback, *Millard Fillmore: Biography of a President* (Buffalo, 1959), pp. 333 ff. Edward Everett to Millard Fillmore, Nov. 26, 1851, Massachusetts Historical Society.

8. Dalzell, *Daniel Webster . . . ,* pp. 246–248.

9. One of the problems involved in aging is that "The covering behavioral systems become superfluous, are given up, and the real personality is revealed beneath." O. S. English and G. H. Pearson, *Emotional Problems of Living* (New York, 1955), p. 449. *Writings,* vol. 13, pp. 498, 507, 511.

10. Daniel Webster to Daniel Fletcher Webster, May, 1832, *Writings,* vol. 16, p. 643. Daniel Webster to Millard Fillmore, May 19, 1852, *Writings,* vol. 18, p. 531.

11. Rayback, *Millard Fillmore,* p. 352.

12. Dalzell, *Daniel Webster . . . ,* pp. 259–277. Rayback, *Millard Fillmore,* pp. 349 ff.

13. Daniel Webster to Richard Blatchford, June 22, 1852, *Writings,* vol. 16, p. 657.

14. Daniel Fletcher Webster to Daniel Webster, Nov. 29, 1851, Van Tyne, p. 504.

15. Robert W. Johannsen, *Stephen A. Douglas* (New York, 1973), p. 350.

16. Dalzell, *Daniel Webster . . . ,* p. 259. Edward Curtis to Peter Harvey, May 25, 1852, Van Tyne, p. 529.

17. *Liberator,* May 10, 1850.

18. Clyde Duniway, "Daniel Webster," in *The American Secretaries of State and Their Diplomacy* (New York, 1958), pp. 78–113. *Writings,* vol. 14, pp. 416–424.

19. Daniel Webster to Richard Blatchford, March 28, 1851, *Writings,* vol. 18, p. 426. Daniel Webster to L. Severance, March 1, 1851, Van Tyne, p. 458. Compare the draft of Webster's memorandum to Pines, Dec. 31, 1851, Van Tyne, p. 508, to the dispatch, Jan. 12, 1852, *Writings,* vol. 14, p. 451.

20. *Writings,* vol. 14, pp. 561–576, Daniel Webster to Millard Fillmore, Sept. 15, 1852, *Microfilm,* 37767.

21. Daniel Webster to Richard Blatchford, April 29, 1851, Daniel Webster to Mrs. Paige, Dec. 29, 1850, *Writings,* vol. 18, pp. 436, 408.

22. Daniel Webster to George Ashmun, undated, *Microfilm,* 38208.

23. S. P. Lyman, *The Public and Private Life of Daniel Webster* (Philadelphia, 1860), vol. 2, p. 112. Daniel Webster to John Latrobe, July 10, 1851, *Writings,* vol. 16, pp. 621, 622.

24. *Writings,* vol. 16, p. 595. Paul Jennings, *A Colored Man's Reminiscences of James Madison* (Brooklyn, 1865).

25. Daniel Webster to Daniel Fletcher Webster, June 27, 1851, *Writings,* vol. 18, p. 446. *Writings,* vol. 13, p. 472.

26. Daniel Webster to unidentified correspondent, Dec. 21, 1851, New York Public Library. Bradford Torrey and Francis Allen, *The Journals of Henry D. Thoreau* (New York, 1962), vol. 2, p. 350.

27. Van Tyne, p. 750. Edward Everett Hale, *Memories of a Hundred Years* (New York, 1904), vol. 2, p. 42. Robert F. Lucid, *The Journal of Richard Henry Dana, Jr.* (Cambridge, Mass., 1968), vol. 2, p. 462. *Writings,* vol. 13, p. 442. The *Lantern,* a New York weekly specializing in political cartoon humor, burlesqued Webster's drinking habits on Aug. 15 and Sept. 14, 1852.

28. James Parton, *Famous Americans of Recent Times* (Boston, 1873), p. 106.

29. *Liberator,* May 3, 1850. Jane Grey Swisshelm, *Half a Century* (Chicago, 1880),

p. 128. The *Saturday Visitor,* May 25, 1850, Feb. 9, 1855. "The Progress of Our Political Virtues," *Putnam's Monthly* (February, 1855), 197–204.

30. When Frank M. Sinnott, who later became chief of police for Marshfield, was a boy, Daniel Webster's coachman, then an old man in his nineties, told him about the alleged affair between Webster and Monica Carty. Mr. Sinnott told me this himself in Marshfield in the summer of 1973. "All honor to Daniel Webster for having had painted, and hung up in a conspicuous place in his house *the portrait of his black cook.* It is the most unique object in it." Fanny Fern, *Ginger-Snaps* (New York, 1857), p. 241.

31. James Ford Rhodes, *History of the United States* (New York, 1913), vol. 1, pp. 143, 160. Henry Cabot Lodge, *Daniel Webster* (Boston, 1883), p. 356.

32. Chales Moore, *Washington Past and Present* (New York, 1929), p. 209.

33. *Liberator,* July 2, 1852. Daniel Webster to Frank Haven, March 9, 1850. *Microfilm,* 29931.

34. Curtis, *Life of Daniel Webster,* vol. 2, p. 496. Fuess, *Daniel Webster,* (Boston, 1930), vol. 2, pp. 392–393. Leroy Graff and Ralph Haskins, *The Papers of Andrew Johnson* (Knoxville, Tenn., 1970), vol. 2, p. 13.

35. Daniel Webster to Frank Haven, July 3, 1851, *Microfilm,* 34063. *Microfilm,* 040608. Daniel Webster to Frank Haven, Sept. 29, 1852, *Writings,* vol. 16, p. 665. Daniel Webster to Corcoran & Riggs, Oct. 20, 1852, *Microfilm,* 038081.

36. Edward Everett to Daniel Webster, June 22, 1852, *Microfilm,* 31704. *Writings,* vol. 13, pp. 535–538.

37. Charles Lanman, *The Private Life of Daniel Webster* (New York, 1852), pp. 60–67. *Writings,* vol. 18, pp. 535 ff.

38. Daniel Webster to B. Clarke, Jr., July 23, 1852, *Writings,* vol. 16, p. 660. *Writings,* vol. 13, pp. 539–544.

39. Daniel Webster to Millard Fillmore, July 25, 1852, *Microfilm,* 37352. Daniel Webster to R. Blatchford, Aug. 24, 1852, *Writings,* vol. 18, p. 550. Daniel Webster to Millard Fillmore, Sept. 12, 1852, *Writings,* vol. 18, p. 552.

40. Dalzell, *Daniel Webster . . . ,* pp. 296–303. The struggle to get an endorsement out of Webster can be followed in the May–Oct., 1852, folder of the Everett Papers, Massachusetts Historical Society.

41. Daniel Webster to Millard Fillmore, Nov. 13, 1850, *Writings,* vol. 18, p. 402.

42. Daniel Webster to Millard Fillmore, *Writings,* vol. 18, p. 554. Curtis, *Life of Daniel Webster,* vol. 2, pp. 671–684. The anecdote concerning Webster's interest in Wellington's death can be found in the James William Paige Mss., #192, Massachusetts Historical Society.

43. B. F. Tefft, *Life of Daniel Webster* (Philadelphia, 1854), p. 454.

44. Curtis, *Life of Daniel Webster,* vol. 2, pp. 684–685.

45. *Ibid.,* vol. 2, p. 692. George Abbot to Mrs. George Abbot, Oct. 20, 22, 1852, Ms. copy, Sterling Library, Yale University.

46. Curtis, *Life of Daniel Webster,* vol. 2, pp. 695 ff. Tefft, *Life of Daniel Webster,* p. 464.

47. *Journals of Ralph Waldo Emerson* (Cambridge, Mass., 1912), p. 336. Curtis, *Life of Daniel Webster,* vol. 2, p. 704.

INDEX